SPECIAL NEEDS
IN SINGAPORE
Trends and Issues

SPECIAL NEEDS IN SINGAPORE
Trends and Issues

Editors

Wong Meng Ee & Levan Lim
National Institute of Education, Nanyang Technological University, Singapore

NEW JERSEY · LONDON · SINGAPORE · BEIJING · SHANGHAI · HONG KONG · TAIPEI · CHENNAI · TOKYO

Published by

World Scientific Publishing Co. Pte. Ltd.
5 Toh Tuck Link, Singapore 596224
USA office: 27 Warren Street, Suite 401-402, Hackensack, NJ 07601
UK office: 57 Shelton Street, Covent Garden, London WC2H 9HE

Library of Congress Cataloging-in-Publication Data
Names: Wong, Meng Ee, editor. | Lim, Levan, editor.
Title: Special needs in Singapore : trends and issues / Wong Meng Ee, Levan Lim.
Description: Hackensack, NJ : World Scientific Publishing Co. Pte. Ltd., [2021] |
  Includes bibliographical references.
Identifiers: LCCN 2020051833 | ISBN 9789814678544 (hardcover) |
  ISBN 9789814667142 (ebook)
Subjects: LCSH: People with disabilities--Singapore. | Special education--Singapore. |
  People with disabilities--Singapore--Social conditions. |
  People with disabilities--Services for--Singapore.
Classification: LCC HV1559.S55 S64 2021 | DDC 371.9095957--dc23
LC record available at https://lccn.loc.gov/2020051833

British Library Cataloguing-in-Publication Data
A catalogue record for this book is available from the British Library.

Copyright © 2021 by World Scientific Publishing Co. Pte. Ltd.

All rights reserved. This book, or parts thereof, may not be reproduced in any form or by any means, electronic or mechanical, including photocopying, recording or any information storage and retrieval system now known or to be invented, without written permission from the publisher.

For photocopying of material in this volume, please pay a copying fee through the Copyright Clearance Center, Inc., 222 Rosewood Drive, Danvers, MA 01923, USA. In this case permission to photocopy is not required from the publisher.

For any available supplementary material, please visit
https://www.worldscientific.com/worldscibooks/10.1142/9546#t=suppl

Desk Editor: Lum Pui Yee

Typeset by Stallion Press
Email: enquiries@stallionpress.com

Endorsements

"What an excellent resource this publication is! Everything that one needs to know or should know about special education in Singapore has been comprehensively captured here. From tracing the genesis of special education to its current state, to acknowledging the key players and watershed moments which have shaped the special education landscape, to covering the issues and challenges pertinent to this sector with such depth and clarity, this volume is a treasure trove of collective wisdom and experience. Whether you are a student, parent, caregiver, teacher, researcher, practitioner or a person interested in finding out more about special education, this publication is for you."

Anita Fam
President of the National Council of Social Service, Singapore

"This is a landmark study of disability and inclusion in Singapore that deserves to be widely read by educators, policymakers, researchers and everyone involved in the 3Ps of special needs — people, private and public sectors. Singapore is a unique and compelling place, a social experiment of great international interest for its stellar achievements and canny and committed way of doing things. Since 2004, disability has been officially part of the strong inclusion story that underpins Singapore's aspirations. This book explores how Singapore has tackled the challenging yet essential task of ensuring people with disabilities are part of the vision of an inclusive society. A hallmark achievement of this book is the fine quality of its essays that offer rigorous, thoughtful, and highly reflective accounts of the long-running efforts to improve the quality of life and inclusion of people with disabilities in Singapore. This book offers a seminal volume that is essential reading for anyone interested in disability in Singapore. It is also a major contribution to the international literature not just because it provides an authoritative account of disability in a country of much global fascination but also advances our contextual understanding of disability and inclusion."

Professor Gerard Goggin
Wee Kim Wee Professor of Communication Studies,
Nanyang Technological University

"Very rarely do we come across a publication that speaks about special needs and disabilities with such breadth and depth that is representative of the diversity of persons being discussed, as has been accomplished by Meng Ee and Levan. The variety of voices from different stakeholders coupled with comprehensive facts is a refreshing take on how far we have come in the space of inclusion, but also a reminder that we owe it to ourselves and future generations of Singaporean learners and educators that much more can, and ought to be done."

J. R. Karthikeyan
CEO, AWWA

"It is my honour and privilege to be invited to provide 'a few words' about this book.

It has been more than 15 years since *Educating Learners with Diverse Abilities* (Lim & Quah, 2004) was released as a source book for teachers in training. Since then, the special education scene has undergone some major changes. While special schools are still with us, the trend is moving more and more towards the provision of opportunities for children with mild special needs to receive a more 'inclusive' education within regular classes within mainstream schools.

This book is timely, not just for those in the profession, but also beyond. It will be a valuable resource for teachers at different levels of training and experience, be they graduate level students, students in their senior years of undergraduate studies, academic staff and professionals in the fields of special educational needs and disability. It also offers the general public some insights into how special education has evolved over the last 20 years.

The 17 chapters contain up-to-date and valuable information about trends and issues in special education in Singapore and should be read by every teacher working alongside these students.

My heartiest congratulations to the authors and editors on producing a very readable and excellent discussion of these trends and issues in special needs education."

Dr Marilyn Mayling Quah
Founding Head of the Department of Education for Children with Special Needs (1982–1991) & Head of the Division of Specialised Education (1991–2002), National Institute of Education

"My colleagues and I at Special Educational Needs Division, MOE, welcome this important contribution to the literature on Special Needs in Singapore. The writers provide valuable and diverse perspectives which combine to bring across the wide range of needs, the progress made thus far in addressing those needs as well as the challenges, opportunities and possibilities ahead. This book will be of great help to the community of stakeholders working together to create a more inclusive Singapore."

Lucy Toh (Mrs)
Divisional Director, Special Educational Needs Division,
Ministry of Education, Singapore

© 2021 World Scientific Publishing Company
https://doi.org/10.1142/9789814667142_fmatter

Contents

Acknowledgements	xvii
Foreword	xix
Preface	xxv
List of Contributors	xxxv

Chapter 1 Special Needs and Inclusion 1
Levan Lim & Wong Meng Ee

Introduction: The Global Context	1
The Singapore Context	3
References	7

Chapter 2 United Nations Convention on the Rights of Persons with Disabilities in Singapore: Considering Some Post-Ratification Implications 11
Wong Meng Ee

Introduction	11
Background to the Convention	12
General Articles of the Convention	14
Key Obligations	15
Promoting and Enforcing Accountability	16
Optional Protocol	17
Implications for Singapore	17

Understanding Disability	18
Advocacy with a Human Rights Influence	19
Defining Inclusive Education	22
Conclusion	24
References	25

Chapter 3 Education as Apprenticeship for the Future: The Evolution of Singapore's Approach and its Impact on Inclusion for Persons with Disabilities — 31
Levan Lim & Thana Thaver

Introduction	31
Education in Singapore	34
Evolution of Education towards Diversification: Impact on the 'Inclusionary Space'	35
The 'Inclusionary Space' vis-à-vis Persons with Disabilities in Singapore	42
The Legacy of Diverse Pathways: Separate Lives?	45
Conclusion	46
References	51

Chapter 4 The Struggle for Merit in Meritocratic Singapore: Implications for Persons with Disabilities — 57
Wong Meng Ee

Introduction	57
Concepts of Meritocracy	60
Features of Meritocracy	61
Considerations of Meritocracy	62
Pitfalls of Meritocracy	63
Value of the Human	64
Emphasis of Ableism in a Meritocracy	65
Meritocracy Legitimising Neoliberal Culture	66
Meritocracy in Singapore	67
Emerging Questions to Consider	68

Concluding Thoughts	70
References	72

Chapter 5   Early Intervention for Young Children with Special Needs in Singapore: History, Development and Future Directions   81
Kenneth K. Poon, Xie Huichao & Yang Xueyan

Introduction	81
Early Intervention in Singapore: Emergence, Development and Consolidation	82
Early Detection in Early Intervention	88
Directions Ahead	89
Conclusion	92
References	93

Chapter 6   Early Childhood Inclusion in Singapore: Inroads and Review   97
Joanna Tay-Lim

Introduction	97
Definition and Significance of Early Childhood Inclusion	97
Early Childhood Inclusive Practices in Singapore	101
Review and Going Forward	106
Conclusion	112
References	112

Chapter 7   Journey of the Heart, Enabling Students with Special Needs   117
Tina Hung

Introduction	117
National Council of Social Service	118
Special Education Schools: Looking Back	119
Special Education Schools: Many Parts to Make a Whole	121
Mainstream Schools and Special Needs Support	127
Transition Management: Support for Early Years	128

xii Contents

Post-Special Education Support	130
Assistive Technology	131
Supporting Parents and Caregivers	133
Inclusion and Socialisation	136
Way Forward	141
References	142
Acknowledgements for the Research of the Paper	147
Appendix I: Listing of Special Education Schools	147

Chapter 8 Psychological Services for Children with Special Educational Needs in Mainstream Schools — **149**

Mariam Aljunied

Introduction	149
The Medical Model	150
The Problem-Solving Approach	153
Enhancing Capability and Resources in Mainstream Schools	156
Linkages with Other Providers of Psychological Services	158
Tiered-System of Support for SEN	160
Conclusion	164
References	165

Chapter 9 Differentiation: Providing for Students with Special Needs in Mixed Ability Classrooms — **169**

Letchmi Devi Ponnusamy

Introduction	169
Mixed Ability Teaching: International and Local Contexts	170
Addressing SEN in Mainstream Education: The Relevance of Mixed Ability Teaching	174
Research on Teaching in Mixed Ability Classrooms	176

A Local Model to Understand Mixed Ability Teaching	179
How the Working Model of Differentiation Can Inform Teachers' Work	181
Conclusion	186
References	186

Chapter 10 Stakeholders' Involvement in the Transition to Adulthood for Youth with Disabilities — 193

Ailsa Goh and Nursidah Malik

Introduction	193
Transition to Adulthood for Youth with Disabilities	194
Stakeholders' Perspectives on Transition to Adulthood	196
Transition to Employment in Singapore for Youth with Disabilities	200
A Methodology for Interviewing	206
Conclusion	210
References	211

Chapter 11 Preparing Persons with Disabilities for the World of Work: The Case of SG Enable Bridging Job Seekers and Employers — 219

Ku Geok Boon

Introduction	219
Background on SG Enable	220
Trends	222
3rd Enabling Masterplan	223
Special Education (SPED) Schools	224
Institutes of Higher Learning	229
Looking Ahead	232
References	233

Chapter 12 Disability and Employment: Confronting Challenges in Contemporary Singapore — 237
Vimallan Manokara

Introduction	237
Background	238
Situation in Singapore	243
International Landscape on Disability Employment	244
Singapore Landscape on Disability Employment: Challenges and Opportunities	247
Conclusion	255
References	255

Chapter 13 Improving the Mental Health of Students with Special Needs in Mainstream Schools — 261
Loh Pek Ru

Introduction	261
Mental Health Problems and SEN	263
Supports for SEN in Mainstream Schools	265
Recognising Mental Health Problems in SEN	267
Adequacy of Training and Programmes	269
Early Intervention at School Level	270
Academic Expectation for SEN in Mainstream Schools	273
Gap between Research and Practice	275
Conclusion	276
References	277

Chapter 14 Educating Students with Hearing Loss: Towards Integration and Inclusion — 283
Christina Michael

Introduction	283
Educational Concerns of Students with Hearing Loss	284
The Singapore Context	297
Conclusion	304
References	305

Chapter 15 Sexuality Development in Persons with Intellectual Disability: A Singapore Perspective — 309
Lohsnah Jeevanandam

Introduction	309
Intellectual Disability: Definition and Prevalence	310
Importance of Considering Sexuality in Persons with Intellectual Disability	311
Comprehensive Sexuality Education	314
Contextual Factors to be Considered in Sexuality Development	314
Current Practices in Singapore Related to Disability and Sexuality	316
Recommendations	318
References	322

Chapter 16 A Perspective from an Educator-Parent — 327
Norman Kee Kiak Nam

Introduction	327
Global Reality of Accelerating Digital Revolution	327
Advances in Advanced Robotics	329
Parents "Outsourcing" Education to Special Education Professionals	330
Sustainable Cost of Living and End of Life Concerns	331
Lifelong Holistic Monitoring, Evaluation of Needs and Support in an Ever Changing Environment	331
Unknown Future Realities	332
Strong Belief, Trust and Reliance on God	333
References	333

Chapter 17 Living a Good Life — 335
Chong Suet Ling

Introduction	335
A National Effort towards Person-Centredness	336
Towards Person-Centred Supports and Services	337

Planning for a Good Life	339
Pathways to a Good Life	339
Realising a Good Life with Paid Supports	343
Transitioning from School to a Good Life	344
Understanding Person-Centredness	346
The Local Context	347
Conclusions	349
References	353
Index	355

Acknowledgements

We wish to thank all the children, students and persons with special educational needs and disabilities, their parents and other family members, as well as all those who serve them in educational, administrative, advocacy, professional and personal roles and capacities. Thank you for teaching and inspiring us!

We would also like to thank Kerri Heng with helping us with the initial editing and formatting of the chapters. To Lum Pui Yee of World Scientific, we truly appreciate your understanding and patience throughout the entire time and process of publishing this book.

I (Levan) am grateful to Professor Lorraine Graham for your warm welcome and generous hospitality at the Melbourne Graduate School of Education, University of Melbourne, where I spent time working on this book during my sabbatical leave.

To our families, especially our parents, we are forever grateful to your guidance, support, encouragement and love throughout our lives. To my dear cousin, Mary Fong (from Levan): God only knows how much you have influenced my life.

Foreword

Professor Dan Goodley

iHuman, School of Education, University of Sheffield

☙❧

I have been visiting Singapore for over twenty years. During that time, I have been lucky enough to work with postgraduate students as part of a team of academics at the University of Sheffield. Our Masters in Education courses — offered through distance learning and study schools held in Singapore — permitted us to explore with Singaporean students questions of curriculum, pedagogy and assessment. And while the modules were set up explicitly to address these big issues so typical of educational research, questions of disability, special and inclusive education usually sat on the edges of our theoretical and methodological discussions. One reason for the peripheral status of disability is explained by the focus of the work that we were engaged with: practice and policy in educational settings. Students came to the course often as teachers from mainstream, public and private schools, colleges and universities. We tailored the course readings accordingly. Hence, the reason for disability's exclusion was explained by the generic and mainstream nature of the educational literature and professional practice that we were engaged with. Disability was simply not a central concern for many of these educators. Another reason for the marginalisation of disability, special and inclusive education considerations relates to a more structural orthodoxy. Disabled students and those with special needs have historically been educated outside of mainstream settings. A consequence of this is that disability becomes constituted as an object of theorisation and educational practice taken up by specialist knowledge and practitioners. Special education has historically been manufactured as *the* disciplinary space in which to deal with these marginalised students who often occupy peripheral places in their communities. This means that many mainstream educators do not consider disability or special educational needs to be their concern. I have to admit that I often found myself frustrated with students and colleagues.

Fortunately, over the last two decades, I have been lucky enough to meet with Singaporean researchers who have introduced me to the ways in which Singaporean society and Singaporean educational systems are engaging with the lives of disabled young people and those with special educational needs. Two of these researchers are the editors of this much-needed text Levan Lim & Wong Meng Ee. During seminars, teaching sessions and conversations over long lunches (the latter a welcome cultural norm within Singaporean society), I have had the pleasure of learning from these colleagues about the specific cultural, historical and economic factors within Singaporean society that contribute to the education of children and young people with disabilities and special educational needs. Alongside these informative discussions with academic colleagues, I have also had the opportunity to meet a number of disabled advocates in Singapore. This has included representatives from deaf, autistic, blind and visually impaired communities as well as people with intellectual disabilities. I remain a student of Singaporean education and disability advocacy and continue to learn much from colleagues (while enjoying the lunches too). As part of my learning curve, I have been forced to decentre my Western European and Anglocentric mindset when it comes to questions of disability and inclusion. British academics are notoriously self-referential in their knowledge production and academic writing. Many of us have been guilty of contributing to a form of cultural imperialism where models, theories and interventions associated with special and inclusive education, generated in the UK, are then utilised as *the* framings, perspectives and epistemologies for understanding special and inclusive education in other national locations. Not only is this tendency deeply colonialist, it also ignores the culturally specific and historically embedded nature of education as its response to disability and diversity. This edited volume does the opposite: it works from a particular geopolitical location and generates a number of theoretical and practical responses that have local and global implications. This text will be an important resource not only for Singaporean researchers and practitioners who want to learn more about issues of disability, special and inclusive education, but should also be required reading for those who work within, say, the UK and Western Europe to revisit their assumptions and theories through a close engagement with the Singaporean context. By drilling down into key concerns and issues in Singapore, the contributors also offer some deep insights into some of the cultural, economic and structural specificities of this city state. Singapore boasts a rich ethnic, religious and cultural diversity. And as a high income nation, boasting economic wealth and advanced technological resources, Singapore provides a unique context in which to consider questions of special and inclusive education. I have long admired the pride that many Singaporeans clearly have for their country. But this pride should not be read as lacking criticality nor an aversion to asking searching questions of their fellow citizens. This text demonstrates there is an urgent need to investigate how best to support students with special educational needs and disabilities in a rapidly expanding and advancing economy. Moreover, because of cultural diversity, many intriguing questions are raised around the vocation of teachers, the role of families, the flexibility of workplaces and the role of different professions in responding to the aspirations of young people.

From my experience, Singaporeans are tremendously generous hosts (did I mention the lunches?). And this generosity of spirit is evident in this book's approach. The text carefully guides the reader through many important issues related to the inclusion of young people with disabilities and special educational needs. These include explorations of:

- The impact of the UN Convention on the Rights of Persons with Disabilities and its impact on Singaporean educators and students.
- The Ableist under-girding of meritocracy
- The relationship between education and a broad notion of apprenticeship
- Early intervention and early childhood education
- The impact of mainstream and special education on the lives of children with disabilities and special educational needs
- The role of parents and educator-parents in advocating for and supporting their children's learning
- The prevalence of different models of disability including medical, social and human rights perspectives
- The impact of psychological services and differentiation on mainstream educational settings
- Transitions in adulthood and the role of stakeholders
- Preparing young people for adulthood, including questions of sexuality, work and independence
- Specific considerations around mental health, hearing loss and intellectual disabilities

A key quality of the text relates to the ways in which each contributor sits with their topic, question or problem and guides the reader through theoretical terrains, the details of educational settings, the relevance of different practical and pedagogical approaches and the wider significance of their work to education and society. While solutions, good practices and changes to educational provision are identified, contributors often pose important questions about education and society that are raised by the presence of disability and special educational needs. In Chapter 16, for example, Norman Kee Kiak Nam (an educator and parent of three adult sons with autism) writes that "The pertinent issue many parents are naturally facing is whether the current special education curriculum and approach will be able to sufficiently equip and empower their children with special needs to be able to function and access all necessary governmental, work support, living and community services, with the skills and independent self-efficacy, within the context of dynamic and constant local and global changes". This quotation hints at just some of the complex challenges that children and young people face in growing up in the Singaporean context. Add into the mix the presence of disability and special educational needs and one gets a sense of some of the extra theoretical and practical work that is necessary to ensure that all children and young people are supported to realise their potential.

This book offers some unique insights into the ways in which advocates and educators are working together to create an inclusive society for all children and young people. Moreover, in focusing on the lives of young people with disabilities and special educational needs, we also proffer opportunities for asking wider questions of the human condition (Goodley, 2020). If educational systems, teachers, curriculum and assessment methods excluded children with disabilities, what does this say about education per se? Moreover, if we take the argument that an educational system is a direct reflection of its national context, then what does this tell us about how disability is understood in that given place? By focusing on the lives of young people, we can contribute to more broader conversations about the ambitions and aspirations of our communities.

Reference

Goodley, D. (2020). *Disability and other human questions*. London: Emerald.

Preface

Wong Meng Ee & Levan Lim

☙❧

The evolution of special education over the past 50 years had modest beginnings but today occupies greater presence in Singapore. Special education is a debatable, emotive and ambivalent topic. Issues in the field such as educational placement in inclusive or special education settings, the categories of disabilities, rights and legal issues, assessment, administration, accommodations, classroom techniques, pedagogies and funding are potentially controversial issues, more so when families are deeply involved.

In the span of the past two decades, mainstream schools have been working to implement tiered systems of support to include students with special educational needs. Mainstream schools today are resourced with allied educators (learning and behavioural support) as well as dedicated groups of Teachers who are trained in Special Needs (TSN). Compulsory education is now extended to include students with disabilities to attend either a mainstream or special school education. A greater number of special schools are partnered with mainstream schools to foster collaboration through satellite arrangements and the special education curriculum framework provides structure and flexibility to guide special education curriculum in special schools. These developments did not happen overnight but were the efforts of multiple stakeholders and agencies that spanned over many years and converged at various propitious periods where timing, leadership, will and climate led to various ministries responding to the disability agenda.

This book is a beginning attempt towards bringing together some enduring issues that are both representative of universal experience as well as those unique to Singapore. The chapters in this book introduce the existing state of special education and, at the same time, discuss controversies surrounding its practices. Some of the content are also drawn from collective years of the editors' experience in teaching the postgraduate course: Issues and Trends in Special Education, a core course in the Master of Education in Special Education at the National Institute of Education, Nanyang Technological University. Students participating in the course are introduced to topical issues in the field where discussions and case studies are explored and in turn, students also bring to the classroom key interests and emergent issues raised from their personal practices for exploration.

Together, this volume offers the reader insight into topics for which significant contributions, both internationally and locally, have shaped our understanding of special needs and special education over the past several decades. The editors have assembled chapters from scholars and practitioners in the fields of special needs education and disability in Singapore. Their interests and expertise span early childhood and early intervention, inclusive and special education, mainstream education, mental health and psychology, social work and social policy, post-school transition, employment and parental perspective. Authors were invited to develop a chapter on their particular expertise area and discuss key and emergent related issues, many of which are enduring. As our understanding of the issues deepen, we will likely find ourselves returning to the same questions in the future.

This collection may also be of interest to global readers as many of the issues related to disabilities are not constrained to legislations, or traditions of any given nation. It is focused primarily on current issues in Singapore, but it includes cultural and international literature, and comparisons and issues not tied to any particular nation or culture. Like other handbooks, it is intended to be a reference volume for students, educators, researchers and administrators in Singapore and in the international arena.

A Word on Terminology

There are two main issues that come into question when writing on disability. Firstly, which is appropriate: 'person with a disability' or 'disabled person'? 'People with disabilities' is referred to as 'person-first' language as it emphasizes the personhood rather than the disability and is seen to be the trend in North America (Goodley, 2011) and generally advocated amongst professionals and professional bodies such as the American Psychological Association to demonstrate respect, sensitivity and to strive towards cultural competence (Dunn & Andrews, 2015). The UN Convention on the Rights of Persons with Disabilities (CRPD) also adopts a person-first language. From Article 1, the CRPD sets out the purpose of the convention with the term 'persons with disabilities' (United Nations Enable, n.d.). By extension, person-first language use is also broadly mandated in scholarly journals and academic programmes (Peers, Spencer-Cavaliere & Eales, 2014). Likewise, this too has been the position taken at the National Institute of Education.

By contrast, there is a growing movement within the disability rights community to question the need for and implications of universal use of person-first language (e.g., Brown, 2012). Instead, authors and activists promote an identity-first posture, one where disability is focused not about bodily impairment, inadequacy, failing or misfortune but considering disability as a culturally composed and shared narrative of the body to study the inequality of distribution of power, resources, status, etc. in society (Brueggemann, 2013). In so doing, the assertion of the identity-first language approach allows for disabled individuals and groups to "claim" the disability as a fact, as well as reframe it as a point of pride.

Claiming disability means valuing disability, that the disabled person chooses his or her identity in lieu of permitting others (e.g., family, peers, employers, medical or rehabilitation professionals, educators, researchers, strangers) to name it. This promotes autonomy, agency and indicates a decision to exercise choice over one's disability destiny (Brueggemann, as cited in Dunn & Andrews, 2015).

Advocates of disability culture and scholars in disability studies are sensitive to the contested nature of International Classification Schemes and do not support describing disabled people as mentioned above (Brueggemann, 2013; Davis, 2013; Goodley, 2011). Disability and Society, a prominent journal in the field, explicitly expresses this as part of the language policy (Taylor & Francis, 2020), for example.

The preference in Singapore is the first-person language and readers will soon discover for themselves that without prompting, an interesting observation is that contributors have adopted the person-first language in this book. One possible explanation to how the preference is part of the field could be the dominance of professionals in the disability space. Until the disability movement gains greater momentum in Singapore, we watch with interest if the terminology shifts towards the identity-first language would align with international trends. Of course, it is also very likely to remain as polarized in Singapore as it already is elsewhere as described above.

Secondly, connected to this use of terminology is the term, special educational needs (SEN). This has been the term adopted in Singapore to describe broadly students with disabilities requiring support in education. In tracing its origins, the term 'special educational needs' originated from the UK, particularly the Warnock Report in the late 1970s. Prior to this term, children were referred to their ten categories of 'handicap' as set out in the regulations of the 1944 Education Act.

The Warnock Report in 1978, followed by the 1981 Education Act (DES, 1981), altered the conceptualisation of special education by emphasizing first the child's educational need instead of their individual learning disability or impairment. Today, in the context of educational provision, the term SEN has a legal definition that refers to children who have learning difficulties and/or disabilities, which make it more difficult for them to learn or access education than most children of the same age (Hodkinson, 2016).

If we look back at historical developments, Singapore too has by and large moved away from the now pejorative but once commonplace terminology such as educationally subnormal, spastic, retarded and crippled (Lim & Nam, 2000; Poon & Wong, 2017). In its efforts to serve the disability population, the government describes its disability schemes and services to support physical disabilities, intellectual disabilities, autism spectrum disorder, hearing impairment and visual impairment (Ministry of Social & Family Development, 2016). The government also acknowledges there is no one uniform definition of disability in Singapore but adopts the one cited in the Enabling Masterplan (2007–2011) where persons with disabilities include all persons "whose prospects of securing, retaining places and advancing in education and training institutions, employment and recreation as equal members of the community are substantially reduced as a result of physical, sensory, intellectual and developmental impairments". (para 3).

Just as the use of terminology at the international stage is diverse, the vernacular adopted in Singapore, as well as in this book, uses the terms 'special educational needs', 'special needs' and 'disability' to describe the population under consideration. This also serves at the most fundamental level to acknowledge that the issues do not only concern those relating to education but extends beyond the strict confines of special education interests.

While we have attempted to include major trends and issues of special education in Singapore, it would be presumptuous of us to believe that we have managed to do just that; there is always more to comment upon. While this book was in the works, the case has been proven unequivocally with the 2019 Coronavirus (COVID-19) impacting the world.

In the spring of 2020, schools around the globe shut down in response to the COVID-19 pandemic. In mid-April 2020, 1.5 billion children and youth from 195 countries from pre-primary to university were affected from school closures. Of the 195 countries, 128 countries had not announced plans for reopening schools (UNESCO,

2019). Singapore suspended school from 8 April to 4 May 2020 following Prime Minister Lee Hsien Loong's 3 April 2020 announcement of the circuit breaker to stop the spread of COVID-19. Within the short period, schools in Singapore scrambled to adapt to new demands such as ensuring physical health and safety of students, implementing quality home-based learning (HBL) and providing technology to families at home. Approximately 12,500 devices, including tablets and laptops, were loaned to students. Additionally, 1,200 internet enabling devices such as dongles were also made available to students. In spite of the circuit breaker measures, the Ministry of Education reported more than 4,000 students, about one percent of students across primary schools, secondary schools and junior colleges who continued to attend school as they either had parents who worked in essential services and did not have alternative care arrangements or needed additional support by way of access to digital devices or required regular face-to-face engagement (TodayOnline, 2020).

Amidst the educational response to the outbreak, little is known about students with special educational needs during the period of the COVID-19 pandemic. The limited literature does, however, report that the emergency remote teaching had increased concerns of educational equity given that students with fewer resources had less access to technology to enable online learning. The emergency situation was also challenging for special education teachers, especially those who teach students with significant support needs (Schuck & Lambert, 2020; Tremmel, Myers, Brunow & Hott, 2020)

The suddenness of the COVID-19 pandemic threatened the stability of education for all students across the world. At the same time, the response to the pandemic has also seen the community stepping up vigorously to the challenges arising from the situation as well as gleaning lessons as data became available. Drawing from similar lessons, where the 1918 influenza imposed a global pandemic to claim the lives of millions of people (Morens & Taubenberger, 2018; Viboud & Lessler, 2018), there were also numerous improvements to public health leading to safety measures taken such as handwashing and sanitation, isolation to avoid spreading the virus, and public education to minimize spread of the pandemic (Martini *et al.*, 2019). Many of these lessons learnt then remain relevant during our fight against the COVID-19 pandemic today.

Underlying the efforts then and now is the momentum of the spirit to drive against seemingly insurmountable odds that may potentially derail the disability agenda in Singapore. In a similar vein, let us keep the momentum in motion to stay the course for persons with disabilities despite the presence of the current outbreak. If the lessons learnt from the 1918 influenza pandemic has contributed in informing us about managing today's COVID-19 pandemic, we look to the continued efforts in staying the course in the present as we grow and seek to flourish the disability and special educational needs fields for the future.

References

Brueggemann, B. J. (2013). Disability studies/disability culture. In M. L. Wehmeyer (Ed.), *Oxford handbook of positive psychology and disability* (pp. 279–299). New York, NY: New York: Oxford University Press.

Brown, L. (2012). Identity-first language. Autistic Self-Advocacy Network. Retrieved from http://autisticadvocacy.org/identity-first-language/

Davis, L. J. (Ed.). (2013). *The disability studies reader* (4th ed.). New York, NY: Routledge.

Department of Education and Science (DES) (1981). *The 1981 Education Act.* London: HMSO.

Dunn, D. S., & Andrews, E. E. (2015). Person-first and identity-first language: Developing psychologists' cultural competence using disability language. *American Psychologist, 70*(3), 255–264.

Goodley, D. (2011). *Disability studies: An interdisciplinary introduction.* Thousand Oaks, CA: Sage.

Hodkinson, A. (2016). *Key issues in special educational needs and inclusion* (2nd Ed.) London: Sage.

Lim, L., & Nam, S. (2000). Special education in Singapore. *Journal of Special Education, 34*(2), 104–109.

Martini, M., Gazzaniga, V., Bragazzi, N. L., & Barberis, I. (2019). The Spanish influenza pandemic: A lesson from history 100 years after

1918. *Journal of Preventive Medicine and Hygiene, 60*(1), E64–E67. https://doi.org/10.15167/24214248/jpmh2019.60.1.1205

Ministry of Social and Family Development (MSF). (2016). *Singapore country report: UN Convention on the rights of people with disabilities.* Singapore: Ministry of Social and Family Development.

Ministry of Social and Family Development (MSF). (2007). *Enabling masterplan 2007–2011.* Singapore: Ministry of Social and Family Development.

Morens, D. M., & Taubenberger, J. K. (2018). Influenza cataclysm, 1918. *The New England Journal of Medicine, 379*(24), 2285–2287. http://doi.org/10.1056/NEJMp1814447

Peers, D., Spencer-Cavaliere, N., & Eales, L. (2014). Say what you mean: Rethinking disability language. *Adapted Physical Activity Quarterly, 31*, 265–282. http://dx.doi.org/10.1123/apaq.2013-0091

Poon, K. K. & Wong, M. E. (2017). Historical development of disability services in Singapore: Enabling persons with disabilities. In R. Hanes, I. Brown, & N. E. Hansen, (Eds.), *The Routledge history of disability.* (pp. 204–215). London: Routledge.

Schuck, R. K., & Lambert, R. (2020). "Am I doing enough?" Special educators' emergency remote teaching in spring 2020. *Education Sciences, 10*(11), 320.

Taylor & Francis (2020). Editorial on language policy: Guidelines for Disability and Society authors. Retrieved from https://www.tandfonline.com/pb-assets/CDSO/LANGUAGE-POLICY-GUIDELINES-1573659845283.pdf

TodayOnline. (2020, April 20). More than 4,000 students continue to go to school during Covid-19 circuit breaker period: MOE students at Dazhong primary school during the circuit breaker period. *TodayOnline.* Retrieved from https://www.todayonline.com/singapore/more-4000-students-continue-go-school-during-covid-19-circuit-breaker-period-moe

Tremmel, P., Myers, R., Brunow, D. A., & Hott, B. L. (2020). Educating students with disabilities during the COVID-19 pandemic: Lessons learned from Commerce Independent School District. *Rural Special Education Quarterly, 39*(4), 201–210.

United Nations Enable. (n.d.). Article1 – purpose. Retrieved from https://www.un.org/development/desa/disabilities/convention-on-the-rights-of-persons-with-disabilities/article-1-purpose.html

UNESCO. (2019). 1.3 billion learners are still affected by school or university closures, as educational institutions start reopening around the world, says UNESCO. Retrieved from https://en.unesco.org/news/13-billion-learners-are-still-affected-school-university-closures-educational-institutions

Viboud, C., & Lessler, J. (2018). The 1918 influenza pandemic: Looking back, looking forward. *American Journal of Epidemiology, 187*(12), 2493–2497. https://doi.org/10.1093/aje/kwy207

List of Contributors

Dr Mariam ALJUNIED is the Principal Educational Psychologist at the Special Educational Needs Division in the Ministry of Education. Concurrently, she is an Adjunct Associate Professor with the NUS Psychology Department and the Office of Education Research in NIE/NTU. Internationally, she is known for her role as Chartered Psychologist and Associate Fellow of the British Psychological Society, and Research Associate in University College London. In recognition of her significant contribution to the field of psychology and special needs, she received the Public Administration Medal from the President of Singapore in 2009 and 2018, and the Fulbright Outstanding Researcher Award in 2011. She is active in several social service organisations and is a board member of the National Council for Social Service (2018–present).

Dr CHONG Suet Ling obtained her doctorate in School Psychology and is a Principal Educational Psychologist at the Ministry of Education. She has devoted a large part of her career to enhancing inclusive supports for students with special educational needs, and has spearheaded key directives and initiatives for quality curriculum and student outcomes in Special Education in the last 10 years. An area she is passionate about is studying and seeing to successful transitions of students with moderate–severe special educational needs to post school settings and life outcomes in living, learning and working. She has forged a successful inter-ministry and multi-agency collaboration to co-create School-to-Work pathways for students with diverse needs in Special Education, and is currently building school capability in person-centred transition planning in collaboration with students and families.

Dr Ailsa GOH is a special education Lecturer in the Psychology and Child & Human Development academic group at the National Institute of Education (Singapore). She received her PhD in Special Education from Lehigh University (USA). She has previously taught at the Texas A&M University-Commerce. Her most recent research projects are in the areas of transition to adulthood for youths with intellectual disabilities, equine assisted learning and positive teacher language. Her work has been published in peer-reviewed journals such as Remedial and Special Education, Education and Training in Autism and Developmental Disabilities and Journal of Positive Behavior Interventions. Her research interests include positive behavioural interventions and supports, social and emotional development of at-risk youth, the effect of in-service professional development on educators and transition to adulthood for individuals with disabilities.

Ms Tina HUNG was the Deputy CEO at the National Council of Social Service (NCSS) from 2007–2020. She led NCSS efforts in service planning, innovation and fund allocation to address service gaps for vulnerable populations. Since 2015, she has provided strategic leadership to pursue research and guide public education efforts to fight stigma and promote social inclusion for people with disability and persons with mental health conditions. In her current role as Senior Consultant at the NCSS, she is passionate about developing future leaders, forging sustainable solutions and pioneering and co-creating person-centred, holistic and user empowered services.

Dr Lohsnah JEEVANANDAM is a Clinical Psychologist who trained at the University of Queensland, Australia. She is currently a Senior Lecturer at the National University of Singapore, where she is also the Director of the Clinical Psychology Programme. She is a Senior Consultant Clinical Psychologist with the Cognitive Health

Consultancy International clinic as well as an expert trainer for a range of topics for mainstream and special needs educators. She previously worked at The Movement for the Intellectually Disabled of Singapore and is strongly passionate about the advocacy for persons with Intellectual Disability. She is a locally well-known trainer for sexuality management in persons with Intellectual Disability. When not working, she enjoys movie nights with her two lovely daughters, exercising and catching up with friends.

Mr Norman KEE Kiak Nam, MTech (NUS), MEd (NTU), BSc, DipEd Tech, DipEd, BCSE, former secondary school teacher, is a Lecturer with the Psychology and Child & Human Development Academic Group at the National Institute of Education, Nanyang Technological University, Singapore. He is Board Certified in Special Education and Board Certified Advocate in Special Education by the American Academy of Special Education Professionals. He is also an elected member of the Omega Gamma Chi, a national honor society for special education teachers of the National Association of Special Education Teachers (NASET) and an affiliate member of Chartered College of Teaching.

Ms KU Geok Boon is the founding Chief Executive Officer of SG Enable, a focal agency dedicated to enabling persons with disabilities. Under her leadership, SG Enable developed the Enabling Village, an award-winning inclusive community space with a focus on inclusive training and employment. Enabling Village has received local and international accolades for universal design and social innovation. She believes that embracing diverse experiences and abilities helps businesses grow and ultimately builds a culture that values every individual. She has guided SG Enable to deliver innovative programmes and services for persons with disabilities in Singapore, especially in inclusive employment and community integration. Prior to her position as CEO of SG Enable, she held several leadership positions at the Ministry of Social & Family Development, Ministry of Education and various schools in Singapore.

Dr Levan LIM is an Associate Professor at the Psychology and Child & Human Development Academic Group at the National Institute of Education, Nanyang Technological University. He obtained his Ph.D. in special education from the College of Education, Lehigh University (Pennsylvania, USA), which awarded him in 2007 the Distinguished Educator Award, and previously worked at Charles Sturt University and the University of Queensland (both in Australia). He was Head of the Early Childhood & Special Needs Education Academic Group from 2009 to 2018 which was the department at NIE responsible for teacher education in special needs at the pre-service, in-service and graduate levels. His research and teaching commitments and interests are focused on the inclusion of persons with disabilities, teacher development for inclusion, and interventions for teaching and supporting individuals with disabilities.

Dr LOH Pek Ru is a Lecturer at the Psychology and Child & Human Development Academic Group at the National Institute of Education, Nanyang Technological University. She has a Ph.D. in Applied Psychology and currently teaches pre-service, in-service and postgraduate courses in Special Needs. She was a practicing psychologist in Australia and Singapore, working with children and adolescents with neurodevelopmental and mental health issues. She was also a Postdoctoral Research Fellow at Curtin University from 2009 to 2012. Her research interests include assessment and measurement, ADHD, mental health in special needs and special needs education.

Ms Nursidah MALIK has a MEd in Special Education from the National Institute of Education, Nanyang Technological University, Singapore. She has participated in research projects on equine therapy for youths at risk, transition to adulthood of youths with intellectual disabilities and the effects of art in special education. Her interest in the use of art with students with special needs has led her to her current job as an art trainer in a special education school.

Mr Vimallan MANOKARA, in his current capacity as Head of MINDS Institute, drives research, innovation, training and curriculum development in Intellectual Disability within MINDS and the disability sector at large. His role also involves working very closely with the rest of the senior management and board at MINDS to drive the organisation's strategic and capability development. He also holds appointments as chair of the social service stream of Agency for Integrated Care (AIC)'s Institutional Review Board (IRB) and co-chair of the Disability Research Coalition. His current research interests include quality of life, inclusive employment, ageing and disability as well as inclusive community living. He is currently undertaking his Doctor of Philosophy (PhD) with the University of Sydney which involves developing a holistic model for successful and sustainable open employment for persons with disabilities.

Ms Christina MICHAEL is an educator with almost 30 years of experience in mainstream education both as a teacher and administrator. In 2013, she was posted to the Special Education Branch at the Ministry of Education (MOE) Singapore, where she served as a Senior Inspector overseeing Special Education Schools. A key area of work at the Ministry was to conduct a review of deaf education in local schools. This included a study of educational supports provided in overseas systems for students with hearing loss in mainstream education. She completed her posting at the MOE in 2016 and is currently the Principal of Canossian School, a Special Education school for primary school-aged children with hearing loss.

Dr Letchmi Devi PONNUSAMY (EdD) currently teaches courses in the High Abilities Specialization for the Master of Education programme as well as initial and continuing teacher education courses on pedagogical practice, differentiation for diverse learners and curriculum innovation processes. Her doctoral dissertation focused on the instructional differentiation strategies and challenges faced by teachers working in mixed ability classrooms across four different subject areas in Singaporean secondary schools. Her experience in educational research began with work in locating trends and issues in teacher education across international contexts. Her other research interests include issues pertaining to differentiation, high ability learner engagement, creativity, concept-focused instruction and teacher learning. She has published on teachers' work including differentiation in mixed ability contexts, curriculum development for high ability learners, creativity and critical thinking approaches as well as on teacher learning during pedagogical change.

Dr Kenneth K. POON is Associate Professor at the Psychology and Child & Human Development Academic Group at the National Institute of Education, Nanyang Technological University. He also serves as Associate Dean (Education Research) at the Office of Education Research, and as Centre Co-Director at the Centre for Research in Child Development. He obtained a PhD specialising in early childhood intervention and autism spectrum disorders. Bringing his training as a psychologist and early childhood special educator, he is currently Principal Investigator of a Tran-SEN, a study of over 600 children with special educational needs in Singapore primary and special schools. He also serves as President of Rainbow Centre, Singapore, a social service agency running three special education campuses and two early intervention centres. He is a board member of the National Council of Social Service. Additionally, he serves as Treasurer on the Board of the International Society for the Scientific Study on Intellectual Disabilities, and on the editorial boards of several international peer reviewed journals.

Dr Joanna TAY-LIM is a Lecturer with the Psychology and Child & Human Development Academic Group of the National Institute of Education, Nanyang Technological University. She conducts courses for pre- and in-service early childhood and primary school teachers in various NIE and professional development programmes. She has also contributed to various early childhood settings here in Singapore through professional talks and in an advisory capacity. She has wide-ranging experiences within the education sector. Prior to entering the early childhood field, she taught in junior college and special needs settings. She has also been an early childhood educator in preschool settings and a teacher educator for early childhood courses before she assumed her present position. Her research interests are focused on young children's learning and well-being, inclusive practices, school transitions, classroom management and programme quality.

Dr Thana THAVER is a Senior Lecturer with the Psychology and Child & Human Development Academic Group, National Institute of Education, Nanyang Technological University, Singapore. She teaches a range of courses from general pedagogies in teaching and learning, educational psychology to inclusive education. She is currently Assistant Dean, Professional & Leadership Development at the Office of Graduate Studies and Professional Learning, NIE. Prior to joining NIE, she was with Singapore's Ministry of Education where she was involved in curriculum development and coaching teachers in the Gifted Education Programme.

Dr WONG Meng Ee received his PhD from the University of Cambridge. He is presently tenured Associate Professor at the Psychology and Child & Human Development Academic Group at the National Institute of Education, Nanyang Technological University. He researches and teaches in areas of special and inclusive education, assistive technology, disability studies and teacher education across diploma and postgraduate courses. He has published in international journals including Asia Pacific Journal of Education, British Journal of Visual Impairment, International Journal of Inclusive Education, Journal of Visual Impairment and Blindness, and Support for Learning. He has also published book chapters with Lexington Books, McGraw-Hill, Springer and Routledge. Additionally, he has reviewed for some of the aforementioned titles. He currently serves on a number of non-profit and charity organisations including SG Enable and iC2PrepHouse serving individuals with disabilities. In 2019, he was appointed Chairman of the Goh Chok Tong Enable Fund. Outside his academic endeavours, he is a keen athlete having completed five full marathons, two biathlons, two 10km open water swims and competed in competitive swimming; participating last at the 2015 ASEAN Para Games with two bronze medals in the Men's S12 50m and 100m freestyle. Today, he is fighting to battle the bulge.

Dr XIE Huichao is an Assistant Professor in the Psychology and Child & Human Development Academic Group at the National Institute of Education, Singapore. She completed her special education teaching licence and PhD training at the University of Oregon, USA. Before that, she worked for ten years with young children at risk of or with developmental disabilities and their families as an early interventionist, consultant and teacher trainer. Her research focuses on developing assessment instruments and procedures for parents and teachers to understand and interact with young children in everyday life and adapting evidence-based pedagogical approaches to support children with diverse needs in community preschools. She serves as an invited reviewer and member on the editorial board for reputable academic journals and as a consultant for the early childhood service providers and universities in the United States, China and Singapore.

Dr YANG Xueyan completed her PhD in Special Education with a focus on Early Childhood at the University of Washington. Guided by the ecological systems framework, her research centres on families in the critical role of supporting children with disabilities and seeks to understand the intersecting systems they interact with, including family-professional collaboration and supporting families in the community. Her work has focused on the critical role of grandparents supporting children with disabilities by examining their roles, experiences and support needs through a series of qualitative and mixed methods research. She has also been involved in research projects on early childhood intervention programmes, inclusive education and transition in Singapore. She currently serves as a research fellow at the Centre for Research in Child Development at the National Institute of Education, Nanyang Technological University, Singapore.

CHAPTER 1
Special Needs and Inclusion

Levan Lim & Wong Meng Ee

ಛಿಲ್

Introduction: The Global Context

Over the past 30 years, the fields of special needs education and disability around the world have increasingly embraced inclusion as a core concept and value in promoting the rights of persons with special needs or disabilities and improving their quality of life outcomes. This global inclusion trend finds its origins in the Universal Declaration of Human Rights (UNDHR) which was proclaimed by the United Nations General Assembly in Paris on 10 December 1948. This milestone declaration represented for the very first time in human history the collective determination of the world community to chart a future for humanity after the horrors of two world wars in the first half of the 20th century. This declaration sets forth common standards for the protection of fundamental human rights for all peoples and all nations including the right of all human beings to education and education's role in promoting and maintaining understanding, friendship and peace among diverse groups and nations (United Nations, 1948).

Over the past 70 years, the UNDHR has continued to wield its influence through new international declarations and initiatives to further protect and uphold human rights, including the basic right of all human beings to education, as fundamentals for nations to evolve progressively towards building just, equitable and inclusive societies. The growth of inclusive education over the past few decades across the globe recognises and credits the UNDHR as providing the foundational impetus for the rights-based approach to education (Opertti, Walker & Zhang, 2014). This rights-based approach to education received particular focus in the 1990s for children, youth and adults with special needs with a salient emphasis on their right to inclusion, membership and belonging within regular schools and communities, as evident in the Salamanca Statement and Framework on Action for Special Needs Education (UNESCO, 1994).

Over a quarter of century has passed since this most prominent international statement on special needs education emerged from the World Conference on Special Needs Education at Salamanca in Spain which was organised by the United Nations Educational, Scientific and Cultural Organisation (UNESCO) and the government of Spain. The momentous milestone achieved at this conference was the agreement by representatives from 92 governments and 25 international organisations to endorse and work towards inclusive education, since it is "the most effective means of combating discriminatory attitudes, creating welcoming communities, building an inclusive society and achieving education for all" (UNESCO, 1994, p. ix). The Salamanca Statement provided the premise upon which inclusive education was extended beyond special needs to all children from marginalised, disadvantaged and excluded communities, as promulgated by new declarations in the 2000s such as the 2000 Education for All (UNESCO, 2000). According to inclusive education scholars (e.g., Ainscow, Slee & Best, 2019), the Salamanca Statement has had and continues to have a major worldwide influence on many countries in adopting and developing inclusion policies and practices for all learners regardless of their diverse backgrounds or profiles.

Another landmark global response to the challenge of protecting and promoting the rights of persons with disabilities is the

Convention on the Rights of Persons with Disabilities (CRPD), an international human rights treaty of the United Nations. The CRPD, which was adopted by the United Nations General Assembly in 2006, builds upon previous international statements and declarations related to people with disabilities by setting out the legal obligations of states to protect and promote the rights of persons with disabilities as equal and full members of society (United Nations, 2006). Acting as a development as well as a human rights instrument, remarkable progress has reportedly been made in the worldwide implementation of the CRPD in guiding and supporting member states in formulating and enforcing their legislations, strategies, policies and programmes to promote the equality, empowerment and inclusion of persons with disabilities in their societies (United Nations, 2016).

These global conventions and statements to uphold the human rights of persons with disabilities and their inclusion within society have contributed much to refuting previous international trends of segregating or separating persons with disabilities from their communities by placing them within institutional arrangements where opportunities to interact and form relationships with others in society were curtailed or limited, or seeking to fit or integrate persons with disabilities into society with the emphasis on changing them instead of changing society and public attitudes to accept and include them. By according universal recognition of the inherent dignity of persons with disabilities and placing the accountability on member states to protect, promote and ensure their full enjoyment of fundamental human rights and freedoms, these latest global developments and trends have contributed to a paradigm shift in approaches and attitudes within the fields of special needs education and disability across many countries around the world, including Singapore.

The Singapore Context

As a country with an exceptional record of economic and social stability achieved over the past five decades, Singapore has moved progressively in joining many global networks as well as adopting international conventions and treaties. Although Singapore did not participate in the World Conference in Special Needs Education at Salamanca and was not a signatory to the Salamanca Statement and Framework for Action on Special Needs Education, Singapore signed the United Nations Convention on the Rights of Persons with Disabilities (UNCRPD) in November 2012 and ratified the convention on 18 July 2013 (Ministry of Social & Family Development, 2016). Significant progress in the fields of special needs education and disability was already noted in the years preceding Singapore's ratification of the UNCRPD, particularly after 2004.

Singapore's historical developments in the fields of special needs education and disability can be categorised into two epochs — before and after 2004. In retrospect, 2004 has been described as the watershed year (Lim & Thaver, 2018) for these fields in light of the explicit mention by Prime Minister Lee Hsien Loong, in his inauguration speech, of persons with disabilities as part of the inclusive society vision for Singapore and his call, about a month later after his inauguration, for better efforts to integrate students with special needs within mainstream schools. The subsequent developments in these fields that soon followed were unprecedented in scope and outreach. For example, the National Institute of Education was tasked with the personnel preparation of a new educator profession — Allied Educators (Learning & Behavioural Support), formerly known as Special Needs Officers — to support students with special needs in mainstream schools, and began a new programme to equip mainstream school teachers with the values, skills and knowledge to include and support students with special needs within mainstream classrooms. The fact that these two programmes have continued to sustain and grow over time till the present bears testimony to Singapore's long-term commitment to investing in resources that support the inclusion of students with special needs in mainstream schools.

On a societal level, the most comprehensive, wide-ranging and longstanding national masterplan ever to have been developed in Singapore for persons with disabilities was launched in 2007. After its initial five-year span (2007–2011), this first Enabling Masterplan was succeeded consecutively by the second (2012–2016) and third (2017–2021) Enabling Masterplans. These Enabling Masterplans essentially aim to build an inclusive society in Singapore where persons with disabilities can be supported and empowered to become integral and contributing members of society. Much progress achieved in the direction towards inclusion during the post-2004 epoch in the fields of special needs education and disability in Singapore can be attributed to these Enabling Masterplans. The consecutive succession of these plans have sustained the momentum of building upon previous efforts and continuing key agendas important to the lives of Singaporeans with disabilities and their families.

In reviewing the literature that has been published about the trends and developments within the fields of special needs education and disability in Singapore, there is clear evidence of changing emphases between the two epochs of developments in these fields. Earlier literature published prior to and during 2004 (e.g., Lim & Nam, 2000; Lim & Quah, 2004; Quah, 1990; Quah, 2004; Quah, Lim & Poon-McBrayer, 2004) highlighted the integration, rather than the inclusion, of students with disabilities into mainstream schools as the prevailing normative philosophy and practice. This emphasis on integration reflected the ideas and beliefs of the pre-2004 epoch which was defined and influenced by the most significant document concerning persons with disabilities at that period: *The Report of the Advisory Council for the Disabled: Opportunities for the Disabled* (1988). On the integration of students with disabilities, this document stated "Whenever appropriate and feasible, special education should be provided within the regular educational system. A child should only be placed in a special school if he cannot be well educated in a regular school" (pp. 37–38). This report also recommended that "integration should fit the disabled child to the most suitable educational environment" (p. 38); but in reality, during that period, special education services were generally provided outside the mainstream education system (Quah, 1993).

This earlier body of literature also noted that special needs education in Singapore was closely associated with and largely defined by the special education system of services consisting of voluntary welfare organisations (currently known as Social Service Agencies) charged with the running of special schools and adult disability services. A dual system of educating students with and without disabilities was clearly in place (Lim & Nam, 2000) which, in itself, posed barriers to integration efforts to promote greater opportunities for interaction between these two groups of students. Prospects for inclusion or inclusive education in Singapore in the first epoch of developments in the fields of special needs education and disability were quite dim (Lim & Nam, 2000; Lim & Tan, 1999).

The literature published in the post-2004 epoch reflect a greater emphasis on using the terms 'inclusive', 'inclusion' and 'inclusive education' in describing the directions, issues involved and efforts to better support the increasing number of students with special needs entering mainstream education (e.g., Lim, 2009; Lim & Thaver, 2018; Lim, Thaver & Strogilos, 2019; Lim, Wong & Tan, 2014; Poon, Musti-Rao & Wettasinghe, 2013; Poon *et al.*, 2016; Strogilos & Lim, 2019; Walker & Musti-Rao, 2016; Wong *et al.*, 2015; Yeo *et al.*, 2016; Zhuang, 2016). Over the past 16 years since PM Lee Hsien Loong's inauguration speech and call for better efforts to support students with special needs within mainstream education, the number of students with special needs attending mainstream schools has increased exponentially and there are many more students with special needs enrolled in mainstream education than in the special education system.

This substantial shift in the special needs education landscape towards greater numbers of students with special needs attending mainstream schools, growing up and interacting with their peers without disabilities is a harbinger of a more inclusive society in the future. With a growing awareness and realisation in Singapore that the well-being, quality of life, social connectedness and interests of persons with disabilities hinge upon their inclusion within regular communities and mainstream society, this shift towards emphasizing inclusion — bolstered and reinforced by the Enabling Masterplans and Singapore's ratification of the UNCRPD — will continue to sustain into the future. This trend towards inclusion, however, needs to be responsibly considered, monitored and managed through sufficient attention, funding and resources to address and handle issues arising from supporting increasing numbers of students and individuals with special needs within mainstream schools and communities.

With this trend towards inclusion framing the backdrop of the special needs education and disability fields in Singapore, this book collection of chapters providing information, knowledge, critical and constructive thought, and research across a wide range of topics and issues relevant to the lives of persons with disabilities within our local context, is timely. The chapter contributors are professionals and academics who are prominent in their respective areas of expertise within the fields of special needs education and disability in Singapore, and we greatly appreciate their sharing of knowledge, perspectives and insights related to their own topics of interest. We hope you, the reader, will be meaningfully enriched by the content of these chapters and be encouraged to re-envision and participate in new ways to create a more inclusive society for persons with disabilities.

References

Advisory Council on the Disabled. (1988). *Opportunities for the Disabled.* Singapore: Advisory Council on the Disabled.

Ainscow, M., Slee, R., & Best, M. (2019). Editorial: The Salamanca Statement: 25 years on. *International Journal of Inclusive Education, 23*(7–8), 671–676.

Lim, L., & Nam, S. (2000). Special education in Singapore. *Journal of Special Education, 34*(2), 104–109.

Lim, L. (2009). Possibilities for an inclusive society in Singapore: Becoming inclusive within. *Journal of Policy and Practice in Intellectual Disabilities, 6*(2), 83–85.

Lim, L., & Quah, M. M. (2004). Foresight via hindsight: Prospects and lessons for inclusion in Singapore. *Asia-Pacific Journal of Education, 24*(2), 193–204.

Lim, L., & Tan, J. (1999). The marketization of education in Singapore: Prospects for inclusive education. *International Journal of Inclusive Education, 3*(4), 339–351.

Lim, L., & Thaver, T. (2018). Inclusion of persons with disabilities in Singapore: An evolutionary perspective. In S. Hsu (Ed.), *Routledge Handbook of Sustainable Development* (pp. 373–393). United Kingdom: Routledge.

Lim, L., Thaver, T., & Strogilos, V. (2019). Contextual influences on inclusivity: The Singapore experience. In M. J. Schuelka, C. J. Johnstone, G. Thomas & A. J. Artiles (Eds.), *The SAGE Handbook of Inclusion and Diversity in Education* (pp. 496–508). London, UK: SAGE Publications.

Lim, S. M. Y., Wong, M. E., & Tan, D. (2014). Allied educators (learning and behavioural support) in Singapore's mainstream schools: First steps towards inclusivity? *International Journal of Inclusive Education, 18*(2), 123–139.

Ministry of Social and Family Development. (2013). Singapore ratifies UN Convention on the Rights of Persons with Disabilities (UNCRPD). Retrieved from: https://www.msf.gov.sg/media-room/Pages/Singapore-Ratifies-UNCRPD.aspx

Opertti, R., Walker, Z., & Zhang, Y. (2014). Inclusive education: From targeting groups and schools to achieving quality education as the core of EFA. In L. Florian (Ed.), *The Sage Handbook of Special Education* (pp. 149–170). Thousand Oaks, CA: SAGE Publications Inc.

Poon, K., Musti-Rao, S., & Wettasinghe, M. (2013). Special education in Singapore: History, trends, and future directions. *Intervention in School and Clinic, 49*(1), 59–64.

Poon, K. K., Ng, Z. J., Wong, M. E., & Kaur, S. (2016). Factors associated with staff perceptions towards inclusive education in Singapore. *Asia Pacific of Education, 36*(1), 84–97.

Quah, M. M. (1990). Special education in Singapore. *International Journal of Disability, Development and Education, 37*(2), 137–148.

Quah, M. L. (1993). Special education in Singapore. In M. L. Quah, S. Gopinathan, & S. C. Chang (Eds.), *A Review of Practice and Research in Education for All in Singapore. Country Report Submitted to the Southeast Asian Research, Review and Advisory Group (SEARRAG)* (pp. 89–102). Singapore: National Institute of Education.

Quah, M. M. (2004). Special education in Singapore. In L. Lim, & M. M. Quah (Eds.), *Educating Learners with Diverse Abilities* (pp. 29–61). Singapore: McGraw-Hill.

Quah, M., Lim, L., & Poon-McBrayer, K. F. (2004). Special education in Singapore: Celebrating the past, envisioning the future. *ASCD (Singapore), 12*(2), 27–33.

Strogilos, V., & Lim, L. (2019). Toward inclusive education in Singapore. In V. Argyropoulos & S. Halder (Eds.), *Inclusion, Equity and Access for Individuals with Disabilities: Insights from Educators Across World* (pp. 365–381). Singapore: Palgrave Macmillan.

Thaver, T., & Lim, L. (2014). Attitudes of pre-service mainstream teachers in Singapore towards people with disabilities and inclusive education. *International Journal of Inclusive Education, 18*(10), 1038–1052.

United Nations. (2006). Convention on the Rights of Persons with Disabilities. https://www.un.org/development/desa/disabilities/convention-on-the-rights-of-persons-with-disabilities.html

United Nations. (2016). 10th Anniversary of the adoption of CRPD: 2006 to 2016. https://www.un.org/development/desa/disabilities/convention-on-the-rights-of-persons-with-disabilities/the-10th-anniversary-of-the-adoption-of-convention-on-the-rights-of-persons-with-disabilities-crpd-crpd-10.html

Walker, Z., & Musti-Rao, S. (2016). Inclusion in high achieving Singapore: Challenges of building an inclusive society in policy and practice. *Global Education Review, 3*(3), 28–42.

Wong, M. E., Poon, K. K., Kaur, S., & Ng, Z. J. (2015). Parental perspectives and challenges in inclusive education in Singapore. *Asia-Pacific Journal of Education, 35*(1), 85–97.

Yeo, L. S., Chong, W. H., Neihart, M. F., & Huan, V. S. (2016). Teachers' experience with inclusive education in Singapore. *Asia-Pacific Journal of Education, 36*(1), 69–83.

Zhuang, K. (2016). Inclusion in Singapore: A social model analysis of disability policy. *Disability & Society, 35*(1), 1–19.

CHAPTER 2

United Nations Convention on the Rights of Persons with Disabilities in Singapore: Considering Some Post-Ratification Implications

Wong Meng Ee

ಅಶಿ

Introduction

The introduction of the United Nations Convention on the Rights of Persons with Disabilities, henceforth CRPD or the Convention, and its ratification by 181 nations as of November 2019 (United Nations Treaty Collection, 2019) offers the global community the legal mandate to "promote and protect the rights of persons with disabilities" (United Nations Department of Economic and Social Affairs, n.d.-a). The CRPD represents a commitment to people with disabilities to respect their basic human rights as citizens and seeks to remove barriers to their participation in society. With Singapore ratifying the CRPD in 2013, the potential of the Convention is already in place for Disabled People's Organisations

(DPOs) and their allies in civil society to engage the government to implement the Convention to turn rights into realities (Wong, Low & Appelhans, 2017).

Background to the Convention

Over several decades, the CRPD and its instruments that many countries have adopted promote and protect the rights of persons with disabilities. From the Universal Declaration of Human Rights in 1948 (Wilson & Daar, 2013), other key landmarks that have influenced the promotion of the rights of persons with disabilities include the World Programme of Action Concerning Disabled Persons (United Nations Department of Economic and Social Affairs, 1982), the principles for the protection of persons with mental illness and the improvement of mental health care by the Office of the United Nations High Commissioner for Human Rights [OHCHR] (OHCHR, 1991), the Standard Rules on the Equalization of Opportunities for Persons with Disabilities (United Nations Department of Economic and Social Affairs, 1993), and the Declaration on the Rights of Disabled Persons (OHCHR, 1975; United Nations Department of Economic and Social Affairs, n.d.-a). The United Nations General Assembly adopted the CRPD in 2006 and it was subsequently entered into force on May 3, 2008 (United Nations Department of Economic and Social Affairs, n.d.-b). The CRPD is the first legally binding international instrument with comprehensive protection of the rights of persons with disabilities, and sets out legal obligations on States to promote and protect the rights of persons with disabilities worldwide (United Nations Department of Economic and Social Affairs, n.d.-a).

With an estimated 15 per cent of the world's population reported to have a disability (World Health Organization & The World Bank Group, 2011), this group continues to face discrimination and fails to be accorded respect for their human rights as compared with others (Inter-Agency, 2008). The CRPD was therefore necessary in order to have a clear reaffirmation that the rights of persons with disabilities are human rights and to reinforce respect for these rights (United Nations Department of Economic and Social Affairs, n.d.-a).

The Convention does not create new rights or entitlements for people with disabilities but states existing rights and is positioned to address the needs and situations of persons with disabilities. The Convention validates their full and equal access to the Universal Declaration of Human Rights promulgated in 1948 (United Nations, 2006). In other words, the CRPD emphasises State discrimination against persons with disabilities and underscores the initiatives States need to employ to realise equal access for all, through a barrier free environment (United Nations Department of Economic and Social Affairs, n.d.-a). This is shaped by the espousal of the social model of disability which highlights the many barriers obstructing the rights of people with disabilities, and ways in which these can be dismantled.

With disability brought alongside other inequalities such as poverty and gender in the international community, UN agencies and organisations have an obligation as set forth by the Convention to include persons with disabilities in all policies and development programmes, especially in the eight Millennium Development Goals where their needs were not previously articulated and brought within the monitoring criteria (Mittler, 2012). Some of the developments include the United Nations Development Group (2011). This coordinating agency oversees 25 regional and country teams and has set out guiding strategies and structures to include persons with disabilities in the provision of UN-sponsored aid and development programmes. Similarly, persons with disabilities confronted with emergencies and humanitarian disasters are acknowledged. A CRPD advocacy tool kit is available for survivors of landmines and cluster bombs (United Nations, 2008). In the area of rights, the OHCHR also takes an interest in the rights of persons with disabilities concerning women, children, torture, racial discrimination and civil and political rights (OHCHR, 2010). Especially with regards to the rights of children, the United Nations International Children's Emergency Fund (UNICEF) Innocenti Research Centre has published a comprehensive periodical titled *Promoting the Rights of*

Children with Disabilities (UNICEF, 2007). UNICEF has also developed a child-friendly version of the Convention (UNICEF, 2009). Children continue to feature strongly in the report of the State of Children with Disability where a call for greater inclusion and the assurance of their protection is asserted (UNICEF, 2013).

General Articles of the Convention

The first nine articles of the CRPD are designed to be considered as the foundation to the rest of the Convention: Article 1 (Purpose), Article 2 (Definitions), Article 3 (General principles), Article 4 (General obligations), Article 5 (Equality and non-discrimination), Article 6 (Women with disabilities), Article 7 (Children with disabilities), Article 8 (Awareness-raising), and Article 9 (Accessibility). The ensuing articles, comprising Article 10 (Right to life) and onwards, are to be understood through the concepts addressed in Articles 1 to 9 (Guernsey, Nicoli & Ninio, 2007). While disability is not explicitly defined, the CRPD states that persons with disabilities "include those who have long-term physical, mental, intellectual or sensory impairments which in interaction with various barriers may hinder their full and effective participation in society on an equal basis with others" (United Nations, 2006, Article 1). In this respect, the Convention views disability through the social model of disability (Kayess & French, 2008; Stein & Lord, 2009).

Especially where countries do not have legislation that explicitly supports persons with disabilities, the CRPD provides a compass to guide a course for change, encompassing various fields and addressing a diversity of human rights, including civil, political rights, as well as economic, social and cultural rights (Quinn, 2009; European Foundation Centre, 2010). In doing so, it has raised the profile of disability (Garcia-Iriarte, McConkey & Gilligan, 2015; Lang, 2009).

With great international espousal of the CRPD — 163 countries have signed it and 181 countries have ratified it as of November 2019 (United Nations Treaty Collection, 2019) — it is reasonable to expect that the Convention will guide and transform the reform of state legislation to strive towards significant equality and non-discrimination for persons with disabilities (Dimopoulos, 2010; Guernsey *et al.*, 2007). Similarly, for a country that is accustomed to inventing the future to stay ahead of the curve, it is critical for Singapore to envisage how the ratification of the Convention will impact upon the subsequent purpose, promotion, protection and assurance that all persons with disabilities will fully enjoy the rights and fundamental freedoms as articulated in the Convention. The following section will put forward broad areas for consideration and explore implications for advancing advocacy and opportunities for persons with disabilities.

Key Obligations

As Lord and colleagues (2010) stress, the Convention is a human rights instrument which has an explicit social development dimension. Mittler (2012) asserts that the fundamental principles which the Convention is built upon inherently provides a framework for monitoring or accountability. These include:

- Respect for inherent dignity, individual autonomy, including the freedom to make one's own choices, and independence of persons;
- Non-discrimination;
- Full and active participation and inclusion in society;
- Respect for difference and acceptance of persons with disabilities as part of human diversity and humanity;
- Equality of opportunity;
- Accessibility;
- Equality between men and women; and
- Respect for the evolving capacities of children with disabilities and respect for the rights of children to preserve their identities (Mittler, 2012, p. 11).

The main articles of the Convention reflect fundamental issues commonly expected to be the norm in mainstream participation, yet persons with disabilities continue to experience barriers to entry.

The articles spell out ideals to guide standards and serve as a platform from which State Parties and non-government organisations can work towards dismantling barriers. The broad areas include: women; children; awareness raising; accessibility; right to life; situations of risk and human emergency; equal recognition before the law; access to justice, liberty and security of the person; freedom from torture, cruel, inhuman or degrading treatment and from exploitation, violence and abuse; protection of the integrity of the person; liberty of movement and nationality; living independently and being included in the community; personal mobility; freedom of expression and opinion and access to information; respect for privacy and home and family; education; health; habilitation and rehabilitation; work and employment; adequate standards of living and social protection; participation in social, political and cultural life, recreation, leisure and sport (Mittler, 2012; United Nations Department of Economic and Social Affairs, n.d.-a).

Promoting and Enforcing Accountability

Especially for countries that have ratified the Convention, State Parties have an accountability to their citizens, particularly persons with disabilities to be involved in and participate in the implementation of the process and outcomes of the Convention. Some of the obligations expected of ratified States include:

- Revising or repealing legislation, laws, policies, customs or practices that discriminate against persons with disabilities;
- Consultation with persons with disabilities and their organisations in implementing the Convention; and
- Including disability in all policies (Mittler, 2012; United Nations Department of Economic and Social Affairs, n.d.-a).

To enable these goals, the social model of disability is the overarching framework. As the CRPD gains traction in more countries and becomes more widespread, guidelines on what may constitute reasonable accommodation are increasingly available (United

Nations Department of Economic and Social Affairs, OHCHR & Inter-Parliamentary Union, 2007). To determine the extent to which States have implemented the Convention, there is an increasing availability of monitoring tools suitable for persons with disabilities (Equalities and Human Rights Commission, 2017; Inclusion International, 2009; World Blind Union, 2012).

Additionally, guidelines on the preparation of civil society reports and submissions are also available (International Disability Alliance, 2010; OHCHR, 2010; United Nations Department of Economic and Social Affairs, n.d.-a). All ratifying states have to submit regular reports on their progress to the new Committee on the Rights of Persons with Disabilities of the OHCHR, which has overall monitoring responsibility for all United Nations conventions. In addition to reports submitted by governments, the Committee is open to submissions by non-governmental and civil society organisations. These are published on the internet, together with the Committee's own report and recommendations on the degree to which the Member State is compliant with the Convention. Since the Committee's recommendations are not legally binding, it is important for national organisations of persons with disabilities to use and publicise the Committee's findings in their advocacy campaigns (Mittler, 2012).

Optional Protocol

For individuals or groups who believe they have had their rights violated, the Optional Protocol is a recourse where a complaint can be formally lodged to the Committee on the Rights of Persons with Disabilities. The Committee has authority to investigate serious or ongoing violations of rights under the CRPD. In this provision, DPOs have avenues by which to report violation of rights under the Convention (International Disability Alliance, 2010; OHCHR, 2010).

Implications for Singapore

The call for greater support and inclusion of persons with disabilities in order for them to be included in society has been advocated for in many parts of the world. While some progress has been made, persons with disabilities remain marginalised in society. The Convention is an opportunity for each country to review and improve the quality of life of its citizens with disabilities and to bring forth this commitment as a priority. This commitment is not only the government's but the collective responsibility of its citizens. Singapore already understands this philosophy through its 'many helping hands' approach to addressing social needs (Report of the Advisory Council of the Disabled, 1988). The following presents three broad topics — understanding of disability, advocacy of human rights, and inclusive education — that are likely to contribute to the shaping of disability rights in Singapore.

Understanding Disability

The definition of disability in Singapore was expressed in the 1988 Advisory Council for the Disabled (ACD), chaired by the then Minister for Education, Dr. Tony Tan. It described persons with disabilities as: "those whose prospects of securing, retaining places and advancing in educational and training institutions, employment and recreation as equal members of the community are substantially reduced as a result of physical, sensory and intellectual impairment" (Enabling Masterplan, 2007, p. 1–1).

This was revised in 2004, where the then Ministry of Community Development, Youth and Sports (MCYS) included the term 'developmental' disability in the ACD's definition and it subsequently read: "those whose prospects of securing, retaining places and advancing in education and training institutions, employment and recreation as equal members of the community are substantially reduced as a result of physical, sensory, intellectual and developmental impairments" (Enabling Masterplan, 2007, p. 1–1). This is also "Singapore's current definition of disability" (Enabling Masterplan, 2007, p, 1–1).

As the Committee of the Enabling Masterplan 2007 has identified, the current definition is based on a medical model. While the Enabling Masterplan committee also claims that the definition is shaped by a socio-functional approach, where disability is viewed as a result of physical, institutional and attitudinal barriers in society, this model recognises that there are also social barriers that prevent an individual from integrating into society. However, this apparent acknowledgement of societal barriers as hindrance to full participation is arguably not sufficiently explicit in its definition. In fact, examined on its own, the adopted definition remains entrenched in a medical model, which is also referred to as the individual, tragedy, deficit or psycho-medical model which locates needs and limitations resulting from the individual's impairment (Thomas, 2014).

In contrast, the social model attributes these constraints and limitations as resulting from society, rejecting the notion of disability as derived from impairment. This questions how existing policies and practices relating to disability are implemented and serves as a reminder to review how to respond to disability through the lens of a social model perspective. As the Convention explicitly espouses the social model of disability, the implication for Singapore to embrace and interpret the social model will take time. As government agencies, DPOs and the wider society adjust to the presence of the social model, the topics raised from the Convention present an immediate lens by which a broad range of issues can be reviewed to improve practices in the immediate future. How this is achieved and put across need to be approached with prudence.

Advocacy with a Human Rights Influence

The Convention represents the first comprehensive human rights treaty introduced this century and is based on the social-ecological model of disability adopted by the WHO (Shogren & Turnbull, 2014). The overarching purpose of the CRPD is to "promote, protect, and ensure full and equal enjoyment of all human rights and fundamental freedoms by all persons with disabilities, and to promote respect for their inherent dignity" (United Nations, 2006). Given that the Convention espouses the social model of disability, embedded within the model is a focus on negative or first generation rights (Stein & Stein, 2006). Negative rights are rights such as freedom of expression, association or religion which cannot be restrained (Jones, 2006). In other words, negative rights require others to abstain from interfering in one's actions, i.e., practising one's religion is a negative right since preventing individuals from doing so is unlawful (Foldvary, 2011). Positive rights on the other hand are to be provided as a good or service, i.e., an obligation to receive service as a customer in a restaurant.

This raises the situation where many anti-discrimination laws do not adequately provide for the positive or second generation rights of persons with disabilities. In this light, there will be some persons with disabilities who will not be able to realise the opportunities provided by the existence of negative rights without first having access to positive rights. Drawing a parallel to the situation in Singapore, while the Singapore Constitution guarantees fundamental liberties of all citizens, it can be argued to be lacking in the case of persons with disabilities, especially in the recommendations put forward by the 1988 ACD where it argued for persons with disabilities to enjoy the same rights as people without disabilities to live normally and independently in society (Report of the Advisory Council of the Disabled, 1988). Though the declaration of rights for persons with disabilities to participate fully in society are in place, Wong and colleagues (2017) posit that in the grand scheme of multiple competing rights, how 'rights' are understood is one issue; the other is that there is a hierarchy of rights, where some rights are given more attention over others.

The human rights paradigm takes into account society's proclivity in constructing barriers which it counters with anti-discrimination legislation commonly found in civil and political rights provisions. In the example where the human rights paradigm calls for universal design, equity cannot be realised by implementing universal design per se. Rather, human rights policies needs to be accessible to all, irrespective of abilities. "The human rights paradigm creates a holistic model which continues to protect negative rights while ensuring that rights generally exogenous to civil rights laws are also protected" (Harpur, 2011, p. 1277). Put differently, Stein and Stein (2006) call for achieving "equal opportunity rather than 'merely' equal treatment" (p. 1206). This highlights the limitations of civil rights legislation, such as the Americans with Disabilities Act (Stein & Stein, 2006).

The international trend to link disability rights to human rights in this instance is that the human rights paradigm "operates from the premise that every person has the right to utilize his or her talents", hence "the contribution that a person can make to society should not guide the extent to which that person is provided the opportunity to exercise his or her rights" (Harpur, 2011, p. 1277).

Therefore, this cautions against the motivation of predicating inclusion based on the legal paradigm. Rather, Harpur (2011) argues that the equal opportunity outcome of the human rights paradigm is achieved by enabling all persons to fulfill their potential regardless of their abilities. The paradigm operates from the premise that every person has the right to utilise his or her talents. The contribution that a person can make to society should not guide the extent to which that person is provided the opportunity to exercise his or her rights.

Similarly, as the human rights paradigm becomes more established in societal discourse in Singapore, one possible outgrowth in response to addressing the need to uphold disability rights is the idea of an anti-discrimination legislation. Whether or not this is realised, the implication of a more conscious human rights climate is that societal interest will grow, and passions will be ignited to initiate advocacy and debate. Persons with disabilities will need to navigate this transition with accountability while existing government agencies as well as NGOs might need to shift from entrenched, outmoded disability-related practices and beliefs to embracing inclusive ones. While a languid, conventional or resistant response will aggravate expectant DPOs and their members, overzealousness on the other hand from overcharged advocates may lead to tensions and even jeopardise collaboration with societal partners. This space needs to be managed as parties seek to arrive at a common consensus; adjustments from various parties may need to be made in the light of greater human rights rhetoric and awareness. Understanding the history of Singaporean civil society and being cognizant of the government's presence in the delicate distinction between civic and civil society is crucial (Wong & Goodley, in-submission). Preempting this human rights paradigm raises the adequacy of self-determination curricular citizenship education and the question of how to prepare young people with disabilities to understand their rights and the ways in which they may engage in responsible advocacy. Persons with disabilities need to be represented beyond superficial involvement in large scale public awareness events and be engaged in critical decision-making opportunities (Wong *et al.*, 2017).

Defining Inclusive Education

Article 24 of the Convention expresses a clear legal declaration and proclaims the right to inclusive education for all individuals (United Nations, 2006). Concerns on how children with disabilities are educated are highlighted in the Convention. It remains questionable whether students with special needs have equal access to learning if education is delivered in segregated environments. General Comment Number Four of Article 24 calls attention for States to implement a fully inclusive education system, that children with special education needs should not be excluded from free and compulsory primary and secondary education as a result of their disabilities. Lack of resources should not be a hindrance in providing access to education. Instead, 'progressive realization' is the desired approach in moving towards a fully inclusive education (United Nations Department of Economic and Social Affairs, n.d.-c).

At the same time, neither the Convention nor Article 24 offers legal clarity on the definition and concept of inclusive education (de Beco, 2016; Ssenyonjo, 2016). This ambiguity is consistent in the literature. Despite the espousal of the concept of inclusion and inclusive education over the past four decades, it has not been without challenges and problems in its conceptualisation and practical implementation (Hornby, 2014; Terzi, 2014). Where definitions and concepts are shaped by societal, pedagogical and policy influences (Terzi, 2014), one argument de Beco (2016) asserts is that in seeking to be inclusive, wealthy countries wind up practising inclusion through segregated education, owing to perceived better provision of education for the disabled as well as addressing mainstream teacher resistance. This situation has often resulted in a lowering of education standards leading to poorer opportunities for students with disabilities. With this practice of segregation in place, de Beco (2016) argues that the transformation into a fully inclusive system will be a colossal task.

The above observations reflect similar issues experienced in Singapore. The provision of education for students with disabilities runs along a continuum spanning total segregation to partial integration to total inclusion, depending on the level of needs and support required (Lim & Nam, 2000). While it is not the place to debate the benefits of inclusive versus segregated education here, we still need to bear in mind that parental aspirations for their children to be educated in mainstream schools are not unusual expectations, especially when societal emphasis in Singapore is historically biased towards reputation and outcome as inherent in a meritocratic system (Wong *et al.*, 2015; Wong, in-submission). Additionally, as compulsory education has been extended to "children with moderate to severe special education needs" in 2019 (Ministry of Education, 2019), it is also not unusual for parents to have their aspirations renewed in light of what the Convention stands for in calling for inclusive education. Despite recent efforts in providing greater support for students with special needs in mainstream and special education, the presence of the Convention will bring forth similar concerns in the Singapore context as the definition of inclusive society is progressively refined (Wong & Wong, 2015).

This debate will likely put forward not only key issues regarding disability but also race, gender and social background, as inclusion encompasses a wider range of interconnected factors. In fact, the principle of inclusion is a catalyst for social justice (Ballard, 2003) as it seeks to surmount obstacles in learning and participation with the aim to close the gaps for all children (Booth & Ainscow, 2011). Inclusion is argued to be transformational in nature, since organisations, communities and societies emerge with a greater sensitivity to diversity (Arnesen, Allen & Simonsen, 2009). Furthermore, where inclusion has been the yardstick to appraise and surmount shortcomings, leading to levers for change (Ainscow, 2005), its definition has expanded to also incorporate social justice, human rights, gender, ethnicity, class and health vis-à-vis access, involvement, achievement and participation (Ouane, 2008).

For Singapore to progress with the aims of the CRPD, it is necessary to clarify the definitions of inclusion and inclusive education to advance educational policy and practice. This will be shaped by social, economic, political, cultural and historical make-up (Mitchell, 2005). At the same time, this also calls to question the future of special education (Hyatt & Hornby, 2017), especially when it is explicitly stated in the CRPD that segregated education is not compatible with inclusive education. As Hyatt and Hornby (2017) also raise the critical question on the moral right to receive an education that is most appropriate to one's needs (especially with regard to students with profound disabilities), Singapore will have to continue to wrestle with how to provide appropriate education for students with diverse special education needs.

Conclusion

The CRPD contains the first legal enshrinement of the human rights of persons with disabilities to be enacted in the 21st century. It is a potential catalyst for paradigm change in disability policy and practice, as it can hold respective governments accountable for the promotion and enforcement of disability rights. While there is promise in the CRPD to improve quality of life for persons with disabilities (Verdugo *et al.*, 2012), it is also well noted that the ratification of the CRPD is no panacea for eradicating discrimination and is challenging to implement (Lang, 2009). This chapter has highlighted three areas for consideration as the presence of the CRPD matures in its progressive realisation in Singapore. With greater dissemination of the social model of disability, there is potential for policy and practice to shift accordingly in an inclusive direction. However, this cannot be driven without advocacy and it is timely to consider how best to embrace greater self-determination, citizenship and advocacy responsibilities amongst persons with disabilities. After all, if the CRPD is to invoke greater participation of persons with disabilities, it is *they* who need to stand alongside fellow advocates to strive for greater inclusion. The question of inclusive and special education will once again go under the spotlight in how the CRPD is interpreted for an evolving Singapore.

This will impact not only the special education sector but also the mainstream landscape as greater expectations will require resources to be in place to support shifting trends and influences. One emergent outcome is the increased consciousness of rights. This is still a relatively under-explored area but is an expected discussion point for persons with disabilities and their advocates, in relation to mechanisms for recourse provided for in the CRPD.

References

Ainscow, M. (2005). Developing inclusive education systems: What are the levers for change? *Journal of Educational Change*, 6(2), 109–124.

Arnesen, A., Allen, J., & Simonsen, E. (Eds.) (2009). *Policies and Practices for Teaching Socio-cultural Diversity. Concepts, Principles and Challenges in Teacher Education.* Strasbourg: Council of Europe.

Ballard, K. (2003). The analysis of context: Some thoughts on teacher education, culture, colonisation and inequality. In T. Booth, K. Nes, & M. Stromstad, *Developing Inclusive Teacher Education.* London: Routledge/Falmer.

Booth, T. & Ainscow, M. (2011). *Index for Inclusion: Developing Learning and Participation in Schools* (3rd edition). Bristol: Centre for Studies on Inclusive Education (CSIE).

de Beco, G. (2014). The right to inclusive education according to Article 24 of the UN Convention on the Rights of Persons with Disabilities: Background, requirements and (remaining) questions. *Netherlands Quarterly of Human Rights*, 32, 263–287.

de Beco, G. (2016). Transition to inclusive education systems according to the Convention on the Rights of Persons with Disabilities. *Nordic Journal of Human Rights*, 34(1), 40–59.

Dimopoulos, A. (2010). *Issues in Human Rights Protection of Intellectually Disabled Persons (Medical Law and Ethics)*. England: Ashgate Publishing Ltd.

Equalities and Human Rights Commission. (2017). The United Nations Convention on the Rights of Persons with Disabilities: What does it mean for you? Retrieved from https://www.equalityhumanrights.com/sites/default/files/the-united-nations-convention-on-the-rights-of-persons-with-disabilities-what-does-it-mean-for-you.pdf

European Foundation Centre. (2010, October). Study on challenges and good practices in the implementation of the UN Convention on the Rights of Persons with Disabilities VC/2008/1214: Final Report. Retrieved November 6, 2019, from https://www.werkhoezithet.nl/doc/kennisbank/good_practices_implementation_UN-Convention.pdf

Foldvary, F. E. (2012). Positive rights. In D. K. Chatterjee (Ed.), *Encyclopedia of Global Justice*. Retrieved November 7, 2019, from https://doi.org/10.1007/978-1-4020-9160-5_359

Garcia-Iriarte, E., McConkey, R., & Gilligan, R. H. (2015). *Disability and Human Rights: Global Perspectives*. Palgrave Macmillan, London.

Guernsey, K., Nicoli, M., & Ninio, A. (2007). Convention on the Rights of Persons with Disabilities: Its implementation and relevance for the World Bank (Publication No. 0712). Retrieved from the World Bank Group website: http://documents.worldbank.org/curated/en/559381468314987023/pdf/399830SP071201PUBLIC1.pdf

Harpur, P. (2011). Time to be heard: How advocates can use the convention on the rights of persons with disabilities to drive change. *Valparaiso University Law Review, 45*(3), 1271–1296.

Hornby, G. (2014). *Inclusive Special Education: Evidence-based Practices for Children with Special Needs and Disabilities*. New York: Springer.

Hyatt, C., & Hornby, G. (2017). Will UN Article 24 lead to the demise of special education or to its re-affirmation? *Support for Learning, 32*(3), 288–304. doi:10.1111/1467-9604.12170

Inclusion International. (2009, July 3). Priorities for people with intellectual disabilities in implementing the United Nations Convention on the Rights of People with Disabilities. Retrieved from https://inclusion-international.org/priorites-for-people-with-intellectual-disabilities-in-implementing-the-un-crpd/

Inter-Agency. (2008, July 1). Convention on the Rights of Persons with Disabilities: Advocacy toolkit. Retrieved from http://www.unhcr.org/refworld/docid/497f04592.html

International Disability Alliance. (2010, May). Guidance document: Effective use of international human rights monitoring mechanisms to protect the rights of persons with disabilities. Retrieved from https://www.internationaldisabilityalliance.org/sites/default/files/documents/crpd-reporting-guidance-document-english-final-print1.pdf

Jones, P. (2006). Human rights. In *Routledge Encyclopedia of Philosophy*. doi:10.4324/9780415249126-S105-1

Kayess, R., & French, P. (2008). "Out of the darkness into light"? Introducing the Convention on the Rights of Persons with Disabilities. *Human Rights Law Review, 8*(1), 1–34.

Lang, R. (2009). The United Nations Convention on the Right and Dignities for Persons with Disability: A panacea for ending disability discrimination? *ALTER: European Journal of Disability Research, 3*(3), 266–285.

Lord, J., Posarac, A., Marco, N., Peffley, K., Mcclain-Nhlapo, C., & Keogh, M. (2010). Disability and international cooperation and development: A review of policies and practices (English) (56092). Retrieved from the World Bank Group website: http://documents.worldbank.org/curated/en/810301468340477288/Disability-and-international-cooperation-and-development-a-review-of-policies-and-practices

Mannan, H., MacLachlan, M., & McVeigh, J. (2012). Core concepts of human rights and inclusion of vulnerable groups in the United Nations Convention on the Rights of Persons with Disabilities. *ALTER — European Journal of Disability Research, 6*, 159–177.

Megret, F. (2008). The disabilities convention: Towards a holistic concept of rights. *International Journal of Human Rights, 12*, 261–277.

Ministry of Education. (2019, April 18). Overview of compulsory education. Retrieved November 6, 2019, from https://www.moe.gov.sg/primary/compulsory-education/overview#:~:text=What%20is%20compulsory%20education%20(CE,school%20regularly%20if%20they%20are%3A&text=Living%20in%20Singapore.

Mittler, P. (2012). It's our convention: Use it or lose it? *Disability, CBR & Inclusive Development, 23*(2), 7–21. doi:10.5463/dcid.v23i2.141

OHCHR. (1975, December 9). Declaration on the rights of disabled persons. Retrieved from: https://www.ohchr.org/EN/ProfessionalInterest/Pages/RightsOfDisabledPersons.aspx

OHCHR. (1991, December 17). Principles for the protection of persons with mental illness and the improvement of mental health care. Retrieved November 7, 2019, from: https://www.who.int/mental_health/policy/en/UN_Resolution_on_protection_of_persons_with_mental_illness.pdf

OHCHR. (2010). Monitoring the convention on the rights of persons with disabilities: Guidance for human rights monitors. Professional training series no. 17. Retrieved from https://www.ohchr.org/Documents/Publications/Disabilities_training_17EN.pdf

Ouane, A. (2008, November). Creating education systems which offer opportunities for lifelong learning. Presented at International Conference on Education: "Inclusive Education: The Way of the Future". Geneva: United Nations Educational, Scientific and Cultural Organization. Retrieved from http://www.ibe.unesco.org/fileadmin/user_upload/Policy_Dialogue/48th_ICE/CONFINTED_48_Inf_2__English.pdf

Quinn, G. (2009). The United Nations Convention on the Rights of Persons with Disabilities: Toward a New International Politics of Disability. *Texas Journal on Civil Liberties & Civil Rights 15*, 33–53.

Report of the Advisory Council on the Disabled. (1988). *Opportunities for the Disabled*. Singapore: Ministry of Education.

Shogren, K. A., & Turnbull, H. R. (2014). Core concepts of disability policy, the Convention on the Rights of Persons with Disabilities, and public policy research with respect to developmental disabilities. *Journal of Policy and Practice in Intellectual Disabilities, 11*(1), 19–26.

Skidmore, D. (1996). Towards an integrated theoretical framework for research in special educational needs, *European Article of Special Needs Education, 11*(1), 33–42.

Ssenyonjo, M. (2016). *Economic, Social and Cultural Rights in International Law (2nd edition)*. Oxford: Hart.

Stein, M. A., & Lord, J. E. (2009). Future prospects for the United Nations Convention on the Rights of Persons with Disabilities. In O. M. Arnardottir & G. Quinn (Eds.), *The UN Convention on the Rights of Persons with Disabilities: European and Scandinavian Perspectives. Volume 100 of International Studies in Human Rights* (pp. 17–40). Netherlands: BRILL.

Stein, M. A., & Stein, P. J. S. (2006). Beyond disability civil rights. *Hastings Law Journal, 58*(6), 1203–1240.

Terzi, L. (2014). Reframing inclusive education: Educational equality as capability equality. *Cambridge Journal of Education, 44*(4), 479–493.

Thomas, C. (2014). Disability and impairment,. In J. Swain, S. French, & C. Barnes (Eds.), *Disabling Barriers: Enabling Environments* (3rd edition). London: Sage.

UNICEF. (2007, October). Promoting the rights of children with disabilities. *Innocenti Digest* (13), i–68. Retrieved November 7, 2019, from https://www.unicef-irc.org/publications/474-promoting-the-rights-of-children-with-disabilities.html

UNICEF. (2009). It's about ability: Learning guide on the Convention on the Rights of Persons with Disabilities. New York: UNICEF. Retrieved November 7, 2019, from https://www.unicef.org/publications/files/Its_About_Ability_Learning_Guide_EN.pdf

UNICEF. (2013, May). The state of the world's children 2013: Executive summary. New York: UNICEF. Retrieved November 7, 2019, from https://www.unicef.org/publications/index_69378.html

United Nations Department of Economic and Social Affairs. (1982, December 3). World programme of action concerning disabled persons. Retrieved November 7, 2019, from https://www.un.org/development/desa/disabilities/resources/world-programme-of-action-concerning-disabled-persons.html

United Nations Department of Economic and Social Affairs. (1993, December 20). Standard rules on the equalization of opportunities for persons with disabilities. Retrieved November 7, 2019, from: https://www.un.org/development/desa/disabilities/standard-rules-on-the-equalization-of-opportunities-for-persons-with-disabilities.html

United Nations Department of Economic and Social Affairs. (n.d.-a). Frequently asked questions regarding the Convention on the Rights of Persons with Disabilities. Retrieved November 8, 2019 from: https://www.un.org/development/desa/disabilities/convention-on-the-rights-of-persons-with-disabilities/frequently-asked-questions-regarding-the-convention-on-the-rights-of-persons-with-disabilities.html

United Nations Department of Economic and Social Affairs. (n.d.-b). Convention on the Rights of Persons with Disabilities (CRPD). Retrieved November 7, 2019, from https://www.un.org/development/desa/disabilities/convention-on-the-rights-of-persons-with-disabilities.html

United Nations Department of Economic and Social Affairs. (n.d.-c). Chapter Two: The convention in detail — Obligations of states parties under the convention. Retrieved November 6, 2019, from https://www.un.org/development/desa/disabilities/resources/handbook-for-parliamentarians-on-the-convention-on-the-rights-of-persons-with-disabilities/chapter-two-the-convention-in-detail-4.html

United Nations Department of Economic and Social Affairs, OHCHR, & Inter-Parliamentary Union. (2007). Handbook for Parliamentarians on the Convention on the Rights of Persons with Disabilities and its

Optional Protocol. Geneva: OHCHR. Retrieved November 8, 2019, from http://archive.ipu.org/PDF/publications/disabilities-e.pdf

United Nations Treaty Collection. (2019, November 5). 15. Convention on the Rights of Persons with Disabilities. Retrieved November 6, 2019, from https://treaties.un.org/Pages/ViewDetails.aspx?src=TREATY&mtdsg_no=IV-15&chapter=4&clang=_en

Verdugo, M. A., Navas, P., Gómez, L. E., & Schalock, R. L. (2012). The concept of quality of life and its role in enhancing human rights in the field of intellectual disability. *Journal of Intellectual Disability Research*, 56(11), 1036–1045.

Wilson, A., & Daar, A. S. (2013). A survey of international legal instruments to examine their effectiveness in improving global health and in realizing health rights. *Journal of Law, Medicine and Ethics*, 41, 89–102.

Wong, M. E. & Goodley, D. (in-submission). *Critical disability studies in the UK and Singapore: Thinking with and across local and national locations*.

Wong, M. E., Low, J. M., & Appelhans, P. (2017). Understanding CRPD implementation in Singapore. In D. L. Cogburn & T. K. Reuter (Eds.), *Making Disability Rights Real in Southeast Asia: Implementing the UN Convention on the Rights of Persons with Disabilities in ASEAN* (pp. 143–166). New York: Lexington Books.

Wong, M. E., Ng, I., Lor, J., & Wong, R. (2017). Navigating through the 'rules' of civil society: In search of disability rights in Singapore. In J. Song (Ed.), *The History of Human Rights Society in Singapore: 1965–2015* (pp. 169–186). London: Routledge.

Wong, M. E., Poon, K. K., Kaur, S., & Ng, Z. J. (2015). Parental perspectives and challenges in inclusive education in Singapore. *Asia Pacific Journal of Education*, 35(1), 85–97.

Wong, R., & Wong, M. E. (2015). Social impact of policies for the disabled in Singapore. In D. Chan (Ed.), *50 Years of Social Issues in Singapore* (pp. 147–166). Singapore: World Scientific.

World Blind Union. (2012). Nothing about us without us! A toolkit for the Disability Rights Convention. New Zealand: World Blind Union. Retrieved November 6, 2019, from http://www.worldblindunion.org/English/resources/Toolkits/CRPD-Toolkit.doc

World Health Organization and the World Bank Group. (2011). World report on disability. Malta: World Health Organization. Retrieved November 7, 2019, from: https://www.who.int/disabilities/world_report/2011/report.pdf

CHAPTER 3

Education as Apprenticeship for the Future: The Evolution of Singapore's Approach and its Impact on Inclusion for Persons with Disabilities

Levan Lim & Thana Thaver

෴

Introduction

We currently live in an age of disruption where the unexpected is expected. Global disrupters to peace and security include geopolitical uncertainties such as the rising tensions in the South China Sea, terrorism, pandemics, and the unsettling displacement of millions of people from their home countries due to conflict, poverty, climate change, and unemployment. Disruptions due to the discrediting of the existing global consensus on economic integration and free trade, the escalation of retaliatory trade wars between countries, and the rapid advances in technology that are disrupting traditional businesses and jobs, contribute further on a global scale to fracturing and destabilising societies around the world.

In such a volatile, uncertain, complex and ambiguous (VUCA) global environment where established political and economic structures and systems are challenged and even overturned, many nations and their citizens are naturally alarmed and frightened for their own futures. Many people the world over wonder about the repercussions of a changing global political and economic order, how relevant or obsolete their skills will be in the new age of disruption, and question their governments' efforts to address the challenges of maintaining or restoring social cohesion, creating jobs and sustaining adequate employment, and reforming education systems to prepare future-ready citizens.

It is ultimately the responsibility of governments to promote stability and security for their citizens through an equitable distribution of resources and benefits across diverse and disparate groups within society; in particular, groups that are disadvantaged or who face disruptions in their livelihoods and further suffer due to a lack of attention and sufficient compensatory safeguards. Governments, therefore, need to be inclusive of the voices, interests and needs of all disparate groups in society so that no one is left behind, thereby minimising the amount of disenchantment and disengagement within society that, if left unattended, can produce deleterious impact and outcomes for individual groups and for society as a whole.

Evermore so, in our turbulent and disruptive epoch in human history, as it is imperative for nations to be inclusive of all its peoples, it is the role of education to support and realise the vision of an inclusive society for all. International conventions and declarations have framed inclusive education as the right of all children and the condition for the development of more inclusive societies (e.g., the Convention of the Rights of the Child, World Declaration on Education for All, Salamanca Statement and Framework for Action on Special Needs Education, Dakar Framework for Action and the United Nations Convention on the Rights of Persons with Disabilities). As a result, many countries have adopted and strengthened the role of inclusive education as an official policy within their education systems.

Unlike many countries around the world that have officially adopted inclusive education as an educational agenda to transform their education systems in order to promote greater access, participation and outcomes for all children, Singapore stands out as an anomaly in that it has yet to officially do so. It may even seem ironic that while inclusive education does not occupy a formal role in Singapore's education system, Singapore does have an explicit aspirational vision to become an inclusive society as officially announced by the Prime Minister in 2004 and since then, has often been referenced by the government and public as a direction for the development of society. Although inclusive education remains elusive as an official educational policy in Singapore, there is no suggestion nor doubt of a lack of commitment on the part of the government to being responsive to the learning needs of diverse and disparate groups of students and the enhancement of their life outcomes. It is the approach taken to responding to student diversity and their inclusion that is examined in this chapter, within the context of a larger socio-historical narrative.

Education in Singapore appears subsumed within the nation's perennial search on how to justify its relevance and excel in a competitive world constantly in flux since its birth as an independent nation. Ingrained and defined by its own inherent and immutable narrative of vulnerability in terms of its size, geography, lack of resources and historical separation from Malaysia (Low & Vadaketh, 2014), Singapore seems permanently saddled with a survival instinct to secure its place in the world and thrive in it.

This chapter charts Singapore's evolutionary journey and approach to how it has continuously reformed and repositioned its education, while learning its own lessons, to achieve its own vision of an inclusive, socially cohesive, prosperous and progressive society that is prepared for the challenges of an uncertain world and future. Through highlighting key historical features of Singapore's educational movements that have created and shaped the nation's responses to diverse and disparate groups of children, this chapter offers a critical understanding of how educational policies and practices, in response to larger global forces and the envisioning of Singapore as an inclusive society, have produced both challenges and opportunities for inclusive education, and, in particular, for students with disabilities.

We have chosen to focus on the inclusive prospects of students with disabilities for two specific reasons: (i) persons with disabilities were explicitly mentioned as part of the inclusive society vision announced in 2004 and this announcement was followed by a slew of measures and efforts to promote their quality of life and inclusion within society; and (ii) based on developments hitherto in Singapore related to persons with disabilities, we seek to understand the 'inclusionary space' afforded within the evolution of Singapore's education and what this space, subject to and shaped by educational reforms, is telling of a larger narrative of Singapore's approach to inclusion and how it can affect persons with disabilities as well as its costs and benefits.

Education in Singapore

In Singapore, education and the economy are 'intertwingled'. This portmanteau of 'intertwined' and 'intermingled' aptly characterises the deep and complex relationship between Singapore's education and its economic fortunes. This intimate nexus between education and the economy hearkens back to Singapore's early days as a fledgling independent and sovereign nation struggling to survive after its separation from Malaysia in 1965. Diminutive in physical size, lacking in natural resources (including water), and besieged by racial tensions, unemployment and economic unrest, the foremost task by its leaders then, headed by Mr Lee Kuan Yew, was to ensure its economic survival. Singapore quickly seized upon the opportunity of attracting foreign investors as the path towards industrialisation, the success of which depended on an educated and skilled workforce (Gopinathan, 1999). This initial impetus for economic survival through education placed an indelible stamp on Singapore's symbiotic relationship between education and economic planning and policy, which in decades to come, would be consistently touted and reinforced as a winning formula for Singapore's thriving accomplishments.

In a little over half a century, Singapore has leapfrogged economically from its dire beginnings to become the third richest country in the world, as listed by Forbes in 2019, based on GDP, after

Qatar and Luxembourg. Singapore is widely considered as a model of successful multiculturalism where diverse races, cultures and religions co-exist and live together in harmony within a densely populated urban city-state. Singapore has an excellent reputation for education and student outcomes. Its top-ranked world-class education system, from the primary level to tertiary education, yield student outcomes and achievements that are consistently the highest achieving in the world, as reflected in the example of student performances in science, mathematics and reading in the Performance for International Student Assessment (PISA) international exercises conducted by the Organisation for Economic Co-operation and Development (OECD).

There are very few education systems in the world that can rival the longevity with which Singapore has systematically built and transformed its education system to continuously align with its economic upgrading and restructuring initiatives that are responsive and relevant to the global economy. Present efforts of educational leaders (i.e., education ministers) are built upon the work of previous leaders to allow a deeper, longer and wider expansion of the impact and scale of implementing policies; unlike the educational upheavals experienced in many countries that occur as a result of government or ministerial change (Corrales, 1999). This systematic and continuous evolution of a singular education system in Singapore has been abetted by Singapore's unique political history of a single ruling government party since independence. Singapore's economic success and educational achievements during the past five decades bear testament that there are important lessons to learn from its educational journey and approach (Ng, 2017).

Evolution of Education towards Diversification: Impact on the 'Inclusionary Space'

There have been key developments in Singapore's history of education that have impacted upon the quality of education, support and inclusiveness for its diverse range of students. In addition, there have been a number of acute and insightful lessons learned from past educational legacies that have been valuable in guiding the evolvement of future educational policy and practice.

The pioneering years of Singapore's education in the 1960s and 1970s relied on a standardised common curriculum, with emphasis on being bilingual (in English and a second language) as well as on science and mathematics. Measures were also taken to ensure a workforce for industrialisation through technical and vocational education (Ho & Gopinathan, 1999; Yip, Eng & Yap, 1990). The educational impact of this standardised one-size-fits-all education system resulted in serious consequences for many students.

An appalling trend of large proportions of students failing their end of primary school exam, i.e., the Primary School Leaving Examination (PSLE) and national examination at the secondary level (i.e., the General Certificate of Education 'O' levels) appeared. It was postulated that among those who could not cope with the pace of the school curriculum and failed in their examinations were children with mild intellectual disabilities (Tan, 1974). This trend coupled with high student attrition rates during the primary and secondary schooling years severely curtailed the employment prospects of many young Singaporeans needed for the nation's industrialisation path. The lesson learned was that a standardised education was inflexible to the learning needs of a diverse range of students; it favoured the above average student and penalised those with less than average academic abilities resulting in low achievement rates and high educational wastage (Goh, 1979).

To meet the diverse learning needs of students, Singapore entered into a phase in the 1980s of ability-based streaming and differentiation of courses and examinations according to ability at both the primary and secondary levels. At primary three (age nine), students would take a school-based streaming examination that would differentiate them into one of three streams with varying academic demands and expectations. Students entering the secondary level would then be streamed again into one of three options based on their performance in the PSLE, again with varying demands and expectations for academic abilities. During this period, the mainstream education system was increasingly focused on academic excellence with its central goal of creating a workforce to propel Singapore onto its next stage of economic development (Yip, Eng & Yap, 1990).

This emphasis on excellence combined with the view by the Advisory Council on the Disabled (1988) that the integration of students with disabilities into mainstream schools should be left to the discretion of these schools did not augur well for the educational access and participation of these students within mainstream school environments. Students, especially those with intellectual disabilities, who were unable to handle the academic challenges of the mainstream streaming options, were redirected to special schools.

The 1980s witnessed the further establishment of the special education system where special schools, operated by voluntary welfare organisations, attended to the learning needs of students with moderate to severe disabilities and those with milder disabilities who could not manage the academic demands of mainstream education. This sorting of children into two systems of education (with children without disabilities attending mainstream schools and children with disabilities attending special schools) developed into a bifurcated education system in Singapore (Lim & Nam, 2000; Lim, Thaver & Poon, 2008; Lim, Thaver & Slee, 2008) was further entrenched with the building of more special schools.

The severe economic downturn that Singapore experienced in 1985 brought about by the larger global recession prompted reforms in educational policy to support and align with the economic priorities of developing a more competitive workforce for the global economy. The 1990s was a period focused on increasing the competitive mindset in education through (i) students competing to do well in schools; (ii) schools competing against each other; and (iii) good schools emerging to show other schools how they can improve (Goh, 1992, p. 31, as cited in Lim & Tan, 1999). This ethos of competitiveness flooded into all aspects of mainstream education and schooling through the introduction of annual school ranking exercises in 1992.

The school ranking exercises led to intense competition among schools in their pursuit of academic excellence, which remained undiminished even after the broadening of ranking indicators in 1995. The public issuance of school ranking results so that parents, students and other stakeholders could make informed decisions on their selection of schools to enter, further exacerbated the competitive education climate. Schools became more selective in their intake of students by courting high achieving students to raise their school rankings in academic league tables. The default of this form of marketisation of education in Singapore in the 1990s was the desirability value cast upon admitting academically weaker students, including those with disabilities who had difficulty coping with the rigour and demands of mainstream education (Lim & Tan, 1999).

The Singaporean colloquial word 'kiasu', literally meaning 'fear of losing' in its Chinese dialectical vernacular, best expresses the local meaning of subscribing to the fear of losing out to others, and is characterised by a 'me-first' attitude. 'Kiasuism' (its noun) entails the desire to be ahead of others by checking out and apportioning to self the best opportunities and advantages in order to stay ahead of the competition. Whether fortunately or unfortunately, 'kiasuism' has become a self-proclaimed national trait, and was particularly pronounced in the 1990s when relentless competitiveness drove and characterised the educational zeitgeist of that period.

By the late 1990s, the intense focus on competitive ranking and academic standing of mainstream schools and students had become a cause for concern as well as a significant reason for rethinking the purpose of education and its outcomes in Singapore. The Ministry of Education published the "The Desired Outcomes of Education" to present a holistic range of attributes and outcomes to establish a common purpose for educators, drive policies and programmes, and provide a gauge to determine how well the education system was doing (Ministry of Education, 2021a).

The then Minister of Education reminded the public and the education community of the greater purpose of education, and stated that while academic achievement was important, it could not be pursued to the exclusion of everything else. The goal of education, as he announced, was on nurturing the whole person and, besides academic achievement, included nurturing high moral ideals as well as a caring spirit for others in the community (Teo, 1998, p. 2, cited in Lim & Thaver, 2018). The emphasis on holistic education was later reinforced in 2014 when the Ministry of Education launched a new framework for 21st century competencies and student outcomes.

This newer framework builds upon the holistic approach to education as stated in the 1997 Desired Outcomes of Education (Ministry of Education, 2021b) to cultivate core values such as integrity, concern for others, resilience, responsibility and active contribution. The framework also emphasises social and emotional competencies and skills such as self-awareness, self-management, social awareness, relationship management and responsible decision-making, all of which are foundations for the young to manage themselves and their relationships with others. To live effectively in society and meet the demands of new and emerging economies of a diverse globalised world in the 21st century, the framework articulates the learning of (i) civic literacy, global awareness and cross-cultural skills; (ii) critical and inventive thinking; and (iii) communication, collaboration and information skills (Ministry of Education, 2021).

The 1997 Asian financial crisis alerted Singapore to relook at its recipe for economic and educational success. The global rules of competition among nations were changing due to a shift towards a global knowledge economy where innovation, creativity and technological advances would provide countries with a competitive edge. A national vision for schools and society known as 'Thinking Schools, Learning Nation' was launched in 1997 by the then Prime Minister, Mr Goh Chok Tong, to foster thinking skills and national commitment on the part of Singaporeans to meet future challenges of the new millennium. It envisaged an education system that could develop creative thinking skills, the engagement of lifelong learning and the commitment of its young citizens to Singapore to enable a paradigm shift in Singapore's education system.

This national vision, foregrounded by the momentous shifts of global education and society at the cusp of the millennium — from knowledge transmission to knowledge generation, and conformity of prescribed standards to creativity, diversity, lifelong learning and innovation for broad populations — kick started a new approach for education in Singapore. The approach consisted of diversifying education itself through the creation of multiple educational pathways to meet the diverse learning needs, interests and abilities of students within the education system. The emergence of multiple educational pathways for students of diverse abilities and interests from the implementation of the 'Thinking Schools, Learning Nation' vision has continued to introduce greater flexibility and new paths into the education system.

Examples of greater flexibility and different pathways that have been introduced into Singapore's education landscape include the Integrated Programme (IP) that offers a seamless education experience where upper secondary students can bypass the GCE 'O' level examination to proceed directly to the junior college years to culminate in either the GCE 'A' level examinations or the International Baccalaureate; the Direct School Admission selection scheme that moves away from academic abilities to aptitude-based admissions (Davie, 2017); greater flexibility for students to gain entry into institutes of higher learning after secondary school (Ministry of Education, 2016); more flexibility in subject offerings for secondary school students to find a better match between their strengths and subject offerings (Ministry of Education, 2013); and wider grade bands instead of absolute points for the PSLE scoring system (Lee, 2013).

The government has also been intentional in enlarging the latitude for defining success beyond the traditional areas such of science and mathematics that Singapore's education is famous for, to the arts and sports, through the establishment of School of the Arts and Singapore Sports School in 2008 and 2004, respectively. These specialised schools offer students gifted in these areas the opportunities to excel in their interests and strengths. Specialised schools have also been established for students who have experienced academic failure in primary mainstream schools, such as in the Primary School Leaving Examinations. Northlight School and Assumption Pathway School were opened in 2007 and 2009, respectively, to cater specifically to students who are unable to access or complete mainstream secondary education. Two other specialised schools — Crest Secondary School and Spectra Secondary School — were opened in 2014 and 2013, respectively, for secondary students in the Normal (Technical) stream who require a more customised and practice-oriented curriculum.

These developments and amendments in educational practice driven by the diversification of education demonstrate the government's efforts to deepen the quality and meaning of education for diverse and disparate groups of students so that all are provided the opportunity and supports to achieve desirable, relevant and meaningful life outcomes that contribute to their personal lives and Singapore's society and economy. The deepening of quality learning and education for diverse learners through the widening of educational pathways represents Singapore's approach to achieving an open and inclusive society, as declared in the Prime Minister's 2004 inauguration speech where he proclaimed the vision of an inclusive society for Singapore:

> We will continue to expand the space the Singaporeans have to live, to laugh, to grow and be ourselves. Our people should feel free to express diverse views, express unconventional ideas, conceive fresh solutions, and open up new spaces. We should recognise many paths of success, and many ways to be Singaporean. We must give people a second chance, to those who have tasted failure may be wiser and stronger among us. Ours must be an open and inclusive Singapore. (Ibrahim, 2004, p. 10)

In recent years, educational thinking in Singapore about the deepening of quality learning and learner engagement in education for diverse learners through the widening of educational pathways has been re-invigorated by the conceptual shift to lengthen the experience of quality lifelong learning and education for every citizen across the individual's lifespan. The national movement SkillsFuture, which the government initiated in 2014, aims to promote and support lifelong learning for every Singaporean, including persons with disabilities, from school to adulthood regardless of academic qualifications.

SkillsFuture represents a major paradigm shift in education and society to move Singaporeans from thinking about education "as a concept of flow, i.e., preparing young students to enter the workforce, to a concept of stock, i.e., helping everyone in society learn throughout their lives" (Ong, 2015). To enhance Singapore's future-readiness to thrive in the challenging global climate of disruptions, rapid technological advancements and the concomitant demand for higher skilled workers, the government has stressed the continuous upgrading and deepening of skills essential for Singapore to stay ahead of the intense global competition for jobs. Beyond school, SkillsFuture reconceptualises the workplace as a major site and source for learning, innovating higher level skills and enhancing productivity.

According to SkillsFuture, partnerships between schools and industries to offer internships to students so that they obtain valuable exposure to and meaningful experience in industry also provide opportunities for the young to arrive at better decisions about career choices and to deepen and integrate the learning and practice of requisite work, relational and communication skills (Ministry of Manpower, 2018). SkillsFuture will purportedly "drive Singapore's next phase of development towards an advanced economy and inclusive society" (Ministry of Manpower, 2018).

The 'Inclusionary Space' vis-à-vis Persons with Disabilities in Singapore

It was in August 2004, in his inauguration speech as Prime Minister of Singapore that Mr Lee Hsien Loong announced the vision of Singapore an inclusive society and explicitly mentioned the inclusion of persons with disabilities within this vision. A month later, he called for greater efforts to integrate people with disabilities into mainstream society, beginning with the integration of students with disabilities (Teo, 2004). The developments that have transpired for persons with disabilities since then have been unprecedented in Singapore's history.

Soon after the Prime Minister's call for the greater integration of students with disabilities in mainstream schools, two new teacher education programmes for the professional development of educational personnel to support students with disabilities were launched in 2005 at the National Institute of Education, Singapore's sole teacher education body. The first programme developed was to prepare a new cadre of personnel, currently known as Allied Educators (Learning & Behavioural Support), to work with teachers to support students with disabilities. The second programme aims at equipping mainstream teachers with the knowledge and skills to better support students with disabilities in mainstream classrooms and schools.

The provision of greater supports for students with disabilities in mainstream schools through additional personnel and the professional development of teachers since the watershed year of 2004 has seen the number of students with disabilities rising considerably from 2,500 students in 2005 (Chan, 2005) to 13,000 in 2013 to 18,000 in 2015 (Lim, 2016) to 24,000 in 2018 (Toh, 2018). For a system of education that has been traditionally dualistic — where students without disabilities went to mainstream schools and students with disabilities went to special schools — the number of students with disabilities in mainstream schools has steadily risen to overtake the number of students with disabilities in special schools.

Singapore has clearly made significant gains towards the inclusion of greater numbers of students with disabilities within mainstream education due to more personnel and systemic support. The specific supports mentioned are part of the ongoing development of infrastructure to support the diversification of and greater flexibility along educational pathways for diverse and disparate groups of students with different abilities and interests within mainstream education. Hence, the broadening of multiple educational options and the provision of greater supports for diverse students have facilitated the expansion of the 'inclusionary space' for more students with disabilities who have as diverse a range of abilities and interests as other regular students.

The inclusion of students with disabilities within an increasingly diversified mainstream education system, however, is still primarily conditional on whether they are able to cope with challenges in mainstream education, namely, the rigour of the mainstream academic curriculum. This caveat indicates that integration is more at work than inclusion. Children with disabilities who cannot manage or benefit from learning the mainstream curriculum are encouraged to seek a special education in special schools run by voluntary welfare organisations [now known as social service agencies (Rashith & Tan, 2019). The students in special schools, ranging from mild intellectual disabilities to moderate, severe and profound disabilities, and their teachers as well, belong to a separate education system which, in turn, present limitations for their access, participation and membership in the 'inclusionary space' within mainstream education.

Singapore ratified the United Nations Convention on the Rights of Persons with Disabilities (UNCRPD) in 2013. According to the UNCRPD, inclusive education is a fundamental right of every child. To realise this human right for every child, State Parties are to ensure that children with disabilities are not excluded from the mainstream education system on the basis of disability and can access an inclusive education on an equal basis with other children from their own communities (UNESCO, 1994; 2016). Although obvious gains have been made in the greater presence and inclusion of students with disabilities within Singapore's mainstream schools, the long-standing features of a strongly entrenched academic emphasis in the mainstream education system and a separate system for educating students with disabilities unable to cope with the rigorous academic demands of mainstream education as well as those with greater support needs, represent barriers according to the UNCRPD's position of non-exclusionary accessibility of these children to mainstream education.

The Salamanca Statement and Framework for Action on Special Needs Education (UNESCO, 1994), which Singapore was not a signatory of, carries a less contravening tone by acknowledging there are "well established systems of special schools" in many countries and these systems "represent a valuable resource for the development of inclusive schools" (UNESCO, 1994, p. 12). Furthermore, the call of the Salamanca Statement and its Framework for Action for the understanding of inclusion as an effective means to include students with special needs within the framework of Education for All (UNESCO, 1990), allows the repositioning of special schools within the inclusive education framework (such as becoming resource centres to promote the participation of students with special needs within mainstream settings).

Unfortunately, the dual education system arrangement per se can pose barriers to the fluidity of movement and membership of students and resources between separate systems. To illustrate, because of the separateness of the dual system arrangement, a continuum of options for special needs within mainstream education such as special classrooms for students with moderate to severe disabilities within mainstream school environments to promote some interaction with their peers without disabilities, is difficult to facilitate (Lim & Quah, 2004).

The Legacy of Diverse Pathways: Separate Lives?

Since the diversification of education in Singapore as it entered the new millennium and the envisioning of Singapore as an inclusive society, the education system has transformed into a variegated education landscape with diverse pathways that respond to differences in abilities, strengths, talents, interests and learning needs among its diverse student population (Ministry of Education, 2015). Singapore's approach to reforming its education system for student diversity through multiple pathways has been likened to building not "a single peak of excellence… but a whole mountain range with many peaks" (Lee, 2011). The government has provided generous amounts of funding for developing diverse educational pathways and the quality of education received by students in each of these pathways. For students who do well in a particular pathway, greater flexibility such as direct entry schemes allow them to gain entry into other educational pathways.

The education system has made tremendous strides during the past 20 years towards becoming much more student-centred in its focus and delivery. Through the deepening, broadening and lengthening of education to foster quality, innovation, excellence and lifelong learning, the education system has evolved into an extensively differentiated network of diverse educational pathways to prepare their respective students, grouped primarily by abilities, interests and learning needs, to enter society as successfully as possible and to learn throughout their lives. This approach to education to respond to diverse students' learning through meaningful and relevant educational experiences is a clear tenet of inclusive education.

A notable concern, however, relates to opportunities for diverse and disparate groups of students to interact across and form understandings of and relationships with other students from other pathways or, in the case of students from special schools, another system. Therefore, a pitfall of this approach to diversifying education refers to limited opportunities for interaction and relationship building among students from different pathways, which is not conducive to building inclusive communities where shared experiences form the basis for inclusion and an inclusive society. This concern has been noted by MOE which established the Satellite Partnership Programme in 2008 to create opportunities for students from mainstream and special schools to mingle and interact through co-curricular activities, games and community projects (Teng, 2019). The Ministry is working towards all 19 special schools having such tie-ups.

Conclusion

In the age of disruption, learning and education are being re-conceptualised to fuel the new economies of the future where broad-based engagement across society with the latest technological developments will determine how advanced the economies of countries are and the types of employment created. The globalisation of trade, the rapid advancement of technology, and the vast movements of people across the globe in search for employment, mean that there is global competition across many jobs from the lowest to the highest skilled.

As one of the freest economies in the world that is deeply interconnected with the global economy, Singapore's survival and success rest on its pragmatic usefulness and relevance to other countries. As the world has continued to diversify its range of goods and jobs as well as the ways in which these can be produced and performed through creative innovations, Singapore's education system has been vigilant in keeping pace through its reforms to 'future-ready' its citizens for a diverse, competitive and uncertain world where disruptions to the existing global order can occur.

Singapore's survival and success lies in staying ahead of other countries in the disruptive global economic climate while remaining a liveable, peaceful and stable home for its citizens. Education has been foundational and instrumental to Singapore's success, peace, stability and prosperity. What Singapore has managed to achieve as a nation and on the world's stage, during its brief history, is remarkable in spite and because of its vulnerability narrative of the odds threatening its survival from its very beginnings.

The narrative of vulnerability, which looms largely in Singapore's national psyche, serves as a permanent reminder and provides a bulwark against complacency and the proclivity to rest on one's laurels. This underlying narrative has consequently shaped the national characteristics of tenacity, determination, hard work, strategy, competitiveness as well as a sense of urgency to stay ahead, constant worry and apprehension for its future, stress, 'kiasuism' and even paranoia. As uttered in the words of Prime Minister Lee Hsien Loong during a dialogue session about a month before Singapore's momentous National Day celebrations of its 50th year of independence:

> We worry all the time. People say we are paranoid, which I suppose we are and we need to be. Because you are at a higher level, you expect to be at a higher level… Is it to be expected that the population of 3.5 million citizens and maybe a million foreign workers will have the best airline in the world, the best airport in the world, one of the busiest ports in the world… and an education, healthcare and housing system which gives us a per capita GDP… higher than America or Australia or Japan. It's an entirely unnatural state of affairs… (Lee, 2015)

The potential for fragility and instability implied in Singapore's vulnerability narrative has also served as the raison d'etre for the government to unify its people, who come from racially, culturally, linguistically and religiously diverse origins and backgrounds. Singapore's outstanding achievements would not have been possible without its government's long-standing commitment to build a socially cohesive, inclusive and peaceful society based on the racial, cultural and religious harmony it has nurtured and enjoyed for decades.

In Singapore, therefore, the concept of inclusivity has been essential to its survival and growth as a nation of diverse races, cultures and religions. As a foundation for a socially cohesive society and a prescription for its sustainability into the future, it appears that inclusivity has primarily been imagined and interpreted upon pragmatic motivations for accommodating diversity in terms of how it relates and adheres to supporting evolving aspirations and visions of Singapore and its relevance in the world. This pragmatic grounding of inclusivity as a legacy of its vulnerability narrative has heavily influenced Singapore's approach to inclusion and its accommodation of diversity. The question this chapter raises is whether this pragmatic approach to inclusion, which has dominated the culture and history of Singapore, and reaped many social and economic benefits that have contributed to its success, is sufficient to achieve its vision of an inclusive society for all.

The response to this question can be revealed in the 'inclusionary space' afforded for diverse students to be in zones of proximal development that can scaffold them, via relationships and networks, to greater membership, participation and significance within mainstream communities. As described earlier, this 'inclusionary space' for students with milder disabilities to be a part of mainstream school communities has grown and strengthened due to greater support, flexibility and diversified pathways in recent educational reforms that have been led by the envisioning of Singapore as an inclusive society. However, other students with disabilities, such as those with mild intellectual disabilities and those with moderate to profound disabilities, face limitations in opportunities to access, participate and acquire membership in this 'inclusionary space'.

A segregated education for these children contradicts the practice of inclusive education, which imparts certain messages on the part of public to the desirability and feasibility of inclusive education in Singapore. A survey conducted by the Lien Foundation in 2016 of the general public revealed that while the majority of Singaporeans (seven in 10) support the idea of inclusive education, only a third "agree that Singapore is an inclusive society when it comes to children with special needs". Significantly, the "majority of respondents (64%) expressed the belief that Singaporeans are willing to share public spaces with special needs children but are not willing to interact with them" (Lien Foundation, 2016). The survey also indicated that only one in 10 Singaporeans expressed confidence in interacting with children with special needs (Lien Foundation, 2016). Among parents surveyed, only half are comfortable with having their own children placed next to a child with special needs in the classroom (Lien Foundation, 2016). This survey highlights that Singaporeans "don't walk the talk" on accepting and including children with special needs (Tai, 2016b). Another survey, which included the views of persons with disabilities, found that six in 10 persons with disabilities do not feel that they are socially included, accepted or given opportunities to reach their potential (Tai, 2016c). Of the general public polled, only 36% indicated they would be comfortable being close friends with a person with a disability (Tai, 2016c).

These survey findings are disappointing in hindsight of the unprecedented amount of attention and work by the government, disability organisations and charities over the past 15 years since the Prime Minister announced persons with disabilities as part of the vision of an inclusive society for Singapore in 2004 (Tai, 2016b). Since his inclusive society envisioning, there have been three national blueprints (known as Enabling Masterplans) developed by the Ministry of Social and Family Development to create an inclusive society for persons with disabilities. The third masterplan to guide the development of policies and services was announced towards the end of 2016 (Seow, 2016; Tai, 2016a), following the previous two five-year masterplans (i.e., 2007–2011 and 2012–2016 respectively) to cultivate greater inclusivity among Singaporeans for their fellow citizens with disabilities.

More recently, two Members of Parliament provided their views on the inclusion of persons with disabilities in education and society during a parliamentary motion titled "Education for Our Future" calling for partnership between government and citizens to ensure accessible, inclusive and lifelong education for all learners (Chia, 2018; Teng, 2018). Member of Parliament Ms Rahayu Mahzam, who has a young son with Down syndrome, stated that while there has been much done in Singapore to promote inclusivity and society is now more open and accepting of person with disabilities, society is still not as comfortable with them and still does not view them as an equal member of a society (Chia, 2018). Ms Chia Yong Yong, a Nominated Member of Parliament, who has a nerve and muscular disorder, called for more to be done to include children with disabilities in mainstream schools and recounted her blessings being included and growing up in a mainstream school environment (Teng, 2018). She advocated, based on her own life experiences, the need for all children to learn, grow and play together to foster acceptance of each other (Teng, 2018).

Singapore's ratification of the UNCRPD in 2013 means that it will need to strengthen the role of inclusive education in the mainstream education system and change existing barriers to inclusion. This task will involve the identification of how educational policies and practices reproduce exclusionary attitudes, and a commitment to reduce and remove these barriers to the inclusion of children with disabilities — a monumental but not impossible endeavour that involves overcoming cultural-historical legacies and systemic inertia. As the UNCRPD affirms the rights-based nature and approach of inclusive education, the motivations and aspirations for envisioning an inclusive society in Singapore will need to be increasingly framed within a rights-based perspective and discourse. This rights-based approach with ensuing legislation for individuals with disabilities to claim entry into the 'inclusionary space' of mainstream education and society is, however, unfamiliar and uncharted territory for Singapore. Without an official inclusive education policy and concomitant legislation (which are common in many countries in their commitment to inclusion), Singapore, moreover, lacks the legal requisite frameworks and platforms to contest and reconsider what may be an appropriate education for individual children or challenge practices that may be deemed exclusionary.

How compatible would a rights-based approach be with Singapore's current modus operandi in building an inclusive education system and socially just society? How would a rights-based approach to inclusion interact with the culture and history of Singapore? What is a culturally relevant rights-based approach for Singapore to support inclusion? These are but a few questions to consider how education in Singapore can be an apprenticeship for all children to have inclusive prospects and futures within a truly inclusive society.

References

Advisory Council on the Disabled. (1988). *Opportunities for the disabled.* Singapore: Advisory Council on the Disabled.

Chan, S. S. (2005, March 9). Reply by Mr Chan Soo Sen, Minister of State, Ministry of Education on resources in schools, special education, pre-school education and education hub. Retrieved from https://www.nas.gov.sg/archivesonline/data/pdfdoc/20050309994.htm

Chia, L. (2018, July 11). Promoting inclusivity in education: Singapore still has some way to go, says MP Rahayu Mahzam. Retrieved from https://www.channelnewsasia.com/news/singapore/promoting-inclusivity-in-education-singapore-still-has-some-way-10520018

Corrales, J. (1999). The politics of education reform: Bolstering the supply and demand; Overcoming institutional blocks. Retrieved from https://web.worldbank.org/archive/website00238I/WEB/PDF/CORRALES.PDF

Davie, S. (2017, March 8). Education focus shifts to students' strengths. Retrieved from https://www.straitstimes.com/singapore/education-focus-shifts-to-students-strengths

Goh, K. S. (1979). *Report on the Ministry of Education 1978.* Singapore: Singapore National Printers.

Gopinathan, S. (1999). Preparing for the next rung: Economic restructuring and educational reform in Singapore. *Journal of Education and Work, 12*(3), 295–308.

Government of Singapore. (1999). *Singapore 21: Together we make the difference*. Singapore: Singapore 21 Committee c/o Prime Minister's Office (Public Service Division).

Goy, P. (2017). People with disabilities given SkillsFuture award to upgrade skills. Retrieved from https://www.straitstimes.com/singapore/people-with-disabilities-given-skillsfuture-award-to-upgrade-skills

Ho, W. K., & Gopinathan, S. (1999). Recent developments in education in Singapore. School effectiveness and school improvement: *An International Journal of Research, Policy and Practice, 10*(1), 99–117.

Ibrahim, Z. (2004, August 13). Let us shape our future together. *The Straits Times*, Prime News section.

Lee, H. L. (2011, July 15). Speech by Prime Minister Lee Hsien Loong at the Official Opening of the School of the Arts. Retrieved from http://www.pmo.gov.sg/newsroom/speech-prime-minister-lee-hsien-loong-official-opening-school-arts-15-july-2011-school

Lee, H. L. (2013). Prime Minister Lee Hsien Loong's National Day Rally Speech 2013. Retrieved from http://www.pmo.gov.sg/newsroom/prime-minister-lee-hsien-loongs-national-day-rally-2013-english

Lee, H. L. (2015, July 2). Transcript of dialogue with Prime Minister Lee Hsien Loong at the SG50+ Conference. Retrieved from http://www.pmo.gov.sg/newsroom/transcript-dialogue-prime-minister-lee-hsien-loong-sg50-conference-2-july-2015

Lien Foundation. (2016). Inclusive attitudes survey. Retrieved from http://www.lienfoundation.org/sites/default/files/FINAL%20-%20Inclusive%20Attitudes%20Survey%20Part%201_30May16.pdf

Lim, J. Q. (2016). Rising number of students with special needs in mainstream schools. Retrieved from https://www.supergeniusiq.com/rising-number-of-students-with-special-needs-in-mainstream-schools/

Lim, L., & Nam, S. S. (2000). Special education in Singapore. *Journal of Special Education, 34*(2), 104–109.

Lim, L., & Quah, M. M. (2004). Foresight via hindsight: Prospects and lessons for inclusion in Singapore. *Asia-Pacific Journal of Education, 24*(2), 193–204.

Lim, L., & Tan, J. (1999). The marketization of education in Singapore: Prospects for inclusive education. *International Journal of Inclusive Education, 3*(4), 339–51.

Lim, L., & Thaver, T. (2018). Inclusion of persons with disabilities in Singapore: An evolutionary perspective. In S. Hsu (Ed.), *Routledge Handbook of Sustainable Development* (pp. 373–393). United Kingdom: Routledge.

Lim, L., Thaver, T., & Poon, K. (2008). Adapting disability studies within teacher education in Singapore. In S. L. Gabel & S. Danforth (Eds.), *Disability and the politics of education: An international reader* (pp. 583–597). New York: Peter Lang Publishing.

Lim, L., Thaver, T., & Slee, R. (2008). *Exploring disability in Singapore: A personal learning journey.* Singapore: McGraw-Hill.

Low, D., & Vadaketh, S. T. (2014). Introduction: Reframing policy and political debates in Singapore". In D. Low & S. T. Vadaketh (Eds.), *Hard choices: Challenging the Singapore consensus* (pp. 1–13). Singapore: NUS Press.

Ministry of Education. (2013, November 14). New scheme to offer more flexibility in secondary schools. Retrieved from https://www.todayonline.com/singapore/new-normal-stream-students-may-offer-higher-level-subjects-12-schools-next-year

Ministry of Education. (2015). *Bringing out the best in every child.* Singapore: Ministry of Education.

Ministry of Education. (2016). Through train pathways: Diverse pathways to fulfil your potential. https://www.plmgss.moe.edu.sg/qql/slot/u173/Programme/Co-Curricular%20Programme/Education%20and%20Career%20Guidance/through-train-pathways-na-students.pdf

Ministry of Education. (2021a). Desired outcomes of education. Retrieved from https://www.moe.gov.sg/education-in-sg/desired-outcomes

Ministry of Education. (2021b). 21st century competencies. Retrieved from https://www.moe.gov.sg/education-in-sg/21st-century-competencies

Ministry of Foreign Affairs. (2004). Swearing in speech by Prime Minister Lee Hsien Loong. Retrieved from https://www.mfa.gov.sg/content/mfa/overseasmission/tokyo/press_statements_speeches/2004/200408/press_200408_5.html

Ministry of Manpower. (2018). SkillsFuture. Retrieved from http://www.mom.gov.sg/employment-practices/skills-training-and-development/skillsfuture

Ng, P. T. (2017). *Learning from Singapore: The power of paradoxes.* New York: Routledge.

Ong, Y. K. (2015, October 14). Speech by Mr Ong Ye Kung, Acting Minister for Education (Higher Education and Skills) at the Opening of the OECD-Singapore Conference on Higher Education Futures, Resorts World Convention Centre, Singapore. Retrieved from https://www.moe.gov.sg/news/speeches/speech-by-mr-ong-ye-kung–acting-minister-for-education-higher-education-and-skills–at-the-opening-of-the-oecd-singapore-conference-on-higher-education-futures–14-october-2015–resorts-world-convention-centre–singapore

Rashith, R., & Tan, T. (2019, July 12). Charities providing social services are no longer called VWOs, but SSAs. Retrieved from https://www.straitstimes.com/singapore/charities-providing-social-services-are-no-longer-called-vwos-but-ssas

Seow, B. Y. (2016, April 3). New roadmap for people with disabilities. *The Straits Times*, April 3. Retrieved from https://www.straitstimes.com/singapore/new-roadmap-for-people-with-disabilities

Tai, J. (2016a, April 6). Third edition of Enabling Masterplan: Inclusive push to improve lives. Retrieved from http://www.straitstimes.com/singapore/third-edition-of-enabling-masterplan-inclusive-push-to-improve-lives

Tai, J. (2016b, May 31). Singaporeans don't 'walk the talk' on special needs kids. Retrieved from http://www.straitstimes.com/singapore/sporeans-dont-walk-the-talk-on-special-needs-kids

Tai, J. (2016c, June 3). People with disabilities in the spotlight. Retrieved from https://www.straitstimes.com/singapore/health/people-with-disabilities-in-the-spotlight

Tan, D. (1974). Parental point of view. Paper presented at the First Regional Conference on Special Education and Mental Retardation. Singapore: Singapore Association for Retarded Children.

Teng, A. (2018, July 11). Parliament: Nominated MP Chia Yong Yong chokes up, recounting her school days. Retrieved from https://www.straitstimes.com/politics/parliament-nominated-mp-chia-yong-yong-chokes-up-recounting-her-school-days

Teng, A. (2019). More schools join hands for lessons on inclusivity, *The Straits Times*. Available at: https://www.straitstimes.com/singapore/education/more-schools-join-hands-for-lessons-on-inclusivity. (Accessed: 30 November 2020).

Teo, C. H. (1998, March 19). Ministerial Statement by the Minister for Education, RADM Teo Chee Hean at the Budget Debate on 19 Mar 1998.

Toh, L. (2018, November 13). Continuing efforts to get students from different groups to interact. Retrieved from https://www.straitstimes.com/forum/letters-in-print/continuing-efforts-to-get-students-from-different-groups-to-interact

UNESCO. (1990). *World declaration on education for all.* Paris, France: UNESCO.

UNESCO. (1994). The Salamanca Statement and Framework for Action in Special Needs Education. World conference on special needs education: Access and quality. Paris: UNESCO. Retrieved from http://www.unesco.org/education/pdf/SALAMA_E.PDF

UNESCO. (2000). Dakar framework for action. Retrieved from http://unesdoc.unesco.org/images/0012/001211/121147e.pdf

UNESCO. (2005). *Guidelines for inclusion: Ensuring access for all.* Paris, France: UNESCO.

UNESCO. (2009). *Policy guidelines on inclusion in education.* Paris, France: UNESCO.

UNESCO. (2010). *EFA Global Monitoring Report 2010: Reaching the marginalized.* Paris, France: Oxford University Press.

United Nations. (2006). The standard rules on the equalization of opportunities for persons with disabilities. Retrieved from https://www.un.org/development/desa/disabilities/standard-rules-on-the-equalization-of-opportunities-for-persons-with-disabilities.html

United Nations. (2006). Convention on the rights of persons with disabilities. Retrieved from https://www.un.org/development/desa/disabilities/convention-on-the-rights-of-persons-with-disabilities.html

Yip, J. S. K., Eng, S. P., & Yap, J. Y. C. (1990). 25 years of educational reform. In S. K. Yip & W. K. Sim (Eds.), *Evolution of educational excellence: 25 years of education in the Republic of Singapore* (pp. 1–30). Singapore: Longman Singapore Publishers.

CHAPTER 4

The Struggle for Merit in Meritocratic Singapore: Implications for Persons with Disabilities

Wong Meng Ee

Introduction

Meritocracy is widely believed to be a set of social values that guides an individual's advancement in society whereby abilities and merits are key determinants rather than social background, family or wealth (Castilla & Benard, 2010; Poocharoen & Brillantes, 2013). Despite Michael Young's original term which was coined in 1958 with a pejorative sense to serve caution against dystopia, many contemporary societies have turned to meritocracy as a positive ideal by which to organise and grow society. Such is the trend when political leaders assert the values of meritocracy as demonstrated in their speeches, i.e., Theresa May aspiring to build Britain as the great meritocracy (May, 2016) and Barack Obama renewing the founding vision that no matter who they are or where they come from, everyone in America can decide their destiny through hard work (Obama, 2013). While meritocracy has somewhat transformed, at the core it "refers to the idea that whatever our social position at birth, society ought to facilitate the means for 'talent' to 'rise to the top'" (Littler, 2013).

As a system in Western societies, meritocracy has been associated positively with capitalism and egalitarianism, values espoused in the 'American Dream' (Sealy, 2010). A key appeal for modern society is that meritocracy offers promise for members from the low status strata to improve their status, economic class and place in the hierarchy, implanting the ideology that everyone has a chance of succeeding if they cultivate the required abilities (Kim & Choi, 2017; Wiederkehr *et al.*, 2015). In this vein, Kim and Choi (2017) go further to assert that meritocracy has served as an engine of meritocratic upward mobility for maintaining social order and calming social unrest.

Meritocracy is one of the core principles that have shaped Singapore's early nation building and remains its modus operandi. Ong Ye Kung, Minister for Education, revisited that meritocracy has helped hundreds of thousands beat the odds — 15 years ago, only half of the students from the bottom 20 per cent of the socioeconomic scale went on to post-secondary education. Today, 9 in 10 do so. In the same period, the proportion of those from this group who went on to get a publicly-funded degree or diploma has risen from 40 to 50 per cent (Ng, 2018).

In spite of the promise of meritocracy, many socio-economic challenges such as globalisation, financial crises and unresolved inequalities experienced in many societies raise doubts on the claims of meritocracy (Corbett, 2013; Hayes, 2012; McNamee & Miller, 2004; Newman *et al.*, 2015; Reynolds & Xian, 2014). The doubts on meritocracy are also manifested in Singapore in terms of inequalities experienced at the lower socio-economic strata as well as in the Gini coefficient rate that indicates disparity in income distribution (Smith *et al.*, 2015; Teo, 2018) within groups, for instance the Malay community (Salahudin, 2019). Different access to resources means not every student has equal access to the range of opportunities (Lim, 2016). In this light, not every school, course or pathway to education is equal (Lim, 2013; Lim, 2016). Some school curricular offer distinctively different citizenship content to different streams suggesting there is a degree of sorting and socialising at play (Ho, 2014). Disadvantaged families have less exposure and experience with cultural competency compared to their upper and middle class peers (Alsagoff & Mohamed, 2019; Osman, 2019).

While the national ethos is that meritocracy remains the architecture which structures Singapore society, how this is portrayed to convey an egalitarian outcome is frequently being redefined to meet the pressures inherent in the ideals of meritocracy. 'Compassionate meritocracy', 'broader meritocracy', 'continuous meritocracy' and 'enabling meritocracy' are just some examples of the realisation of how meritocracy is imperfect and needs tweaking to avoid elitism (Goh, 2013; Tharman, 2013; Today Online, 2019). Ong Ye Kung admitted while the meritocratic doctrine has been embraced to introduce fairness, there is a paradox in that this has resulted in systemic unfairness — as uplifted families invest in their children, they have a head start over those from humble backgrounds (Ong, 2018). Acknowledging that meritocracy is in danger of being viewed as a "dirty word", Ong remarked that "I stress there is no contradiction between meritocracy and fairness, nor reducing inequality and raising our collective standards. Instead, we should double up on meritocracy, by broadening its definition to embrace various talents and skills. We should not cap achievement at the top, but work harder to lift the bottom" (Ong, 2018).

Given that Singapore is not spared from non-meritocratic elements, what are the implications confronting persons with disabilities? As persons with disabilities have endured disadvantaged positions in society throughout history, this chapter seeks to raise pertinent questions arising from Singapore's long-term embrace of meritocratic principles in light of seeking greater inclusion. There is a serious need to discuss, understand and consider the contemporary aspects of meritocracy as envisioned in Singapore. The following sections will review the literature, describe aspects and characteristics of meritocracy and reflect on how disability features in a meritocratic society.

Concepts of Meritocracy

A review of literature examining meritocracy typically points to Michael Young's 1958 book, *The Rise of the Meritocracy*, where the term 'meritocracy' was first coined. Young described 'merit' as consisting of IQ plus effort, and 'meritocracy' of a society as the elite class mingling only with those from similar social backgrounds and economic classes. Young's satire was a critique of societal dystopia where merit is limited to IQ and effort, arguing the proclivity that widespread inequality is a result of one's measurable merit. However, Littler (2013) uncovered that it was Alan Fox instead whose 1956 article "Class and Equality" in the journal *Socialist Commentary* was where 'meritocracy' was first cited. As an industrial sociologist, Fox researched the history of trade unions and in this piece, he examined the policies, social apparatuses and ideologies that reproduced and legitimised social stratification. Examining the role of 'the four scales' of income, property, education and occupation, Fox asserted these to determine one's inequality of position. While he posited even if mechanisation and unionisation were to improve workers' livelihoods, Fox argued that social stratification will remain if the assumed law of nature continues, where those with higher occupational status enjoy superior education and income. Society then is divisible between the blessed and unblessed; those who get the best of everything and those who get the poorest and the least. Meritocracy then is a process to sift out "the gifted, the smart, the energetic, the ambitious and the ruthless" to arrive at their destined dominant positions where they are subsequently rewarded for their endowments (Fox as cited in Littler, 2013).

Both Fox's and Young's initial descriptions of meritocracy were couched with negative connotations that reflected societal stratification. Despite these overtones, the contemporary understanding of meritocracy connotes an equal society (Lipsey, 2014). Generally, success is believed to be a valid indicator of personal effort and performance (Wiederkehr *et al.*, 2015) and has since gained widespread support even from the lowest of the social ladder (Chong, 2014; Newman *et al.*, 2015). Given this general belief, there is a strong call for meritocracies to provide 'equality of opportunity' for all members of society regardless of gender, race, class and social position (Lipsey, 2014; Martin *et al.*, 2014; So, 2015; Talib & Fitzgerald, 2015).

With meritocracy gaining positive traction in the West, the concept was soon linked to political ideology, capitalism and the familiar association with the 'American Dream' (Newman *et al.*, 2015; Wiederkehr *et al.*, 2015). This is also part of the Singapore narrative where a meritocratic system is a core principle that has allowed Singapore to successfully mature as a society and arrive at its modern state (Bellows, 2009). In many westernised societies such as Singapore, meritocratic ideals are also commonly practiced in organisations. Companies determine promotion largely through performance management and contributions to the organisation (Barbosa, 2014). Human resource policies are designed to promote fair recruitment and promotion aligned to meritocratic ideals to avoid partial appointments and promotion of staff (S'liwa & Johansson, 2014)

In general, it can be understood that meritocracy is a system and an ideology commonly accepted in contemporary society. This broad acceptance couched in aspirations of success through hard work has replaced the original dystopic undertones. Arguably, pit against systems of aristocracy, nepotism, patronage and corruption, meritocracy emerges as the superior system that ostensibly promotes equity.

Features of Meritocracy

Two fundamental features of meritocracy are 'impartial competition' and 'equality of opportunity' (Talib & Fitzgerald, 2015). Without equality of opportunity, meritocracy will fail to realise its inherent objective. So (2015) argues that 'equality' and 'fairness' are often adopted in many western corporations. To this end, meritocratic principles are framed to justify the use of talent as a means to drive goal setting at the individual and corporate levels (Panayotakis, 2014). Meritocratic principles are also extended to generate staff competition with the objective to increase productivity (Barbosa, 2014).

As to how meritocracy is expressed in terms of merit and individual achievement, achievement tests or 'testocratic merit' are common practices (Guinier, 2016). Yet, especially in a school setting, Mijs (2016) queries how truly similar schools are, calling to question the disparity in quality of instruction and student population between public and private schools. While achievement testing suggests hard work and merit offers a fair chance to success regardless of a person's class, gender and cultural background (Au, 2013; Guinier, 2016), failure to achieve is attributed to lack of ability or deficits (Alon & Tienda, 2007).

Despite how meritocracy is presented as a fair means of determining talent through meritocratic elements such as hard work, ambition and good education, Reynolds and Xian (2014) point out that non-meritocratic elements such as family wealth, background and connections may enhance one's social capital (Clycq et al., 2014; Warikoo & Fuhr, 2014). For this reason, it is not surprising that some observers define meritocracy as an adapted aristocracy (Meroe, 2014; Patel, 2015). With this observation, how hidden non-meritocratic elements are perceived is important for maintaining transparency, which is associated with the fundamentals of meritocracy.

Generally, the literature discussing meritocracy highlights its function to enable social mobility by encouraging individuals to strive to achieve the goals of society. Another function of meritocracy is that it clarifies how resources are allocated through the system of rewarding talent and merit, which in turn reduces corruption. Despite these inherent functional features of meritocracy, the literature also reveals that family background and sociocultural contexts cannot be ruled out from meritocratic outcomes. These non-meritocratic elements are considered next.

Considerations of Meritocracy

One of the key features of meritocracy is equality of opportunity. This is significant in establishing harmony (Panayotakis, 2014; Lipsey, 2014; Martin et al., 2014; Talib & Fitzgerald, 2015). Kim and

Choi (2017) assert that there are two prerequisites for a meritocratic society: transparency and impartiality. It is only through these prerequisites that equality of all members can be achieved so that societal growth can occur. In fact, the principle of 'noblesse oblige' is expected of those with more, given their social position and economic class. Another important feature of meritocracy is the consensus of what is merit and how to measure it (S'liwa & Johansson, 2014). What is deemed meritable will differ across nations and organisations (Park & Liu, 2014). With this subjective interpretation, it is not unusual then to also expect that beliefs about meritocracy are mutable (Reynolds & Xian, 2014). It is with these challenges that the problems of meritocracy will next be considered.

Pitfalls of Meritocracy

Given that the concept of meritocracy is by and large embraced as a positive means to organise society, Littler (2015) asserts five flaws of meritocracy to illustrate its pitfalls. These will be shared below with further expansion. Firstly, there is an assumption inherent in the logic of meritocracy that 'talent' or 'intelligence' is congenital; i.e., these apparently merit-based qualities are biological. Where bolstering of these qualities is necessary, cultural resources such as wealth enable opportunities (Meroe, 2014). This implies that those who fail to meet these standards or who do not have access to the necessary cultural resources are relegated to social Darwinistic perspectives (Meroe, 2014). This notion of merit is singular, linear and smacks of eugenics. Secondly, meritocracy endorses a competitive, linear and hierarchical system. Therefore, arising from this definition, there will be a group of people who will be left behind. For as long as there is a top, there will be a bottom. Not everyone can 'rise' to the top. Unrealised talent is therefore both the necessary and structural condition of its existence. Talent shows are one such example of such displays of meritocracy. This can be likened to a ladder system of social mobility where self-interest and competitive drive run the risk of fostering a socially corrosive ethic that both legitimises inequality and damages community by pitting individuals against one another. Thirdly, meritocracy inevitably introduces a hierarchical ranking of valued professions and status. History has demonstrated that at different time points, what have been deemed desirable characteristics have shifted. For instance, where Arnold Schwarzenegger and Sylvester Stalone were once seen as machismo models of success, Jeff Bezos, Warren Buffett and Bill Gates have since moved into the foreground as successful products of meritocracy in the contemporary world. Fourthly, there is an affirmation of upper-middle class values as norms to aspire towards while working-class cultures are to be broken away from and avoided. Fifthly, meritocracy functions as an ideological myth. There is not only an obscuring of socio-economic inequalities but also a curtailing of social equality. Research is uncovering that effort and talent are not always salient determinants of social mobility; instead, material and cultural resources, in other words, economic and social capital, are strong influences (Lin *et al.*, 2001; McNamee & Miller, 2004).

As we begin to deconstruct meritocracy, it is possible to identify the essentialised and exclusionary notion of 'talent', competitive individualism and the need for social mobility. These three overarching issues are at the core of meritocracy and when these are juxtaposed against disability, the fundamental value of the human being, underscoring of ableism and neoliberalist socio-economic forces further stress the place of individuals with disabilities.

Value of the Human

In the first instance, meritocracy and both its implicit and explicit definitions raise questions on the value of the human being. In examining how individuals with disabilities are valued, this brings forth the good, bad and ugly examples of societal treatment of the disabled. Infanticide of children with disabilities has been historically accepted and is not uncommon in some societies; it is even argued for in some situations (Kuhse & Singer, 1988; Morgan, 1987). In other societies, institutions and state asylums for individuals with disabilities are believed to be appropriate rehabilitation;

these are, however, often degraded with detrimental outcomes when supervision is negligent and resources are lacking (Scheerenberger, 1983). Perhaps most tellingly, under adverse situations such as war, where there is scarcity of food and resources, the stark choices of allocation are reduced to a simple division of productive or unproductive, curable or incurable; in other words, resource allocation can, at times, exacerbate the binary distinction between the disabled and non-disabled. Pushed to extremes, it was people with disabilities who were faced with the fate of sanctioned genocide in Nazi Germany. When economic viability is linked to human worth, people with disabilities are perceived as burdensome, not contributing but taking from society, and these notions spark ethical debates concerning euthanasia and sterilisation (Mostert, 2002). If such a rationale represents one extreme depravity, it is arguably far less vulgar and even a vast improvement that there is a chance for people with disabilities to participate in the mainstream, never mind if they only occupy the bottom rung of the social ladder. After all, what is important is that society has demonstrated humanity. This is evidenced in much of societal participation. Considering employment, research reports have shown that people with disabilities continue to be concentrated in lower paid service jobs and under-represented in better paid managerial and professional positions (Barnes & Mercer, 2005; Stevens, 2002). Ill-founded, stereotypical employer perceptions of persons with disabilities often fuel discrimination (Bonaccio et al., 2019). The system of meritocracy therefore features a further structure to legitimise the position of the disabled in the bottom rung of the social ladder.

Emphasis of Ableism in a Meritocracy

As we contend with histories and beliefs about ability and disability contributing to exclusion, one emerging concept is ableism. "Ableism is a set of beliefs, processes and practices that produce — based on abilities one exhibits or values — a particular understanding of oneself, one's body and one's relationship with others of humanity, other species and the environment, and includes how one is judged by others" (Wolbring, 2008). What is particularly salient in the issue of meritocracy is the sentiment of certain social groups and social structures that value and promote certain abilities. In the case of a largely free market economy such as Singapore, productivity and competitiveness are valued abilities. Wolbring (2008) warns that "this preference for certain abilities over others leads to a labelling of real or perceived deviations from or lack of 'essential' abilities as a diminished state of being, leading or contributing to justifying various other isms".

In the case of persons with disabilities, ableism reflects a preference for species-typical normative abilities, leading to discrimination against 'less able' and/or 'impaired' disabled people (Wolbring, 2004, 2005). This echoes the perspective of disability understood from the medical model, where disability is seen as a deficit, impairment and medical condition requiring treatment and normalisation, and is surrounded by an attitude against having further reproduction of such individuals (Wolbring, 2008).

Different social groups have historically also used ableism to justify their rights and status in relation to other groups. Women have been viewed as incapable of voting and owning property as a result of their apparent emotional fragility (Silvers *et al.*, 1998). Here we observe ableism manifested in sexism, where the apparent lack of certain abilities justifies sexism and leads to male domination over females (Wolbring, 2008). Parallels can also be drawn between the able-bodied and disabled, leading to discrimination and hegemony between groups.

Meritocracy Legitimising Neoliberal Culture

With ableism entrenched in meritocracy — Littler (2017) asserts that meritocracy is the key cultural means of legitimation for the contemporary neoliberal culture — and whilst it promises opportunity, it in fact creates new forms of social division. Neoliberalism has its roots from Adam Smith who espoused classical liberalism to abolish government intervention in manufacturing, commerce and tariffs for free trade and free enterprise to instead have resources efficiently allocated through market mechanisms (Clarke, 2005; Munck, 2005). Neoliberalism has also been argued to have occupied the economic theories of centrists (Palley, 2005). In recent times, Saad-Filho and Johnston (2005) assert that the dominant ideology that shapes contemporary world economies is neoliberalism where the concentration of wealth and power resides with transnational corporations and global elite groups. This is observed with the ideology associated with the Washington Consensus that espouses capitalism, free trade and laissez-faire market economy widely practiced since the early 1980s and commonly adopted in supranational organisations such as the World Bank, the World Health Organization (WHO) and the Organisation for Economic Co-operation and Development (OECD). Thirty of the countries in the OECD are among the richest in the world that embrace western style democracy and capitalist principles (Richardson, 2005; Vislie, 2003). Under this paradigm, the presence of the state is 'rolled back', unproductive welfare spending is curtailed, and public services and social provisions are subject to business principles. Economic rationality driven by competition informs social welfare reform (Rizvi & Lingard, 1996). While these principles and practices serve to drive outcomes, to what extent do these emerge as cold, result-oriented initiatives that overlook individuals who are unable to participate in the competitive environment?

Meritocracy in Singapore

Singapore experienced remarkable capitalist transformation especially from the late 1960s through to the early 1980s. By and large, this brought material and social improvements to the nation, catapulting it from third world to first world status. One of the commonly cited ingredients that has led to the Singapore success story is the meritocratic principle. Since gaining independence in 1965, meritocratic ideals have shaped governance and educational distribution in Singapore (Lee, 2000; Mauzy & Milne, 2002; J. Tan, 2008). The competitive education system, through evidence of meritorious results, has been the machinery by which government scholarships and entry to the upper echelons in the civil service and political leadership are determined (Barr & Skrbis, 2008; Quah, 2010). Meritocracy is also a deeply-ingrained ideology that shapes the Singaporean way of life (Goh & Gopinathan, 2006; Lim, 2013). Yet, as evident in the literature examining meritocracies, there are inherent contradictions between the concept and practice of meritocracy, as seen in egalitarian and elitist strains, and this is no different in Singapore (cf. Lim, 2013; J. Tan, 2008; K.P. Tan, 2008).

As much as we desire to uphold the meritocratic ideal that talents and qualifications should determine individuals' suitability for positions, rather than race, class or gender, it is also these very categories that emerge as unequal advantages or disadvantages (Mills, 2008; Lareau, 2003; Pateman, 1988). Where meritocracy and multiracialism are national ideals upheld to underscore that the opportunity for and access to success is possible through one's hard work regardless of one's socioeconomic, parental and ethnic background (Mauzy & Milne, 2002), commentators argue that contradictions are also observed in Singapore in areas of income inequalities and access to differentiated educational curricula (Lim, 2016; Joseph & Matthews, 2014; Salahudin, 2019; Teo, 2018). While meritocracy gives an impression of fair and equal chance of success, it also serves to disguise the disparity in differential distribution across society (Jencks, 1988). One negative outgrowth is biological cultural determinism (Barr, 1999), where underserved groups have the proclivity to blame themselves for not succeeding as a consequence of lack of hard work, as Rahim (1998) has observed among the Malay community.

Emerging Questions to Consider

The formula of effort equals reward in meritocracy is not without other influencing factors. The 'starting point of the race' begins with the nature versus nurture debate. The natural endowment of talent is beyond one's control and raises once again the issue of disability. In a competitive meritocratic society, it is not unusual to ask how persons with disabilities have a chance to compete in the mainstream when the odds are stacked against them. Without a social model perspective, it is understandable how disability can be tragically construed. Where nurture is concerned, typical considerations such as which school to attend, access to tuition/enrichment classes and social networks are universal parental concerns. In the case of students with disabilities, however, additional considerations such as access to resources, for instance, therapy services and enrollment at an appropriate school (whether special or mainstream) are two examples of parental concerns. These are just a few barriers that parents need to contend with throughout their children's educational and life journeys.

Where examination results are the meritocratic measure and means that determine reward, Singapore's educational streaming process affords or limits opportunities to the individual throughout his or her life. The higher one's academic performance and grades, the greater one's chances of gaining entry to prestigious schools and courses. Lim (2016) argues this point when examining the teaching of critical thinking skills differently in an elite school and a mainstream school, and explains how one's family culture also carries through the learning culture thereafter. Hence, being in an elite school avails one to quality resources and invaluable alumni networks which contribute to subsequent social capital. Further, Ho (2014) reports a sorting of citizenship roles between academic students and those on the vocational track in the citizenship curriculum. Students on academic tracks demonstrated higher levels of civic knowledge in areas such as the roles and responsibilities of citizens, citizenship rights and democratic principles. In contrast, students on the vocational track lacked knowledge of democratic processes and structures, and failed to display confidence with regard to affecting change in their school or society.

What about special schools which are on a totally different trajectory? How do these different resources, experiences and opportunities impact students with disabilities? In general, citizens who engage in work, military service, and/or parenthood are rewarded with entitlements and support provisions while those with poor education, health, mental illness and disability are at risk of social exclusion, reinforcing the presumption that only able-bodied individuals can fulfil active citizenry (Turner, 2009). This again shines a negative light on persons with disabilities with preconceived notions of their contributing roles and ability to participate in society.

It was from 2004 when Lee Hsien Loong became Prime Minister that Singapore witnessed steady attention paid to the special education and disability sector (Wong & Wong, 2015; Wong et al., 2017). Prior to increased attention to the sector, special education was confronted with greater disparity and fewer resources in terms of physical structures, teacher salaries and training opportunities (Lim & Nam, 2000). In spite of increased resources in the special education sector and social services supporting disability, the employment rate of a mere 4.9 per cent among persons with disabilities in Singapore (Tai, 2019) queries the efforts and efficacy of programmes undertaken vis-à-vis societal readiness for inclusion. Once again, it raises the question of meritocracy: is this the harsh reality of the disabled being relegated to their lot in a meritocratic system, or are there forces at play that further disable them?

Concluding Thoughts

In Singapore society where meritocracy has been the nation-building blueprint, this social infrastructure has served the city-state well. Issues raised in this chapter, however, highlight that meritocracy is not without flaws. Having a notion that meritocracy is an ideal system that leads to success can be misleading. Doing so overlooks conspicuous and less conspicuous conditions that may lead to witting or unwitting discrimination and a culture of self-blame. Are our positions in society singularly attributable to hardwork and talent? Are there other societal forces that have promoted or hindered advancements of persons with disabilities? At the same time, in the absence of another system able to include diverse abilities and talents in society, meritocracy still remains the ideal that shapes and organises the allocation of resources. Fundamentally, two broad fronts need to be addressed. Firstly, mechanisms need to be in place to enable marginalised individuals to compete on a level playing field. Dismantling inequalities not only needs to remove socially disadvantageous conditions, but also disabling barriers such as stereotypes of the disabled that, while subtle, carry with them profound impact. While change can come from society, it is also imperative that people with disabilities step forward to take on a larger role to advocate for greater disability rights. With Singapore's 2013 ratification of the UN Convention on the Rights of Persons with Disabilities (CRPD), the legal framework to champion disability rights is already in place. After 50 years of nation building, Singapore has matured as a society and is ready to engage in widening and deepening its rights-related issues. The mantra of 'nothing about us without us' can begin to permeate all levels of societal discourse. Yet, how this is carried forth is critical and needs to be delivered with care to ensure cooperation from the incumbent. Consensus rather than contentious engagement is a reliable way forward in the Singaporean civil society (Wong & Goodley, in submission).

As a related approach, when dealing with wider institutional issues such as education, economic and employment policies, inclusive disability conscious values need to be brought into the general way of life. Where 'every school is a good school' is the Ministry of Education's vision for every school, 'every school is an inclusive school' should be an ideal to strive towards. Likewise, 'every service as an inclusive service' and 'every job as an inclusive job' need to be driving thrusts that permeate all aspects of society. A suggested support framework can be found in the field of critical disability studies. This is an arena populated by people who advocate building upon the foundational perspectives of disability studies whilst integrating new and transformative agendas. Where ableism is so much entangled in the issue of meritocracy, critical disability studies is one way to help disentangle the otherwise Gordian knot (Wong & Goodley, in submission).

At the 2018 debate on the President's Speech, Prime Minister Lee highlighted four broad questions to ensure that meritocracy remains relevant and progressive:

> First of all, every child must have a good start in life, regardless of which family you are born into. Secondly, every talent has to be recognised and developed to the fullest. Thirdly, every opportunity has to be open to anyone with the right attitude and ability. Finally, a capable person must face minimal social impediments to being accepted, to contribute, to be in a position to lead in society. (Lee, 2018)

In other words, these questions are couched in meritocratic ideals. The upside is the government has declared its commitment in upholding these ideals. The challenge is to ensure opportunity is available and not to perpetuate inequalities. Society needs to be re-aligned with inclusive practices. Where Singapore has made effort to separate non-meritocratic elements such as family background and social networks from talent and merit, inclusive disability conscious practices are less easy to marry with the fundamentals of a meritocratic society.

This chapter raises questions in need of further dialogue. With meritocracy here to stay, the questions to ask are: How is merit defined through a disability lens? How can we apply inclusion to meritocratic policies? How is meritocracy operationalised through inclusive contexts and cultures? From the examination of these questions, we can begin to redefine a more inclusive meritocratic Singapore.

References

Abdullah, F. Z., & Mustapha, S. A. (2019). A re-look at the efficacy of 'alternative pathways' to educational and social mobility in Singapore. *MENDAKI Policy Digest*, 81–90.

Allen, A. (2011). Michael Young's The rise of the meritocracy: A philosophical critique. *British Journal of Educational Studies*, 59(4), 367–382.

Alon, S., & Tienda, M. (2007). Diversity, opportunity, and the shifting meritocracy in higher education. *American Sociological Review*, 72, 487–511.

Alsagoff, S. S. H., & Mohamed, M. K. (2019). The Singapore perspective: Supporting social mobility through education and acquiring future skills. *MENDAKI Policy Digest*, 91–98.

Au, W. (2013). Hiding behind high-stakes testing: Meritocracy, objectivity and inequality in U.S. education. *The International Education Journal: Comparative Perspectives*, *12*(2), 7–19.

Baldridge, D. C., Beatty, J. E., Konrad, A. M., & Moore, M. E. (2016). People with disabilities. In *The Oxford Handbook of Diversity in Organizations* (pp. 469–498).

Barbosa, L. (2014). Meritocracy and Brazilian society. *RAE-Revista de Administração de Empresas*, *54*(1), 80–85.

Barnes, C. (2004). Disability, disability studies and the academy. In J. Swain, S. French, C. Barnes & C. Thomas (Eds.), *Disabling Barriers, Enabling Environments* (2nd Ed.). (pp. 28–33). London: Sage.

Barnes, C., & Mercer, G. (2005). Disability, work, and welfare: Challenging the social exclusion of disabled people. *Work, Employment and Society*, *19*(3), 527–545.

Barr, M. D. (1999). Lee Kuan Yew: Race, culture and genes. *Journal of Contemporary Asia*, *29*(2), 145–166.

Barr, M. D., & Skrbis, Z. (2008). *Constructing Singapore: Elitism, Ethnicity and the Nation-building Project*. Copenhagen: Nordic Institute of Asian Studies Press.

Bellows, T. J. (2009). Meritocracy and the Singapore political system. *Asian Journal of Political Science*, *17*(1), 24–44.

Bonaccio, S., Connelly, C. E., Gellatly, I. R., Jetha, A., & Ginis, K. A. M. (2019). The participation of people with disabilities in the workplace across the employment cycle: Employer concerns and research evidence. *Journal of Business and Psychology*, 1–24.

Castilla, E., J., & Benard, S. (2010). The paradox of meritocracy in organizations. *Administrative Science Quarterly*, *55*(4), 543–676.

Chong, T. (2014). Vocational education in Singapore: Meritocracy and hidden narratives. *Discourse: Studies in the Cultural Politics of Education*, *35*(5), 637–648.

Clarke, S. (2005). The neoliberal theory of society. In A. Saad-Filho & D. Johnston (Eds.), *Neoliberalism — A Critical Reader* (pp. 50–59). London: Pluto Press.

Clycq, N., Ward Nouwen, M. A., & Vandenbroucke, A. (2014). Meritocracy, deficit thinking and the invisibility of the system: Discourses on educational success and failure. *British Educational Research Journal*, *40*(5), 796–819.

Corbett, R. J. (2013). The fading promise of a more meritocratic society. *Perspectives on Political Science, 42*(4), 212–216.

Davies, K., Gray, M. & Webb, S. A. (2014). Putting the parity back into participation: An integrated model of social justice. *International Journal of Social Welfare, 23*(2), 119–127.

Goh, C. B., & Gopinathan, S. (2006). The development of education in Singapore since 1965. Background paper prepared for the Asia Education Study Tour for African Policy Makers, June 18–30. Retrieved from http://siteresources.worldbank.org/EDUCATION/Resources/278200-1121703274255/1439264-1153425508901/Development_Edu_Singapore_draft.pdf

Goh, C. L. (2013, July 27). Meritocracy works but beware of elitism: ESM Goh. Retrieved from https://www.straitstimes.com/singapore/meritocracy-works-but-beware-of-elitism-esm-goh

Guinier, L. (2016). *The Tyranny of the Meritocracy: Democratizing Higher Education in America*. Boston, MA: Beacon Press.

Hayes, C. (2012). *Twilight of the Elites: America After Meritocracy*. New York: Broadway Books.

Ho, L. C. (2014). Meritocracy, tracking, and elitism: Differentiated citizenship education in the United States and Singapore. *Social Studies, 105*(1), 29–35.

Hyde, M. (1998). Sheltered and supported employment in the 1990s: The experiences of disabled workers in the UK. *Disability & Society, 13*(2), 199–215.

Jencks, C. (1988). Whom must we treat equally for educational opportunity to be equal? *Ethics, 98*, 518–533.

Jones, G. E. (1997). Advancement opportunity issues for persons with disabilities. *Human Resource Management Review, 7*(1) 55–76.

Joseph, C., & Matthews, J. (2014). Understanding the cultural politics of Southeast Asian education through postcolonial theory. In C. Joseph & J. Matthews (Eds.), *Equal Opportunity and Education in Postcolonial Southeast Asia*. London: Routledge.

Kim, C. H., & Choi, Y. B. (2017). How meritocracy is defined today? Contemporary aspects of meritocracy. *Economics and Sociology, 10*(1), 112–121. doi: 10.14254/2071-789X.2017/10-1/8

Konrad, A. M., Moore, M. E., Ng, E. S. W., Doherty, A. J., & Breward, K. (2013). Temporary work, underemployment and workplace accommodations: Relationship to well-being for workers with disabilities. *British Journal of Management, 24*(3), 367–382.

Kuhse, H., & Singer, P. (1988). *Should the Baby Live? The Problem of Handicapped Infants (Studies in Bioethics)*. Oxford University Press.

Lareau, A. (2003). *Unequal Childhoods: Class, Race, and Family Life*. Berkeley: University of California Press.

Lee, H. S. (2018, May 16). PM Lee Hsien Loong at the debate on the President's Speech 2018. 2018. Retrieved from the Prime Minister's Office: https://www.pmo.gov.sg/Newsroom/pm-lee-hsien-loong-debate-presidents-speech-2018

Lee, K. Y. (2000). *From Third World to first: The Singapore Story 1965–2000*. Singapore: Times Publishing.

Lim, L. (2016). Analysing meritocratic (in)equality in Singapore: Ideology, curriculum and reproduction. *Critical Studies in Education, 57*(2), 160–174.

Lim, L. (2013). Meritocracy, elitism, and egalitarianism: A preliminary and provisional assessment of Singapore's primary education review. *Asia Pacific Journal of Education, 33*(1), 1–14.

Lim, L., & Nam, S. S. (2000). Special education in Singapore. *Journal of Special Education, 34*(2), 104–109.

Lin, N., Cook, K. S., & Burt, R. S. (2001). *Social Capital: Theory and Research*. New Brunswick, NJ: Transaction Publishers.

Lipsey, D. (2014). The meretriciousness of meritocracy. *The Political Quarterly, 85*(1), 37–42.

Littler, J. (2017). *Against Meritocracy: Culture, Power and Myths of Mobility*. Abingdon, Oxon, New York, NY: Routledge.

Littler, J. (2013). Meritocracy as plutocracy: The marketising of 'equality' under neoliberalism. *New Formations, 80/81*, 52–72. doi:10.3898/NewF.80/81.03.2013

Martin, G., Dymock, D., Billet, S., & Johnson, G. (2014). In the name of meritocracy: Managers' perceptions of policies and practices for training older workers. *Ageing and Society, 34*(6), 992–1018.

Mauzy, D. K., & Milne, R. S. (2002). *Singapore Politics Under the People's Action Party*. New York: Routledge.

May, T. (2016, September, 9). Britain, the great meritocracy: Prime Minister's speech. Department for Education, 10 Downing Street: London. Retrieved from https://www.gov.uk/government/speeches/britain-the-great-meritocracy-prime-ministers-speech

McNamee, S. J. & Miller, R. K., Jr. (2004). *The Meritocracy Myth*. Lanham, MD: Rowman and Littlefield.

Meroe, A. S. (2014). Democracy, meritocracy and the uses of education. *The Journal of Negro Education, 83*, 485–498.

Mijs, J. J. B. (2016). The unfulfillable promise of meritocracy: Three lessons and their implications for justice in education. *Social Justice Research, 29,* 14–34. doi:10.1007/s11211-014-0228-0

Mills, C. (2008). *The Racial Contract.* New York: Cornell University Press.

Morgan, S. (1987). *Abuse and Neglect of Handicapped Children.* Boston, MA: Little, Brown and Company.

Mostert, M. P. (2002). Useless eaters: Disability as a genocidal marker in Nazi Germany. *Journal of Special Education, 36,* 155–168.

Munck, R. (2005). Neoliberalism and politics, and the politics of Neoliberalism. In A. Saad-Filho & D. Johnston (Eds.), *Neoliberalism: A Critical Reader* (pp. 60–69). London: Pluto Press.

Newman, B. J., Johnston, C. D., & Lown, P. L. (2015). False consciousness or class awareness? Local income inequality, personal economic position, and belief in American meritocracy. *American Journal of Political Science, 59*(2), 326–340.

Ng, C. (2018, October, 24). Meritocracy is best model for Singapore, but needs to evolve to meet new challenges: Ong Ye Kung. Retrieved from https://www.straitstimes.com/singapore/ong-ye-kung-meritocracy-is-best-model-for-singapore-but-needs-to-evolve-to-meet-new

Obama, B. (2013, February, 15). President Obama speaks on building ladders of opportunity into the middle class. The White House. Retrieved from https://obamawhitehouse.archives.gov/photos-and-video/video/2013/02/15/president-obama-speaks-strengthening-economy-middle-class#transcript

Ong, Y. K. (2018, July 11). Parliamentary motion: "Education for our future". Response by Minister for Education, Ong Ye Kung. Retrieved from https://www.moe.gov.sg/news/speeches/parliamentary-motion-education-for-our-future–response-by-minister-for-education–mr-ong-ye-kung

Osman, M. F. (2019). Keeping the Singapore dream alive: Breaking the link between family background and educational attainment. *MENDAKI Policy Digest,* 53–68.

Palley, T. I. (2005). From Keynesianism to Neoliberalism: Shifting paradigms. In A. Saad-Filho & D. Johnston (Eds.), *Neoliberalism: A Critical Reader* (pp. 20–29). London: Pluto Press.

Panayotakis, C. (2014). Capitalism, meritocracy, and social stratification: A radical reformulation of the Davis-Moore thesis. *American Journal of Economics and Sociology, 73*(1), 126–150.

Patel, L. (2015). Desiring diversity and backlash: White property rights in higher education. *The Urban Review, 47,* 657–675. doi:10.1007/s11256-015-0328-7

Pateman, C. (1988). *The Sexual Contract.* Stanford, CA: Stanford University Press.

Poocharoen, O., & Brillantes, A. (2013). Meritocracy in Asia Pacific: Status, issues, and challenges. *Review of Public Personnel Administration, 33*(2), 140–163.

Quah, J. S. T. (2010). *Public Administration Singapore Style.* Singapore: Talisman.

Rahim, L. Z. (1998). *The Singapore Dilemma: The Political and Educational Marginality of the Malay Community.* Kuala Lumpur: Oxford University Press.

Reynolds, J., & Xian, H. (2014). Perceptions of meritocracy in the land of opportunity. *Research in Social Stratification and Mobility, 36,* 121–137.

Richardson, D. (2005). Desiring sameness? The rise of a neoliberal politics of normalisation. Antipode, *37*(3), 515–535.

Rizvi, F., & Lingard, B. (1996). Disability, education and the discourses of justice. In C. Christensen and F. Rizvi (Eds.), *Disability and the Dilemmas of Education and Justice* (pp. 9–26). Buckingham: Open University Press.

S'liwa, M., & Johansson, M. (2014). The discourse of meritocracy contested/reproduced: Foreign women academics in UK business schools. *Organization, 21*(6), 821–843.

Saad-Filho, A., & Johnston, D. (2005). *Neoliberalism: A Critical Reader.* London: Pluto Press.

Salahudin, M. H. (2019). The education factor of inequality in Singapore. *MENDAKI Policy Digest,* 69–80.

Scheerenberger, R. (1983). *A History of Mental Retardation.* Baltimore, MD: Paul H. Brookes.

Sealy, R. (2010). Changing perceptions of meritocracy in senior women's careers. *Gender in Management: An International Journal, 25*(3), 184–197.

Silvers, A., Wasserman, D., & Mahowald, M. B. (1998). *Disability, Difference, Discrimination: Perspective on Justice in Bioethics and Public Policy (Point/Counterpoint: Philosophers Debate Contemporary Issues).* Landham, Bolder, New York, Oxford: Rowman & Littlefield.

Smith, C. J., Donaldson, J. A., Muclaliar, S., Md Kadir, M., & Lam, K. (2015). A handbook on inequality, poverty and unmet social needs in Singapore. *Social Insight Research Series,* 1–86.

So, B. W. Y. (2015). Exam-centred meritocracy in Taiwan: Hiring by merit or examination? *Australian Journal of Public Administration, 74*(3), 312–323.

Stevens, G. R. (2002). Employers' perceptions and practice in the employability of disabled people: A survey of companies in Southeast UK. *Disability & Society, 17*(7), 779–796.

Tai, J. (2019, February, 11). Just 5 in 100 people here with disabilities have jobs. *The Straits Times*, A6.

Talib, N., & Fitzgerald, R. (2015). Inequality as meritocracy: The use of the metaphor of diversity and the value of inequality within Singapore's meritocratic education system. *Critical Discourse Studies, 12*(4), 445–462.

Tan, J. (2008). Whither national education? In J. Tan & P.T. Ng (Eds.), *Thinking Schools, Learning Nation* (pp. 72–86). Singapore: Prentice Hall.

Tan, K. P. (2008). Meritocracy and elitism in a global city: Ideological shifts in Singapore. *International Political Science Review, 29*(1), 7–27.

Teo, Y. Y. (2018). *This is What Inequality Looks Like*. Singapore: Ethos Books.

Tharman, S. (2013, April 20). Towards a broader meritocracy. *The Straits Times*, A40.

Today Online. (2019, July, 20). Singapore's approach to tackling inequality is to build "enabling meritocracy": Indranee. *TODAY Online*. Retrieved from https://www.todayonline.com/singapore/singapores-approach-tackling-inequality-build-enabling-meritocracy-indranee

Turner, B. S. (2009). T.H. Marshall, social rights and English national identity. *Citizenship Studies, 13*(1), 65–73.

Vislie, L. (2003). From integration to inclusion: Focusing on global trends and changes in the Western European societies. *European Journal of Special Needs Education. 18*, 17–35.

Warikoo, N. K., & Fuhr, C. (2014). Legitimating status: Perceptions of meritocracy and inequality among undergraduates at an elite British university. *British Educational Research Journal, 40*(4), 699–717.

Wiederkehr, V., Bonnot, V., Krauth-Gruber, S., & Damon, C. (2015). Belief in school meritocracy as a system-justifying tool for low status students. *Frontiers in Psychology. 6*(1053).

Wolbring, G. (2008). The politics of ableism. *Development, 51*, 252–258. doi:10.1057/dev.2008.17

Wolbring, G. (2004). Solutions follow perceptions: NBIC and the concept of health, medicine, disability and disease. *Health Law Review, 12*(3), 41–46.

Wolbring, G. (2005). HTA Initiative #23 The triangle of enhancement medicine, disabled people, and the concept of health: A new challenge for HTA, health research, and health policy'. *Institute of Health Economics*. Retrieved from https://www.ihe.ca/publications/the-triangle-of-enhancement-medicine-disabled-people-and-the-concept-of-health-a-new-challenge-for-hta-health-research-and-health-policy

Wong, M. E. & Goodley, D. (in submission). *Critical Disability Studies in the UK and Singapore: Thinking with and Across Local and National Locations.*

Wong, M. E., Ng, I., Lor, J., & Wong, R (2017). Navigating through the 'rules' of civil society: In search of disability rights in Singapore. In J. Song (Ed.), *The History of Human Rights Society in Singapore: 1965–2015* (pp. 169–186). London: Routledge.

Wong, R., & Wong, M. E. (2015). Social impact of policies for the disabled in Singapore. In D. Chan (Ed.), *50 Years of Social Issues in Singapore* (pp. 147–166). Singapore: World Scientific.

CHAPTER 5

Early Intervention for Young Children with Special Needs in Singapore: History, Development and Future Directions

Kenneth K. Poon, Xie Huichao & Yang Xueyan

ಆಕ್ಟ

Introduction

Approximately 3.2 per cent of preschool children in Singapore have been identified with special needs (Enabling Masterplan Steering Committee, 2011). The largest group of children identified with special needs were those with speech and language delays (34 per cent), followed by those with autism spectrum disorder (21 per cent), behavioural problems (17 per cent), and then global developmental delay (13 per cent) (Ho, 2018). Early intervention targets these issues in a child's health, well-being and development, both cognitive and socioemotional (Poon & Lim, 2012). Besides promoting child development, it also seeks to minimise the likelihood of detrimental outcomes in later life. Early intervention includes support for those with an identified special needs and/or known biological or environmental risk factors. Since the genesis of the earliest services for young children with special needs starting as a downward extension of special education in the late 1980s, early intervention services have proliferated in both numbers and form. This chapter will provide an outline of the development of early intervention services in Singapore, tracking its emergence, development and its current state of service consolidation of programmes for children with special needs. It will also reflect upon the directions that lie ahead for early intervention services.

Early Intervention in Singapore: Emergence, Development and Consolidation

Early intervention has a relatively short history in Singapore. However, its development has been rapid and the sector has, in a short history of over 35 years developed from a fledging downward extension of special education to one that is comprehensive and integrated with preschool education.

Emergence (1983–2002): Downward extension of special education by charities

The first services for young children with special needs was provided by the Singapore Association of Retarded Citizens (now termed the Movement for the Intellectually Disabled of Singapore) when they started offering a programme for young children with intellectual and developmental disabilities in 1983 (Quah, Lim & Poon-McBrayer, 2004). This programme was subsequently formalised as the Early Intervention Programme for Infants and Children (EIPIC) when it was transferred to Margaret Drive Special School (MDSS) in 1987 (Tham-Toh & Poon, 2012). EIPIC was also offered by the Asian Women's Welfare Association (AWWA) and at Rainbow Centre's Balestier Special School (Quah, Lim & Poon-McBrayer, 2004).

Development (2003–2017): Centralisation of funding and support by the government

Whilst the establishment of EIPIC by special schools led to the emergence of early intervention services in Singapore, it was not until the centralisation of funding and support by what was then the Ministry of Community Development and Sports (which was subsequently named the Ministry of Social and Family Development) in 2003 that led to the proliferation and development of the sector (Lee, 2018). The number of such centres for young children with developmental needs increased in the subsequent two decades with new social service agencies such as the Thye Hwa Kuan Moral Charities, Fei Yue Community Services and the Spastic Children's Association of Singapore establishing new EIPIC centres for the broad spectrum of children, and with the Autism Resource Centre and the Autism Association of Singapore running specialised EIPIC services (Enabling Masterplan Steering Committee, 2006).

In addition, the Integrated Childcare Programme (ICCP) was established in 2003. Unlike EIPIC centres, ICCPs are operated by childcare providers (Ministry of Community Development and Sports, 2003). Thus, ICCPs are selected childcare centres that serve children aged two to six and receive additional resources to further provide support to young children with mild to moderate developmental needs. The introduction of the ICCP was significant as it heralded the first effort to provide early intervention to children with special needs in preschool environments. There are currently 14 childcare centres that offer the ICCP to children with mild to moderate needs. The nature of the supports varies from centre to centre but ICCPs, like the Development Support (DS) and Learning Support (LS) programme, offers support in addition to the opportunities for young children with special needs to be educated alongside their peers (Poon & Yang, 2016).

Another turning point in early intervention service provision took place in 2006 with the publication of the first Enabling Masterplan for Persons with Disabilities 2006–2011 (EM1; Enabling Masterplan Steering Committee, 2006). With one of the focal points of EM1 being on early intervention and education, it proposed a need for (a) a leadership revamp with increased role of the government in early intervention and in special education, (b) the adoption of a continuum approach to the development of services in early intervention and special education, (c) a focus on the quality of programme and professionals, (d) a review of funding within EIPIC programmes, (e) the empowerment of family caregivers, and (f) planned transition management at key points. The subsequent Enabling Masterplan for Persons with Disabilities 2012–2016 (EM2; Enabling Masterplan Steering Committee, 2011), in its study of the needs of the early intervention sector, highlighted the following as their priorities: (a) the establishment of an early detection network, (b) enabling access to more early intervention services, (c) promoting family involvement, and (d) the establishment of a framework for service quality and effectiveness.

The most recent Enabling Masterplan for Persons with Disabilities (EM3; Enabling Masterplan Steering Committee, 2016) proposed four key thrusts for 2017 to 2021. The first thrust promoted the quality of life of persons with disabilities. The recommendations accompanying this thrust included (a) flexible service models, (b) improved transition management, (c) timely and effective detection of developmental needs, and (d) enhanced integration and inclusion of children with special needs in education. The next thrust of supporting caregivers had embedded within it the recommendation to (a) improve caregivers' well-being and enhance their caregiving capabilities and (b) support them in future care planning. The third thrust of building the community proposed to build the capacity and capability of disability service providers to enhance service quality. The fourth thrust of building an inclusive community proposed to (a) build positive attitudes towards persons with disabilities and improve knowledge on how to interact with them and (b) include persons with disabilities in all settings. In response to these recommendations, refinements to the early intervention landscape were introduced bringing the sector to a greater level of maturity and consolidation of services.

Consolidation (2018–present): A continuum approach to the development of services in early intervention

With the development of the basic early intervention services established after 35 years of history, the next step that was undertaken sought to consolidate and broaden the suite of services. One of the most significant recent developments, perhaps addressing this need, is the transfer of oversight of early intervention from the Ministry of Social and Family Development (MSF) to the Early Childhood Development Agency (ECDA; Lee, 2019). As ECDA currently regulates the preschool sector, this move potentially facilitates the coordination of the early childhood education and early intervention service. Additionally, with ECDA being the regulatory and developmental authority on early childhood in Singapore, it will be able to address and coordinate the professional development of early childhood educators and professionals in early intervention. This also further extends the continuum of early intervention services beyond EIPIC and ICCP. In the sections below, the current continuum of early intervention services for young children with special needs is presented. As seen in Figure 1, the needs of young children with mild to severe levels of special needs vary. Corresponding to the levels of risk is the types of early intervention programmes described in levels of specialised support. This section ends with a description of the current state of early detection network, a critical entry point into the early intervention system.

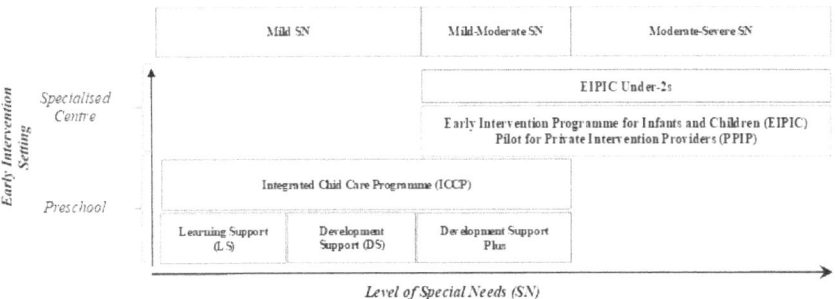

Figure 1: The continuum of early intervention services (adapted from MSF 2019).

Early intervention for children with mild to moderate levels of special needs

The ideal early intervention setting for young children with mild special needs is the preschool environment. This is an important environment as children with special needs, particularly those in childcare centres, spend a substantial amount of their day hours there. Additionally, the preschool environment is also one that offers opportunities to practice and generalise learnt skills. There are two major national initiatives supporting young children with mild to moderate needs in preschools, namely the DS and LS Programme, as well as the ICCP programme.

The DS and LS programme was introduced to support young children with mild developmental or learning needs (SG Enable, 2019). These are targeted short-term interventions delivered by therapists and Learning Support Educators (LSEds). DS is provided to children with mild to moderate special needs who need the intervention of an occupational therapist, speech and language therapist, psychologist, or needing further literacy and learning support. It is provided weekly but with a longer duration of ten to 15 weeks.

LS, on the other hand, is a programme where an LSEd provides support in literacy, language, social and handwriting skills for approximately an hour a week for a period of six to ten weeks. LSEds are teachers with at least two years of teaching experience who also hold a Specialist Diploma in Early Childhood Learning Support (SDELS). The SDELS is a post-Diploma Certification provided through the National Institute of Early Childhood Development (NIEC), a major training and professional development institute for early childhood educators in Singapore (NIEC, 2019b).

Children are identified for DS or LS by teachers in participating preschools. These 550 preschools are typically run by not-for-profit organizations. Following identification, the LSEds will screen the child and, if needed, will be seen by a developmental paediatrician from the Child Development Programme.

Early intervention for children with moderate to severe developmental needs

Children with moderate to severe developmental needs are supported through the Early Intervention Programme for Infants and Children (EIPIC), a specialised setting provided at 21 early intervention (EI) centres run by 10 Social Service Agencies (SSAs). Depending on their individual needs, children receive up to 12 hours of EIPIC a week from specially trained EI teachers (SG Enable, 2019). EI teachers have at least one year of working with children with special needs and hold an Advanced Diploma in Early Childhood Intervention, Special Needs (ADESN) from NIEC, which is the only certification recognised by the National Council for Social Service for training early intervention teachers (NIEC, 2019a). EI teachers in EIPIC work as part of transdisciplinary teams comprising also therapists, psychologists and social workers (Poon & Yang, 2016). An alternative option is the Pilot for Private Intervention Providers (PPIP) programme. In this programme, services are provided through accredited private EI centres but children are similarly subsidised (SG Enable, 2019).

More recently, a specialised early intervention service for children from birth to 24 months old was announced (Lee, 2019). As young children spend a lot more time with their families and caregivers, the EIPIC Under-2 programme requires parents and/or caregivers to be also present so that intervention strategies may be embedded in the child's daily routines at home. With learning opportunities embedded within the children's daily lives, there is a greater opportunity for functional application within the home and community. This model has also been conducted within home environments with positive results (Leong *et al.*, 2017).

Children in EIPIC who make progress to the point where they can be supported within preschools may be placed in the Developmental Support Plus (DS Plus) programme. DS Plus is a programme providing intervention about twice a week for about 6 months in preschools (SG Enable, 2019). The purpose of this programme is to introduce and help children adapt to preschool settings so they are better equipped with the skills needed for learning in a larger class setting. Children are supported by both preschool teachers as well as early interventionists in this programme.

Early Detection in Early Intervention

Critical to accessing needed supports and early intervention services is the early identification of children with special needs or who are at risk. An early detection network for identifying young children who need intervention has been described in the Enabling Masterplan (EM3; Enabling Masterplan Steering Committee, 2016). This early detection network consists of developmental screening efforts from three sectors: (a) primary care agencies such as community clinics and hospitals, (b) families and caregivers, and (c) other community partners such as early childhood care and education and family service centers. However, most developmental screening practices reported in the literature took place in only one of the three sectors — the primary care agencies. For example, a recent survey study by Koh and colleagues (2016) reported that most parents did not use the developmental checklist in the Health Booklet to monitor their child's developmental status.

A gap in timely identification of young children who need intervention services can be found in the literature. Ho (2018) indicates that the number of young children identified with developmental problems has been increasing with approximately 4,900 new cases seen by the Child Development Programme at two hospitals in 2017. The Enabling Masterplan 2017–2022 indicates that 2.1 per cent of the student population was diagnosed with a disability (Enabling Masterplan Steering Committee, 2016), a figure consistent with the previous figure of 2.5 per cent reported in EM2 (Enabling Masterplan Steering Committee, 2011). When contrasted against the 3.25 per cent of children aged birth to 2 years, and 6.44 per cent of children aged 3 to 5 years covered by the USA Individuals with Disabilities Act 2017/2018 (Office of Special Education Programmes, 2018), the figures indicate that there remains a gap in the identification of young children with special needs.

To strengthen the non-healthcare sectors in the early detection network and increase the effectiveness and efficiency of this system, developmental screening services have been recently delivered in some early childhood care and education programmes. For example, the DS and LS professionals conduct developmental screening with children red-flagged by early childhood educators to determine whether an evaluation of early intervention eligibility is needed. Once developmental concerns are confirmed and an eligibility evaluation is considered necessary, the parents will be advised to take their child to one of the two hospitals for a comprehensive assessment of vision/hearing, motor, cognition, communication, social-emotional and adaptive skills (Ho, 2018).

Directions Ahead

As this short account of the development of early intervention in Singapore suggests, the current continuum of early detection and early intervention services represent a significant advance in policy and sector development since our previous review (Poon & Lim, 2012) and over the past 35 years. However, there remains room for growth within the early intervention sector. As a framework to guide analysis, relevant recommendations within EM3 will be employed to reflect upon future directions.

Flexible service models

With early intervention services being established to serve the continuum of needs, EM3 called for a greater exploration of service models and for there to be more review of services to "ensure that services remain relevant and responsive to the changing needs" (Enabling Masterplan Steering Committee, 2016, p. 34) for children with special needs. The role of research and standardised assessment tools was underscored as one of the means of achieving this goal.

Improved transition management

Transitions between life stages and service providers can be particularly stressful for children with special needs. Children with special needs attending EIPIC would receive some support in making the transition as part of the broader support process but the support provided by preschools is unclear. More research to understand the service provision across the spectrum of needs is needed.

Timely and effective detection of developmental needs

As the DS and LS programmes are being rolled out among more preschools in Singapore, children increasingly receive developmental screening in early childhood care and education settings rather than in healthcare. However, challenges to accurate and efficient developmental screening are different in educational and healthcare settings (Bricker *et al.*, 2013). Research is needed to examine and identify evidence-based practices that facilitate sustainable developmental screening in early childhood care and education settings.

Another future direction for progress remains with the untapped potential of using the Health Booklet in Singapore. One way to improve the current application of the Health Booklet is to update the developmental checklist with a more rigorous instrument with evidence supporting its cultural relevance to Singaporean children (Koh *et al.*, 2016).

Inclusion of children with special needs in education

With the introduction of ICCPs and the DS and LS programmes, early intervention services have been extended to preschool environments for children with mild to moderate levels of special needs. The more recent introduction of DS-Plus further supports children from EIPIC who would benefit from support within preschools. However, there are also children with more significant levels of special needs in preschool environments. In an effort to address this issue, a cross-sectoral workgroup was introduced to better understand the issues of including young children with moderate to severe special needs and to propose recommendations for supporting them (MSF, 2019). The broadening of support for increasing numbers of young children with special needs to meaningfully participate in preschool environments will enable them to learn and develop with and alongside their peers. Additionally, typically developing peers will have more opportunities to understand, appreciate and work with peers with different abilities.

Improve caregivers' well-being and enhance their caregiving capabilities

In the call to support caregivers, EM3 proposed both formal as well as informal supports. Formal supports proposed takes the form of greater training options for caregivers to enhance their information and care needs and easier access to counselling and other support services. In terms of informal supports, more opportunities for building new and positive relationships with experienced caregivers and befrienders were proposed. Likewise, the need to enhance family relationships was also highlighted. Taking reference from the work of Poon and colleagues (2014), other areas that may merit consideration include knowledge of how to advocate for their child as well as providing families with ideas for participating in the community with their child.

Building capacity and capability of disability service providers to enhance service quality

With the sector rapidly growing in both capacities of supporting more children and in terms of scope to better serve children on both sides of the continuum, the issue of quality becomes a pivotal issue that requires attention. The EM3 proposed three recommendations relevant for young children under the key thrust of capacity and capability building.

First, the need to identify strategies to attract and retain the human capital within the early intervention sector was proposed by EM3. Whilst it was mentioned as a strategy that allied health professionals be cross-deployed between sectors, this too can be the case for early interventionists who are typically first trained as early childhood educators. With early childhood education as one of the foundational disciplines of early intervention, cross deployment of early childhood educators across both inclusive as well as specialised environments is possible. However, the current state where the training between the early interventionists is a barrier merits consideration. For instance, an EIPIC teacher seeking to work as an LSEd will need to be retrained by attending the SDELS. Further, while early childhood educators in preschool settings indicate positive attitudes toward inclusion of children with special needs, many highlight the need for additional formal training and professional development in supporting students with additional learning and behavioural needs (Lian et al., 2008; Nonis, 2006; Nonis et al., 2016).

Next is a proposal to have the sector guided by evidence-based practices. The current practices adopted within the sector such as multidisciplinary teaming and family centred practices (Chong et al., 2012; Tang et al., 2012) are practices based on the corpus of research. As these practices were developed in a different ecological context and were implemented in differently supported classrooms by professionals with a different pathway of training, the degree to which these practices are applicable and may be directly implemented in Singapore would merit investigation. Likewise, the instrumentation for the measurement of both practices and outcomes needs verification. Work in this area is underway examining the applicability of instruments such as the Family Outcomes Survey (Poon et al., 2014) and Family Quality of Life Scale (Waschl et al., 2019).

Conclusion

Once a downward extension of special education, early intervention is now a comprehensive system providing a continuum of support. Likewise, the focus on capacity has shifted, as evident from the issues highlighted by EM3, to one of quality. Evident from the preceding description is how the field of early intervention in Singapore has grown in the short span of 35 years. However, the adage that Rome was not built in one day also holds true for the field of early intervention. The recommendations of the EM3 serve as signposts for further development within the field of early intervention. Just as early intervention emerges and progresses through the combined efforts of service providers and government, the continued involvement of these stakeholders is required. Furthermore, as the sector matures, the support of research is needed to further guide and evaluate the development of this sector.

References

Bricker, D., Macy, M., Squires, J., & Marks, K. (2013). *Developmental Screening in Your Community: An Integrated Approach for Connecting Children with Services*. Baltimore, MD: Paul Brookes.

Chong, W. H., Goh, W., Tang, H. N., Chan, W. P., & Choo, S. (2012). Service practice evaluation of the early intervention programs for infants and young children in Singapore. *Children's Health Care, 41*(4), 281–301.

Enabling Masterplan Steering Committee. (2006). Enabling Masterplan (2007–2011). Retrieved from https://www.msf.gov.sg/policies/Disabilities-and-Special-Needs/Pages/EM per cent201.pdf?utm_source=website

Enabling Masterplan Steering Committee. (2011). Enabling Masterplan. (2012–2016). Retrieved from https://www.msf.gov.sg/policies/Disabilities-and-Special-Needs/Enabling-Masterplan-2012-2016/Pages/default.aspx

Enabling Masterplan Steering Committee. (2016). Enabling Masterplan 2017–2021: Caring Nation, Inclusive Society. Retrieved from https://www.ncss.gov.sg/NCSS/media/NCSS-Documentsand-Forms/EM3-Final_Report_20161219.pdf

Ho, L. Y. (2007). Child development programme in Singapore 1988 to 2007. *Annals of the Academy of Medicine, 36*, 898–910.

Ho, L. Y. (2018). *Building an Inclusive Early Childhood Intervention Ecosystem in Singapore, 1988–2017*. Singapore: KK Women's and Children's Hospital, Department of Child Development.

Koh, H. C., Ang, S. K. T., Kwok, J., Tang, H. N., Wong, C. M., Daniel, L. M., & Goh, W. (2016). The utility of developmental checklists in a parent-held child health record for identifying children with developmental issues in Singapore. *Journal of Developmental and Behavioural Pediatrics, 37*(8), 647–656.

Lee. D. (2018, Apr 27). Speech by Minister Desmond Lee at Early Intervention Conference. Retrieved from https://www.msf.gov.sg/media-room/Pages/Early-Intervention-Conference.aspx

Lee, D. (2019, Apr 10). More integrated support for children with developmental needs under ECDA. Retrieved from https://www.msf.gov.sg/media-room/Pages/More-Integrated-Support-for-Children-with-Developmental-Needs-Under-ECDA.aspx?fbclid=IwAR1y2Xl1JTLZ6GbevlcUEsNQ1_eWg_cYagNLcGt_57EIzFjPO0gcyvqnQI

Leong, J., Chew, K., Chay, P. Y., & Xie, H. (2017, November). Implementing and evaluating a transdisciplinary team approach to early intervention in Singapore. Poster session presented at the International Association for the Scientific Study of Intellectual and Developmental Disabilities Asia-Pacific Regional Congress, Bangkok, Thailand.

Lian, W. B., Ho, S. K. Y., Choo, S. H. T., Chan, D. K. L., Yeo, C. L., & Ho, L. Y. (2008). Pre-school teachers' knowledge, attitudes and practices on childhood developmental and behavioural disorders in Singapore. *Journal of Paediatrics and Child Health, 44*(4), 187–194.

Ministry of Community Development and Sports. (2003). Integrated childcare programme. Retrieved from https://www.msf.gov.sg/publications/Pages/Integrated-Childcare-Programme.aspx

Ministry of Social and Family Development. (2019). Supporting your child with developmental needs. Retrieved from https://www.msf.gov.sg/media-room/Documents/Infographic_Enhanced%20Early%20Intervention.png

National Institute of Early Childhood Development. (2019a). Advanced Diploma in Early Childhood Intervention (Special Needs) (ADESN). Retrieved from https://niec.edu.sg/courses/postdiplomas/advanced-early-childhood-intervention-special-needs/

National Institute of Early Childhood Development. (2019b). Specialist Diploma in Early Childhood Learning Support (SDELS). Retrieved from https://niec.edu.sg/courses/postdiplomas/specialist-early-childhood-learning-support/

Nonis, K. P. (2006). Integrating children with special needs: Singapore preschool teachers share their feelings: A preliminary investigation. *The Journal of the International Association of Special Education, 7*(1), 4–10.

Nonis, K., Chong, W. H., Moore, D. W., Tang, H. N., & Koh, P. (2016). Preschool teacher's attitudes towards inclusion of children with developmental needs in kindergartens in Singapore. *International Journal of Special Education, 31*(3), 1–30.

Office of Special Education Programs. (2018). IDEA Section 618 data products: Static tables. Retrieved from https://www2.ed.gov/programs/osepidea/618-data/static-tables/index.html

Poon, K. K., & Lim, A. K. (2012). Current provision, recent developments, and future directions for early childhood intervention in Singapore. *Infants and Young Children, 25*(4), 1–11.

Poon, K. K., Ooi, N., Bull, R., & Bailey, D. B. (2014). Psychometric validation of the Family Outcome Survey-Revised in Singapore. *Research in Developmental Disabilities, 35*, 1534–1543.

Poon, K. K., & Yang, X. (2016). The student profile, service delivery model, and support practices of four early childhood intervention environments in Singapore. *Asia Pacific Journal of Education, 36*, 437–449. doi: 10.1080/02188791.2014.940030

Quah, M. L., Lim, L., & Poon-McBrayer, K. F. (2004). Special education in Singapore: Celebrating the past, envisioning the future. *ASCD (Singapore) Review, 12*(2), 27–33.

SG Enable. (2019). Development Support (DS) and Learning Support (LS). Retrieved from https://www.sgenable.sg/pages/content.aspx?path=/for-children/development-support/

Tang, H. N., Chong, W. H., Goh, W., Chan, W. P., & Choo, S. (2012). Evaluation of family-centred practices in the early intervention programmes for infants and young children in Singapore with measure of processes of care for service providers and measure of beliefs about participation in family-centred service. *Child: Care, Health and Development, 38*(1), 54–60.

Tham-Toh, S. Y. J., & Poon, K. K. (2012). The development of special education in Singapore. In J. S. Y. Tham-Toh, K. Lyen, K. K. Poon, E. H. Lee, & M. Pathnapuram (Eds.), *Rainbow Dreams: A Holistic Approach to Helping Children with Special Needs* (3rd Ed.) Singapore: Rainbow Centre.

Waschl, N., Xie, H., Chen, M., & Poon, K. K. (2019). Construct, convergent, and discriminant validity of the Beach Centre Family Quality of Life Scale for Singapore. *Infants & Young Children, 32*(3), 201–214.

CHAPTER 6

Early Childhood Inclusion in Singapore: Inroads and Review

Joanna Tay-Lim

Introduction

This chapter first outlines the definition and significance of early childhood inclusion in order to provide the conceptual backdrop for the ensuing discussion of the early childhood inclusion landscape in Singapore. The presentation of the early childhood inclusion in Singapore will include an overview and critical look at the evolution of inclusive practices, and to conclude by advocating for the need to draw up quality indicators to provide concrete direction for the field to establish inclusive practices.

Definition and Significance of Early Childhood Inclusion

Scoping the definition of inclusive education

The definition of inclusive education has taken on a milieu of different meanings. The discourses on what is inclusive education are clouded. In fact, many institutions, organisations and advocacy groups have furnished their own definitions. Clough and Corbett (2000) rightly classified it as a "contestable term" (p. 6). It is therefore imperative to note the specific definition which will be adopted by this discussion to avoid ambiguity. A good place to start the discussion is the UNESCO's (2005a) definition:

> Inclusion is a process of addressing and responding to the diversity of needs of all learners through increasing participation in learning, cultures and communities, and by reducing exclusion within and from education. It involves changes and modifications in content, approaches, structures and strategies, with a common vision which covers all children of the appropriate age range and a conviction that it is the responsibility of the regular system to educate all children. (p. 13)

The important point to note in the UNESCO's definition is that inclusive practices should take place within the regular system or alternatively know as mainstream education. In other words, for a classroom to be considered inclusive, the children in focus (i.e., those with needs to be included) have to be educated alongside their typically developing peers. Without a critical mass of typically developing children, it will be difficult to implement values pertaining to inclusion and belonging. In addressing inclusive practices, UNESCO additionally emphasises the need to include all children who are vulnerable to marginalisation and exclusion, and advocates that they be accorded the rights to be supported in their development in the regular school system. This constitutes the *broader* definition of inclusion and articulates the right of every child to feel belong and to be educated to his/her highest potential (Booth, Ainscow & Kingston., 2008; DEC/NAEYC, 2009; Sandall & Schwartz, 2008).

The other commonly held definition relates more specifically to the provisions made for children with special educational needs (SEN) in mainstream school settings (Poon & Khaw, 2007; Odom *et al.*, 2004, UN General Assembly, 2016). This constitutes the *basic* definition of inclusion (UNESCO, 2005a) and it relates to the social model of disability (Jones, 2005). The context of this article is in line with this focus of inclusion of children with SEN, and posits that an inclusive class is one in which the school responds to their needs through providing a "sense of belonging and membership, positive social relationships and friendships, and development and learning to reach their full potential"(DEC/NAEYC, 2009, p. 2). This has a different philosophical stance from the concept of mainstreaming/integration of children with special needs. Though having a diverse range of interpretations, mainstreaming and/or integration generally focuses on providing access into mainstream education in which the onus is on the child to fit into the system.

The United Nations Convention on the Rights of Persons with Disabilities (UNCRPD) strongly advocates inclusive education to be a fundamental right of every child, and clearly distinguishes between the concept of inclusion and integration. In contrast to inclusion, which was conceived as a process of systematic reforms to ensure children with SEN have access to equitable and participatory education experiences in mainstream environments, integration was predominantly viewed as a viable option for children with disabilities as long as they can adjust to the standardised mainstream curriculum (United Nations, 2016). In other words, the children are expected to 'be ready' to be integrated into mainstream. This was the case in many of the earlier efforts (Allen & Cowdery, 2005). However, the "resounding theme for the 21st century is that programmes, not children, have to be ready for inclusion" (Odom, 2000, p. 25).

Significance of early childhood inclusion

The call for inclusion is a compelling one. This probably emanates from the influential Salamanca Statement: Framework for Action for Special Needs Education (UNESCO, 1994) that heightened the rights of children with SEN to have equal access to education and participation in inclusive settings, and foregrounded inclusive education as "the most effective means of combating discriminatory attitudes, building an inclusive society and achieving education for all" (p. iv). A total of 92 governments and 25 international organisations were represented in this critical discussion leading to a new dynamism that saw a shift towards greater endorsement for inclusive practices and a multinational commitment towards the education of children with SEN in inclusive settings rather than in segregated facilities. It resulted in greater awareness of governments in many nations to re-look and re-assess the education of children with SEN in their countries in order to embrace more inclusive practices — a move which has ramifications for both policy directions and practical implementations. Since then, there have been renewed calls and discussions on the need and value of inclusive education (OECD, 2001; UNESCO, 2000, 2005a, 2009; UN General Assembly, 2016).

The benefits of early childhood inclusion are well-attested to in the research literature. Odom *et al.* (2004) reviewed research studies on early childhood inclusion from 1990 to 2002. The result shows that overall both children with and without disabilities benefited positively in terms of their developmental and behavioural outcomes. Other studies have also documented similar trend which shows successful preschool inclusion with positive outcomes for including children with mild SEN (Li, 2008; Mogharreban & Bruns, 2009; Odom, Buysse & Soukakou, 2012). This is true as well for those who have explored the outcomes of inclusive education for preschool children with moderate to severe disabilities (Cross *et al.*, 2004; Downing & Peckham-Hardin, 2007; Jones, 2005). Although there are also research studies which have pointed to preschool children with SEN experiencing peer difficulties (Buysse, Goldman & Skinner, 2002; Odom *et al.*, 2004), there are also studies which have investigated empirically-supported peer strategies which generated positive outcomes as a result (Diamond & Tu, 2009; Gena, 2006; Hollingsworth & Buysse, 2009; Kim, 2005).

Nutbrown and Clough (2004) have contended that early education at its best is inclusive education. The early years have been regarded as critical for children's development. This is therefore an excellent time for children to learn inclusive values. Lim, Thaver and Slee (2008) underlined this as the key to transforming a nation into one that is open towards including the needs of those with special needs. They mentioned emphatically that "in our view, the vision of an inclusive society hinges upon the vision of how inclusive schools and teachers are" (p. 6). Given that disposition can and should be nurtured in the early years (Katz, 2002), the early childhood educational platform is probably the optimum place to build a strong disposition towards including the needs of others who may have special needs.

Early Childhood Inclusive Practices in Singapore
A nation's call to inclusion

The education landscape in Singapore has evolved in the last 15 years to embrace the concept of inclusive practices. The impetus for this has come from socio-political factors.

The advocacy for greater inclusivity stems from a nation-wide appeal to transform Singapore into a more caring, compassionate and inclusive state. In 2004, the Singapore Prime Minister issued Singapore's strongest call for inclusion as an integral societal value which its citizens can imbibe as part of the nation's new vision (Teo, 2004). It was also the first time that the government openly advocated for people with special needs. The people of Singapore were to embrace diversities which go beyond age, wealth and ethnicity dimensions to include people with special needs (Lim, Thaver & Slee, 2008). In August 2013, Singapore ratified the UNCRPD. This initiative garnered more traction to transform Singapore to be an inclusive nation. Since 2007, three Enabling Masterplans, which are roadmaps chartering guidelines and pathways to enable Singapore to realise her vision to become a caring and inclusive society, have been drawn up (MSF, 2018a).

This top-down approach set in motion a succession of coordinated efforts by the Ministry of Education which paved the way for children with mild SEN to be educated in the mainstream primary and secondary schools instead of in segregated settings. This was in recognition of the strategy that the shaping of an inclusive society has to start with our young when they are still in school. Since 2005, the progress made has been perceptible — a slew of new initiatives was seen at several levels of our educational milieu to support children with mild special needs in mainstream primary and secondary schools. These included training of mainstream teachers and specialised allied professionals in supporting the needs of children with SEN. More resources were also provided (materials and assistive devices) and some schools were designated and empowered to be resource centres for specific disabilities (Lim *et al.*, 2008).

How has this call to be an inclusive nation being translated at the preschool level in Singapore? The scenario that emerges is not as cohesive and fast-moving. Preschool in the Singapore context are early childhood settings comprising infant-care, childcare and kindergarten settings for children up to 6 years of age before they enter mainstream primary schooling. Early childhood settings in Singapore did not have the privilege of having the kind of support seen at the mainstream schools when the nation's call for inclusion was made in 2004, and therefore efforts towards inclusion paled somewhat in comparison to the inroads which had been made at the mainstream primary and secondary school level. The call for inclusive education at the preschool level was also visibly absent in all the three Singapore Enabling Masterplans. Instead, the recommendations veered towards studying approaches to foster greater interaction between mainstream preschools and children with SEN in Early Intervention Programme for Infants and Children (EIPIC) centres, which fell short of being an inclusive education approach. In addition, unlike mainstream education which is nationalised in Singapore and come under the sole purview of the Ministry of Education, the preschools are run by a plethora of operators. Overall, efforts have been more sporadic probably because there is no central body to coordinate or advocate for greater inclusivity in the preschool sector. The next section describes some of these sporadic efforts to support the needs of children with SEN at the preschool level.

Initiatives in supporting children with SEN in preschools

Towards the end of the 20th century and into the millennium, pockets of independent efforts had been seen from several quarters launching support and integration programmes which went beyond the EIPIC provided by hospital child clinics and some social service agencies (previously known as voluntary welfare organisations). This paved the way for some preschool children with mild disabilities to be educated and supported in mainstream preschool settings. One of these pioneering attempts was initiated by the National Council of Social Services (NCSS) in the late 1990s. The Council conducted a pilot study known as Project ASSIST (Assisted Integrated Support) for 40 preschoolers with mild disabilities to determine the extent they could be integrated into the mainstream classes (Quah, 1998). Although it was framed as a feasibility study, the project nevertheless created the opportunity for these children who were previously denied admission into mainstream preschools to experience school together with their typically developing peers in a supported environment.

Another laudable effort came from the Asian Women's Welfare Association (AWWA)'s Therapy and Educational Assistance for Children in Mainstream Education (TEACH ME) programme. It is currently known as their school integration programme (AWWA, 2018). The main objective is to provide relevant support to preschool children with mild SEN in order that they have a better opportunity to be integrated into mainstream education. Its service delivery includes having a transdisciplinary team to provide rehabilitative, educational and social-emotional needs to the targeted children. First launched in 1990, the programme is still proactive in its vision and mission.

Joining the fold to facilitate the support of children with SEN in mainstream preschools, the KK Women's and Children's Hospital (2018) mounted its Therapy Outreach Programme (TOP) in 2006. The programme comprises a multi-disciplinary team and its main aim is to partner preschools to bring early intervention and therapy for children with mild learning and development needs to the classroom.

The first notable government's efforts to promote early childhood inclusion was the implementation of the Integrated Child Care Programme (ICCP) (SG Enable, 2018). The Ministry of

Community, Youth and Sports (currently known as the Ministry of Social and Family Development) embarked on this programme in 2003. The ICCP enables children aged 2–6 years with mild SEN to be educated alongside their typically developing peers in existing childcare centres. ICCP centres will have at least one teacher with some training in supporting children with SEN in their care. These are para-educators who are not professionally trained special needs personnel. Thus far, the programme has not been well-received with only about 1% of the preschool establishments in Singapore adopting the ICCP in 2017. A probable reason for this is the limited resources at the centres' disposal for this programme, with the lack of professional personnel to support the needs of children with SEN being a key reason.

Thus far, the majority of the efforts described in the preceding section to support preschool children with SEN are not only limited in its influence, but they also do not point to a clear indication that these efforts could be categorised as inclusive practices. Re-visiting our definition of inclusive education which requires the school system to make transformative adjustments to flexibly respond to the diverse needs of children with SEN, the various initiatives seem to focus on early intervention support to enable the child with SEN be more adaptive and/or functional in existing school systems. In other words, the approaches are more aligned with the concept of integration rather than inclusion. Additionally, many of these efforts are focused on preschool children with mild SEN. Preschool children who have been diagnosed with more severe needs are generally excluded from having a place in mainstream preschool.

These limitations have been recognised in some quarters and to buck this trend which rides on the integration model, a small number of mainstream preschools have boldly embarked on a more inclusive mode of operations in supporting preschool children with special needs. A prominent effort was made in 2016 by AWWA in partnership with the Lien Foundation and SG Enable. It envisioned Kindle Garden as an inclusive preschool model (AWWA, 2018). Touted as the first inclusive preschool in Singapore, it promulgates a values-based, inclusive and non-discriminatory learning environment.

Thirty per cent of its student population are allocated for children with SEN, and these can include children with severe SEN as well. The preschool operationalises inclusion though a whole-school approach which sets forth inclusive policies, create inclusive cultures and provides inclusive pedagogical practices. It has a team of allied health professionals which work alongside the teachers in supporting children with additional needs, primarily through an embedded teaching and learning system.

More efforts by the government to support the needs of children with SEN at the preschool level were seen in recent years. In 2012, the Ministry of Social and Family Development launched the Development Support Programme (DSP) to provide targeted short-term support for preschool children with mild SEN (MSF, 2018b). It is conceived as a two-pronged approach. After screening, the children undergo a focused intervention by therapists. This is followed by in-class support by trained early childhood professionals known as Learning Support Educators. The programme incorporates features such as curriculum modifications and development of individual education plans (IEPs). The primary outcome is to equip these children with functional and developmentally appropriate skills to reach their potential in mainstream preschool environment. To better reflect the two-tiered support, the programme is currently known as the Development Support and Learning Support (DS and LS) programme (MSF, 2019a).

With more qualified personnel providing the support, interventions and increased government subsidies, it is easy to see that the DS-LS programme has greater reach in the early childhood field compared to the earlier ICCP. Even then, the DS-LS programme is still not widespread and is taken up by mainly anchor-operator preschools such as My First Skool from NTUC First Campus and Sparkletots from PAP Community Foundation (MSF, 2019a). This pales in comparison to some nations in which the majority of children with SEN are educated in mainstream preschool settings (Ferguson, 2008). In July 2019, the Ministry of Social and Family Development initiated the Development Support-Plus (DS-Plus) programme to work with Early Intervention (EI) centres to identify children who have made sufficient progress in EI centres to transition to preschool setting (MSF, 2019b). These children will receive the necessary support by trained health professionals who will work with the school teachers to enable them to adapt to the mainstream preschool setting. Another effort towards improving the services for children with SEN is that the government has assigned the Early Childhood Development Agency (ECDA), which is the main regulatory authority for the early childhood sector in Singapore, to take over the responsibility of early intervention services from the Ministry of Social and Family Development. The main aim is "to undertake a more coordinated approach toward manpower and capability development of both early childhood educators and EI professionals" (MSF, 2019c, para 3).

All early intervention services will come under the purview of ECDA by end 2020. The latest effort taking place in 2020 is the formation of a cross-sectoral workgroup comprising of professionals from the public and private sectors to further study how to better support children with SEN in mainstream preschools. In particular, the workgroup will focus on how children with moderate to severe developmental needs can be included in mainstream classrooms as well (MSF, 2020).

Review and Going Forward

It is heartening to see the support for children with SEN in preschools picking up at an aggressive pace with the government spearheading several initiatives and pumping in millions of dollars for its programmes. However, considering the review thus far, it could be said that the field of early childhood inclusion in Singapore is still very much in its nascent stage for several reasons. First, the most extensive programme to date is the DS-LS programme. Even then, at this point of writing, this is still limited in its influence in the early childhood field in Singapore. Second, as mentioned earlier, the majority of the programmes, including the DS-LS programme, is still very much an integrated model rather than an inclusive model — the child with SEN is expected to fit into a mainstream classroom with appropriate intervention. In other words, these programmes orientate towards an outside-in paradigm. For successful inclusion to take place, it has to be conceptualised as an inside-out and not just an outside-in paradigm, reiterating the assertion by Odom (2000) — the "resounding theme for the 21st century is that programmes, not children, have to be ready for inclusion" (p. 25). The class/school has to be ready for inclusion, and not just the child with SEN. An inclusive classroom is one in which the class is established as a community of learners where teachers and children embrace and are effectively equipped to value and respond to differences. Only in such a safe and inclusive environment will the child with SEN feel a strong sense of belonging, an essential criteria of inclusion. Third, most of the efforts thus far have focused only on children with mild developmental needs. Given the current state of developments, this is an appropriate focus for early efforts. However, the field needs to mature to include children with moderate and even severe disabilities who have the potential to receive mainstream education. It is good to know that the government has set up a workgroup to look into this (MSF, 2020).

Going forward, in response to the review, there is a need for the field to understand that merely 'including' children with SEN in mainstream preschool by providing early intervention services for the child is not good enough, and does not automatically constitute what quality inclusion should be. This then begs the questions of why quality inclusion is important, and what constitutes a 'good' inclusive model in Singapore, bringing us to consider the need to draw up quality indicators which could provide clear direction for quality inclusive practices in the Singapore context, and the concurrent need for quality training, especially for preschool teachers to have this vision materialised at the ground level. These points are elaborated in the following sections.

The need for localised quality preschool inclusive practices

The potential for positive outcomes for early childhood inclusion is undeniable but the pertinent question we need to ask is what it takes to reap these beneficial outcomes from our inclusive practices. Inclusion alone does not guarantee the reaping of these desirable outcomes (Cate *et al.*, 2010). The question of quality naturally comes into play. In a more generic sense, UNESCO (2005b) identified quality as the cornerstone supporting successful educational practice — "Quality is at the heart of education. It influences what students learn, how well they learn and what benefits they draw from their education." Referring to early childhood inclusive practices, Ferguson (2008) reiterated the same sentiment in a more practical sense. Noting the 'success' of widespread reforms in some countries in the European block towards the implementation of early childhood inclusion which resulted in 80 to 90 per cent of the children with special needs being educated in inclusive settings, he cautioned against the tendency to view achievements in terms of mere attendance. He stressed that numbers game at best tells a partial story because numbers itself cannot reflect what actually occurs in the classroom. The issue of quality of an early childhood inclusive programme matters a great deal because the success of the programme hinges upon it.

In determining what constitutes quality early childhood inclusion, it has to go beyond the quality standards that have been drawn up for determining quality early childhood programme, i.e, beyond global early childhood education quality indicators. These standards of global quality are not able to adequately reflect the required/desired practices which define inclusive programme quality (Buysse & Hollingsworth, 2009). The joint position statement by NEC/NAEYC (2009) affirms this standpoint when it underscores the need to construct quality framework as the basis for informing and guiding inclusive practices.

Internationally, there has been increasing efforts from professional bodies and researchers to draw up quality indicators for inclusive practices (e.g., Booth, Ainscow & Kingston, 2008; Cate *et al.*, 2010). However, this stimulus to develop quality standards reflected the dominant philosophies and culture of the nations they represent. Relying on studies in other nations to determine for us what the important elements are in support of early childhood quality inclusive practices will not be entirely adequate because of the existence of differences in terms of context. Unlike natural laws which have universal rules governing its functioning, the rules of culture and society are fluid and more applicable in a certain location and time. The watershed Salamanca statement discussed earlier had reiterated the importance of considering local factors in the effective implementation of inclusive practices in the various nations (UNESCO, 1994). The literature review conducted by Odom *et al.* (2004) revealed that cultural factors shaped the practical outworking of inclusive practices within the classrooms. Such views were also echoed by Nutbrown and Clough (2004) when they did a comparative study of inclusionary practices in four European countries — Denmark, Greece, Italy and the UK. Having delineated common dimensions through which they attempted to analyse the data, they advocated the "need to find ways of understanding and relating (within the generalisations) the locally specific phenomena that are emerging within the larger picture" (p. 314). These discourses acknowledge the subjective nature of the concept of quality. In addressing reforms in inclusive education in the Asia-Pacific region, Forlin and Lian (2008) underscored the careful and cautious applications of ideas of quality inclusion which came from Western countries. Because of cultural and other contextual variables, the conceptualisation of what inclusion should look like in the Asia-Pacific region would probably be different. What constitute as best practices in one part of the world need not necessarily work well in another part of the world. Furthermore, they also pointed out that the route to inclusive practices in the West is far from perfect. In a certain sense then, they are still evolving, just like us.

As Singapore is beginning to focus on early childhood inclusion, an understanding of quality issues and requirements will enable those who want to embark on inclusive practices to start off right in implementing and delivering inclusive experiences that will have positive outcomes for all the stakeholders. In other words, a quality programme framework is necessary to propagate effective practice. Currently in Singapore, there is no quality indicators for early childhood inclusive practices. Singapore has put into place global quality indicators through the Singapore Pre-School Accreditation Framework (SPARK), which is a quality assurance framework introduced in 2011 to raise the quality of preschool education in Singapore (ECDA, 2015). As pointed out in the preceding section, this is insufficient to guide inclusive practices. The SPARK quality indices reflect primarily overall programme quality, and with limited reference made to include children with special education needs. Dimensions of inclusive programme quality should be developed over and above global programme quality. Delineating what constitutes dimensions of quality inclusive practices has been deemed crucial in the evaluation, regulation and improvement of inclusive practices (Buysse & Hollingsworth, 2009).

So a necessary inroad into fostering quality early childhood inclusion in Singapore is to construct quality indices which can be used as a basis not only to set up a preschool inclusive model for Singapore, as well as to guide current practices in the field. To determine what works for the Singapore context, a critical starting point is to conduct research into local practices and perspectives which can inform the development of a quality framework. Many of the existing research in Singapore (e.g., Lian *et al.*, 2008; Nonis, 2006; Poon & Yang, 2016; Quah, 1998; Yeo *et al.*, 2011; Yong & Cohen, 2008) were either survey studies to examine teachers' knowledge, attitudes and perceptions in relation to preschool inclusion or investigative studies of intervention and/or therapy support in early childhood settings. However, Cate *et al.* (2010) suggested that "Ideally, quality inclusive system is developed intentionally and 'planfully' from the start rather than after other aspects of the system are already in place" (p.3). Hence, a more targeted research into investigating whole-school approach to inclusive education is required. An announcement was made by the government to advocate for a feasibility study on an inclusive model for Singapore (MSF, 2017). Such a feasibility study should look into conducting relevant research in Singapore to inform on the development of localised quality indices.

The need for more robust training for preschool teachers

As inclusion takes place in a mainstream classroom environment, the preschool teacher is a key player. If he or she does not have the necessary dispositions, skills and knowledge to set up an inclusive classroom, placing a child with SEN, even with the input of allied health professionals, may end up with a scenario of integration instead of inclusion. Implementation of quality inclusive practices has implications in terms of not only equipping allied health professionals such as the Learning Support Educators in the DS-LS programmes, but also preschool teachers to have strong foundations in setting up inclusive practices in their classes. The role of training in contributing to quality education is well established — "the most important single factor for the quality of education and thus for the efficiency and quality of the pupils' learning is the quality of the teachers' training" (Qvortrup, cited in NIE, 2009, p. 11). Survey studies which have been conducted in Singapore to explore early childhood professionals' perspectives on inclusion has foregrounded training as a key factor in strengthening the expertise and efficacy of preschool teachers to effect inclusive practices. Nonis (2006) investigated 50 kindergarten teachers in including children with SEN, and the results indicated that while the participants held positive attitudes toward inclusion, they highlighted training as a major concern. The lack of knowledge to include children with SEN also resonated as a key theme in the survey conducted by Lasse, Lynn and Lim (2019) of 35 leaders in the field. The following narrative from a participant echoed this sentiment in a compelling manner: "If teachers on the ground do not think that they can do inclusion, then they wouldn't. Or they think that inclusion is just too fuzzy or it's just beyond me. Or they need more training or someone trained to be in this school to do it. It will never happen" (p. 68). The study concluded that the majority of early childhood teachers in Singapore are not adequately equipped to work with children with SEN. For the government to realise the vision of an inclusive society first put forth in 2004, and for this to start with the very young in our schools, then a pre-requisite, one that cannot be compromised, is to allocate resources into training for both pre-service and in-service preschool teachers. Quality inclusive practices cannot take place without a quality workforce who embrace such a vision and have the competency to bring it to fruition where they are placed.

Conclusion

While education in Singapore has progressively evolved during the past 15 years towards greater systemic support to include more students with special needs within mainstream primary and secondary schools, a similar trend of pervasive corresponding change within the preschool education sector has yet to be realised. Although there have been many efforts and inroads in the recent years to support and include students with special needs at the preschool level, as described in this chapter, various salient issues such as inadequate teacher preparation and the lack of a comprehensive quality framework as well as an intentional system-wide movement towards inclusion, mean that preschool inclusion in Singapore is just at its incipient stage.

References

Allen, K. E., & Cowdery, G. E. (2005). *The Exceptional Child: Inclusion in Early Childhood Education*. New York, NY: Thomson Delmar Learning.

Ang. L. (2000). Special education in Singapore: A reflection on inclusion. *The Journal of Special Education, 4*(2), 104–109.

AWWA. (2018). Kindle Garden. Retrieved September 21, 2018 from http://www.kindlegarden.com.sg/

Booth, T., Ainscow, M., & Kingston, D. (2008). *Index for Inclusion: Developing Play, Learning and Participation in Early Years and Childcare*. Bristol, UK: Centre for Studies in Inclusive Education (CSIE).

Buysse, V., Goldman, B. D., & Skinner, M. L. (2002). Setting effects on friendship formation among young children with and without disabilities. *Exceptional Children, 68*(4), 503–517. doi: 10.11770014402902068000406

Clough, P., & Corbett, J. (2000). *Theories of Inclusive Education: A Student's Guide*. London: Paul Chapman.

Cross, A. F., Traub, E. K., Hutter-Pishgahi, L., & Shelton, G. (2004). Elements of successful inclusion for children with significant disabilities. *Topics in Early Childhood Special Education, 24*(3), 169–183. doi: 10.1177/02711214040240030401

DEC/NAEYC. (2009). *Early childhood inclusion: A joint position statement of the Division for Early Childhood (DEC) and the National Association for the Education of Young Children (NAEYC)*. Chapel Hill, NC: The University of North Carolina, FPG Child Development Institute.

Diamond, K., & Tu, H. (2009). Relations between classroom context, physical disability and preschool children's inclusion decisions. *Journal of Applied Developmental Psychology, 30*(2), 75–81. doi: 10.1016/j.appdev.2008.10.008

Downing, J. E., & Peckham-Hardin, K. D. (2007). Inclusive education: What makes it a good education for students with moderate to severe disabilities. *Research & Practice for Persons with Severe Disabilities, 32*(1), 16–30. doi: 10.2511/rpsd.32.1.16

Early Childhood Development Agency (ECDA). (2015). About SPARK. Retrieved September 20, 2018 from https://www.ecda.gov.sg/SPARKinfo/Pages/AboutSPARK.aspx

Ferguson, D. L. (2008). International trends in inclusive education: the continuing challenge to teach each one and everyone. *European Journal of Special Needs Education, 23*(2), 109–120. doi:10.1080/08856250801946236

Forlin, C., & Lain, M. J. (2008). *Reform, Inclusion and Teacher Education: Towards a New Era of Special Education in the Asia-Pacific Region*. London: Routledge.

Gena, A. (2006). The effects of prompting and social reinforcement on establishing social interactions with peers during the inclusion of four children with autism in preschool. *International Journal of Psychology, 41*(6), 541–555. doi: 10.1080/00207590500492658

Hollingsworth, H. L., & Buysse, V. (2009). Establishing friendships in early childhood inclusive settings: What roles do parents and teachers play? *Journal of Early Intervention, 31*(4), 287–307. doi: 10.1177/1053815109352659

Jones, P. (2005). *Inclusion in the Early Years: Stories of Good Practice*. London: David Fulton Publishers.

Katz, L. G. (2002, August). Engaging children's heart and minds. Paper presented at A Public forum conducted by the RTRC Asia International Advisory Panel, Singapore.

Kim, S. G. (2005). Kevin: "I gotta get to the market": The development of peer relationships in inclusive early childhood settings. *Early Childhood Education Journal, 33*(3), 163–169. doi: 10.1007/s10643-005-0041-3

KK Women's & Children's Hospital. (2018). Child development. Retrieved September 21, 2018 from https://www.kkh.com.sg/services/children/childdevelopment/Pages/Home.aspx

Lasse, L., Lynn, A., & Lim, S. (2019). *Vital Voices for Vital Years (2): Perspectives on Early Childhood Development in Singapore*. Singapore: Lien Foundation.

Li, L. (2008). Parents and teachers' beliefs about preschool inclusion in P.R. China. *Dissertation Abstracts International Section A: Humanities and Social Sciences, 68*(12A), 4972.

Lian, W. B., Ho, K. Y. S., Choo, H. T. S., Chan, K. L. D., Yeo, C. L., & Ho, L. Y. (2008). Preschool teachers' knowledge, attitudes, and practices on childhood developmental & behavioural disorders in Singapore. *Journal of Pediatrics and Child Health, 44*, 187–194, doi: 10.1111/j.1440-1754.2007.01231.x

Lim, L., & Nam, S.S. (2000). Special education in Singapore. *Journal of Special Education 34*(2), 104–109. doi:10.1177/002246690003400205

Lim, L., Thaver, T., & Slee, R. (2008). *Exploring Disability in Singapore: A personal learning journey*. Singapore: McGraw-Hill Education (Asia).

Ministry of Social & Family Development (MSF). (2017). Opening speech by Mr Tan Chuan-Jin at the Committee of Supply 2017. Retrieved September 20, 2018 from https://www.msf.gov.sg/media-room/Pages/Opening-Speech-By-Mr-Tan-Chuan-Jin-At-The-Committee-Of-Supply-2017.aspx

Ministry of Social and Family Development (MSF). (2018a). Disabilities and special needs: Enabling master plan. Retrieved September 21, 2018 from https://www.msf.gov.sg/policies/Disabilities-and-Special-eeds/Pages/default.aspx

Ministry of Social and Family Development (MSF). (2018b). Development support and learning support. Retrieved September 21, 2018 from https://www.msf.gov.sg/assistance/Pages/Development-Support-and-Learning-Support.aspx

Ministry of Social and Family Development (MSF). (2019a). Development support and learning support. Retrieved July 12, 2019 from https://www.msf.gov.sg/assistance/Pages/Development-Support-and-Learning-Support.aspx

Ministry of Social and Family Development (MSF). (2019b). Enhanced early intervention: Better support for children with developmental needs. Retrieved July 12, 2019 from https://www.msf.gov.sg/media-room/Pages/Enhanced-Early-Intervention.aspx

Ministry of Social and Family Development (MSF). (2019c). More integrated support for children with developmental needs under ECDA. Retrieved July 12, 2019 from https://www.msf.gov.sg/media-room/Pages/More-Integrated-Support-for-Children-with-Developmental-Needs-Under-ECDA.aspx?fbclid=IwAR1y2Xl1JTLZ6Gbe-v1cUEsNQ1_eWg_cYagNLcGt_57EIzFjPO0gcyvqnQI

Ministry of Social and Family Development (MSF). (2020). More integrated support for children with developmental needs under ECDA. Retrieved from https://www.msf.gov.sg/media-room/Pages/More-Integrated-Support-for-Children-with-Developmental-Needs-Under-ECDA.aspx

Mogharreban, C., & Bruns, D. (2009). Moving to inclusive pre-kindergarten classrooms: Lessons from the field. *Early Childhood Education Journal, 36,* 407–414. doi: 10.1007/s100643-008-0301-0

National Institute of Education (NIE). (2009). *A Teacher Education Model for the 21st Century:* Singapore: National Institute of Education, an Institute of Nanyang Technological University.

National Professional Development Center on Inclusion (NPDCI). (2009). Why programme quality matters for early childhood inclusion: Recommendations for professional development. Retrieved September 21, 2018 from https://npdci.fpg.unc.edu/

Nonis, K. P. (2006). Integrating children with special needs: Singapore preschool teachers share their feelings: A preliminary investigation. *The Journal of the International Association of Special Education, 7*(1), 4–10.

Nutbrown, C., & Clough, P. (2004). Inclusion and exclusion in the early years: Conversations with European educators. *European Journal of Special Needs Education, 19*(3), 301–315. doi: 10.1080/0885625042000262479

Odom, S. L. (2000). Preschool inclusion: What we know and where we go from here. *Topics in Early Childhood Special Education, 20*(1), 20–27. doi:10.1177/027112140002000104

Odom, S. L., Buysse, V., & Soukakou, E, (2012). Inclusion for young children with disabilities: A quarter of century of research perspectives. *Journal of Early Intervention, 33*(4), 344–356. doi: 10.1177/1053815111430094

Odom, S. L., Vitztum, J., Wolery, R., Lieber, J., Sandall, S., Hanson, M. J., Beckman, P., Schwartz, L., & Horn, E. (2004). Preschool inclusion in the United States: A review of research from an ecological systems perspective. *Journal of Research in Special Educational Needs, 4*(1), 17–49. doi:10.1111/J.1471-3802.2004.00016.x

Organization for Economic Cooperation and Development (OECD). (2001). *Starting strong: Early childhood education and care.* Paris: OECD.

Poon, K. K., & Khaw, J. (Eds.). (2007). *Supporting Students with Special Needs in Mainstream Schools: An Introduction.* Singapore: Pearson Education South Asia.

Poon, K. K., & Yang, X. (2016). The students profile, service delivery model, and support practices of four early childhood intervention environments in Singapore. *Asia Pacific Journal of Education, 36*(3), 437–449. doi: 10.1080/02188791.2014.940030

Quah, M. M. (1998). Early intervention for pre-schoolers with mild disabilities. *Early Child Development and Care, 144*, 101–111. doi: 10.1080/0300443981440111

Sandall, S. R., & Schwartz, I. S. (2008). *Building Blocks for Teaching Preschoolers with Special Needs.* Baltimore, MD: Paul H. Brooks Publishing.

SG Enable. (2018). Integrated Childcare Programme. Retrieved September 21, 2018 from https://www.sgenable.sg/pages/content.aspx?path=/for-children/integrated-child-care-programme-iccp/

Teo, L. (2004, 19 September). $220m school aid for disabled kids. *The Straits Times*, p.1. United Nations (UN) General Assembly. (2016). Convention on the rights of persons with disabilities. Retrieved September 20, 2018 from https://www.un.org/development/desa/disabilities/convention-on-the-rights-of-persons-with-disabilities.html

United Nations Educational, Scientific and Cultural Organisation (UNESCO). (1994). *The Salamanca Statement and Framework for Action on Special Needs Education.* Spain: OECD.

United Nations Educational, Scientific and Cultural Organisation (UNESCO). (2000). *The Dakar Framework for Action.* Dakar: OECD.

United Nations Educational, Scientific and Cultural Organisation (UNESCO). (2005a). *Guidelines for Inclusion.* Retrieved September 20, 2018 from http://unesdoc.unesco.org/images/0014/001402/140224e.pdf

United Nations Educational, Scientific and Cultural Organization (UNESCO). (2005b). Education for all: The qualitative imperative. Retrieved from https://en.unesco.org/gem-report/report/2005/education-all-quality-imperative"https://en.unesco.org/gem-report/report/2005/education-all-quality-imperative

United Nations Educational, Scientific and Cultural Organisation (UNESCO). (2009). *Policy Guidelines on Inclusion in Education.* Paris: UNESCO.

Yeo, L. S., Neihart, M., Tang, H. N., Chong, W. H., & Huan, V. S. (2011). An inclusion initiative in Singapore for preschool with special needs. *Asia Pacific Journal of Education, 31*(2), 143–158. doi: 10.1080/02188791.2011.566990

Yong, M., & Cohen, L. (2008). Preschool inclusion using consultation in Singapore: A case study. *Special Education Perspectives, 17*(2), 20–32.

CHAPTER 7

Journey of the Heart, Enabling Students with Special Needs

Tina Hung

ᙅᙏ

Introduction

Special education as we know it today is the foundational work of many pioneers in the social service sector for the past 50 years since Singapore's independence. I had agreed to contribute this chapter so that I may honour the many unsung heroes, staff and volunteers, who have contributed their expertise, creativity and often personal resources. The pioneers were determined to grow the range and quality of disability services over time. Countless individuals, corporate donors, foundations and funders have contributed to the cause of special education and made it possible for thousands of children with special needs to have an education.

It is not the purpose of this chapter to debate the success of special education. This chapter attempts to share some of the progress and highlights in Singapore's special education journey. Pioneers in the area of special education have identified and addressed the needs and gaps and closed many gaps over the decades. This chapter, written from the viewpoint of National Council of Social Service

(NCSS), does not attempt to be exhaustive or comprehensive. It is not a research document but rather tells the story of special education from my experience.

I hope this short chapter sparks your interest to find out more about these unsung heroes and inspires you to offer your treasure, talent and time to the many social service agencies providing critical services and helping children with special needs and their caregivers.

National Council of Social Service

NCSS celebrated 60 years of structured social services in 2018. NCSS began its journey as the Singapore Council of Social Service (SCSS). SCSS was formed in 1958 to coordinate and promote the roles and contributions of social service agencies (NCSS, 2008; 2020a). SCSS brought together organisations and individuals with an interest in community service and social welfare. SCSS became a statutory body in 1968 and was restructured as the NCSS in 1992 in order to respond to social service needs, to provide leadership in social service delivery and to support agencies meeting social needs (NCSS, 2008; 2020a).

Pursuant to the NCSS Act (1992), NCSS's mission is to provide leadership and direction in enhancing the capabilities and capacity of our members, advocating for social service needs and strengthening strategic partnerships, for an effective social service ecosystem (NCSS, 2020b). Following the launch of the Social Service Sector Strategic Thrusts (4ST) in 2017, the work at NCSS is focused on three strategic themes: (i) Effective social purpose entities that deliver quality, innovative and sustainable solutions; (ii) Quality, innovative and sustainable solutions for an impactful sector; and (iii) Caring, collaborative and impactful social service ecosystem (NCSS, 2020b). The collective social service sector vision captured in 4ST articulates that every person is empowered to live with dignity in a caring and inclusive society. Social service agencies providing services for persons with special needs, such as in the area of special education, are NCSS members and also come under the umbrella of the NCSS.

The Community Chest, the centralised fund-raiser arm of the NCSS was established by Dr Ee Peng Liang and Dr Tan Bee Wan in 1983. Dr Ee's wish and purpose was to relieve social service agencies of fund-raising activities and burdens so that professional staff can concentrate on providing better care and services for the service users (NCSS, 2020a). Funds raised through the Community Chest have benefited thousands of children with special needs so they could receive educational support. Between the fiscal year 2003 to fiscal year 2014, the Community Chest had raised approximately $176.6 million for special education services alone.

Special Education Schools: Looking Back

Social service agencies started pioneering education and related services for children with special needs since the 1950s. Between the 1950s and 1960s, the focus was on those with sensory impairment, and physical and intellectual disabilities. Among the early pioneers were the Singapore Association for the Deaf (SADeaf), Canossa Mission Singapore (formerly known as Canossian Daughters of Charity), Singapore Association of the Visually Handicapped (formerly known as the Singapore Association for the Blind), Cerebral Palsy Alliance Singapore (formerly known as the Spastic Children's Association of Singapore) and the Movement for the Intellectually Disabled of Singapore (formerly known as the Singapore Association for Retarded Children) (Canossian School, 2020; CPAS, n.d.; MINDS, n.d.; SADeaf, 2018; SAVH, 2017).

In the 1970s, the Association for Persons with Special Needs (formerly known as Association for the Educationally Subnormal) closed an important service gap by initiating education and related services for children with mild intellectual disability (APSN, 2020).

Educational and related services for children with multiple disabilities and autism spectrum disorder only became available between 1970s and 1980s. These were pioneering efforts by the

AWWA and the Margaret Drive Special School (AWWA, 2019a; Rainbow Centre, 2019). The latter was a pioneer project of the NCSS and has grown to include an array of disability services under the leadership of Rainbow Centre.

During the 2000s, two additional schools were set up by the Metta Welfare Association and Presbyterian Community Services, as they saw the need and demand, to join the community of service providers to serve children with mild intellectual disability (GOS, 2020; MWA, 2013). Similarly, in 2000s, the Autism Association (Singapore), the Autism Resource Centre (Singapore) and the St. Andrew's Mission Hospital (AAS, 2020; Pathlight School, 2020; SAMH, n.d.) saw the need to provide educational services for children with autism spectrum disorder and answered NCSS's call to meet this need. Pathlight School was a significant milestone, being the first special education school to provide mainstream curriculum. Many of the parents involved in the pioneering efforts continue to serve fervently and passionately in leadership and various capacities. Among them are pioneering giants including Ms Denise Phua, Mr Eddie Koh, Mr Ho Sweet Huat, Dr Kenneth Lyen and the late Dr Dixie Tan. Former Anglican Bishop John Chew was instrumental in mobilising the St. Andrew's Mission Hospital leadership to take on a more prominent role in meeting the needs of children and adults with autism spectrum disorder by setting up the St. Andrew's Autism Centre.

This impressive list of NCSS member agencies which stepped forward to set up the various special education schools and related services did so on their own accord. It was very much a bottom-up approach. The special education schools you see today are the efforts of many pioneering leaders and giants including Mr Peng Tsu Ying, Mrs Leaena Tambyah, Sister Anne Tan, Venerable Chao Khun Fa Zhao, Prof Nather Aziz, Prof Tan Ser Kiat, Prof Lee Eng Hin, Mr Laurence Wee and many others. Mr Tan Guan Heng and the late Mr Ron Chandran Dudley were the first and second blind Presidents of the Singapore Association for the Visually Handicapped which used to operate the School for the Blind, renamed Lighthouse School. It has been my deep honour and privilege to have worked with many of these pioneering giants and indefatigable leaders and I apologise for not being able to list all of them here.

Special Education Schools: Many Parts to Make a Whole

A major milestone in the evolution of special education was the setting up of the Advisory Council on the Disabled (ACD) in 1988 (Ng, 2010). Dr Tony Tan, then Minister of Ministry of Education (MOE) chaired the ACD and looked into the needs of persons with disabilities with the aim of helping them to integrate into society (Ng, 2010). Recommendations were submitted to the government in the *Report of the Advisory Council on the Disabled: Opportunities for the Disabled* in November 1988 (Quah, 1990). One major recommendation was for MOE to take over the administration of special education schools (Quah, 1990). Post-ACD, the per capita grant for each child attending special education school increased to four times that of the cost of mainstream primary education. The government also set aside land to accommodate purpose-built special education schools and subsequently increased its financial support for the capital cost of special education school buildings from 90% to 95% of approved costs (MOE, 2004). A taskforce was set up and recommended better teacher-student ratios to cater to the different student profiles and having more psychologists and rehabilitative staff to support the work of teachers and to enhance the quality of education for the students (Quah, 1990). The recommendations depicted the government's commitment to provide greater affordability, accessibility and quality education for students with special needs.

A Co-ordinating Committee for Special Education (CCSE) was set up by MOE in 1989 to coordinate special education schools (NCSS, 2010a). The role of the CCSE was to set policy direction and provide guidance to the special education schools (NCSS, 2013a). The committee also spearheaded efforts to raise the quality of education and identified resources required to meet the educational needs of students with special needs (NCSS, 2013a).

A notable development was the delineation of roles between MOE and NCSS with regards to special education. In 2001, MOE and NCSS agreed to the delineation of roles in special education, based on their respective strengths and domain expertise. Since then, there have been several developments in special education towards MOE playing a major role in enhancing the quality of education for children with special needs. In March 2007, MOE announced several initiatives towards raising the quality of education for children with special needs (MOE, 2007). It emphasised its focus in being more involved in the overall management of special education schools, particularly on educational areas, providing more differentiated educational opportunities for students with special needs and lending greater support in the training and professional development in special education schools (MOE, 2007).

In view of MOE's greater involvement and focus in special education, MOE and NCSS further refined the delineation of roles in special education and signed an inaugural Memorandum of Understanding (MOU) on 14 July 2009.

Refinements to the role delineation between MOE and NCSS continued to be guided by the core business and expertise of each organisation. The arrangement has largely been for MOE to oversee education matters including curriculum and pedagogy while NCSS to oversee the therapy and social support services. Both MOE and NCSS were highly committed to an effective partnership in the "Many Helping Hands" approach, and worked in collaboration with the special education schools towards enhancing the learning environment in all special education schools. Strong collaboration and partnership between NCSS and MOE at the national level has helped to ensure that children with special needs have opportunities to maximise their potential and educational outcomes, regardless of their disability.

It was not a relationship without disagreements and differences in views. However, the commitment on both sides to discuss, deliberate and keep forging the way forward for the best interests of the children, kept both sides going strong. Both sides made the conscientious decision to always be respectful, to seek each other's views and hear each other out, even through difficult circumstances and complex issues.

Many differences in views were resolved through discussions, research, data and consultations with stakeholders including with parents, children and special education schools. Such resolutions and progression in turn gave both sides confidence to bring up and tackle complex and challenging issues from time to time. In times of disagreement, both sides were able to leverage and apply different strengths to enrich the final outcome and be even more committed to the joint solutions. Such solutions also tend to present rich opportunities to co-create what each would not be able to accomplish alone, and to achieve deeper impact.

Special education schools are unique in that they combine academic and cognitive development with social, psychological and behavioural management, in addition to the various physical and developmental therapies which some of the students also require. Special education schools do much more than just teach. They weave a web of family and community-based support structures for each child and his or her family.

Children with special needs have varying functioning levels which are better served by a specialised approach that combines academic development with therapies and social support. In 1999, NCSS and MOE visited Blue Ribbon special schools in the USA in an effort to learn and improve special education efforts in Singapore. One of the learning points was that, while legislations required the admission of students with special needs into mainstream schools, the schools had to find their own way to fund the cost of supporting the students with special needs adequately. This differs from the Singapore model where MOE and NCSS provide fully for special education schools. Approved allied health professional positions such as social workers, psychologists, occupational therapists, physiotherapists and speech therapists are fully funded. As needed, special education schools also received funding for audiologists. In fiscal year 2005, MOE requested NCSS to administer the government share of the special education funding. NCSS went on to introduce funding by disability types in order to customise, respond to and better meet the varied needs of students with different abilities and functioning. Over the years, MOE and NCSS had introduced changes to the funding norms, including staff ratio to number of children served, in order to provide adequate resources to serve students better.

By fiscal year 2019, there were 19 special education schools serving 6,500 students. The funding provided by MOE, Tote Board Social Service Fund and NCSS totalled $230.5 million. Please see Appendix I for a full listing of the schools.

The MOE-NCSS collaboration has allowed students with special needs to have access to special education in an environment which nurtures their growth and development. It is an imperfect system and there remains much work to be done to address the issues of transition from special education to mainstream schools, from education to employment etc. The next generation of leaders, volunteers and staff must continue to build upon the good work. Many parts are needed for the whole, so that students with special needs can thrive, achieve and succeed.

Capacity building and competencies

As part of a larger national effort to improve client outcomes for services and programmes, NCSS developed a Programme Evaluation System (PES) in 2001 and the Enhanced Programme Evaluation System (EPES) in 2004 (NCSS, 2020c). The EPES provided a tool to capture critical inputs, outputs and client outcomes. NCSS and its member agencies believe in delivering quality services to ensure that the interests and welfare of the service users are safeguarded. The EPES outcome indicators for special education schools were developed by the NCSS in consultation with MOE, NIE and the special education schools.

NCSS later assisted MOE to develop a framework customised for special education schools (MOE, 2007) which replaced the EPES. The quality assurance framework (QAF) was subsequently piloted in the special education schools to improve student outcomes and align service quality of special education schools. Refinements to the framework were made periodically to ensure that the QAF remained comprehensive and relevant.

Capability and competency are of paramount importance to the running of quality special education schools. In addition to the annual budget and funding for each special education school, MOE set up the Steering Committee for Teaching and Learning (SCTL) in 2005. The purpose of the Teaching and Learning fund is to enhance the capability of special education schools in curriculum design and development, pedagogy in classroom management and teaching, and innovative ideas in teaching and learning (NCSS, 2014). The SCTL is fully funded by MOE and NCSS administers it. The SCTL has since been renamed the Sector Professional Development Fund.

In 2006, MOE supported NCSS's suggestions to second principals and teachers to special education schools, and to fund the cost of relief teachers so that special education teachers can attend critical training programmes to increase their competencies. Such improvements, and many others, together with regular salary reviews helped to stabilise the challenging special education school manpower situation and strengthen the capability and professionalism for special education schools in the long run.

To recognise the hard work, achievements and valuable contributions of special education teachers, NCSS suggested an outstanding teachers' award for special education teachers. The inaugural Outstanding Special Education Teacher Award (OSTA) was held jointly by MOE and NCSS in 2007 (Gan, 2007). Thanks to MOE's leadership and commitment, this initiative has grown from year to year and has evolved into an inspiring event where special education educators, professionals and staff are able to network, learn from experts, celebrate and be appreciated for their contributions in changing lives. The 2014 SPED Conference and 7th OSTA was attended by approximately 1,900 participants. The 2018 SPED Conference was attended by 3,024 attendees and reflected the growth and camaraderie in this sector.

Each year at the award ceremony, the students performed on stage, showcasing their diversity, and wowed the audience with their creativity, discipline and talents. The deep sense of pride felt among the audience towards the students' accomplishments was palpable. As at 2020, 31 teachers have been conferred with the prestigious OSTA Awards and there have been 29 Innovation Award winners. Many educators in special education schools continue to give their talent and effort selflessly as they believe fervently in the cause and this keeps them going year after year.

Over the last few special education conferences, it is clear that MOE has made continuous efforts to improve the affordability, accessibility and quality of special education.

Training and professional development are two critical factors for the attraction and retention of skilled manpower. Under Dr Gerard Ee's leadership, NCSS set up the Social Service Training Institute (SSTI) in 2003 to ensure there would be training for staff and professionals in the social service sector and those who wished to join the sector but were untrained (NCSS, 2020a). In celebration of its 10th Anniversary in 2013, SSTI was renamed Social Service Institute (SSI) to reflect an enhanced role, going beyond training and serving as the focal point for learning and manpower development for the social service sector (NCSS, 2020a). For professionals in the special education sector, whether they are newcomers or existing social service personnel, SSI offers a range of courses for those who wish to receive more specialised special education training or shorter certificates to gain specific skills to support children with special needs. Feedback is regularly gathered, and improvements are systematically made to enhance the relevance and effectiveness of the training courses offered.

Another aspect of professional development is through networking with people who are engaged in similar work in the sector. NCSS established the Social Workers' Network in September 2010, the Psychologists' Network in March 2011 and Community of Practice to create platforms for networking and building competencies among professionals in and beyond special education schools. Over time, NCSS expanded the Social Workers' and Psychologists' Networks to include the Early Intervention Programme for Infants and Children (EIPIC) practitioners, and invited experts and senior practitioners from social service agencies, EIPIC centres and special education schools to share their experiences and exchange best practices.

To upskill special education teachers and allied health professionals so that they can better support the students and their caregivers, NCSS initiated the First Line of Care programme in collaboration with MOE, Ministry of Social and Family Development (MSF) and the Institute of Mental Health in 2015 (NCSS, 2015). Talks and guidance provided by MSF on child abuse and neglect were made available to all special education educators and professionals. Intermediate training on managing challenging and difficult family situations were also given to psychologists and social workers from the special education schools by SSI.

Mainstream Schools and Special Needs Support

Students with special needs also attend mainstream schools and are part of the mainstream school system. For those who need it, some support services are available to them.

For example, the Dyslexia Association of Singapore (DAS) has been providing support services for students attending mainstream schools since the 1990s (DAS, 2020).

Students with special needs who attend mainstream schools are able to access the Community Integration Service in AWWA (formerly known as TEACH ME). Since 1991, Community Integration Service has been providing educational, rehabilitative and social support to children with special needs to better integrate into their schools and community (AWWA, 2019b).

SADeaf set up the Itinerant Support Service for Deaf persons and those with hearing loss to equip them with appropriate skills to cope with the demands of education and to meet their individual developmental milestones (SADeaf, 2018). This support service continues to be relevant today.

Asst Prof Wong Meng Ee, Adj A/Prof Audrey Looi, A/Prof Ang Beng Ti and Ms Lee Lay Hong approached NCSS regarding their vision to pioneer a new service for students with visual impairment who attend mainstream schools. With the unwavering commitment and passion of the leadership, iC2 PrepHouse Limited was incorporated and succeeded in starting the Vision Education and Rehabilitation Programme in 2012. Their efforts focus on educating, rehabilitating and equipping students with low vision in order to enable them to live confidently and with dignity in a sighted community. Parents and caregivers also receive support.

The purpose of setting up and growing such community-based services is to provide a range of critical social support to students with special needs, so they can overcome the many challenges they face and do well in the mainstream school system. Such services must continue to evolve and grow over time as we learn from our own local experiences.

There is room to identify, explore and resource the type of support and services currently unavailable but are critical to helping our students with special needs from primary schools and beyond, including the Institutes for Higher Learning, so they can achieve their potential and be successful in their chosen careers and vocations.

Transition Management: Support for Early Years

While special education schools have existed for many years, structured support for infants and children below school going age comes much later. Parents and service providers understand the paramount importance to provide appropriate support to infants and children as early as possible once the special needs have been identified and diagnosed.

To bridge this gap, NCSS consulted MOE, special education schools, the Departments of Child Development (DCD) in KK Women's and Children's Hospital (KKH) and National University Hospital (NUH). Subsequently, NCSS developed and championed the service model for the Early Intervention Programme for Infants and Children or EIPIC to be funded and implemented all over the island. The EIPIC domains that were developed by NCSS, in consultation with experts, practitioners, doctors and academics and which were used for intervention, included: (i) fine and gross motor skills; (ii) cognition and perception; (c) communication and language; (d) social; (e) self-help skills (including adaption to and use of assistive equipment).

In the early days, EIPIC was adapted from successful overseas experiences and services and improvements were made through trials and errors. We have since embarked on local reviews and enhancements to improve user outcomes. The approved EIPIC model has received funding from MSF and NCSS since 2003.

With government support and funding, services available has grown to 21 EIPIC centres providing a full range of physiotherapy, occupational therapy, speech therapy, social work and psychological services to those diagnosed with special needs from birth to age six. These EIPIC centres are currently under the purview of the Early Childhood Development Agency.

Special education educators provide NCSS with feedback regarding the value and benefits of EIPIC for the very young ones. Hence EIPIC has become a critical and developmental component of the special needs landscape of disability services in Singapore. According to anecdotal reports and the EIPIC baseline study conducted by the NCSS, KKH and Nanyang Technological University in 2010 (Goh, Chong & Chan, 2010), EIPIC has clearly contributed towards optimising the potential of the children and to better prepare them for school. For some, EIPIC opened the door to integration into mainstream schools. The EIPIC baseline study also pinpointed many areas of improvements that were acted upon by the EIPIC service providers, NCSS and the DCD at KKH and NUH to improve the children's developmental outcomes. Creating EIPIC and scaling EIPIC was a tough but necessary journey and everyone involved contributed selflessly and generously to pioneer and scale this critical service in the early years. Among the many contributors, Prof Ho Lai Yun was a champion among champions. He tirelessly advocated support for EIPIC, and NCSS efforts in this area would not have been possible without his leadership.

Post-Special Education Support

In 2001, NCSS started surveying students from special education schools just prior to their graduation, to assist the students and their parents to plan ahead for suitable post-special education school options. The survey findings also guided NCSS to forecast the potential support services needed, such as pre-vocational pathways. Schools were advised to collaborate with parents to determine the students' potential and possible matches for placements. Given the usefulness of the survey information, NCSS had been sharing the survey data and findings with MOE.

MOE and NCSS carried out a pilot programme in 2007 on vocational training in Metta School and Delta Senior School for students aged 16 years and above (Gan, 2007; MOE, 2010). In the pilot phase, the programme enabled 70 students to secure employment (MOE, 2010). The programme offered both off and on-the-job training opportunities to students, in areas such as food and beverage, housekeeping and landscaping operations. Students were able to work at renowned businesses around Singapore, such as Han's (F&B) Pte Ltd., Holiday Inn Singapore Orchard City Centre, etc. Through this programme, students were able to graduate with national certification in specific industries (MOE, 2010).

The pilot programme was subsequently adopted by MOE and NCSS as a permanent component of special education to benefit those students who were able to pursue this pathway. 1 in 4 special education graduates successfully found employment after graduation from this pathway (Sim, 2014).

In 2014, special education schools embarked on the School-to-Work (S2W) Transition Programme (Sim, 2014). The programme co-developed by MOE, MSF and SG Enable was to develop work and training options for students from special education schools who were not able to acquire the relevant work certifications but still have potential for work (MOE, 2014). This was a two-year pilot and expected to be rolled out to more special education schools in phases from 2016 (MOE, 2014).

Special education graduates who are work-ready are assisted by the job placement and job support agencies in their transition from school to work. A variety of options, including sheltered workshops, vocational training courses and internship opportunities, have been created for special education graduates who require more time to hone their job-related skills. SG Enable was set up on 1 July 2013, with one of its key function being to enhance the employability and employment options for persons with special needs (SG Enable, 2015a). NCSS continues to co-fund employment initiatives run by social service agencies and support relevant programmes to fill gaps in the employment landscape for persons with special needs.

For those not suitable for open or sheltered employment, day activity centres provide life skills training, activities for independent living and socialisation opportunities (SG Enable, 2015b). MSF has also rolled out home-based care services to provide home based therapy and personal care services for persons with special needs at their home settings (MSF, 2014).

In 2015, NCSS, together with AWWA, Autism Association (Singapore) and Movement for the Intellectually Disabled of Singapore piloted Me Too! Club to create opportunities for persons with moderate to severe disabilities to interact with the community through social recreational activities (NCSS, 2015). The pilot project aimed to reduce the effects of social isolation often faced by persons with special needs and promote social inclusion.

Assistive Technology

Assistive technology is a barrier breaker that helps students with special needs in rehabilitation, mobility or be more independent in their daily life, including school. For example, a student who is visually impaired may use screen reader software in order to do research online or complete online assignments. A student with speech impairment may need augmentative and alternative communication devices to be able to participate fully in class.

In the early days when computers were hard to come by and not included in the funding for special education schools, NCSS persuaded donors and volunteers to give and to set up computers with appropriate software for students from special education schools so that they would not be left out of the global push to leverage IT.

The situation is much improved today with all special education schools having access to desktop computers and iPads for lessons, music, projects and assignments.

SPD implemented the Assistive Technology Centre (ATC) in 2001 (SPD, 2018), a pioneering initiative conceptualised by NCSS and then Infocomm Development Authority, to benefit persons with special needs through the use of assistive technology. In 2005, SPD was appointed by NCSS as the Specialised ATC (NCSS, 2008). The Specialised ATC provided consultation, assessment, intervention and training on the use of assistive technology equipment for persons with special needs and their families. The Specialised ATC was co-funded by NCSS and MSF to help persons with special needs overcome their disabilities and participate fully in society. From October 2015, to broaden its reach and to centralise services at the one-stop centre for persons with special needs, SPD Specialised ATC transitioned to be part of a collaborative effort at Tech Able centre at the Enabling Village.

SPD also managed the Infocomm Accessibility Centre (IAC) to provide IT training for persons with special needs so as to enhance their employability (SPD, 2014a). The centre was formed as a result of people-public-private collaboration between SPD, then Infocomm Development Authority, MSF, NCSS, Tote Board and Microsoft Singapore (SPD, 2014a). Through the IAC, SPD offered a vocational training programme, named the IAC Certificate in Office Skills (ICOS). SPD ICOS provided basic Information and Communication Technology (ICT) and corporate skills training to equip and prepare persons with special needs for employment (SPD, 2014b). The programme enabled persons with special needs to perform office administrative tasks and acquire industry recognised work skills that were transferable and of value to potential employers in the open market (SPD, 2014b).

More could be done to leverage technology to enable students with special needs. For example, in the United States, students who require special education have individualised education plans (IEP) which includes assessment of the student's need for assistive technology.

Technology has great potential to level the playing field for students with special needs. Greater utilisation and application of technology for persons with special needs will require focused efforts, trans-disciplinary collaboration, time and resources devoted to this end. Going forward, SG Enable will play a critical and leadership role in this and many other aspects of disability matters and to improve the lives of persons with special needs.

Supporting Parents and Caregivers

To alleviate caregivers' stress as their children with special needs progress through the developmental phases in life and transit across different services, it is important to have good data and information management in place. Having a coordinated system in place will help detect emerging trends and facilitate better planning.

NCSS in consultation with its member agencies, created the electronic case management system or eCMS (NCSS, 2005). eCMS was a voluntary system for social service agencies to effectively manage client information, systematically track client progress and development over time and to enhance casework supervision. Such electronic case files would overcome the problem of the caseworker or supervisor or allied health professionals having access one at a time to the case file. Issues of confidentiality were overcome with controlled access by use of passwords. eCMS had potential to further aid service providers and partner agencies in their collaborative and trans-disciplinary efforts in the provision of services to the clients. It is a happy development that the eCMS has been replaced by the MSF SSNet with far better capabilities and potentials.

With the creation of the eCMS, NCSS also set up the Developmental Disability Registry (DDR) in 2006 (NCSS, 2006). A key goal was to enable the social service sector to have better information and statistics for planning and forecasting service gaps and needs. Due to the low participation rate by service providers, the

DDR did not achieve its goal of better service planning for the social service sector.

Nevertheless, the DDR has made it possible for NCSS to implement or expand critical community initiatives which gave caregivers support and assistance in times of need.

The Appropriate Adult (AA) Scheme is one such community initiative. The Committee on Assisting Offenders with Mental Disabilities, chaired by Mr Wong Kok Weng from the Attorney General's Chambers, trialled the AA Scheme at the Bedok Police Division in 2013. The AA Scheme uses AAs to provide support and assistance to persons alleged of crimes and suspected of having intellectual disability, autism spectrum disorder or mental health issues during police investigations (Hoe, 2014). AAs are trained volunteers activated through the Law Society of Singapore formerly, and currently through SG Enable. The Police utilises DDR as a form of identification in ascertaining if a detainee may require an AA volunteer to be activated. The AA Scheme was piloted at police stations island wide from January 2015.

The AA Scheme is renamed the Appropriate Adult Scheme for Persons with Mental Disabilities or AAPMD. Feedback to NCSS highlighted that the AA Scheme has been meeting a critical gap in our society and provides direct and useful support to persons with special needs and their families.

Another example of drawing practical value from data is the DDR Identity Card (DDRID), formerly known as Identity Card for People with Special Needs. This project was first developed in 2002 (NCSS, 2003) at the request of parents and caregivers. The intent is to provide better support for persons with intellectual disability and their families. This initiative provides a source of identification for individuals who were lost but not able to articulate their contact information. Persons with special needs could register through participating NCSS member agencies for an identity card. The Singapore Police Force (SPF) receives 24/7 support from SG Enable to access the DDR. The DDR has made it possible for the DDRID project to grow and include another vulnerable population. As at 2019, 10,200 persons with special needs had registered with the DDRID project. An additional 2,266 persons diagnosed with dementia had registered with the Safe Return Card, modelled after the DDRID. The Safe Return Card project has since been divested to the Alzheimer Disease Association.

Another project which NCSS implemented to support parents and caregivers is the Emergency SMS service. In 2008, Member of Parliament and Mayor, Ms Denise Phua and the SPF approached NCSS to provide an avenue for communication between Deaf or hard of hearing persons and the Police in times of emergency. The Emergency SMS service was launched and the number to contact the SPF is 71999 (SPF, 2020). However, there was no dedicated helpline for those who needed to contact the Singapore Civil Defence Force (SCDF). In 2014, NCSS worked with the SCDF to develop a targeted Emergency SMS service, 70995, to enable Deaf and hard of hearing individuals to contact SCDF directly in the event of a fire or when they need an emergency ambulance service (SCDF, 2020). NCSS worked closely with SADeaf, TOUCH Community Services' Silent Club, Canossian School, Lighthouse School and SG Enable to bring these projects to fruition.

To increase the financial security and well-being of persons with special needs, the Special Needs Trust Company Limited (SNTC) was set up by NCSS in June 2008, with support from MSF (SNTC, 2014). SNTC was the first of its kind, an independent Company Limited by Guarantee to provide non-profit trust services. Prof Lim Pin was the first and founding chairman and chaired the SNTC Board till 2018. In 2010, the Special Needs Savings Scheme, complementary to the SNTC, was announced to enable parents to set aside their CPF savings for the long-term care of their children with special needs upon their demise (Balakrishnan, 2010). Both initiatives started as a result of recommendations from MINDS and the Parents' Workgroup on Enhancing the Financial Security of Persons with Special Needs, led by Ms Denise Phua. A significant milestone was the SNTC taking over the administration of the Special Needs Savings Scheme in 2014. Mr Moses Lee took over the chairmanship on Jan 2019. As of 30 Sept 2020, SNTC has reached out to 15,383 parents and caregivers, community partners and professionals. It has completed 2,832 care plans and set up trust accounts for 795 persons with special needs.

Another programme which is directly helpful for parents and caregivers is the Signposts for Building Better Behaviour. Signposts helps families manage their children with special needs aged 3–15 years who have behavioural issues. NCSS supported the Signposts programme for a 3-year pilot from 2011. The programme was adapted for local implementation with the help of Prof Ho Lai Yun and his team of dedicated doctors and staff at the KKH DCD, together with the Parenting Research Centre in Australia. Signposts provides a structured, tried and tested curriculum to train caregivers, parents and staff from social service agencies. Signposts continues to be available to caregivers and staff from social service agencies as a useful training tool. Staff training is available through the SSI.

Three Enabling Masterplans (EM) were developed through the 3P approach, with active participation from the people, private and public sectors as well as service users and caregivers. The EMs are five-year national roadmaps to improve the quality of life of persons with special needs, support for caregivers, and build a caring and inclusive society (NCSS, 2020d). These Masterplans have guided many of the initiatives covered earlier. NCSS played a critical role in conceptualising and implementing some of the key recommendations in the three Enabling Masterplans (2007–2011, 2012–2016, 2017–2021). In particular, significant efforts were made by NCSS to organise focus group discussions and consultations with service users, caregivers, leaders and professionals in the disability sector so that their views could be heard and included.

Mr Chua Chin Kiat and Ms Anita Fam were the Chairpersons for Enabling Masterplans 2012–2016 and 2017–2021 respectively. All these were done with the aim to build a more inclusive society in which persons with special needs are included as contributing members.

Inclusion and Socialisation

Persons with special needs will not be able to achieve their fullest potential or lead their lives with dignity, if they are not able to participate fully in society or if they are not embraced by society and treated as peers with something unique and valuable to offer our community.

The movement to promote the inclusion of persons with special needs in Singapore has been slow but is gathering momentum. Progress is possible when parents, caregivers, persons with special needs, professionals, social service providers, donors, funders, volunteers, policy makers, planners and politicians embrace inclusion as a fundamental value for our society.

When the Edusave Scheme was launched in 1993, NCSS and AWWA advocated for students from special education schools to be included in the scheme. Dr Aline Wong, then Minister of State for Education, announced in Parliament the government policy to include students from special education schools for Edusave payouts in 1996 (NCSS, 2008). Mrs Leaena Tambyah (AWWA's founding board member) must be credited for her lifelong advocacy for children with special needs and her repeated appeals regarding Edusave. Many others have spoken up and continue to speak up to share their observations and advocate for an inclusive society to be extended to all aspects of our daily life and interaction.

Given the deep and lasting impact of social interaction and socialisation as well as the inspiring and successful model of the Canossian Eduplex, a brainchild of Sister Anne Tan and the Canossian Sisters, NCSS advocated for various satellite models and the co-location of special education schools with mainstream schools. In 2007, MOE announced that more opportunities for interactions would be encouraged through co-locating special education schools with mainstream schools and there were plans to build more satellite school models (MOE, 2007).

This was a significant milestone, as it helps students with special needs learn socially acceptable behaviour in the natural environment and to do so as early as possible. This arrangement also benefits the mainstream students who rarely have the opportunity to interact or befriend students with special needs and so feel very awkward about how to behave around persons with special needs. This social awkwardness is also evident among adults. Parents and caregivers sometimes share stories about how others would stare at their charges in public places, causing embarrassment and even pain. This type of behaviour would be less likely to occur if we are all more aware and less ignorant towards disability issues and have greater understanding towards persons with special needs.

Social interaction and socialisation are important steps towards understanding others. Understanding others is a critical step towards embracing diversity and building an inclusive society.

Inclusive playground

Playgrounds for children with special needs can be found within the confines of special education schools. However, existing outdoor playgrounds in Singapore lack the appropriate physical structures and equipment which are accessible for children with special needs. This minimises the opportunities for children with special needs and their non-disabled peers to interact with one another through play. The lack of inclusive playgrounds therefore deepens the segregation between the children with special needs and their non-disabled peers.

With this in mind, NCSS worked closely with NParks to build an inclusive playground in Bishan-Ang Mo Kio Park that included features such as a wheelchair-accessible swing and merry-go-round (Ng, 2015). The Bishan-Ang Mo Kio Park inclusive playground, supported by the Care & Share Movement, was officially opened by then Minister for Social and Family Development, Mr Tan Chuan-Jin on Saturday, 22 August 2015 (Ng, 2015). Ten more of such inclusive playgrounds was planned to be built across Singapore by 2017 (Ng, 2015). This playground has created an inclusive space and platform for children with special needs and their non-disabled peers to socialise and learn from one another through play. The inclusive playground was a community-based, community owned project and succeeded because the various local community groups, including schools, town councils, grassroots organisations, social service agencies, businesses and residents in the local community, actively utilised it. Ms Fazlin Abdullah, a former NCSS staff had suggested this and other pioneering ideas to promote an inclusive society.

Buddy'IN

NCSS recognises the importance of social inclusion and has pioneered a new programme to socially integrate graduating students from special education schools with their peers at Institutes of Higher Learning (IHLs) (Khew, 2014; NCSS, 2015). The programme — Buddy'IN prepared the graduating students with special needs to communicate and interact with the community. At the same time, it provided opportunities for students without special needs to learn, accept and work with others with special needs.

Financial assistance

In times of need, families with special needs children often face financial hardships. In 2008, Singapore underwent a devastating economic downturn. To help low-income students attending special education schools to remain in school and receive critical services despite the economic downturn, NCSS administered the Trailblazer — Chan Chiew Ping Special Schools Fund worth $603,000 (NCSS, 2010b). Both service users and social workers were very grateful for this injection of funds by the Trailblazer Foundation Ltd and other corporate donors. The timely financial assistance helped tide the families over a very difficult period.

The 'Many Helping Hands' approach when appropriately activated can mean that more children and their families can access help and get it faster.

The Straits Times School Pocket Money Fund (SPMF) is a community project co-initiated by The Straits Times and NCSS in 2000. The aim is to provide children from low-income families with school pocket money so that they may continue schooling and successfully complete school (SPMF, 2019). The SPMF supports about 10,000 children yearly in their school-related expenses, such as buying meals and paying for public transport (SPMF, 2019). Cumulatively, over 170,000 children have benefited from the school pocket money since SPMF started in 2000 (SPMF, 2019).

NCSS actively guided the policy, criteria, and annual budgets for the SPMF till it was incorporated as a charity with IPC in 2012.

Disbursements continue through NCSS member agencies such as the network of family service centres, special education schools and children's homes.

Public awareness and understanding

Alongside the transformation in the special needs sector through the years, efforts were also made to increase public awareness and understanding towards persons with special needs. Such efforts are important as persons with special needs form an integral part of our society but are often not socially included. On 30 November 2012, Singapore signed the United Nations Convention on the Rights of Persons with Disabilities (UNCRPD) (NCSS, 2013b). The Agreement was then ratified on 18 July 2013 and came into effect for Singapore on 18 August 2013 (NCSS, 2013b). UNCRPD focuses on ensuring that persons with special needs have the opportunity to live a dignified life and be given access to all areas of life: including health, physical environment, education and employment (NCSS, 2013b).

To raise awareness of the UNCRPD, on 22 March 2013, NCSS launched a year-long campaign with the tagline, "We are Able! Enhancing Possibilities, Celebrating Abilities". It encouraged the community, including persons with special needs, to play their part and to take action towards building an inclusive society. A total of 26 champions, comprising of social service agencies, persons with special needs and business leaders, collaborated with NCSS to raise public awareness through the campaign. NCSS produced an easy-read guidebook (NCSS, 2013b) which explained the 50 Articles in the UNCRPD in simple terms that are easily understood by the general public and students. To cap the year-long campaign, NCSS organised the "We Are Able!" conference on 18 January 2014 (NCSS, 2014). 340 participants attended to listen to people with special needs who took centre stage to share their experiences, hopes and aspirations. Attendees were moved by the many stories shared candidly and expressed their commitment to play their part in celebrating the abilities of and enhancing the possibilities of persons with special needs.

Another movement that supports inclusion and celebrates the abilities of persons with special needs is the Purple Parade, the brainchild of Ms Denise Phua. Support for the Purple Parade continues to swell every year since 2013. In 2020, despite the Purple Parade events being conducted online, there were over 200 partner agencies and over 50,000 viewers and participants (The Purple Parade, 2020).

Way Forward

In our quest to be a better society, to be more compassionate and to build a better future for all our children, there are no simple answers. The journey is as important as the destination.

We have to consider our own unique history, culture, social and political aspirations to forge a way forward that is efficacious for us, and which we will be proud of in the next 50 years.

As Singapore celebrates 50 years of nation building, national pride and achievements, we must keep searching for ways and means to build upon what we have already put in place. While it is often easier to see what is not there, what is not yet perfect, it is also important to celebrate the advances and accomplishments, however small, which have improved our lives collectively.

The talents, potentials and challenges of our children with special needs are not homogenous. Special education schools therefore have to forge ahead and continue to adapt and adopt what works best for our students. While the schools need adequate support and resources to deliver quality education, the pathway and curriculum for each school could differ. In order to bring out the best from our students with special needs, we have to keep charting the path forward with knowledge and evidence.

We must learn how to teach by learning how the students learn and do more of what works. Part of the answer lies with taking a student-centric approach. Educators should be empowered to stop doing what does not work for the particular child or the particular class. Can we see a child for who he or she is? Each child is unique and different from the next person. Can we see who he or she can become, with our support and nurturing?

How do we achieve inclusion and embrace diversity? If becoming confident, value-centered members of society is one of the goals for education, what would we do differently going forward? What changes would we make to achieve this long-term outcome? Policies and programmes put in place may have served the purpose for which they were first created, but we must have the courage and humility to regularly disrupt, to create anew and to climb the next mountain. We have taken the approach of integration as much as possible. The next mountain may be to aim for full integration so that every child with special needs is able to attend a school in his or her local neighbourhood and community.

It is important to listen to the hearts and minds of our children with special needs. How might we enable a child with special needs to achieve his or her potential, lead a life of dignity and to achieve success?

My wish as we celebrate our nation's 56th birthday is Ohana. Ohana means family and family means nobody gets left behind or forgotten.

References

Association for Persons with Special Needs (APSN). (2020). About us. Retrieved 12 November 2020 from https://www.apsn.org.sg/about-apsn/

Autism Association (Singapore) (AAS). (2020). Overview of Autism Association (Singapore). Retrieved 12 November 2020 from https://www.autismlinks.org.sg/about-us/overview

AWWA. (2019a). AWWA school. Retrieved 12 November 2020 from https://www.awwa.org.sg/our-services/school-going-7-to-18-years-old/awwa-school/

AWWA. (2019b). Community integration service. Retrieved 12 November 2020 from https://www.awwa.org.sg/our-services/school-going-7-to-18-years-old/community-integration-service/

Balakrishnan, V. (2010, March 10). Speech by Dr Vivian Balakrishnan, Minister for Community Development, Youth and Sports, at Committee of Supply 2010 — Opening Speech on 10 March 2010 at 3.40pm at Parliament House. Retrieved 12 November 2020 from https://www.nas.gov.sg/archivesonline/data/pdfdoc/20100318001.htm

Canossian School. (2020). Our journey. Retrieved 12 November 2020 from http://www.canossian.edu.sg/ourjourney/

Cerebral Palsy Alliance Singapore (CPAS). (n.d.). Overview. Retrieved 12 November 2020 from https://cpas.org.sg/overview/

Dyslexia Association of Singapore (DAS). (2020). History of DAS family. Retrieved 12 November 2020 from https://www.das.org.sg/about-das/about-us/history-of-das.html

Gan, K.Y. (2007, November 16). Speech by Mr Gan Kim Yong, Minister of State, Ministry of Education and Ministry of Manpower, at the MOE-NCSS SPED Teacher Award held on 16 November 2007 at 2.30pm at the Marina Mandarin Hotel. Retrieved 12 November 2020 from https://www.nas.gov.sg/archivesonline/data/pdfdoc/20071116999.htm

Goh, W.H., Chong, W.H., & Chan, W.P. (2010). *Study to Establish the Baseline of Early Intervention Programme for Infants and Children.* Singapore: National Council of Social Service, KK Women's and Children's Hospital.

Grace Orchard School (GOS). (2020). Milestones. Retrieved 12 November 2020 from https://go.edu.sg/milestone/

Hoe, P.S. (2014, May 18). Help for 'vulnerable' suspects during probes. *The Sunday Times*, p. 18.

Khew, C. (2014, January 18). New programme to pair up special needs students with peers from mainstream schools. *The Straits Times*. Retrieved 12 November 2020 from https://www.straitstimes.com/singapore/new-programme-to-pair-up-special-needs-students-with-peers-from-mainstream-schools

Metta Welfare Association (MWA). (2013). Annual report 2012/2013. Retrieved 12 November 2020 from http://www.metta.org.sg/pdf_courses/about_metta/AnnualReport/Year1213/AR_2013.pdf

Ministry for Education (MOE). (2004). Enhancing support for children with special needs. Press release, MOE, Singapore. Retrieved 12 November 2020 https://www.nas.gov.sg/archivesonline/data/pdfdoc/2004091894.htm

Ministry for Education (MOE). (2007). Levelling up opportunities — Raising the quality of education for children with special needs. Press release, MOE, Singapore. Retrieved 12 November 2020 from https://www.nas.gov.sg/archivesonline/data/pdfdoc/20070307986.pdf

Ministry of Education (MOE). (2010). New framework for vocational education in special education (SPED) schools. Press release, MOE,

Singapore. Retrieved 12 November 2020 from https://www.nas.gov.sg/archivesonline/data/pdfdoc/20101119003/press_release_voc_ed.pdf

Ministry of Education (MOE). (2014). Five special education schools onboard School-To-Work Transition programme. Press release, MOE, Singapore. Retrieved 12 November 2020 from https://www.moe.gov.sg/news/press-releases/five-special-education-schools-onboard-school-to-work-transition-programme

Ministry of Social and Family Development (MSF). (2014). MSF pilots home-based care services for persons with disabilities. Press release, MSF, Singapore. Retrieved 12 November 2020 from https://www.msf.gov.sg/media-room/Pages/MSF-pilots-home-based-care-services-for-Persons-with-Disabilities.aspx

Movement for the Intellectually Disabled of Singapore (MINDS). (n.d.). About us. Retrieved 12 November 2020 from https://www.minds.org.sg/about-us/

National Council of Social Service (NCSS). (2003). *NCSS Annual Report 02/03*. Singapore: National Council of Social Service.

National Council of Social Service (NCSS). (2005). *NCSS Annual Report 04/05*. Singapore: National Council of Social Service.

National Council of Social Service (NCSS). (2006). *NCSS Annual Report 05/06*. Singapore: National Council of Social Service.

National Council of Social Service (NCSS). (2008). *For All We Care: 50 Years of Social Service in Singapore*. Singapore: Epigram.

National Council of Social Service (NCSS). (2010a). *Rapport Nov 2009 – Feb 2010*. Singapore: National Council of Social Service.

National Council of Social Service (NCSS). (2010b). *NCSS Annual Report FY2009*. Singapore: National Council of Social Service.

National Council of Social Service (NCSS). (2013a). NCSS annual report FY2012. Retrieved 12 November 2020 from https://www.ncss.gov.sg/Press-Room/Publications/Detail-Page?id=National-Council-of-Social-Service-Annual-Repo-(2)

National Council of Social Service (NCSS). (2013b). Understanding the United Nations Convention on the Rights of Persons with Disabilities. Retrieved 12 November 2020 from https://www.ncss.gov.sg/Press-Room/Publications/Detail-Page?id=Understanding-the-United-Nations-Convention-on-The

National Council of Social Service (NCSS). (2014). NCSS annual report FY2013. Retrieved 12 November 2020 from https://www.ncss.gov.sg/Press-Room/Publications/Detail-Page?id=National-Council-of-Social-Service-Annual-Repo-(1)

National Council of Social Service (NCSS). (2015). NCSS annual report FY2014. Retrieved 12 November 2020 from https://www.ncss.gov.sg/Press-Room/Publications/Detail-Page?id=National-Council-of-Social-Service-Annual-Report-F

National Council of Social Service (NCSS). (2020a). Our story. Retrieved 12 November 2020 from https://www.ncss.gov.sg/Who-We-Are/Our-Organisation

National Council of Social Service (NCSS). (2020b). Our mission. Retrieved 12 November 2020 from https://www.ncss.gov.sg/Who-We-Are/Our-Mission

National Council of Social Service (NCSS). (2020c). NCSS standards framework. Retrieved 12 November 2020 from https://www.ncss.gov.sg/GatewayPages/Social-Service-Agencies/Capability-Building/Consultancy-Support

National Council of Social Service (NCSS). (2020d). Adults with disabilities. Retrieved 12 November 2020 from https://www.ncss.gov.sg/GatewayPages/Social-Services/Adult-with-Disabilities

Ng, E.H. (2010, April 27). Speech by Dr Ng Eng Hen, Minister for Education and Second Minister for Defence, at the Official Opening of the New Pathlight School Site on 27 April 2010 at 10.30am. Retrieved 12 November 2020 from https://www.nas.gov.sg/archivesonline/data/pdfdoc/20100504001/minister_speech.pdf

Ng, H. W. (2015, August 23). Their turn at the playground. *The Sunday Times*, pp. 1, A10.

Pathlight School. (2020). Milestones. Retrieved 12 November 2020 from http://www.pathlight.org.sg/about-us/milestones

Quah, M.M. (1990). Special education in Singapore. *International Journal of Disability, Development and Education, 37*(2), 137–148.

Rainbow Centre. (2019). Our history. Retrieved 12 November 2020 from https://www.rainbowcentre.org.sg/about-us/

SG Enable. (2015a). About us. Retrieved 12 November 2020 from https://www.sgenable.sg/pages/content.aspx?path=/about-us/

SG Enable. (2015b). Day activity centres. Retrieved 12 November 2020 from https://www.sgenable.sg/pages/content.aspx?path=/for-adults/day-activity-centres

Sim, A. (2014, November 12). Address by Ms Sim Ann, Minister of State, Ministry of Education & Ministry of Communications and Information at the Special Education (SPED) Conference 2014 on 12 November 2014 at 9.00am at Resorts World Convention Centre. Retrieved 12 November 2020 from https://www.moe.gov.sg/news/speeches/

address-by-ms-sim-ann--minister-of-state--ministry-of-education-and-ministry-of-commuunications-and-information-at-the-special-education-sped-conference-2014-on-12-nov--900am--resorts-world-convention-centre

Singapore Association for the Visually Handicapped (SAVH). (2017). Milestones. Retrieved 12 November 2020 from https://savh.org.sg/milestones/

Singapore Civil Defence Force (SCDF). (2020). SMS 70995 Emergency Service. Retrieved 12 November 2020, from https://www.scdf.gov.sg/home/about-us/information/sms-70995-emergency-service

Singapore Police Force (SPF.) (2020). SMS 71999. Retrieved 12 November 2020 from https://www.police.gov.sg/SMS-71999

SPD. (2014a). Infocomm Accessibility Centre ramps up efforts to increase opportunities for people with disabilities. Press release, SPD. Retrieved 12 November 2020 from https://www.spd.org.sg/infocomm-accessibility-centre-ramps-up-efforts-to-increase-opportunities-for-people-with-disabilities/

SPD. (2014b). Infocomm technology and office skills training help increase employability of people with disabilities. Press release, SPD. Retrieved 12 November 2020 from https://www.spd.org.sg/infocomm-technology-and-office-skills-training-help-increase-employability-of-people-with-disabilities/

SPD. (2018). Specialised assistive technology centre. Retrieved 12 November 2020 from https://www.spd.org.sg/specialised-assistive-technology-centre/

Special Needs Trust Co. (SNTC). (2014). Establishment of SNTC. Retrieved 12 November 2020 from https://www.sntc.org.sg/Pages/sntc_about.aspx?MainMenu=What%20Drives%20Us

St. Andrew's Mission Hospital (SAMH). (n.d.). History. Retrieved 12 November 2020 from https://www.samh.org.sg/history/

The Purple Parade. (2020). Quick facts of 2020. Retrieved 12 November 2020 from https://www.purpleparade.sg/

The Singapore Association for the Deaf (SADeaf). (2018). History. Retrieved 12 November 2020 from https://sadeaf.org.sg/about-us/history/

The Straits Times School Pocket Money Fund (SPMF). (2019). About us. Retrieved 12 November 2020 from https://www.spmf.org.sg/about

Acknowledgements for the Research of the Paper

My deepest gratitude to Ms. Lim Woan Yun, Sector Strategy Group (NCSS) who ably assisted me. Without Woan Yun's help, this chapter would not have been possible. My appreciation to Service Planning and Funding Group (NCSS), MOE Special Education Branch, General Manager (SNTC), General Manager (SPMF) for providing me with the relevant data.

Appendix I: Listing of Special Education Schools

Social Service Agency	School
Association for Persons with Special Needs	Chaoyang School
	Delta Senior School
	Katong School
	Tanglin School
Metta Welfare Association	Metta School
Presbyterian Community Services	Grace Orchard School
Movement for the Intellectually Disabled of Singapore	Fernvale Gardens School
	Lee Kong Chian Gardens School
	Towner Gardens School
	Woodlands Gardens School
AWWA	AWWA School
Rainbow Centre	Rainbow Centre — Margaret Drive School
	Rainbow Centre — Yishun Park School
Cerebral Palsy Alliance of Singapore	Cerebral Palsy Alliance Singapore School
Autism Resource Centre (Singapore)	Pathlight School
Autism Association (Singapore)	Eden School
St. Andrew's Mission Hospital	St. Andrew's Autism School
Canossa Mission Singapore	Canossian School
Singapore Association of the Visually Handicapped	Lighthouse School

CHAPTER 8

Psychological Services for Children with Special Educational Needs in Mainstream Schools

Mariam Aljunied

ఝ

Introduction

November 2016 represented a significant milestone in the landscape of support for students with Special Educational Needs (SEN) in Singapore, i.e., the announcement of the inclusion of students with SEN in the Compulsory Education act (CE for SEN). From 2019, all children with SEN born on or after 2 January 2012, must attend in national primary schools, that is, either a mainstream primary school or a government-funded special education (SPED) schools. Then Minister for Education, Mr Ng Chee Meng, predicated this announcement of the extension of Compulsory Education Act for Students with SEN by re-affirming the strong commitment of the Ministry of Education (MOE) on ensuring quality support for SEN:

> "MOE remains committed to enhancing support for children with special needs … always ensuring that our children — whatever their background, current circumstances, educational challenges,

can and will be an integral part of who we are and what we can achieve as a society and as a country." (MOE, 2016)

The current SEN provisions in Singapore are grounded in the belief of the need for a continuum of provisions for SEN, so that the diverse needs of children with SEN can be adequately and appropriately met. Many strides and significant improvements have been achieved in the inclusion of students with SEN in mainstream schools. As at December 2017, there were about 30 000 students with a reported SEN; about 80 per cent of them are in mainstream schools and 20 per cent are in SPED schools (NAS, 2018).

It is against this backdrop of developments in SEN support that the role of professionals and psychologists as providers of psychological services for children with SEN in mainstream schools is discussed in this chapter. This chapter also describes the development and evolution of psychological services for children with SEN in mainstream schools in Singapore in the last three decades, highlighting the influencing factors in the larger social and educational landscape as well as the implications for the professional development of psychologists. Several phases of development are identified and described, highlighting the dominant model or approach that has shaped the practice of psychologists serving children in Singapore mainstream schools, namely: the initial medical model; the problem-solving approach; the phase of enhancing schools' capability; and the tiered system of support.

The Medical Model

The genesis of psychological services for children with SEN can perhaps be dated to 1970, when the MOE was reported to have established the Schools Social Work (Tham-Toh *et al.*, 2012). Little is known or recorded about these services and by the 1980s, the service no longer existed. During those early years of 1970s and 1980s, children with SEN in mainstream schools would access the services of psychologists at the Child Psychiatric Clinic (later renamed the Child Guidance Clinic or CGC), which was established by the Ministry of Health in 1970. Schools or parents could refer the children under their care to the CGC for assessment and diagnosis, and if appropriate be referred to SPED schools, or to seek treatment at the CGC for social and emotional disorders.

From the perspective of the mainstream schools at that time, the role of psychologists and the service they provide for students were clear and circumscribed, i.e., as diagnostician and important gatekeeper to the access to SPED schools and specialised treatment provided in specialised medical centres or hospitals, which were clearly apart from the confines of the school. This approach was predicated on the medical model, where problems were conceptualised as residing primarily within patients (i.e., the students), and the role of the clinician (i.e., psychologists or therapists) was to treat the illness (i.e., the SEN) and to maximize human functioning and adjustment. Thus, the model was reactive, waiting for problems to occur and then responding to them. It was also an approach that focused solely on individual students (or cases) most often, as opposed to groups or systems. This origin of psychological services in Singapore was not unique; the model or approach used in psychological services in many other developed countries began very much as clinical services within the framework of a medical model, and this remained a common feature of psychological services in many developing countries (Deluca, 2003).

For Singapore (then also a developing economy), this model of psychological services served well the needs of children with SEN in mainstream schools for the first few decades after independence (1960s–1980s). During those initial years, the SEN landscape was divided starkly into two clearly defined and separate systems — mainstream schools which had no specialised provision for children with SEN, and SPED schools which, albeit received some funding from government, were run with a fair degree of independence by charitable organisations or social service agencies.

In that context, where mainstream schools found children under their care with needs that they were unable to support, these children ('patients') were referred for diagnosis, and a key treatment outcome could be the placement of the child in an alternative school setting, i.e., SPED school. The first few psychologists in MOE HQ (headquarters) in the late 1980s were recruited in the MOE's 'Reading Clinic'; reflecting an approach towards addressing literacy skills that was deeply embedded in this medical model (Tan, 2002). Nonetheless, this reflected the beginning of a slight shift in the role of psychologists from one that was mainly concerned about school placement decisions, to one which included making specific educational recommendations for interventions for individual cases. Today, however, the SEN landscape is markedly different. There is a wide and comprehensive range of specialised support for children with SEN in mainstream schools, and the range of alternative educational options has also diversified greatly (these will be discussed in later sections).

As the provisions for SEN developed and the distinction between students who could be supported in mainstream and those that could not be became less clear to teachers and parents, the medical model of psychological services very quickly became insufficient. On the one hand, there would always be a role for psychologists as diagnosticians and gate-keepers to costly specialised resources; however, at the same time, mainstream schools began raising questions and issues that went beyond the scope of diagnosis and referral to SPED, such as:

- "How do we know which children are likely to have SEN? What can we do to help them early, i.e., before the problem worsens?"
- "These children do not meet the criteria for SPED, but they still experience much difficulty; what do we do with them?"
- "Some of the children with SEN have the same educational needs as their non-SEN peers; how do we help both groups in school?"

These issues reflected the fact that schools needed a more diverse range of services from psychologists; one that helped schools to solve the problems that they were facing in supporting children with SEN. With better awareness of the range of profiles of children with SEN, schools were interested in strategies that could help them address the needs of groups of students, and not just individual cases. This was the impetus for a change from the medical model to psychological services that was characterised by the problem-solving approach.

The Problem-Solving Approach

The first challenge in evolving from a medical model to one where psychologists become problem-solving partners of the schools was the creation of a service model where the psychologists were a part of the school system, and not apart from it. This structural reform came in 1991 in the form of the School Psychological Services (SPS) in the MOE HQ, with a small group of educational psychologists employed in HQ to provide direct services to children in 10 mainstream primary schools.

In the 1990s, in the larger international scene, the practice of educational and school psychologists grew and matured. The value proposition of educational psychologists going beyond diagnostics was illustrated clearly by the inclusion of specific competencies relating to problem-solving approaches for school psychology that was articulated in the UK's Consultation Model for service delivery (Wagner, 1995), and the United States' National Association of School Psychologists (NASP) in their 'Blueprint for Training and Practice III' and Standards for School Psychological Services (NASPE, 2000), which highlighted that:

> "Practice guidelines state that school psychologists use a decision making process in collaboration with other team members to identify academic and behavior problems, collect and analyse information to understand the problems, make decisions about service delivery, and evaluate the outcomes of the service delivery. School psychologists ... translate research into practice through the problem-solving process, and use research design and statistics skills to conduct investigations to develop and facilitate effective services."

It was therefore unsurprising that the development of the psychological service in MOE HQ in the initial decade (1990s to 2000) reflected an approach where the service model was designed to facilitate the implementation of problem-solving approaches in applied psychology. Some of the key elements of the SPS at MOE HQ at that time included (Weerasinghe, Ong & Cockburn, 2002):

- **Implementation of a universal screening for students who needed support for learning in primary schools.** Students were identified based on specific needs-based criterion and selection was conducted by trained teachers and not 'expert clinicians'. This provided schools with the flexibility to identify students that needed learning help, regardless of whether the need for support arose from socio-economic disadvantage or a medical condition/disability.
- **Implementation of the school-based intervention programmes** to provide school-based intervention for primary students identified to have learning needs through the screening and/or teachers' observation, such as the Learning Support Programme.
- **Employing a team of Reading Specialists and Educational Counsellors** as part of the service team alongside the psychologists in MOE HQ. The role of these professionals was to provide direct intervention and advice for students referred to the SPS for learning and/or behavioural difficulties. The Reading Specialists subsequently moved to join other curriculum specialists in the curriculum division in MOE, while the role of Educational Counsellors was subsequently taken over by Full-Time School Counsellors based in all schools.

In the first decade of the SPS, a new value proposition for psychological services for students with SEN was established, i.e., as a service that aimed to help mainstream schools implement school-based interventions for students with SEN. This was also reflected in the next iteration of the name of the psychological service in MOE HQ, i.e., from 'School Psychological Services' to the 'Specialised Pupils Programmes Branch' (or SPPB) in 1995. (Note: The service was later re-organised and renamed as the 'Psychological and Guidance Services Branch' in 2000, and subsequently as the 'Psychological Services Branch' in 2006.)

Within the perspective of the problem-solving approach, when a child was referred to the educational psychologist by the school, the aim was not simply to seek a diagnosis and treatment. Instead, the goal was to collaboratively unpack the problem presentation, explore hypotheses for its continuation, and finally arrive at a series of possible in-school solutions to be tried out and evaluated over time to check for efficacy. It should be noted that in this approach, the psychologists' role in assessment and diagnosis of children with SEN remained relevant; but over time, the additional role of psychologists as partners in problem-solving for teachers in schools was expected to grow.

In its initial years, the problem-solving approach that characterised the MOE HQ psychological services was valuable for schools. It provided the structures necessary for framing school-based problems and for analysing the effectiveness of these solutions. The problem-solving approach facilitated schools and teachers to evaluate objectively whether the interventions being applied to students were working.

However, the problem-solving approach did not completely replace the medical model; instead the two co-existed. Over time the two roles of the psychologists — as diagnostician and problem-solver — became equally dominant, and this often created a tension in the demands for psychological services for SEN in schools. While schools could see the benefit in the consultative problem-solving process of unpacking and re-framing children's problems and identification of new ways of addressing them themselves (with expert help), the expediency of referring children with problems to the educational psychologist for expert advice and recommendations (with a spoken or unspoken desire for the psychologist to 'fix' the problem) was also appealing to busy teachers and school personnel.

Additionally, another limitation that was inherent in the problem-solving approach also surfaced. As discussed by several writers (Tilly, Reschly & Grimes, 1999; Marston *et al.*, 2003), what the problem-solving approach lacked was a supportive context for implementation and structures within schools that embraced and promoted evidence-based practices. Most teachers in schools were not trained in application of the problem-solving methods in psychology, and most educational structures (e.g., methods for problem identification, referral processes and service delivery structures) and practices were not driven using evidence-based or student outcome data as a guide.

In the Singapore context, the early application of the problem-solving approach in the delivery of MOE HQ psychological services for SEN relied heavily on external professionals or 'experts' (i.e., psychologists, reading specialists and educational counsellors based in MOE HQ) to bring the good SEN practices to schools, to facilitate their application, and at the same time, for these 'experts' to provide assessment and intervention services when referrals for individual students were received.

As a result, most often, cases that were referred to the psychologists for problem-solving were those with significant or severe problems, i.e., after these problems had manifested in the school environment for some time. As such, the role of psychologists as partners in problem-solvers was not positioned well to address problems early, i.e., when the problems were most workable. There was very little scope for preventative work with schools, and in some cases, where the school teacher and the psychologist had agreed on solutions to address the needs of children with SEN in the school, there were no school-based structures in place to address the SEN students' learning and behavioural needs.

What was needed to lift the psychological services for SEN to the next level was a leap in the structural changes within mainstream schools, such that the capacity of mainstream schools to support SEN was raised at the systems level. One important structural change was the introduction of the additional resources and specialised manpower for SEN in mainstream schools and the Tiered System of Support (TSS) framework for SEN in mainstream schools.

Enhancing Capability and Resources in Mainstream Schools

The year 2004 was a significant year for several reasons. It was the year that Mr Lee Hsien Loong took office as Singapore's 3rd Prime

Minister (PM). In his inaugural speech as PM, he painted a vision for Singapore that signalled a watershed in how individuals with disabilities were positioned in society:

> "We should recognise many paths of success, and many ways to be Singaporean. We must give people a second chance, for those who have tasted failure may be the wiser and stronger among us. Ours must be an open and inclusive Singapore." (NAS, 2004).

As highlighted by other writers, such as Poon, Musti-rao and Wettasinghe (2013), the PM's vision of Singapore as an inclusive society was a key event that paved the way for changes in policy and service delivery for students with disabilities in unprecedented proportions. The changes resulted in several new measures that were instituted in 2005 within the mainstream school system to better support students with SEN (Aljunied, 2012).

These measures included a significant increase in funding allocation for professional development, the introduction of new professionals ('Special Needs Officers' or SNOs, who later became known as 'Allied Educators for Learning and Behaviour Support' or AEDs [LBS]) in mainstream schools to support students with SEN, as well as the training of general education teachers to support students with SEN in all mainstream schools.

The collective impact of these initiatives provided the impetus for the leap that was needed for the next evolution in the focus of psychological services for SEN, i.e., building schools' capacity for supporting children with SEN. Some of the significant initiatives during this phase (2005 to 2015) were:

- The training of 'Teachers trained in Special Needs' (TSNs), where the goal was to equip every school 20 per cent of teachers serving as TSNs, and have all teachers receive awareness training in SEN as part of their pre-service teacher training;
- The implementation of School-Based Dyslexia Remediation programme for students with persistent literacy difficulties in all primary schools; and

- The introduction of school-based itinerant support services for students with hearing loss, visual impairment and physical impairment in all mainstream schools.

Linkages with Other Providers of Psychological Services

In tandem with developments of the psychological services in MOE HQ, beyond the confines of schools, other providers of psychological services for children with SEN in mainstream schools also developed and evolved; these too impacted the work of psychologists in MOE HQ with school-going children.

For example, the paediatric Developmental Assessment Clinic (DAC) which was developed in public hospitals in 1991 also provided services for preschool children with disabilities to help them transition from early intervention services to formal schooling (Ho, 2007). It was later named the Department for Child Development (DCD) in 1997, and by the mid-2000s, the KK and National University Hospitals' DCDs were reported to see about 1,000 pre-schoolers at risk for developmental delays each year (Lian et al., 2012)

Additionally, services for children and adolescents at the outpatient clinic at CGC were remodelled in 2007 as a community-based mental health services with direct access by schools (Fung et al., 2013). Renamed as 'REACH — Response, Early Intervention and Assessment in Community Mental Health', one of its key goals was to build the capacity of schools and other community partners to detect and manage children's mental health related problems through support and training. Almost 40 per cent of cases referred for support by REACH are school-going children with SEN, including those with ADHD and developmental disorders (Choon et al., 2017).

The need to work more closely with psychological service providers outside of the school system made it necessary to have a clear common understanding and shared framework for professional practice among psychologists from the different sectors. This was to ensure that when parents and teachers received advice and guidance about their children with SEN, there would be some consistency in professional standards and common reference points. This prompted the development and promulgation of the Professional Practice Guidelines (PPG) for Psycho-educational Assessment and Placements for Students with SEN in 2011. The PPG represented the consensus of multi-disciplinary professionals from the relevant education, health and social service sectors in Singapore (MOE, 2018). Notably, it was in the first edition of the PPG in 2011 that a clear definition for SEN used in Singapore schools was publicly articulated, as well as a standard framework of SEN categorisation, and relevant provisions available for each category were described, along with best practice guidelines for the assessment and diagnosis of common disability conditions seen in school-going children in Singapore.

As the PPG was developed through consensus by professionals from different sectors, the guidelines and framework in the PPG had to be coherent when seen through the lenses of practitioners in education, health and social service sectors, and be implementable across all these different sectors. Consequently, while the PPG's focus was on the psycho-educational assessments and placements of students with SEN, it also took reference from several clinical practice guidelines (CPG) developed by Singapore's Academy of Medicine and Ministry of Health, e.g., CPG for ADHD (Fung *et al.*, 2014). These cross-disciplinary references meant that psychologists who traditionally worked within the confines of schools had to embrace the best practices arising from health and social service sectors (and vice versa). This initial challenge presented an opportunity for cross-disciplinary training and professional development for psychologists; however, across many training courses for psychologists available locally, there seemed to be a lack of emphasis in the development of competencies needed by psychologists to work effectively with professionals in cross- or multi-disciplinary contexts.

As the complexity of service provision for SEN increased in response to the needs of children with SEN in mainstream schools, the competencies needed by providers of psychological services grew. This has continued into the next phase, which is the latest iteration of the enhancements in supporting students with SEN in the mainstream, namely, the Tiered-System of Support for SEN.

Tiered-System of Support for SEN

Resources and additional specialised manpower are not enough to realise the vision for all mainstream schools to increase their capacity to support children with SEN. This was a key message in PM Lee's speech to teachers as he paints his vision for education in Singapore:

> "It's not just a matter of putting in the resources and the people or the money. It's finding the dedication, the commitment, the team: setting the goals for our education system and motivating and inspiring our teachers, our principals, our staff, to go ahead, give of their best and make it happen and change the lives of the students." (NAS, 2006).

With the additional resources and manpower, mainstream schools are poised to do more; but what can psychologists do to help schools develop the structural and process capabilities that are needed to optimise and utilise these resources? How can psychologists help schools translate these additional resources to implement effective support for children with SEN? These present new challenges for the role of psychological services for children with SEN. However, this could also be a window of opportunity for another evolution of the role of psychological service providers for SEN in Singapore, i.e., systems coaching.

Systems coaching involves collaborating with educators and school leaders to facilitate an educational environment that improves student outcomes (Frederickson & Cline, 2009; March *et al.*, 2016). When psychologists play the role of 'systems coaches' for SEN support, they focus on issues such as establishing whole-school processes and procedures that promote the implementation of support for SEN. These would require a shift in how schools view the framework of support for SEN, i.e., quality of SEN support rests on the fidelity and strength of whole-school support processes for all students. It is

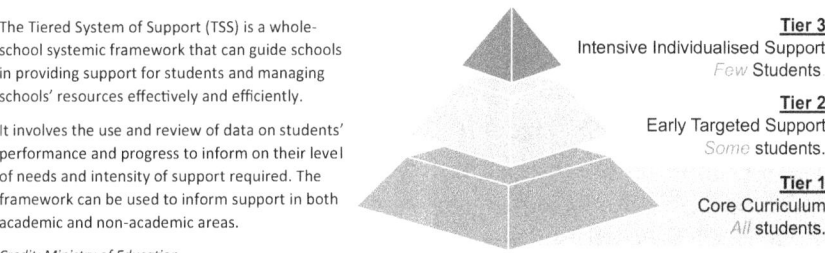

Figure 1: TSS framework for SEN support in mainstream schools.

against this backdrop that the psychological service in MOE HQ introduces the Tiered System of Support for SEN to all mainstream schools (see Figure 1).

The key ideas in the MOE's TSS framework resonate strongly with school-based frameworks for inclusive educational practices that have been established internationally, e.g., the School-based Community Intervention Framework (Goldman, 2010); and the Collaborative Strategic Planning Framework (Stollar *et al.*, 2006). The fundamental basis in the TSS framework is the assignment of the level of support to the students based on their observed needs, rather than diagnostic labels *per se*. This would allow support to be customised and catered to the students as well as ensure that resources within schools are efficiently and effectively utilised. Using this framework, students need not wait to be diagnosed before early help is given, and students with diagnoses but who are coping well and whose needs are adequately met by the class-teacher at Tier 1, do not get unduly highlighted for specialised attention.

The operationalisation of the TSS framework draws from the core principles of 'Response-To-Intervention' (Batsche *et al.*, 2005), which include the emphasis on using a problem-solving method to make decisions within a multi-tier model of service delivery, and to monitor students' progress to inform instructions and use data to make instructional and educational decisions. Hence, conceptually, the TSS framework is not totally new to the mainstream schools, rather it builds on and enhances the existing problem-solving approaches. More importantly, the TSS framework provides the structural mechanisms and school processes that are needed to enable the problem-solving approach to be effective.

Within the TSS structure, the role of the schools' Case Management Teams (CMTs) is critical in making clear and consistent decisions about assigning of students' needs and allocation of resources across the three tiers. Typically led by a member of the school leadership team, the school's CMT comprises key personnel in the school who are responsible for making decisions about support for students with SEN as well as those with additional needs, and oversee the implementation of the interventions. Psychologists from the psychological service in MOE HQ have a critical link with the CMTs in every school, and through regular meetings and training sessions, they have a role in developing the capacity of the CMTs in ensuring a robust and effective TSS-based intervention for SEN.

The implementation of the TSS framework for SEN to mainstream schools in Singapore is a work in progress and at times is unevenly operationalised across different schools. Beyond structures and capacity building, effective implementation of the TSS framework requires a significant change in the perceived relationship between the psychological service providers and individual schools. It is no longer where one is the 'expert problem-solver' and the other a 'client'. Rather, the relationship could be characterised as a strategic alliance between a 'school system' (be it of one school or a cluster of schools within a district), with a 'consultant' who facilitates data-based planning and problem solving, and provides training and technical assistance to stakeholders for SEN support in schools.

This relationship will also demand new sets of competencies for professionals, especially psychologists, who are involved in provision of psychological services for SEN in schools. Some of these competencies include knowledge and skills that may not be adequately emphasised in the traditional professional training courses for psychologists, for example, competencies relating to the provision of systems-based service delivery. This is an issue that is not unique to Singapore. For example, in its description of the system-based competencies for school psychologists, the NASP Blueprint III emphasised that school psychologists can no longer focus exclusively on intervening at the individual level but to the systems charged with addressing the learning problems of students so as to enhance student outcomes and build schools' capacity. This would include competencies in working with school leaders and school leadership teams to develop schools as safe, caring, inviting places where there is a sense of community, the contributions of all persons (e.g., families, teachers) are valued, and there are high expectations of excellence for all students, including students with SEN (Ysseldyke *et al.*, 2006).

It has been noted by several writers (e.g., Ysseldyke *et al.*, 2006; Bashste *et al.*, 2005) that the developmental opportunities in these competencies have not been widely available for many psychologists in many countries; this is also true for psychologists in Singapore. To be a competent 'systems-coach' and an influencer of schools' systems and processes, psychologists would require deep knowledge and understanding of the operational details of schools (i.e., how schools work), and how decisions are made in schools (i.e., how school leaders think). Additionally, the soft-skills of persuasion and negotiation are critical in order for psychologists to influence school leadership teams to recognise the need for changes and implement them in their schools. These competencies are typically not emphasised or adequately addressed in the local professional training programmes for psychologists. Consequently, many newly trained psychologists may find a frustrating gap between the basic skills and knowledge that they have post-training and the competencies required when working with schools.

Looking ahead, the role of psychologists serving students with SEN will continue to change and evolve rapidly. The systems approach necessitates a close working relationship between providers of psychological services and school leadership teams. An important alliance between these two professional groups is emerging which sees one strengthening the other with their respective knowledge of leadership and culture and practices among school leadership on the one hand, and knowledge and skills for delivery of school-based intervention for SEN on the other. Beyond school, with recent enhancements of SEN and disability support at institutions of higher learning and preschool years (UNCRPD, 2018), psychologists would need to be able to work more effectively alongside specialists from other fields. These changes mean that psychologists need to be able to work alongside other specialists and other personnel in MOE HQ to embed sound approaches to SEN across the system. Competencies for trans-disciplinary approaches are needed, and psychologists, even the relatively inexperienced ones, need to develop the dispositions and skills for collaborative work.

Thus, as the roles of providers of psychological services in Singapore evolve, a constant challenge is ensuring that local professional training programmes for psychologists are kept abreast of the wider systems change and updated in tandem with the new service demands.

Conclusion

In the last 30 years, the shape and focus of psychological services for children with SEN in mainstream schools have undergone significant changes. These waves of evolution are in tandem with the changes in the larger landscape of SEN support, as well as new developments in the practice of educational and school psychology internationally. Each wave of change brings new challenges, as well as opportunities. The different phases are not discrete; rather each reflects the most dominant approaches that have shaped or influenced the practice of psychologists serving school-going children in mainstream schools. What remains consistent is the need for the providers of psychological services of SEN, especially psychologists working with schools, to continually keep abreast with evidence-based practices, and remain flexible to respond to new demands of service delivery in an ever-evolving field. Availability of and access to appropriate professional development opportunities are vital, be it at initial training or continual professional development levels, to ensure that psychologists have the requisite competencies for the roles that they are expected to fulfil.

References

Aljunied, M. (2012). The child with special needs in the school-going years. In J. S. Y Tham-Toh, K. Lyen, & K. Poon (Eds.), *Rainbow Dreams* (3rd Edition). Singapore: Rainbow Centre.

Batsche, G., Elliott, J., Graden, J. L., Grimes, J., Kovaleski, J. F., Prasse, D., Schrag, J., & Tilly, W. D. (2005). *Response to Intervention: Policy Considerations and Implementations.* Alexandria, VA: National Association of State Directors of Special Education.

Deluca, M. (2003). Diversity, inclusion and equity: Insights from special needs provision. In *Education Policy Analysis.* OECD: Paris.

Deno, S. L. (2002). Problem solving as "best practice". In A. Thomas & J. Grimes (Eds.), *Best Practices in School Psychology IV* (pp. 37–56). Washington DC: National Association of School Psychologists.

Department for Education and Employment. (2000). Educational psychology services: Current role, good practices and future directions. In *Report on the Working Group.* Nottingham: DfEE Publications.

Frederickson, N., & Cline, T. (2009). *Special Educational Needs, Inclusion and Diversity* (2nd Edition). UK: McGraw Hill.

Fung, D. S., Lim, C. G., Wong, J. C. M., Ng, K. H., Cheok, C. C. S., Kiing, J. S. H., Chong, S. C., Lou, J., Daniel, M. L., Ong, D., Low, C., Aljunied, S. M., Choi, P. M., Mehrotra, K., Kee, C., Leung, I., Yen, L. C., Wong, G., Lee, P. Y., Chin, B., & Ng, H. C. (2014). Academy of Medicine-Ministry of Health clinical practice guidelines: Attention deficit hyperactivity disorder. *Singapore Medical Journal, 55*(8), 411–415.

Fung, D., Ong L. P., Tay, S. L., & Sim, W. H. (2013). *REACH Chronicles — a Community Mental Health Model for Children and Adolescents in Singapore. Singapore:* World Scientific.

Ho, L. Y. (2007). Child development programme in Singapore 1988 to 2007. *Annals of Academy of Medicine Singapore, 36*, 898–910.

Lian, W. B., Ho, S. K. Y., Choo, S. H. T., Shah, V. A., Chan, D. K. L., Yeo, C. L., & Ho, L. Y. (2012). Children with developmental and behavioural concerns in Singapore. *Singapore Medical Journal, 53*(7), 439–445.

Lim, C. G., Loh, H., Renjan, V., Tan, J., & Fung, D. (2017). Child community mental health services in Asia Pacific and Singapore's REACH Model. *Brain Sciences, 7*, 126. doi:10.3390/brainsci7100126

Marston, D., Muyskens, P., Lau, M., & Canter, A. (2003). Problem-solving model for decision making with high incidence disabilities. The

Minneapolis experience. *Learning Disabilities Research & Practice, 18*, 187–200.

Ministry of Education (MOE). (2018). Professional practice guidelines: Psycho-educational assessment and placement for students with special educational needs. Retrieved from https://www.moe.gov.sg/docs/default-source/document/education/special-education/files/professional-practice-guidelines.pdf

Ministry of Education (MOE). (2019). Provisions and support in mainstream schools. Retrieved from https://www.moe.gov.sg/education/special-education/mainstream-schools#Provisions-and-Support-in-Mainstream-Schools

Monsen, J., Graham, B., Frederickson, N., & Cameron, R. J. (1998). Problem analysis and professional training in educational psychology: An accountable model of practice. *Educational Psychology in Practice, 13*(4), 234–244.

National Archives of Singapore (NAS). (2004). PM Lee Hsien Loong Swearing In Ceremony Speech. Retrieved from http://www.nas.gov.sg/archivesonline/data/pdfdoc/20040812-PMO.pdf

National Archives of Singapore (NAS). (2006). PM Lee Hsien Loong Teacher's Day Rally Speech. Retrieved from https://www.nas.gov.sg/archivesonline/data/pdfdoc/20040812-PMO.pdf

National Archives of Singapore (NAS). (2018). Parliamentary Debates Singapore Official Report 2018, Volume 24, Number 81. Retrieved from https://www.nas.gov.sg/archivesonline/data/pdfdoc/20180806015/WQ-6Aug2018.pdf

Poon, K. K., & Cohen, L. (2008). Assessing students with special needs: Applications in Singapore schools. In K. K. Poon, J. Khaw & J. Y. Li (Eds.), *Supporting Students with Special Needs in Mainstream Schools*. Singapore: Pearson, Prentice Hall.

Poon, K., Musti-Rao, S., & Wettasinghe, M. (2013). Special education in Singapore: History, trends, and future directions. *Intervention in School and Clinic, 49*(1), 59–64.

Robinson, V. M. J. (1993). *Problem-based Methodology: Research for the Improvement of Practices*. Oxford: Pergamon.

Stobie, I., Boyle, J., & Woolfson, L. (2005). Solution-focused approaches in the practice of educational psychologists: A study of the nature of their applications and evidence of their effectiveness. *School Psychology International, 26*(1), 5–28.

Stollar, S. A., Poth, R. L., Curtis, M. J., & Cohen, R. M. (2006). Collaborative strategic planning as illustration of principles of systems change. *School Psychology Review*, 35(2), 181–197. doi: 10.1080/02796015.2006.12087986. Retrieved from http://www.nasponline.org/publications/spr/pdf/spr 352stollar.pdf

Tan, A. G. (2002). Development of psychology in Singapore: Some perspectives. In A. G. Tan & M. Gog (Eds.), *Psychology in Singapore: Issues of an emerging Discipline*. Singapore: McGraw Hill Education.

Tham-Toh, J., Yuen, S., Lyen, K., Poon, K., Lee, E. G., & Pathnapuram, M. (2012). *Rainbow Dreams — a Holistic Approach to Helping Children with Special Needs* (3rd Edition). Singapore: Armour Publishing.

Tilly, W. D., Reschly, D. J., & Grimes, J. (1999). Disability determination in problem-solving systems: Conceptual foundations and critical components. In D. J. Reschly, W. D. Tilly, & J. P. Grimes (Eds.), *Special Education in Transition: Functional Assessment and Noncategorical Programming* (pp. 221–254). Longmont, CO: Sopris West.

Wagner, P. (1995). *School Consultation: A Handbook for Practising Educational Psychologists*. London Borough of Kensington and Chelsea: Educational Psychology Consultation Service.

Weerasinghe, D., Ong K. W., & Cockburn, L. (2002). Development of educational psychology in Singapore: Some perspectives. In A. G. Tan & M. Goh (Eds.), *Psychology in Singapore: Issues of an Emerging Discipline*. Singapore: McGraw-Hill Education.

Ysseldyke, J. E., Burns, M., Dawson, P., Kelley, B., Morrison, D., Ortiz, S., Rosenfield, S., & Telzrow, C. (2006). *School Psychology: A Blueprint for Training and Practice III*. Retrieved from https://www-s3-live.kent.edu/s3fs-root/s3fs-public/file/Blueprint%20NASP%20III_0.pdf

CHAPTER 9

Differentiation: Providing for Students with Special Needs in Mixed Ability Classrooms

Letchmi Devi Ponnusamy

ೞ

Introduction

The dual economic forces of globalization and the knowledge economy have resulted in a networked, knowledge-driven world (Giddens, 2002). At the same time, such connections have resulted in a more informed populace that recognises that schools are inhabited by learners with dissimilar readiness levels and interests, and that public institutions need to work to address diversity (Cole, 2008; Friend & Pope, 2005). This focus on real world expectations and greater inclusivity in classrooms affects the work of teachers (Schumm & Avalos, 2009). Teachers now need to be aware of and work in increasingly diverse classrooms, while they promote and contextualise learning for a wide range of abilities and interests (Perez, 2013). This is true for larger nations such as the USA and Europe as much as for small nation states like Singapore. However, while research has found that mixed ability classrooms can be empowering for both the learner and the teacher (Boaler, Wiliam & Brown, 2000; Reid *et al.*, 1981), there is little knowledge about how teachers could go about planning and teaching in such complex contexts. This chapter explores this conundrum, suggesting that while differentiation is seen as a good thing, the task of doing this is a complex challenge for the teacher, especially in the midst of educational systems that have high stakes examinations.

This chapter firstly explores the historical contexts and current trends in differentiation and mixed ability teaching, looking at the international environment and then focusing on Singapore. It also considers how greater inclusion of learners with special educational needs (SEN) into the mainstream classroom is very challenging for teachers. It then presents a working model of teachers' implicit attempts at differentiation and the resources that they relied on to manage the everyday demand of meeting different learners' needs. The elements of the model, developed from a study of how secondary school teachers dealt with teaching in mixed ability classes (Ponnusamy, 2010), is then discussed, with an explication of the kinds of resources and specific strategies teachers used in their efforts at differentiation. The chapter ends with a discussion of the merits of embracing a working model for differentiation, arguing that this engenders teacher agency with respect to dealing with the current calls for greater inclusivity in their classrooms. Finally, the chapter proposes that using a working model for differentiation during professional conversations at workshops and in learning communities enhances teachers' attempts at inclusion as it deepens teachers understanding of their decisions and actions, which could otherwise remain dormant and untapped.

Mixed Ability Teaching: International and Local Contexts

In almost every school, regardless of the national contexts, learners are grouped according to age and grades. Hargreaves (2003) points out that the division of classes into age and grades has allowed schools and teachers to make assumptions about student's prior knowledge and skills, and this has arguably resulted in the adoption and acceptance of transmission-based pedagogy as a way to teach everyone. In such pedagogy, the emphasis is on creating habits through rote and drill to enable learners to acquire the appropriate content and procedures so that they can achieve in tests. Porter and Brophy (1988) point out that such a transmission-based model of instruction often results in little or no instructional or resource adaptation to the needs of specific learners and contexts, giving rise to the 'one-size-fits–all' curriculum and teaching. However, Hargreaves points out this 'factory floor model' of teaching is not suited to our future needs. In fact, teachers are expected to embrace diversity amongst students, rather than treating it superficially (Darling-Hammond & Friedlaender, 2008) and adopt a more complex idea of learning, that of learners being active participants, creators of knowledge and seekers of engaging, personal experiences during lessons (McLoughlin & Lee, 2008).

Local educational initiatives and the mixed ability movement in Singapore

Much of the teaching in Singapore has been centered on the need for learners to acquire the fundamental knowledge and skills required to perform in national examinations (Deng, Gopinathan & Lee, 2013). Tracking or streaming has been used traditionally to customise education for students of different abilities at the end of primary schools in Singapore and began as a policy initiative in 1979 to reduce attrition rates and ensure learners complete secondary education (Goh, 1979). The streams offered different curricula and longer education pathways, so that more learners had the opportunity to leave school with minimum educational qualifications and therefore gain suitable employment (Gopinathan, 2001). Since its inception, the three-decade long streaming policy has been tweaked numerous times, and is now focused at the secondary level, where at the end of primary school, learners are streamed into three different tracks based on an overall aggregate score obtained at the Primary School Leaving Examinations (PSLE). Learners are placed into four different streams according to ability[1] (Goh & Gopinathan, 2008). The streams differ in terms of lengths of secondary education, curricula and expected higher education trajectories. Students sit for different national examinations, referred to as the General Certificate of Education examinations[2], or GCEs in short, at the end of secondary school, and their performance determines their entry to higher education, vocational training or employment.

Streaming has been a cornerstone of the local education system, and proponents point out that it is instrumental in Singapore having one of the highest secondary school graduation rates in the world (OECD, 2011). However, critics have pointed out that streaming has created a rigid educational pathway (Yuen, 2020). To the system's credit, the streaming policy has been constantly tweaked to address such criticism. One such change was in 2004 where students in Normal (Academic) stream were allowed to offer up to two GCE (O) level subjects at Secondary 4 and sit for these examinations at the end of the fourth instead of the fifth year (Ministry of Education, 2006; Teo, 2000). This was justified on the grounds that more than 90 per cent of the Sec 4N (Academic) students, who took (O) level subjects from 2001 to 2004, passed the examinations, with over 25 per cent of students scoring distinctions (Shanmugaratnam, 2004). Besides this, greater flexibility in pathways was also introduced to allow students who scored well to move to another stream that was considered academically more challenging. Schools were given more autonomy in deciding how to best create transition points between academic streams in the secondary level, so that late developers could move to "academically rigorous streams that allow them

---

[1] The four streams are the Normal-Technical, Normal-Academic, Express and Special respectively. The streams offered increasing academic challenge, so that Express stream subjects dealt with content that is more complex. The T-score, a statistically computed composite score that compares the total mark scored by the pupil against the performance of the entire cohort for that year, is used to place students into different streams.

[2] These are jointly drawn up by the Ministry of Education in Singapore and University of Cambridge International Examinations Syndicate.

to take more academically complex subjects and complete secondary school in a shorter time" (Shanmugaratnam, 2006).

However, despite these adjustments, streaming and the over emphasis on performance is seen to be detrimental to learners in many ways. For a start, instructional priority is placed on covering the syllabus and churning out efficient test-takers. Research about the instructional practices in local classrooms has found that teachers tended to focus on factual and procedural knowledge, and knowledge transmission (Hogan *et al.*, 2013; Kaur & Yap, 1997). Hogan *et al.* (2013) referred to these instructional practices as having a "performative orientation to instruction" (p. 57), where teachers placed more emphasis on covering the national syllabus. The teacher-student interaction was reported to be predominantly initiation-response-evaluate/feedback (IRE/IRF) (Coulthard & Sinclair, 2013; Mehan, 1979), with limited opportunities for students to participate in expression and deliberation of key ideas. The exceptional performance of Singapore students in international comparative studies (Martin, Mullis & Hooper, 2016; OECD, 2016) have led some observers to caution against removing streaming and performative pedagogies completely or seeing them as having no value in building understanding and increasing educational attainment.

However, recent social commentary has pointed to other systemic issues for the weak learners. Some point out that streaming as an educational differentiation tool is too blunt, as it does not help teachers determine the real needs of weaker learners and late developers. At the same time, the curriculum offered to learners in the Normal (Academic) and Normal (Technical) streams are consistently less challenging, as simplified content is offered in the Mathematics, Languages, Science or Humanities. There are concerns that such over-simplification of content does not serve these learners in the future, as they are effectively locked out of university pathways, resulting in further disenfranchisement with the educational process and reduced life and career potential. There are also concerns that tracking results in labelling by other stakeholders and that when it is internalised by the learners, may result in reduced self-esteem, such that they see themselves as less able or failures (Mokhtar, 2019).

In an effort to refine the system, MOE recently announced that full subject-based banding (SBB) will be rolled out as a replacement to the current streaming process in secondary schools by 2024 (Ong, 2019). The SBB is seen as an attempt to reduce the negative socio-emotional impact of streaming and provide a more level playing field for all learners (Ong, 2019). Firstly, full SBB will involve getting learners to be banded by subjects, rather than the current practice of streaming learners by their total scores. Hence, all Secondary 1 students in the 2024 batch will take subjects at three levels — G1, G2 or G3, with G standing for 'General'. The new SBB grouping arrangement will arguably result in classrooms that are more diverse. This is because, while the SBB will allow learners who show capacity in one subject to be placed together, the concerns of these learners in terms of what they might want to do with the subject in terms of higher education or employment will be very different.

The pace of learning in the Express stream is generally faster, and teachers in such classrooms traditionally focus on learners achieving high scores in examinations. However, with full SBB, even where students with strengths in a subject are banded together, their pace of learning might differ widely. Thus, teaching in the SBB environment will demand greater differentiation on the part of the teacher, as they have to take different intellectual capacities and cognitive abilities into consideration. At the same time, diversity in classrooms in Singapore schools today has also been heightened by recent moves to make classrooms more inclusive to SEN learners. Clearly, meeting the needs of learners with SEN through inclusivity is putting a new dimension to mixed ability teaching, and therefore placing a greater spotlight on differentiation.

Addressing SEN in Mainstream Education: The Relevance of Mixed Ability Teaching

Educational inclusion, where learners with SEN are given the same opportunities in education, is a worldwide phenomenon. The concept of SEN is an umbrella term, describing a wide range of difficulties which may impair children's ability to achieve during their time in school (Stakes & Hornby, 2012). Although the phrase is relatively new, awareness of the problems faced by such children in school has been widespread (Fuchs & Fuchs, 1994; Slee, 2008). Given that legally, the term 'Special Educational Needs' refers to learning problems or disabilities that can impede learning, inclusion has placed the ball squarely in the teacher's court. In the UK, the Warnock Report (Warnock Committee, 1978) was an important milestone in the development of education for children with SEN, whereas in the United States, meeting the needs of SEN learners in the mainstream classroom was made mandatory in 1975 via the Education for All Handicapped Children Act (EAHCA)(Congress, 1975).

The idea behind such inclusion is that as different groups learn, play and grow together, they learn to value one another. Provisioning for pupils with SEN in mainstream schools has developed gradually over the years around the world (Avramidis & Norwich, 2002), and in the local context, 2004 was a turning point for inclusion in schools. Prime Minister Lee Hsien Loong instated an inclusion policy in all public institutions, including schools that would ensure "all communities will progress and no one will be left behind..." (Lee, 2004). Thus, the five-year Enabling Masterplan (Steering Committee on the Enabling Masterplan, 2007) put forth six key recommendations, which included development and training of staff in mainstream schools and an intentional focus on transition planning and management within schools to support the life-long needs of the SEN learner. The main teacher-training institute in Singapore, The National Institute of Education, in consultation with the Ministry of Education, has since 2005 created and conducted specific programmes, such as the Teachers Trained in Special Needs (TSN) and the Diploma in Special Education (DISE) for Allied Educators (LBS).[3]

However, while educational inclusion has been hailed as a milestone, teachers have to teach in classrooms that are more mixed in

---

[3] For Allied Educators, who provide much needed support for learners with SEN in school, the DISE also offers the alternative Allied Educator-Learning and Behavioral Support (AED-LBS) certification course.

terms of ability, particularly when they have to address the needs of learners with SEN. This is indeed a major issue in mainstream schools, as evidence points to teachers struggling with managing lesson activities so that learners with SEN are better integrated with typical learners (Yeo, Chong, Neihart, & Huan, 2016). Researchers point out that the support offered to teachers working in mainstream schools to be inclusive is not deep and comprehensive enough, with factors such as the short duration of training (the Diploma is only one year long) and the traditional emphasis on achievement in mainstream education rather than on learning (Walker & Musti-Rao, 2016; Yeo *et al.*, 2013). Preservice teachers' views of inclusion are also limited by their experiences and prior training with persons with disabilities (Thaver, Lim & Liau, 2014), and since such teachers are products of the achievement-focused mainstream culture, they would indeed feel challenged by the expectations of inclusion.

Yet, the Ministry of Education sets out that 80 per cent of SEN students, or 24,000 students, including those with sensory and physical impairments, currently attend mainstream schools in Singapore (Toh, 2018). Thus, there is a need to provide greater support for teachers to address multiple learners' needs as they go about their work and to examine additional factors which influence the formation of positive attitudes towards inclusion (Avramidis & Norwich, 2002; Stakes & Hornby, 2012). The most important role of teachers at the primary school level is to identify children who are experiencing difficulties at school. Identification of such difficulties is the vital first step. At the same time, in building greater support for teachers to address multiple learners' needs, a more specific way by which they can actually go about differentiation would be more invaluable. There is a clear need for a more holistic model of how teachers can get a chance to reflect on their own practices.

Research on Teaching in Mixed Ability Classrooms

A review of the literature about teaching in mixed ability classes point to several large-scale comparative studies that investigated the effect of different types of grouping practices across different subjects[4]. Hallam and Ireson (2005) carried out a multi-school study involving 1,500 teachers from 45 British secondary schools where they compared teachers' practices across three types of class groupings: mixed-ability, partially streamed (along two subjects only) and completely streamed (in more than four subjects). Based on data collected through questionnaires, classroom observations and interviews with Mathematics, Science and English teachers, they found that less differentiation of pedagogical practices occurred in mixed ability classes. Struggling learners in mixed ability classes were found to receive more opportunities for repetition and rehearsal, more structured work, more practical work, less homework with less detailed feedback, and less access to the curriculum compared to their more able peers. Pace wise, the lessons in mixed ability classes also proceeded slowly when compared to streamed and partially streamed ones. Teachers who taught both mixed-ability and homogenous classes reported that their classroom practices differed significantly, and therefore it was concluded that class grouping patterns led teachers to change their teaching practices rather than their own personal teaching styles. This therefore pointed to significantly different patterns of instruction that teachers used in mixed ability classes, although the study did not indicate how the specific instructional strategies were used by the teachers to manage teaching different students in such classes.

In a similar study, Smith and Sutherland (2003) compared the instructional practices of 30 English, Mathematics, Science and Modern Languages classes (both tracked and de-tracked) from different schools in Scotland. The study reported that class work was more purposeful and focused in tracked classes. Whole class teaching occurred in both tracked and de-tracked classes. However, in this study, the researchers found that teachers in both heterogeneous and homogenous classes used small group teaching and individual tuition as much as whole class teaching. This implies that a 'one size-fits-all'

---

[4] In research, the terms 'streaming' and 'tracking' were used interchangeably, whilst classes that were mixed ability were termed "de-tracked".

method of instruction was not useful, and that teachers needed to differentiate the instruction further in both types of classes. Both groups of teachers reported that including strategies such as providing more learner encouragement, employing support staff and incorporating independent learning opportunities resulted in greater student learning during direct teaching sessions. However, the teachers working in mixed ability classes indicated they were acutely aware of the range of abilities within their classes and modified direct instruction to cater to the greater diversity. Teachers also reported tensions when teaching mixed ability classes, specifically pointing to their inability to cater adequately to everyone and uncertainty with how to motivate slower pupils in these classes.

Humphrey *et al.* (2006) analysed semi-structured interview data obtained from five primary school teachers teaching in mixed ability classrooms, and found that teachers adopted more inclusive attitudes even as they facilitated greater inclusivity and solidarity in pupils. Two significant themes: the building of collaborative networks and the use of 'responsive' teaching, described specific teaching strategies that enables the teachers. Other studies that looked at mixed ability teaching identified the selective use of teacher- and learner-centered instructional methods as well as providing support for student learning (Hootstein, 1999; Xanthou & Pavlou, 2008; Zimmerman & Dibenedetto, 2008). Some of the studies found that teachers were expected to think about the content depth and breadth and appropriate strategies to use as they planned and carried out their lessons in mixed ability classes (Watanabe *et al.*, 2007; Xanthou & Pavlou, 2008).

It must also be pointed out that researchers also recognise that teachers face challenges in carrying out such instruction (Darling-Hammond & Friedlaender, 2008; Villegas & Lucas, 2002). Teachers have to possess a deeper understanding of the learner (Brown *et al.*, 1993) and have to apprehend what the learner holds as background knowledge (Cochran-Smith, 2004). In addition to this, managing learning in a complex environment requires the development of a culture of learning with specific relations between the teacher, the learner, the subject and conceptions of learning held by both teacher and learner (Watkins & Mortimore, 1999).

Clearly, teaching in a diverse environment calls for more from the teacher and the studies discussed so far have pointed to some of these multiple challenges. The educational trend of providing for the learner with SEN within mainstream schools has thrust mixed ability pedagogies such as differentiation and pedagogical conversations into the limelight. This is especially so in the Singapore context.

Gaps in addressing mixed abilities teaching

Despite looking at the practices of teachers in mixed ability classrooms, few studies have documented the processes and experiences of teachers designing and implementing lessons in mixed ability classes. Research about instructional processes (Good & Brophy, 2002; Lieberman & Miller, 1984) has shown that classroom teaching is complex. In mixed ability classes, ensuring that lessons are tailored to meet every learner's needs all the time is more challenging. In order to improve pedagogy, researchers (Berliner, 2001; Moon, 2004) point out that a clearer understanding of the principles that teachers use to keep learners engaged and of the strategies that work well is needed. Specifically, Tomlinson (2008) points out that we do not have a clear picture of how instructional differentiation is carried out to suit learner readiness, interest and profiles, mirroring an earlier call by Rios (1996), who argues for the development of practitioner-relevant teaching theory or model that united the dimensions of teachers' action with classroom learning. This gap in the research is addressed by the local model described below.

A Local Model to Understand Mixed Ability Teaching

Given that teaching in mixed ability contexts is complex, researchers point out that developing a model requires a nuanced exposition of how teachers decide and act on the many decisions they make in order to manage learners with diverse knowledge, readiness levels and interests (Good & Brophy, 2002; Lieberman & Miller, 1984). An overarching schema therefore could be developed from retrospectively studying the types of knowledge and strategies teachers use

Figure 1: A working model of teaching in mixed ability classrooms

and the decisions that are made during practice. Such an approach is utilised in a local study (Ponnusamy, 2010) and the resultant working model of teachers' decisions and actions in the context of teaching in mixed ability classes is shown in Figure 1 above.

Figure 1 highlights the dynamic links that exist between the three significant themes that are identified in this study about how teachers dealt with mixed ability teaching. The first theme of 'building knowledge' represents the tacit compiling and storing of information about learners that teachers gained during classroom interaction and when assessing learners' work. The second theme refers to the active use of three strategies, i.e., pitching, scaffolding and remediation that the secondary school teachers in the sample used to enable learning in diverse classrooms. The third theme signifies the tensions that teachers face as they go about dealing with the diverse class. This last theme is unique, as it picks out tensions as an end-product of the teachers' reflection of what they feel is not going well in the mixed ability classroom. Hence, dealing with mixed ability teaching is a process where teachers interact with and assist learners in a dynamic manner, utilising several bits of information.

Put simply, Figure 1 illustrates a working model of differentiation and how this might take place in mixed ability teaching contexts. The interaction between the three elements draws a link between the problem finding and problem solving agentic behaviour that exists in teachers' work (Berliner, 2001). It is argued that the complex context of mixed ability classrooms generates conditions that require the teachers to make sense of the complex stimuli that then allows them to develop maps of specific knowledge. Being mindful of the tensions that they face with differing needs, the teachers in this study then reflect agentic behaviours so that they could make the lessons qualitatively different for each learner. Thus, this framework allows practitioners to be mindful of the complex interactions that mixed ability classrooms engender and that it requires them to be adaptive and reflective. It also draws attention to the kinds of knowledge and strategies that are utilised when teachers differentiate in mixed ability contexts, which is discussed in detail next.

How the Working Model of Differentiation Can Inform Teachers' Work

Building knowledge

The working model of differentiation in Figure 1 presents a clear pattern of interaction between knowledge, action and reflective thought when teachers work in mixed ability classes. This pattern means that teachers collect specific types of knowledge and employ a finite set of strategies to ensure that all learners are able to achieve significant gains in learning. In terms of knowledge types, a wide range are identified as being significant in teaching in mixed ability classes. The notion of teachers requiring a more nuanced set of knowledge bases was first conceptualised by Shulman (1987). Specifically, Shulman posits the idea of pedagogical content knowledge (PCK) as the blending of content and pedagogy into an

Table 1: Types of teacher knowledge used in mixed ability teaching (Ponnusamy, 2010)

Commonly used in the study	Less commonly mentioned
Substantive Knowledge About Teaching The Subject And Education System	Syntactic Knowledge
Knowledge About Common Beliefs About The Subject	Curriculum Knowledge
General Pedagogical Knowledge	Knowledge/ Models Of Teaching
Knowledge Of Contexts	Knowledge Of Educational Ends
Knowledge Of Learners: Empirically Gained	Knowledge Of Self
Knowledge Of Learners: Cognitive	

understanding of how particular aspects of subject matter are organised, adapted and represented for instruction. Later theorists have also postulated the differentiated, subject specific and dynamic nature of teacher knowledge (Hashweh, 2005; Tsui, 2003; Turner-Bisset, 1999, 2001). Turner-Bisset's (2001) representation of PCK in expert teachers theorises a multi-layered, dynamic model of PCK made up of all 11 parts as shown in Table 1.

However, the study has found that specific types of knowledge are more commonly used by the teachers during mixed ability teaching, as is shown in Table 1. Specifically, teachers point to the key role that empirical observation of the learners' interests, learning preferences and cognitive abilities has on their work. Clearly, observations made in direct or indirect interaction with the children provides the teachers with a store of background knowledge that the teachers use to understand what their learners could do. Given the complex, multifaceted and situated nature of this knowledge, it will be difficult to prescribe to teachers what they should 'collect'. However, the implication of this finding is that there is a need for teachers to be inveterate pupil watchers in the classroom as they teach. They should be encouraged to take note of their empirical observations and use this knowledge in their practice. This expertise, i.e., the acquisition and formatting of a complex map of learners' empirical and cognitive knowledge, is crucial to appropriate pitching. Magnusson, Krajcik and Borko (1999) point out that teachers with differentiated and integrated knowledge will have greater ability than those whose knowledge is limited and fragmented to plan and enact lessons that help students develop deep and integrated understandings. Thus, within the mixed ability classroom, the teacher arms herself not only with knowing what each person knows, but also how each persons' ability and interests differs. Thus, her knowledge map is fluid, growing with future interaction with the class. This fluid knowledge map enables the teacher to differentiate instruction.

Other studies have also reported a similar interactive pattern in teachers gathering specific types of knowledge about students' skills and thinking when teaching in mixed ability classes. Bartolo *et al.* (2005) report that teachers gain and use knowledge from a wide range of sources such as test scores, self-reports, school records and teacher observations. Smith and Sutherland (2003) also find that teachers working in mixed ability classes are exceptional in this respect, as they find that their primary school teacher-participants are constantly adjusting when working in mixed ability, semi-streamed and completely streamed classes.

Strategy choice and use

Clearly, dealing with teaching in mixed ability classes requires the skill of identifying and matching strategies to learning needs. Puntambekar and Kolodner (2005) point out that in a dynamic and complex classroom environment, one scaffold is usually not sufficient in achieving a learning goal. Instead, researchers argue that a complex interaction of multiple scaffolds is used by teachers when they teach in diverse classrooms (Kolodner *et al.*, 2003; Puntambekar & Hubscher, 2005; Puntambekar & Kolodner, 2005; Tabak, 2004). Investigations of teachers in this Singaporean study has found that teachers rely on the strategy of pitching, scaffolding and remediation to manage mixed ability teaching. In terms of scaffolding, a range of scaffolds is employed each time rather than just one, so that multiple needs are met. One such set of scaffolds used in one mixed ability class in shown in Figure 2 below.

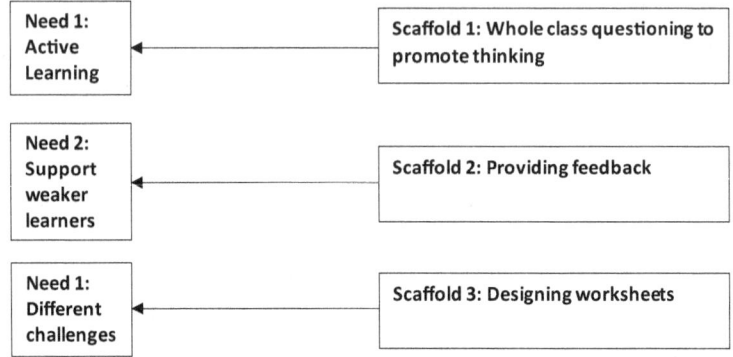

Figure 2: Strategies and scaffolding when teaching in mixed ability classrooms

Figure 2 shows, as Grumbine and Alden (2006) found, that a multiple strategy implementation approach is best suited to meet different needs in the mixed ability classroom. Hence, while Scaffold 1 of "Whole Class Questioning" is used, Scaffolds 2 and 3 are needed to achieve wider gains. This fits in with recommendations made in learner-centered lessons where higher order thinking processes (Biggs, 1999), in-class discussions (Weld, 2002) and questioning and feedback (Weimer, 2002) are advocated. However, more significantly, teachers working in mixed ability classes report that it has taken them time to figure out selectively the order of scaffolding needed, and that once this is done, it enhances their efforts at ensuring learning takes place for all learners.

While the teachers in this study use a variety of strategies to manage mixed ability teaching, it must also be noted that learning is "enhanced when teachers recognise and teach to diverse learning styles and strengths" (Grumbine & Alden, 2006, p. 27). The teachers mention that they often have to use one strategy to address the educational difficulties that the learners have, and another one when preparing them for examination achievement. This is difficult and the indication in the working model of the tensions faced by teacher points to this problem, especially that of the demand of having to use multiple strategies each time to help diverse learners (Ponnusamy, 2010).

Teachers also constantly face issues of figuring out who has learned in mixed ability classrooms. Marble, Finley and Ferguson

(2000) find that determining if learning truly happens in the classroom is a significant tension for teachers and that this tension has two dimensions. In most cases, teachers constantly deliberate if learning is best achieved by knowledge transmission or knowledge construction during lessons. The other tension teachers face is doubts about whether learning is best supported by a didactic or facilitative teacher role. Clearly, teachers' tension is indicative of deeper issues that go beyond instructional decisions. The teachers in this study have to make decisions constantly about the optimal methods to bring about learning so that they are able to allow learners to achieve examination success. The task of designing learning experiences in the mixed ability classroom therefore requires the teacher to apprehend the varying readiness levels of the learners, manage different levels of teacher-learner interactions and meet educational outcomes. Such demands require teachers to be more observant in determining what the learners could do and this then led to the building up of more knowledge. The working model in Figure 1 therefore depicts differentiation as a cyclical process.

Meeting SEN needs in mixed ability contexts

This working model has shown that differentiation can happen implicitly as a dynamic process. The three distinct dimensions: the building of knowledge, trialling strategies and identifying and addressing tensions, interact during differentiation. Such a model offers important insights about how teachers can differentiate for learners with SEN in diverse classrooms. In preparing lessons that would meet the needs of all learners, teachers' decisions should come from knowledge that is progressively built over time. This store of knowledge is drawn from observations of the learners during lessons as well as some background knowledge of the learners in general. This sets up an imperative for how teachers can be helped to ensure greater differentiation. Teachers need to be provided with tools to build up a map of the needs of the learners through formal and informal channels. There also should be a way for such knowledge to be updated and shared. While this might seem like an onerous task for one teacher to do, the idea is to set up a system for the knowledge to grow organically through pedagogical conversations teachers can have with their peers as they plan and implement lessons.

Planning the conversations around questions about how learners are learning should help teachers build a credible store of knowledge. In as far as helping teachers' use a range of strategies, schools and departments could start by creating a less threatening environment where teachers are open to adopting innovative teaching practices and sharing them with others. This increases teacher inquiry and builds on their adaptive capacity. Finally, encouraging mindful attention to and careful observation of how learning is taking place, it would create spaces for teachers to identify tensions in how they are able to meet learners' needs. Such mindful attention to detail and open inquiry are crucial to enabling greater differentiation for SEN learners during mixed ability teaching.

Conclusion

To conclude, while teaching in mixed ability environments can challenge the teacher and help them to understand the craft and technique of differentiation, using a model allows teachers to investigate their actions and decisions openly. This chapter has illustrated how differentiation can be seen as a cyclical process that incorporates the everyday work of teachers that involve strategy choice and implementation with that of studying how this affects the learners and creating a fluid knowledge base about the learner. Once the teacher is able to see differentiation as a workable process and succeed at its implementation, their appreciation for differentiated instruction will grow. This will ultimately be a win-win situation for both the teacher and the learners.

References

Avramidis, E., & Norwich, B. (2002). Teachers' attitudes towards integration/inclusion: A review of the literature. *European Journal of Special Needs Education, 17*(2), 129–147.

Bartolo, P., Humphrey, N., Lous, A. M., & Wetso, G. M. (2005). European teachers' concerns and experiences in responding to diversity in the classroom. Paper presented at the 30th Annual Conference of Association for Teacher Education in Europe, Amsterdam. Retrieved from http://www.atee2005.nl/download/papers/04_ac.pdf

Berliner, D. (2001). Learning about and learning from expert teachers. *International Journal of Educational Research, 35*(5), 463–482.

Biggs, J. B. (1999). What the student does: Teaching for enhanced learning. *Higher Education Research & Development, 18*(1), 57–75.

Boaler, J., Wiliam, D., & Brown, M. (2000). Students' experiences of ability grouping — dDsaffection, polarisation and the construction of failure. *British Educational Research Journal, 26*(5), 631–648. doi:10.1080/713651583

Brown, A., Ash, D., Rutherford, M., Nakagawa, K., Gordon, A., & Campione, J. C. (1993). Distributed expertise in the classroom. In G. Saloman (Ed.), *Distributed cognition: Psychological and educational considerations*, Cambridge, UK: Cambridge University Press.

Cochran-Smith, M. (2004). *Walking the road: Race, diversity, and social justice in teacher education.* New York: Teachers College Press. New York: Routledge.

Cole, R.W. (2008). *Educating Everybody's Children: Diverse Teaching Strategies for Diverse Learners.* Alexandria: VA: ASCD.

Coulthard, M., & Sinclair, J. (2013). Towards an analysis of discourse. In *Advances in Spoken Discourse Analysis* (pp. 7–40). New York: Routledge.

Darling-Hammond, L., & Friedlaender, D. (2008). Creating excellence and equitable schools. *Educational Leadership, 65*(8), 14–21.

Deng, Z., Gopinathan, S., & Lee, C. K. E. (2013). The Singapore curriculum: Convergence, divergence, issues and challenges. In Z. Deng, S. Gopinathan, & C. K. E. Lee (Eds.), *Globalisation and the Singapore Curriculum* (pp. 263–275). Singapore: Springer.

Friend, M., & Pope, K. L. (2005). Creating schools in which all students can succeed. *Kappa Delta Pi Record, 41*(2), 56–61.

Fuchs, D., & Fuchs, L. S. (1994). Inclusive schools movement and the radicalization of special education reform. *Exceptional Children, 60*(4), 294–309.

Giddens, A. (2002). *Runaway World: How Globalisation is Reshaping our Lives* (Second Edition). London: Profile Books Ltd.

Goh, C. B., & Gopinathan, S. (2008). Education in Singapore: Developments since 1965. In B. Fredriksen & T.J. Peng (Eds.), *An African Exploration of the East Asian Experience.* Washington D.C.: The World Bank.

Goh, K. S. (1979). *Report on the Ministry of Education 1978*. Singapore: Singapore National Printers.

Good, T. L., & Brophy, J. (2002). *Looking into Classrooms* (9th Ed.). Boston: Allyn & Bacon.

Gopinathan, S. (2001). Globalisation, the state and education policy in Singapore. In M. Bray & W.O. Lee (Eds.), *Education and Political Transition: Themes and Experiences in East Asia* (pp. 21–36). Hong Kong: Comparative Education Research Centre (CERC).

Grumbine, R., & Alden, P. B. (2006). Teaching science to students with learning disabilities. *The Science Teacher, 73*(3), 26–31.

Hallam, S., & Ireson, J. (2005). Secondary school teachers' pedagogic practices when teaching mixed and structured ability classes. *Research Papers in Education, 20*(1), 3–24.

Hargreaves, A. (2003). *Teaching in the Knowledge Society: Education in the Age of Insecurity*. New York: Teachers College Press.

Hashweh, M. Z. (2005). Teacher pedagogical constructions: A reconfiguration of pedagogical content knowledge. *Teachers and Teaching: Theory and Practice, 11*(3), 273–292.

Hogan, D., Chan, M., Rahim, R., Kwek, D., Khin, M. A., Loo, S. C., ... Luo, W. (2013). Assessment and the logic of instructional practice in secondary 3 English and Mathematics classrooms in Singapore. *Review of Education, 1*(1), 57–106. doi:10.1002/rev3.3002

Hootstein, E. (1999). Differentiation of instructional methodologies in social studies at the secondary level. *Journal of Social Studies Research 23*(1), 11.

Humphrey, N., Bartolo, P., Ale, P., Calleja, C., Hofsaess, T., Janikova, V., ... Wetso, G. M. (2006). Understanding and responding to diversity in the primary classroom: An international study. *European Journal of Teacher Education, 29*(3), 305–318.

Kaur, B., & Yap, S. F. (1997). *Kassel Project (NIE-Exeter Joint Study) Second Phase*. Singapore: National Institute of Education.

Kolodner, J. L., Camp, P. J., Crismond, D., Fasse, B., Gray, J., Holbrook, J., ... Ryan, M. (2003). Problem-based learning meets case-based reasoning in the middle-school science classroom: Putting learning by design (tm) into practice. *Journal of the Learning Sciences, 12*(4), 495–547.

Lee, H. L. (2004). *Our future of opportunity and promise*. Speech presented at the National Day Rally 2004 at the University Cultural Centre, National University Of Singapore on 22 August 2004. Retrieved 30 June 2017, from National Archives of Singapore http://www.nas.gov.sg/archivesonline/speeches/view-html?filename=2004083101.htm.

Lieberman, A., & Miller, L. (1984). *Teachers, Their World, and Their Work.* Virginnia: Association for Curriculum Development.

Magnusson, S., Krajcik, J. S., & Borko, H. (1999). Pedagogical content knowledge: An introduction and orientation. In J. Gess-Newsome & N. G. Lederman (Eds.), *Examining Pedagogical Content Knowledge* (pp. 95–132). Dordrecht, The Netherlands: Kluwer.

Marble, S., Finley, S., & Ferguson, C. (2000). *Understanding Teachers' Perspectives on Teaching and Learning: A Synthesis of Work in Five Study Sites.* Austin, TX: Southwest Educational Development Laboratory.

Martin, M. O., Mullis, I. V., & Hooper, M. (2016). Methods and procedures in TIMSS 2015. Retrieved from http://timssandpirls.bc.edu/publications/timss/2015-methods.html

McLoughlin, C., & Lee, M. (2008). Future learning landscapes: Transforming pedagogy through social software. *Innovate, 4* (5). Retrieved from http://www.innovateonline.info/index.php?view=article&id=539

Mehan, H. (1979). 'What time is it, Denise?": Asking known information questions in classroom discourse. *Theory Into Practice, 18*(4), 285–294.

Ministry of Education. (2006, October 14). Towards ability-driven education. *Contact.* Retrieved from http://www3.moe.edu.sg/corporate/contactonline/2006/issue14/sub_BigPicture_Art01.htm

Mokhtar, F. (2019). The Big Read: Streaming — the good, the bad and the ugly side of an outdated policy. Retrieved from https://www.channelnewsasia.com/news/singapore/the-big-read-streaming-the-good-the-bad-and-the-ugly-side-of-an-11332116

Moon, J. (2004). *A Handbook of Reflective and Experiential Learning: Theory and Practice.* New York: Routledge Falmer.

OECD. (2011). Singapore: Rapid improvement followed by strong performance. In OECD (Ed.), *Lessons from PISA for the United States* (pp. 159–176). Paris: OECD Publishing.

OECD. (2016). PISA 2015 Results. Excellence and Equity in Education (Volume 1), 1. Retrieved from http://dx.doi.org/10.1787/9789264266490-en

Ong, Y. K. (2019). Learn for life — One secondary education, many subject bands. MOE FY2019 Committee of Supply Debate Response by Minister for Education Ong Ye Kung: Ministry of Education Singapore.

Perez, K. (2013). *The New Inclusion: Differentiated Strategies to Engage All Students.* New York: Teachers College Press.

Ponnusamy, L. D. (2010). Teaching mixed ability classes. Doctor of Education Thesis, University of Western Australia, Perth.

Porter, A. C., & Brophy, J. (1988). Synthesis of research on good teaching: Insights from the work of the Institute for Research on Teaching. *Educational Leadership*, *45*(8), 74–85.

Puntambekar, S., & Hubscher, R. (2005). Tools for scaffolding students in a complex learning environment: What have we gained and what have we missed? *Educational Psychologist*, *40*(1), 1–12.

Puntambekar, S., & Kolodner, J. L. (2005). Toward implementing distributed scaffolding: Helping students learn science from design. *Journal of Research in Science Teaching*, *42*(2), 185–217.

Reid, M. I., Clunies-Ross, L. R., Goacher, B., & Vile, C. (1981). Mixed ability teaching: Problems and possibilities. *Educational Research*, *24*(1), 3–10.

Rios, F. (Ed.). (1996). *Teacher Thinking in Cultural Contexts*. Albany: State University of New York Press.

Schumm, J., & Avalos, M. A. (2009). Responsible differentiated instruction for the adolescent learner. In K. D. Wood & W. E. Blanton (Eds.), *Literacy Instruction for Adolescents: Research-based Practice*. New York: Guilford Press.

Shanmugaratnam, T. (2004). To light a fire: Enabling teachers, nurturing students.Retrieved from http://www.moe.gov.sg/media/speeches/2004/sp20040929.htm

Shanmugaratnam, T. (2006). Opening address by Mr Tharman Shamugaratnam, Minister for Education at the MOE Workplan Seminar 2006 on Wednesday 28 September 2006. Retrieved from http://www.moe.gov.sg/media/press/2006/pr20060928.htm

Shulman, L. (1987). Knowledge and teaching: Foundations of the new reform. *Harvard Educational Review*, *57*(1), 1–22.

Slee, R. (2008). Beyond special and regular schooling? An inclusive education reform agenda. *International Studies in Sociology of Education*, *18*(2), 99–116.

Smith, C., & Sutherland, M. (2003). Setting or mixed ability — Teachers' views of the organisation of pupils for learning. *Journal of Research in Special Educational Needs*, *3*(3), 141–146.

Stakes, R., & Hornby, G. (2012). *Meeting Special Needs in Mainstream Schools: A Practical Guide for Teachers*. London: David Fulton Publishers.

Steering Committee on the Enabling Masterplan. (2007). Enabling Masterplan, 2007–2011. Singapore: Ministry of Social and Family Development. Retrieved from http://app1.mcys.gov.sg/Publications/EnablingMasterplan20072011.aspx

Tabak, I. (2004). Synergy: A complement to emerging patterns of distributed scaffolding. *Journal of the Learning Sciences*, *13*(3), 305–335.

Teo, C. H. (2000, September 23). Ability-driven education — Putting the system in place. Paper presented at the Ministry of Education Workplan Seminar at Nanyang Polytechnic Auditorium.

Thaver, T., Lim, L., & Liau, A. (2014). Teacher variables as predictors of Singaporean pre-service teachers' attitudes toward inclusive education. *Published by International Association of Social Science Research*, *1*(1), 1–8.

Toh, L. (2018, November 13). Continuing efforts to get students from different groups to interact. *The Straits Times*.

Tomlinson, C. A. (2008). Differentiated instruction. In J. Plucker & C. Callahan (Eds.), *Critical Issues and Practices in Gifted Education* (pp. 167–177). Waco; Texas: Prufrock Press.

Tsui, A. B. M. (2003). *Understanding Expertise in Teaching*. Cambridge: Cambridge University Press.

Turner-Bisset, R. (1999). The knowledge bases of the expert teacher. *British Educational Research Journal*, *25*(1), 39–55.

Turner-Bisset, R. (2001). *Expert Teaching*. London: Fulton.

United States Congress. (1975). The Education of All Handicapped Children Act, PUBLIC LAW 94-142—NOV. 29, 1975.

Villegas, A. M., & Lucas, T. (2002). Preparing culturally responsive teachers: Rethinking the curriculum. *Journal of Teacher Education*, *53*(1), 20–32. doi:10.1177/0022487102053001003

Walker, Z., & Musti-Rao, S. (2016). Inclusion in high-achieving Singapore: Challenges of building an inclusive society in policy and practice. *Global Education Review*, *3*(3).

Warnock Committee (1978). Special educational needs: The Warnock report. London: DES.

Watanabe, M., Nunes, N., Mebane, S., Scalise, K., & Claesgens, J. (2007). Chemistry for all, instead of chemistry just for the elite: Lessons learned from detracked chemistry classrooms. *Science Education*, *91*(5), 683–709.

Watkins, C., & Mortimore, P. (1999). Pedagogy: What do we know? In P. Mortimore (Ed.), *Understanding Pedagogy and Its Impact on Learning* (pp. 1–19). London: Paul Chapman Publishing Ltd.

Weimer, M. (2002). *Learner-centered Teaching: Five Key Changes to Practice*. San Francisco, CA: Jossey Bass.

Weld, J. (2002). Learner-centred teaching. In R. W. Bybee (Ed.), *Learning Science and the Science of Learning: Science Educators' Essay Collection* (pp. 77–85). Arlington, VA.: NSTA Press.

Xanthou, M., & Pavlou, P. (2008). Strategies of accommodating mixed ability classes in EFL settings: Teachers' armour in an ongoing battle. *Humanising Language Teaching Magazine, Year 10*(1). Retrieved from http://www.hltmag.co.uk/jan08/

Yeo, L. S., Neihart, M., Chong, W. H., & Huan, V. S. L. (2013). Inclusive education in Singapore primary school classrooms. Retrieved from http://hdl.handle.net/10497/15002

Yeo, L. S., Chong, W. H., Neihart, M. F., & Huan, V. S. (2016). Teachers' experience with inclusive education in Singapore. *Asia Pacific Journal of Education, 36*(sup1), 69–83.

Yuen, S. (2020). Intan Azura Mokhtar: Academic glad efforts to phase out streaming paid of. Retrieved 31st October 2020, from Singapore Press Holdings https://www.straitstimes.com/politics/academic-glad-efforts-to-phase-out-streaming-paid-off

Zimmerman, B., & Dibenedetto, M. (2008). Mastery learning and assessment: Implications for students and teachers in an era of high-stakes testing. *Psychology in the Schools, 45*(3), 206–216.

CHAPTER 10

Stakeholders' Involvement in the Transition to Adulthood for Youth with Disabilities

Ailsa Goh and Nursidah Malik

Introduction

The transition from school to adulthood is a crucial period of preparation for all youths, and in particular, for youth with disabilities. This chapter discusses the significance of this phase of transition to adulthood for youth with disabilities, the importance of multiple stakeholders' involvement in contributing towards the success of post-school life outcomes for students with disabilities, and local transition-related research and developments in recent years within Singapore's special education landscape. This chapter concludes with a practical methodology derived from the research literature for use with interviewing youth with intellectual disabilities and key stakeholders, such as parents, siblings and school personnel, for the purpose of obtaining relevant input into the transition process.

Transition to Adulthood for Youth with Disabilities

In the area of special education for youth with disabilities, people often think of transition as transition from school to work. However, according to the Council of Exceptional Children's Division on Career Development and Transition, transition refers to a change in status from behaving primarily as a student to assuming emergent adult roles in the community (deFur, Todd-Allen & Getzel, 2001). As an emerging adult, youth with disabilities require more than just having employment to function well in the community, they would also need to contribute to maintaining a home, engage in appropriate community participation, and experience satisfactory personal and social relationships, and for some youth with disabilities, taking on an emerging adult role may also include participating in postsecondary education (Wehman, 2006).

Transition to adulthood is challenging, not just for the youth with disabilities themselves, but for their families and the larger community as well. When these youth transition out of school to postschool environments, they will move from a structured environment with clear daily routines, with school personnel who are tasked to teach and support them, to environments where ongoing support and services may not be readily available. Some of these youth with disabilities enter work environments that can be impersonal and most of them are unprepared for the level of independence that is required of them (Sitlington, Frank & Carson, 1992). Many of them will find difficulty forming social networks as an adult and feel isolated in the community (Amado *et al.*, 2013; Scuccimarra & Speece, 1990).

Many youth with disabilities leave school with no employment in the near future (Nord *et al.*, 2013) and to further complicate matters, there may be limited places at alternative day activity centers for them (Ministry of Social and Family Development [MSF], 2012). These group of youth with disabilities may be inactive, socially isolated and will continue to rely on family for any social and community interaction (Lichtenstein & Michaelides, 1993; Mithaug, Horiuchi & Fanning, 1985; Ow & Lang, 2000; Sitlington & Frank, 1990).

Transitioning to adulthood is therefore more than just vocational transition. Other important facets of transition to adulthood include possibly the change in living arrangements, appropriate community participating, mobility in the community, some levels of financial independence, building social relationships, sexuality, self-determination and having fun (Wehman, 2006). However, schools and other service delivery models often neglect various facets of young peoples' lives beyond work (Whitney-Thomas & Hanley-Maxwell, 1996). Thus, a youth with disability may be well-trained to perform a job competently, but if he or she is unable to build and maintain satisfactory relationships within the workplace and maintain a personal network of friends outside of work, this youth may experience poor quality of life and may eventually drop out of work due to lack of motivation. Heal and colleagues (1999) have found that social relationships are a predictor of postschool quality of life. As quality of life indicators are inter-related, the failure to address one or more domains of adult life can result in problems manifesting in other realms (Whitney-Thomas & Hanley-Maxwell, 1996).

Increasingly, non-work related aspects on transition to adulthood for youth with disabilities are highlighted in research to improve their quality of life (e.g., Dyke *et al.*, 2013; Rehm *et al.*, 2012). Youths and parents have emphasised the need to identify meaningful transition programmes that will enable youth with disabilities to harness their unique abilities, develop their social relationships, and allow them to be part of the community (Rehm *et al.*, 2012). Non-work related factors to successful transition include: (a) participation in leisure and recreation activities; (b) having interpersonal relationship with others beyond the family; (c) community participation; (d) lifelong learning and personal development (Dyke *et al.*, 2013; Rehm *et al.*, 2012). While improving the quality of life of these youth have been highlighted in research, they have seldom been included as part of the transition programmes to adulthood (Powers *et al.*, 2008; Rehm *et al.*, 2012). As such, barriers to their inclusion would provide critical information for future successful transition programmes.

Therefore, even as we work on equipping youth with disabilities with job skills for employment, we will also need to equip them with skills to develop and maintain social relationships that will ensure that they have quality of life which will work towards a healthier work-life balance for them. Careful transitional planning for youth with disabilities would therefore better prepare them for the complex world of adulthood. Schools, families and adult disability service agencies would need to work collaboratively to ensure that ongoing support and services are in place as they prepare youth with disabilities to transition to adulthood (Whelley et al., 2003).

Stakeholders' Perspectives on Transition to Adulthood

As the African proverb says "It takes a village to raise a child"; similarly, it also takes a village to raise a child with disability to adulthood. Many people need to be involved in the transition of youth with disabilities to adulthood. These stakeholders would include the youth with disabilities themselves, their families (e.g., parents, siblings, extended family members), community members (e.g., neighbours, religious leaders), school personnel (e.g., teachers, school leaders, job coaches) and local agencies (e.g., job support coordinators, mental health workers).

A relatively large body of research has been conducted in the area of transition to adulthood of youth with disabilities from the perspectives of parents (e.g., Davies & Beamish, 2009; Dyke et al., 2013; Henninger & Taylor, 2014; Whitney-Thomas & Hanley-Maxwell, 1996), siblings (e.g., Burke, Fish & Lawton, 2015; Chambers, Hughes & Carter, 2004; Saaltink et al., 2012), school personnel such as teachers and job coaches (e.g., Finn & Kohler, 2010; Goupil et al., 2002; Park, 2008; Lindstrom et al., 2007; Scheef, Walker & Barrio, 2017; Trainor et al., 2008), and employers (e.g., Ju, Zhang & Pacha, 2012). There are research studies on the issue of transition to adulthood from the perspectives of youth with disabilities; some of these studies focused on youth with intellectual disabilities (e.g., Mill, Mayes & McConnell, 2010; Saaltink et al., 2012) while other studies included youth with diverse disabilities, which included intellectual disabilities among other disability categories (e.g., Benz, Lindstrom & Yovanoff, 2000; Hogansen *et al.*, 2008; Lindstrom *et al.*, 2007; Trainor *et al.*, yyyy?; Whitney-Thomas & Moloney, 2001). The next section will briefly discuss the transition to adulthood within these two focus areas: (a) envisioning the future of youth with disabilities, and (b) enablers and challenges to successful transition to adulthood.

Envisioning the future of youth with disabilities

Whitney-Thomas and Hanley-Maxwell (1996) surveyed 93 parents of students with disabilities and 111 parents of students without disabilities on their experiences as their children prepare to leave high school. They found that parents held a complex vision of their children's future, which included the home leaving process, employment, building social relationships and increased independence. In comparison with parents of students without disabilities, parents of students with disabilities expressed greater levels of discomfort and pessimism in their visions of their child's future.

Blue-Banning, Turnbull and Pereira (2002) conducted focus group interviews with 38 Hispanic parents of youth with intellectual and developmental disabilities on their visions for the future of their child with disabilities. The parents had diverse hopes and expectations for their child with disabilities but five themes emerged. Some of the more common themes were employment, daily living skills and future living arrangement. Other less commonly discussed themes were leisure activities and acceptance by the community. The parents envisioned a future where their child would be involved in meaningful leisure activities with friends and be accepted in the community.

Another study on parental expectations and hopes for their child's future looked at the experiences of Korean American parents with children with disabilities (Kim, Lee & Morningstar, 2007). The researchers interviewed ten Korean American parents. One interesting finding that emerged from this study was that a majority of the Korean American parents had considered group home as a living arrangement for their child with disabilities. While group homes are a common living arrangement in the U.S. for adults with disabilities, this living arrangement is uncommon in Asian countries. The researchers posited that parents' expectations for the child with disabilities appeared to be tampered by society's expectations for individuals with disabilities based on the severity of the disability.

Enablers and challenges to successful transition to adulthood

Henninger and Taylor (2014) surveyed 198 parents of individuals with intellectual and developmental disabilities on their perspectives on successful transition to adulthood. They found that although parents did define successful transition in the traditional areas of independence in work, living and relationships, parents often described the criteria of success subjectively using terms like 'reaching his or her full potential' or 'maximising his or her strengths'. When researchers approach stakeholders on factors that promote successful transition to adulthood, these are the enablers that are commonly discussed:

- *Parental involvement.* Many research studies have emphasised the importance of parental and family involvement during the transition of youth with disabilities to adulthood (e.g., Dyke *et al.*, 2013; Lindstrom, Doren & Miesch, 2011).
- *Transition planning.* Parents believed that individualised transition planning that starts early and is well coordinated is an important enabler in helping their child with disabilities during the transitional period (e.g., Bhaumik *et al.*, 2011; Davies & Beamish, 2009; Lindstrom, Doren & Miesch, 2011).
- *Early work experiences.* One of the enabling factors leading to successful transition to employment is early work experience for youth with disabilities (e.g., Benz, Lindstrom & Yovanoff, 2000; Hogansen *et al.*, 2008; Lindstrom, Doren & Miesch, 2011).
- *Transition programmes.* Stakeholders have opined that the participation of youth with disabilities in transition programmes have many benefits (e.g., Lindstrom *et al.*, 2007). The youth with disabilities

shared that they had opportunities to explore career option, learn specific skills and gain confidence in transition programmes. Transition programmes also prepares youth with disabilities for community participation (e.g., Davies & Beamish, 2009).

- *Supportive school personnel.* Youth with disabilities have noted that the individualised attention, consistent support and staff persistence were the main helpful factors of the transition programmes (Benz, Lindstrom & Yovanoff, 2000). Parents have voiced that if the personal connection and relationship between school personnel and their child is poor, their child will not be engaged in the transition process (Hogansen *et al.*, 2008).
- *Peer mentors.* Adolescence is a period where youth move away from the family and develop increased ties with peers and peer groups (Chipuer & Pretty, 2000; Jager *et al.*, 2015). Peers become primary sources of support; however, when the youth with disabilities graduates from school, this important source of social support may be lacking. In a study on the effectiveness of youth transition programmes, the youth with disabilities that participated in the programme suggested that peer mentors would be beneficial as they transition to postschool environments (Whitney-Thomas & Moloney, 2001).

Wehman (2006) deliberated that special education services for youth with disabilities occur in a 'vacuum' where the students are shielded from the realities of the world where multiple pressures will affect the students. The pressures of the world that Wehman highlighted include violence in the community, high-stakes testing access to alcohol and drugs, continual poverty and unemployment and peer pressure. Stakeholders perceive the following factors as challenges that they face during the transitioning of youth with disabilities to adulthood:

- *Lack of participation.* Youth with disabilities often do not contribute in a significant way during the transition planning process (e.g., Davies & Beamish, 2009). Youth with disabilities who do not have meaningful contribution to the transition planning may not be invested in the programmes that have been put in place for them. School personnel have also voiced their concerns with the lack of parent assistance during the preparation for transition (e.g., Hogansen *et al.*, 2008).

- *Lack of information.* Parents often lack information regarding post-school options for their child with disabilities (e.g., Bhaumik *et al.*, 2011), and they have acknowledged that they rarely discussed post-school matters with other family members (Chambers, Hughes & Carter, 2004).
- *Limited access to services.* Parents have implored that adult service agencies need to be more flexible and reduce the level of bureaucracy required for the parents to access the needed services (Bhaumik *et al.*, 2011).
- *Lack of post-school options.* Parents noted that there is a lack of post-school options for their child with disabilities (e.g., Davies & Beamish, 2009). Youth with disabilities have also shared that their peers without disabilities have more advantages and opportunities when it comes to employment (Hogansen *et al.*, 2008).

Transition to Employment in Singapore for Youth with Disabilities

In Singapore, the transition landscape from school education to employment for youth with disabilities has gone through significant changes in the recent years. The government has worked with various organisations, companies and special education (SPED) schools to improve vocational and career pathways for students with disabilities. The third Enabling Masterplan (2017–2021), a five-year blueprint that serves as a guide in the development of programmes, policies, services and other support for people with disabilities in Singapore, aims to work towards building an inclusive society where people with disabilities can reach their potential and be an integral member of the society (Hassan, 2016).

One of the strategic directions of this masterplan is to enhance pathways for employment and provide lifelong learning opportunities for people with disabilities (MSF, 2016a). Adding to this, the steering committee of the Enabling Masterplan acknowledges the need to develop employment opportunities and job support programmes as well as offering better support to potential employers of people with disabilities. To achieve this, recommendations are made. The Enabling Masterplan recommends the development of a range of open and customised employment models, which leads to the enhancement of vocational and employment pathways, and boosts efforts in providing lifelong learning opportunities for people with disabilities. Employers' capabilities in hiring and managing employees with disabilities must also be improved (MSF, 2016a).

In 2010, the Ministry of Education (MOE) released a 'Framework for Vocational Education in SPED schools' to all the SPED schools. This framework maps the vision, philosophy, processes and learning outcomes of vocational education for students with disabilities (MOE, 2017). A series of guides are provided in this framework to support SPED schools to develop a structured vocational programme that can equip their students with skills, so they can be gainfully employed and have an independent life. To prepare the students for the working world, vocational education must encompass a customised curriculum and resources that suit the diverse needs of students with disabilities. This also means that there is a need for more effective procedures in vocational assessment, guidance and attainment of work habits and skills from structured and authentic work experiences (MOE, 2017).

Post-secondary and vocational schools

There are three SPED schools and one vocational school that are catered for students with disabilities until the age of 21. Metta and Delta Senior schools enroll students with mild intellectual disabilities from the age of 16 years and provide vocational certification programmes that equip them with the skills and certification to enter open employment market or pursue further education in any of the Institutes of Technical Education (ITE), if they meet the courses' requirements (MOE, 2017). Metta School offers the ITE Skills Certificate (ISC), which is awarded by ITE, while Delta Senior

School provides the Singapore Workforce Skills Qualifications (WSQ). Pathlight School is an autism-specific school offering mainstream curriculum that leads to PSLE, GCE-O Level and GCE-N Level certifications. Pathlight also has a vocational track for students who are better suited for a vocational curriculum. These students with autism learn skills that help them to function independently and have opportunities to go to a sheltered, supported or open employment (Pathlight School, 2014). There is one vocational school that provides an alternative vocational training for a diverse range of students with disabilities. Similar to Metta School, the Mountbatten Vocational School also offers a training programme that leads to the attainment of ISC and work-based placements (Mountbatten Vocational School, 2015). This vocational school accepts students with disabilities from the age of 14 years old.

The School-to-Work transition programme

There are students with disabilities who are not eligible to enter the vocational certification programmes. To help these students gain employment, the Ministry of Social and Family Development (MSF), MOE and SG Enable with partnerships from selected SPED schools developed the School-to-Work (S2W) Transition Programme (MOE, 2017). This programme aims to provide customised training with work options for students with mild intellectual disability and autism who are not suitable for the vocational certification programmes, and gives them the support to transition from school to the working world. Students start this programme during their final schooling year and continue for another year after they graduate from school. These students with diverse disability profiles must have the potential to work and this programme helps to facilitate the job training pathways. SG Enable and potential employers work together with SPED schools and families to ensure that job training options and placements match the students' interests, strengths and preferences (MOE, 2017). In order to have a smooth transition to job training and placement, this matching process is done before the students graduate from school.

The S2W Transition Programme was piloted in 2014 with five SPED schools for two years. Since 2016, this programme has been implemented in other SPED schools in phases (Mokhtar, 2016). There were 30 students in this programme in 2016 and the number of students is expected to increase to 60 by 2019 (Tan, 2017). During his Budget statement, Finance Minister Mr. Heng Swee Keat announced that this programme would be extended to students with moderate intellectual and multiple disabilities (Lam, 2017). Supporting the expansion of this programme, the then Minister for Social and Family Development Mr. Tan Chuan-Jin shared that "employment is integral to enabling persons with disabilities to live independently and integrate with society" (Tan, 2017). The joint efforts by the ministries in partnership with SG Enable, SPED schools and participating employers had enhanced the landscape for transition to employment for students with disabilities in Singapore.

Even though the programme was piloted in five SPED schools, it had proven to play an important part in the transition journey to employment for students with disabilities. At the end of 2016, MSF released a press statement that reported positive outcomes for the first graduating cohort of students, their parents and employers (MSF, 2016b). According to the press release, 80 per cent of students in this pilot transition programme were successfully employed with 83 per cent of them staying employed for a minimum of 6 months. These students also described having a sense of self worth from being able to earn a salary and contribute to their families. Parents of these students also noted that the programme helped their child to attain work skills and habits as well as gain more self-confidence, independence and capabilities in their daily activities. Employers shared that the programme encouraged an inclusive culture that allowed their staff to develop more positive attitudes towards people with disabilities (MSF, 2016b). Such positive feedback from the various stakeholders indicated that the appropriate support and partnership from government, relevant agencies, schools and employers, coupled with a well-developed training programme, could help students with disabilities be gainfully employed and contribute to the economy.

SG Enable

SG Enable is an agency that is dedicated towards enabling people with disabilities. This agency aims to empower people with disabilities and their caregivers by giving them access to various information and referral services, grants and support. It is also committed to enhance the employment and work options for people with disabilities. SG Enable engages family, community, stakeholders and the public in supporting people with disabilities to be contributing members of society (SG Enable, 2015). SG Enable plays a crucial role in providing support and information at various transition stages, especially in employment.

Wong, Chong and Ng (2020) presents a joint SG Enable and MOE collaborative school-to-work pilot programme. Components of this programme include an 'individual transition planning process', a 'student vocational profiling tool' and a 'group internship model'. The authors describe the collaboration needed between schools, teachers and employers in implementing the programme, and concludes their chapter with an evaluation of this school-to-work pilot programme to consider the value that it brought to different stakeholders such as parents and students,

Local research

There is limited published research related to transition in Singapore (e.g., Ow & Lang, 2000; Poon, 2013; Scheef, Walker & Barrio, 2017; Soh & Lim, 2015). Poon explored the expectations of 20 parents regarding the postschool social attainments of their adolescent child with autism spectrum disorders (ASD). He found that most parents expected their child to be working either in a sheltered workshop or be unemployed. None of the parents expected their child would be able to have any independent access to the community. However, due to the small sample size and the narrow profile of the sample of students in this study, which was ASD with intellectual disabilities and challenging behaviours, these findings are not generalisable to the larger population of youth with disabilities in Singapore.

Ow and Lang (2000) interviewed 17 elderly parents (mean age = 63 years) with adult children with intellectual disabilities (mean age = 30 years) in Singapore to investigate parental planning of long term care for their children with learning disabilities. They highlighted systemic and subjective factors that influenced parental preparation for their child's long term care. *Systematic* concerns included family's income level and assets, the availability of working adult siblings to provide care after parents' demise and the lack of formal provisions (e.g., educational or recreational services). *Subjective* concerns included parental over-protection for the child with disability and parental consideration on whether they were 'fair' to their other offspring by burdening the offspring with the responsibility of looking after the sibling with disability. Ow and Lang (2000) also emphasised that planning and intervention for long term care (e.g., daily living skills, social emotional wellbeing, financial plans) should start early in the life span of a child with disability when the parents have the opportunity to prepare their child for the future.

Soh and Lim's (2015) descriptive case study of the development of a transition programme for students with mild intellectual disabilities documented the process of establishing a prototype for school-to-work transition in Singapore. This descriptive research illustrated, through a retrospective account using an action learning and research framework, the chronological evolution of the key processes and practices leading to the development of a field-tested transition programme at Delta Senior School, one of the three SPED schools mentioned earlier with transition programming for their students until the age of 21. This illustrative case study contributed toward the understanding of the development work involved for setting up transition programmes — an area of study that is sorely lacking in the international and local research literature.

Scheef, Walker and Barrio (2017) interviewed 12 job developers (otherwise known as job coaches) to understand their perspectives on what they thought were salient employability skills needed by youth with intellectual and developmental disabilities to be successful in the Singaporean workplace. The majority of the job developers (10 of them) were employees of four different special schools serving students with intellectual disabilities and autism spectrum disorder in Singapore and the remaining two were from a government agency. Findings from the interviews with the job developers revealed that soft skills, such as dependability, attitude, stamina, communication and flexibility were valued over skills which were more technical and job-specific.

Further research is needed on the transition of youth with disabilities in Singapore. One critical need is to explore the perspectives of various stakeholders as they plan and prepare youth with disabilities to transition to adulthood. Another important research direction is to include of the voice of the youth with disabilities in the research process (Benz, Lindstrom & Yovanoff, 2000; Trainor et al., 2011; Whitney-Thomas & Hanley-Maxwell, 1996). As the research literature on transition to adulthood for youth with disabilities has highlighted the importance of involving the perspectives of multiple stakeholders, including listening to the voice of the youth with a disability during the transition process, the next section of this chapter will discuss a practical methodology for conducting interviews with various stakeholders, including youth with disabilities, in order to understand their respective views on: (i) envisioning the future of youth with disabilities; (ii) the preparation of youth with disabilities for transition to life after school; and (iii) what are the enablers and barriers to successful transitioning to adulthood. As many special schools in Singapore primarily serve students with intellectual disabilities, research studies on transition involving students with intellectual disabilities have been used to inform the methodology for interviews with relevant stakeholders.

A Methodology for Interviewing

Many qualitative research studies have been conducted with individuals with intellectual disabilities participating in interviews as the target sample population (e.g., Broer, Doyle & Giangreco, 2005; Hall, 2013; Liu et al., 2014; Mactavish, Lutfiyya & Mahon, 2000;

Saaltink *et al.*, 2012). While many of these studies were conducted in Western countries, Chen and Shu (2012) conducted a study in Taiwan that involved interviewing youth with intellectual disabilities on their experiences of being stigmatised. Understandably, there are concerns about conducting interviews with individuals with intellectual disabilities, particularly with regards to the comprehension of interview questions and the issue of acquiescence when the individuals provide answers that they feel is what the interviewer wants (Finlay & Lyons, 2001). However, Finlay and Lyons (2001) have also noted that many individuals with mild intellectual disabilities would not have a problem understanding interview questions meant for the general population.

As noted in the research literature, there are challenges conducting interviews with individuals with intellectual disabilities; however, the knowledge gained from gathering and gleaning from their experiences is invaluable. As Knox, Mok and Parmenter (2000) have noted, "…people with an intellectual disability are experts on their own experiences" (p. 57). When interviewing students with intellectual disabilities, the research literature report some general issues, including problems associated with (a) comprehending questions, (b) responding to open-ended questions, (c) repeating same answer to different questions, (d) pleasing the interviewer by saying what they think the interviewer is expecting, and (e) significant others influencing or filtering participant responses during interviews (Biklen & Moseley, 1988; Walker, 1999).

To support the inclusion of individuals with intellectual disabilities in the interview process, special considerations would need to be in place to ensure that their rights are protected, and that the qualitative data gathered are rich and reliable. Recommendations for interviewing individuals with intellectual disabilities include: (a) building rapport to ensure that they are comfortable with sharing information about their experiences and their opinions; (b) planning adequate time for interviews to allow for longer wait-time for responses; (c) adding probing questions and rephrasing questions when the individuals are not able to comprehend the original interview questions; (d) scheduling several shorter interview sessions across a period of time as the individual may be fatigued if the interview is completed in one long session, and the additional sessions also allow the individual to provide additional information after a period of reflection; (e) allowing the participant to have an advocate around during the interview session; and (f) using focus group to allow peers to interact naturally with one another during the interview (Finlay & Lyons, 2001; Hall, 2013; Knox *et al.*, 2000; Mactavish *et al.*, 2000). Table 1 below contains interview questions that can be used to understand the transition to adulthood from the viewpoint of the youth with an intellectual disability.

As mentioned, it is also important to understand the perspectives of relevant stakeholders involved in the transition to adulthood process. Interviews can also be conducted with other significant stakeholders such as parents, siblings and school personnel using the following interview questions listed below in Table 2.

Table 1: Interview questions for youth with intellectual disabilities

1. Tell me what your life would be like after you graduate from school.
2. Tell me more about your work experience in the workplace.
3. Are you ready to graduate from school? Why or why not?
4. Tell me what you need to learn from school to be successful in the workplace. Why do think that it is important to learn that?
5. What are the difficulties that you will face to be successful in life after school?
6. How have you been prepared for adult life?
7. What are your hopes or dreams for yourself as an adult?

Table 2: Interview questions for parents, siblings and school personnel

For parents

1. Can you tell me about your caregiving responsibilities to your child?
2. What are your family's routines like during the weekdays? What are your family's routines like during the weekends?
3. Can you tell me about your involvement in school meetings or activities?
4. What do you think your child's life would be like after s/he graduates from school?
5. Will your family life be the same or different when your child graduates from school? Why do you say so?

Table 2: *(Continued)*

For parents

6. What is your child's experience during his/her attachment in the workplace?
7. Is your child ready to graduate from school? If yes or no, why?
8. What do you think your child will need to graduate from school and be successful in the workplace? Why do you think so?
9. What do you think will be barriers for your child to be successful in life after school? Why do you think so?
10. How have you been preparing your child for life after school? Why do you put these things in place?
11. How have you been preparing your family for when your child graduates from school? Why do you put these things in place?
12. What can be done to help your child transition smoothly from school to the workplace? Why do you think these are important?
13. What are your hopes or dreams for your child as an adult?

For siblings

1. What are your responsibilities in terms of taking care of your sibling? What activities do you do together with your sibling?
2. What do you think your sibling's life would be like after s/he graduates from school?
3. Will your family life be the same or different when your sibling graduates from school? Why do you say so?
4. What is your sibling's experience during his/her attachment in the workplace?
5. Is your sibling ready to graduate from school? If yes or no, why?
6. What do you think your sibling will need to graduate from school and be successful in the workplace? Why do you think so?
7. What do you think will be barriers for your sibling to be successful in life after school? Why do you think so?
8. How have you been helping in preparing your sibling for life after school? Why do you do these things?
9. What can be done to help your sibling transition smoothly from school to the workplace? Why do you think these are important?
10. What are your hopes or dreams for your sibling as an adult?

(Continued)

Table 2: (*Continued*)

For school personnel

1. What is your role in supporting your student during this transitional period? Can you describe the things you do with your student on a regular basis?
2. What do you think your student's life would be like after s/he graduates from school?
3. What is your student's experience during his/her attachment in the workplace?
4. Is your student ready to graduate from school? If yes or no, why?
5. What do you think your student will need to graduate from school and be successful in the workplace? Why do you think so?
6. What do you think will be barriers for your student to be successful in life after school? Why do you think so?
7. How have you been preparing your student for life after school? Why do you put these things in place?
8. What has the school done to help your student transition smoothly from school to the workplace?
9. What else can be done to help your student transition smoothly from school to the workplace? Why do you think these are important?
10. What are your hopes or dreams for your student as an adult?

Conclusion

Current best practices in special education for children with disabilities involve the provision of individualised planning by a multidisciplinary team to determine service to meet the needs of the child with a disability. This usually come in the form of an individualised education plan for the middle childhood and adolescence years, and an individualised transition plan for the later adolescence years. Unlike the school-age years where special schools offers special education services and a safe haven for children with disabilities, there exist however insufficient work opportunities and support services for adults with disabilities. This hinders the development of a strategic transition plan for life after school where clear goals and delineated services could be outlined.

Families end up shouldering the full responsibility of caring for their adult child with disabilities, and for many families, the default placement setting for their adult child is often the home, with few opportunities for community participation. The government and the voluntary welfare organisations are working towards creating more opportunities for adults with disabilities (MSF, 2016a). While we may lament the lack of adult disability services that exist today, with aspiration and determination we can create in our tomorrow an inclusive society with ample opportunities for people with disabilities to participate meaningfully in all aspects of Singapore life.

Ultimately, for the transition to a meaningful and inclusive adult life for youth with disabilities, we need to work closely with the families. The families' hopes and dreams for their child with disabilities are often clouded by society's expectations for people with disabilities. Therefore, the mindset, beliefs and attitudes of the society towards people with disabilities must change. Take a moment to ponder the expectations you have for individuals with disabilities in Singapore. They could be your student, your family member, your neighbour or the random stranger you see in the train. What are your hopes and dreams for them and for this society? What is your stake in this?

References

Amado, A. N., Stancliffe, R. J., McCarron, M., & McCallion, P. (2013). Social inclusion and community participation of individuals with intellectual/developmental disabilities. *Intellectual and Developmental Disabilities, 51*, 360–375.

Benz, M. R., Lindstrom, L., & Yovanoff, P. (2000). Improving graduation and employment outcomes of students with disabilities: Predictive factors and student perspectives. *Exceptional Children, 66*, 509–529.

Bhaumik, S., Watson, J., Barrett, M., Raju, B., Burton, T., & Forte, J. (2011). Transition for teenagers with intellectual disability: Carers' perspectives. *Journal of Policy and Practice in Intellectual Disabilities, 8*, 53–61. doi:10.1111/j.1741-1130.2011.00286.x

Biklen, S. K., & Moseley, C. R. (1988). 'Are you retarded?' 'No, I'm Catholic': Qualitative methods in the study of people with severe handicaps. *Journal of the Association for Persons with Severe Handicaps, 13*, 155–162.

Blue-Banning, M., Turnbull, A. P., & Pereira, L. (2002). Hispanic youth/young adults with disabilities: Parents' visions for the future. *Research and Practice for Persons with Severe Disabilities, 27*, 204–219. doi:10.2511/rpsd.27.3.204

Broer, S. M., Doyle, M. B., & Giangreco, M. F. (2005). Perspectives of students with intellectual disabilities about their experiences with paraprofessional support. *Exceptional Children, 71*, 415–430.

Burke, M. M., Fish, T., & Lawton, K. (2015). A comparative analysis of adult siblings' perceptions toward caregiving. *Intellectual and Developmental Disabilities, 53*(2), 143–157. doi:10.1352/1934-9556-53.2.143

Chambers, C. R., Hughes, C., & Carter, E. W. (2004). Parent and sibling perspectives on the transition to adulthood. *Education and Training in Developmental Disabilities, 39*, 79–94.

Chen, C., & Shu, B. (2012). The process of perceiving stigmatization: perspectives from Taiwanese young people with intellectual disability. *Journal of Applied Research in Intellectual Disabilities, 25*, 240–251.

Chipuer, H. M., & Pretty, G. H. (2000). Facets of adolescents' loneliness: A study of rural and urban Australian youth. *Australian Psychologist, 35*, 233–237. doi:10.1080/00050060008257484

Davies, M. D., & Beamish, W. (2009). Transitions from school for young adults with intellectual disability: Parental perspectives on "Life as an adjustment". *Journal of Intellectual & Developmental Disability, 34*, 248–257.

deFur, S., Todd-Allen, M., & Getzel, E. (2001). Parent participation in the transition planning process. *Career Development for Exceptional Individuals, 24*, 71–88.

Dyke, P., Bourke, J., Llewellyn, G., & Leonard, H. (2013). The experiences of mothers of young adults with an intellectual disability transitioning from secondary school to adult life. *Journal of Intellectual & Developmental Disability, 38*, 149–162.

Finlay, W. L., & Lyons, E. (2001). Methodological issues in interviewing and using self-report questionnaires with people with mental retardation. *Psychological Assessment, 13*, 319–335. doi:10.1037/1040-3590.13.3.319

Finn, J. E., & Kohler, P. D. (2010). Transition outcomes project: Perceptions of school personnel explored through a multiple case study. *Journal of Ethnographic & Qualitative Research, 4*, 95–107.

Goupil, G., Tasse, M. J., Garcin, N., & Dore, C. (2002). Parent and teacher perceptions of individualised transition planning. *British Journal of Special Education, 29*, 127–35.

Hall, S. A. (2013). Including people with intellectual disabilities in qualitative research. *Journal of Ethnographic & Qualitative Research, 7,* 128–142.

Hassan, N. J. (2016, April 2). Committee to develop new enabling masterplan for disabled in Singapore. *Channel NewsAsia.*

Heal, L. W., Khoju, M., Rusch, F. R., & Harnisch, D. L. (1999). Predicting quality of life of students who have left special education high school programs. *American Journal on Mental Retardation, 104,* 305–319. doi:10.1352/0895-8017(1999)104<0305:PQOLOS>2.0.CO;2

Henninger, N. A., & Taylor, J. L. (2014). Family perspectives on a successful transition to adulthood for individuals with disabilities. *Intellectual and Developmental Disabilities, 52,* 98–111.

Hogansen, J. M., Powers, K., Geenen, S., Gil-Kashiwabara, E., & Powers, L. (2008). Transition goals and experiences of females with disabilities: Youth, parents, and professionals. *Exceptional Children, 74,* 215–234.

Jager, J., Yuen, C. X., Putnick, D. L., Hendricks, C., & Bornstein, M. H. (2015). Adolescent-peer relationships, separation and detachment from parents, and internalizing and externalizing behaviors: Linkages and interactions. *Journal of Early Adolescence, 35,* 511–537. doi:10.1177/0272431614537116

Ju, S., Zhang, D., & Pacha, J. (2012). Employability skills valued by employers as important for entry-level employees with and without disabilities. *Career Development and Transition for Exceptional Individuals, 35,* 29–38.

Kim, K., Lee, Y., & Morningstar, M. E. (2007). An unheard voice: Korean American parents' expectations, hopes, and experiences concerning their adolescent child's future. *Research and Practice for Persons with Severe Disabilities, 32,* 253–264.

Knox, M., Mok, M., & Parmenter, T. R. (2000). Working with the experts: Collaborative research with people with an intellectual disability. *Disability & Society, 15,* 49–61. doi:10.1080/09687590025766

Lam, L. (2017, February 20). Singapore Budget 2017: Integrating disabled into workforce and supporting caregivers focus on new Govt masterplan. *The Straits Times.* Retrieved from https://www.straitstimes.com/singapore/health/singapore-budget-2017-integrating-disabled-into-workforce-and-supporting-caregivers

Lichtenstein, S., & Michaelides, N. (1993). Transition from school to young adulthood: Four case studies of young adults labeled mentally retarded. *Career Development for Exceptional Individuals, 16*, 183–195.

Lindstrom, L., Doren, B., & Miesch, J. (2011). Waging a living: Career development and long-term employment outcomes for young adults with disabilities. *Exceptional Children, 77*, 423–434.

Lindstrom, L., Paskey, J., Dickinson, J., Doren, B., Zane, C., & Johnson, P. (2007). Voices from the field: Recommended transition strategies for students and school staff. *Journal for Vocational Special Needs Education, 29*(2), 4–15.

Liu, E. X., Carter, E. W., Boehm, T. L., Annandale, N. H., & Taylor, C. E. (2014). In their own words: The place of faith in the lives of young people with autism and intellectual disability. *Intellectual and Developmental Disabilities, 52*, 388–404. doi:10.1352/1934-9556-52.5.388

Mactavish, J. B., Mahon, M. J., & Lutfiyya, Z. M. (2000). 'I can speak for myself': Involving individuals with intellectual disabilities as research participants. *Mental Retardation, 38*, 216–227. doi:10.1352/0047-6765(2000)038<0216:ICSFMI>2.0.CO;2

Mill, A., Mayes, R., & McConnell, D. (2010). Negotiating autonomy within the family: The experiences of young adults with intellectual disabilities. *British Journal of Learning Disabilities, 38*, 194–200.

Ministry of Education. (2017). Vocational education and School-to-Work pathways. Retrieved from https://www.moe.gov.sg/education/special-education/vocational-education

Ministry of Social and Family Development. (2012). Enabling masterplan 2012–2016. Retrieved from https://www.msf.gov.sg/policies/Disabilities-and-Special-Needs/Pages/default.aspx.

Ministry of Social and Family Development. (2016a). 3rd Enabling masterplan 2017–2021: Caring nation, inclusive society. Retrieved from https://www.msf.gov.sg/policies/Disabilities-and-Special-Needs/Pages/default.aspx

Ministry of Social and Family Development. (2016b, November 2). Positive outcomes of the School-To-Work transition programme (Press release). Retrieved from https://www.msf.gov.sg/media-room/Pages/Positive-Outcomes-of-the-School-to-Work-Transition-Programme.aspx

Mithaug, D. E., Horiuchi, C. N., & Fanning, P. N. (1985). A report on the Colorado statewide follow-up survey of special education students. *Exceptional Children, 51*, 397–404.

Mokhtar, F. (2016, March 22). Do more to prepare special needs students for the workforce. *Channel NewsAsia.* Retrieved from http://www.channelnewsasia.com/news/singapore/do-more-to-prepare-special-needs-students-for-the-workforce-deni-8148230

Mountbatten Vocational School. (2015). Curriculum. Retrieved from http://mvs.edu.sg/index.php/cirriculum/

Nord, D., Luecking, R., Mank, D., Kiernan, W., & Wray, C. (2013). The state of the science of employment and economic self-sufficiency for people with intellectual and developmental disabilities. *Intellectual and Developmental Disabilities, 51,* 376–384.

Ow, R., & Lang, F. J. (2000). Permanency planning: Families of children with intellectual disability. *Asia Pacific Journal of Social Work and Development, 10,* 73–85.

Park, Y. (2008). Transition services for high school students with disabilities: Perspectives of special education teachers. *Exceptionality Education International, 18,* 95–111.

Pathlight School. (2014). Vocational track. Retrieved from http://www.pathlight.org.sg/programmes/vocational-track

Poon, K. K. (2013). Parental expectations regarding postschool social attainments of adolescents with autism spectrum disorders in Singapore. *American Journal on Intellectual and Developmental Disabilities, 118,* 95–107.

Powers, K., Hogansen, J., Geenen, S., Powers, L. E., & Gil-Kashiwabara, E. (2008). Gender matters in transition to adulthood: A survey study of adolescents with disabilities and their families. *Psychology in the Schools, 45*(4), 49–364. doi: 10.1002/pits.20297

Rehm, R. S., Fuentes-Afflick, E., Fisher, L. T., & Chesla, C. A. (2012). Parent and youth priorities during the transition to adulthood for youth with special health care needs and developmental disability. *Advances in Nursing Science, 35*(3), 57–72. doi: 10.1097/ANS.0b013e3182626180

Saaltink, R., MacKinnon, G., Owen, F., & Tardif-Williams, C. (2012). Protection, participation and protection through participation: Young people with intellectual disabilities and decision making in the family context. *Journal of Intellectual Disability Research, 56,* 1076–1086.

Scheef, A. R., Walker, Z. M., & Barrio, B. L. (2017). Salient employability skills for youth with intellectual and developmental disabilities in Singapore: The perspectives of job developers. *International of Developmental Disabilities, 65,* 1–9.

Scuccimarra, D. J., & Speece, D. L. (1990). Employment outcomes and social integration of students with mild handicaps: The quality of life two years after high school. *Journal of Learning Disabilities, 23*(4), 213–219. doi:10.1177/002221949002300403

SG Enable. (2015). Vision and mission. Retrieved from https://www.sgenable.sg/pages/content.aspx?path=/about-us/vision-and-mission/

Sitlington, P. L., & Frank, A. R. (1990). Are adolescents with learning disabilities successfully crossing the bridge into adult life? *Learning Disability Quarterly, 13*, 97–111. doi:10.2307/1510654

Sitlington, P. L., Frank, A. R., & Carson, R. (1992). Adult adjustment among high school graduates with mild disabilities. *Exceptional Children, 59*, 221–233.

Soh, M. C., & Lim, L., (2015). Enhancing the postschool outcomes of students with intellectual disabilities in Singapore. In R. G. Craven, A. J. S. Morin, D. Tracey, P. D. Parker & H. F. Zhang (Eds.), *Inclusive Education for Students with Intellectual Disabilities* (pp. 73–93). Charlotte, North Carolina: Information Age Publishing Inc.

Tan, J. (2017, March 9). Ministry looking at inclusive preschool model for special needs children. *The Business Times.* Retrieved from https://www.businesstimes.com.sg/government-economy/singapore-budget-2017/ministry-looking-at-inclusive-preschool-model-for-special

Trainor, A. A., Carter, E. W., Owens, L. A., & Swedeen, B. (2008). Special educators' perceptions of summer employment and community participation opportunities for youth with disabilities. *Career Development for Exceptional Individuals, 31*, 144–153. doi:10.1177/0885728808323717

Trainor, A. A., Carter, E. W., Swedeen, B., Owens, L., Cole, O., & Smith, S. (2011). Perspectives of adolescents with disabilities on summer employment and community experiences. *Journal of Special Education, 45*, 157–170.

Walker, P. (1999). From community presence to sense of place: Community experiences of adults with developmental disabilities. *Journal of the Association for Persons with Severe Handicaps, 24*, 23–32.

Wehman, P. (2006). Transition: The bridge from youth to adulthood. In P. Wehman (Ed.), *Life Beyond the Classroom: Transition Strategies for Young People with Disabilities* (4th Ed., pp. 3–40). Baltimore, MD: Paul H. Brookes Publishing Co., Inc.

Whelley, T. A., Radtke, R., Burgstahler, S., & Christ, T. W. (2003). Mentors, advisers, role models and peer supporters: Career development relationships and individuals with disabilities. *American Rehabilitation, 27*, 42–49.

Whitney-Thomas, J., & Hanley-Maxwell, C. (1996). Packing the parachute: Parents' experiences as their children prepare to leave high school. *Exceptional Children, 63*, 75–87.

Whitney-Thomas, J., & Moloney, M. (2001). "Who I am and what I want": Adolescents' self-definition and struggles. *Exceptional Children, 67*, 375–389.

Wong, M. E., Chong, S. L., & Ng, H. L. (2020). School-to-Work transition: Support for students with moderate-to-severe special educational needs in Singapore. In M. Yuen, W. Beamish, & V. S. Solbergg (Eds.), *Careers for students with special educational needs: Perspectives on development and transition from the Asia-Pacific region* (pp. 249–260). Singapore: Springer.

CHAPTER 11

Preparing Persons with Disabilities for the World of Work: The Case of SG Enable Bridging Job Seekers and Employers

Ku Geok Boon

Introduction

Individuals with disabilities experience considerable difficulties in gaining employment compared to their able-bodied peers. From the point when students with disabilities complete formal education, they face an uncertain future. This uncertainty is exacerbated the longer they remain unemployed. While qualifications are an implied promise of securing employment in meritocratic Singapore, qualified persons with disabilities experience a different outcome. With the multiple challenges confronting this population, SG Enable is set up to improve the employment outcomes of persons with disabilities.

This chapter first introduces SG Enable with its background, followed by an overview of its employment initiatives and programmes. This chapter then comments on the key programmes that have been successful in supporting persons with disabilities in the transition to employment. Given the diverse profile of persons with disabilities, this chapter also discusses the barriers and success factors in securing gainful employment for persons with disabilities in different education pathways. These will be juxtaposed against two major influences — employers' mindset and readiness, and shifting socio-economic trends. Finally, the chapter will conclude with suggestions on how SG Enable can work with government agencies and other disability sector players to support persons with disabilities to remain employable in a time of volatility in the future economy.

Background on SG Enable

SG Enable is an agency dedicated to enabling persons with disabilities in Singapore. Set up in 2013 by the Ministry of Social and Family Development, SG Enable's key functions include:

- Enhancing information and referral services for child and adult disability schemes;
- Administering grants and support to persons with disabilities and their caregivers;
- Improving transition management across different life stages;
- Enhancing employability and employment options for persons with disabilities; and
- Rallying stakeholder support in enabling persons with disabilities.

SG Enable approaches the employment of persons with disabilities through a 'Ready Employees, Ready Employers, Ready Environment' framework:

- To support persons with disabilities to become 'ready employees', SG Enable works closely with different training partners to customise and provide a variety of pre-vocational and vocational training targeted at industry needs. Funding is also provided to help the jobseekers attend these courses. At the same time, SG Enable works closely with its Job Placement and Job Support

(JPJS) partners, namely Autism Resource Centre, Movement for the Intellectually Disabled of Singapore (MINDS) and SPD (formerly Society for Physically Disabled), to provide job matching and job support services;

- To enable more employers to become 'ready employers' to hire persons with disabilities, SG Enable supports employers through assessment, training and self-help resources. As a first step, employers are encouraged to use the Workplace Disability Inclusive Index to conduct a self-assessment to identify areas of improvement. To train employers on how to hire, support and integrate persons with disabilities into their workforce, SG Enable conducts disability awareness talks and the High Impact Retention & Employment (HIRE) workshop series (SG Enable, 2016b), and also makes available online supplementary resources such as Human Resource Management (HRM) toolkits (SG Enable, 2016d). SG Enable organises signature events like the Enabling Employers Award and the Inclusive Business Forum to facilitate sharing of best practices and recognise inclusive employers. SG Enable also partners employer networks such as the Singapore Business Network on DisAbility (SBNoD) and Singapore Business Federation Foundation (SBFF). Beyond education and outreach, SG Enable also administers the Open Door Programme (ODP) which is a funding grant provided by the government that aims to encourage employers to hire, train and integrate persons with disabilities (SG Enable, 2016a); and
- To build a 'ready environment', SG Enable sees that the quality and sustainability of each job placement is often dependent on the skills of the disability employment professionals. To build their capabilities, SG Enable has embarked on initiatives such as a Community of Practice for job coaches, the joint development of an Advanced Certificate in Supported Employment with the Social Service Institute, as well as the SkillsFuture Study Award for Disability Employment Professionals to encourage continuous learning and upskilling. SG Enable also operates the Tech Able facility in collaboration with SPD to provide advice and funding on assistive technology to persons with disabilities and potential employers.

While SG Enable and its partners have helped more than 1,400 persons with disabilities find jobs since 2014 (SG Enable, 2014, 2015, 2016c), it is also important to provide transition support to students transitioning from school to work. Students with disabilities may find the transition from school into employment challenging, especially if they are not properly equipped with relevant technical and soft skills, confidence and people network, which are critical factors to advance in today's competitive labour market. SG Enable runs four key transition initiatives to support students with disabilities in their transition from school to the world of work. The four initiatives are:

- *For students graduating from SPED Schools*:
    o School-to-Work (S2W) Transition Programme, and
    o Job Shadowing Day.
- *For students graduating from Institutes of Higher Learning (IHLs)*:
    o IHL Internship Programme, and
    o RISE Mentorship Programme.

These transition programmes provide students with the opportunity to gain necessary skills, confidence, work exposure and experience and build their professional networks, and are described later in this chapter.

Trends

Several key economic trends could impact on the disability employment landscape.

Firstly, the nature of jobs in Singapore could change as trends like the 'gig economy' gain traction, taking the place of more permanent and traditional jobs. The 'gig economy' is also supported by new online-labour or capital sharing platforms, which serve to match or connect people who are looking to buy a service with workers who are willing to provide the said job. Examples of these platforms would be food delivery service Deliveroo and transport/food delivery service Grab. While there are challenges and concerns over job security and protections of workers in the gig economy, this may open up new employment opportunities for persons with disabilities, especially those who may require more flexibility.

Secondly, employers could rely on technological advances and automation to do away with lower-skilled jobs to raise productivity and raise bottom lines. Digital transformation and widespread adoption of technology would also impact skills sets required of employees (HumanResources, 2017). Persons with disabilities may be at risk from economic restructuring, and more efforts have to be put in to help them to remain employable.

Thirdly, the Committee for Future Economy (CFE), which is set up to help drive the growth and transformation of Singapore's economy, has proposed seven strategies to guide Singapore in the next 10 years (CFE, 2017). Of these seven, two notable ones are for workers to acquire deep skills, and to build strong digital capabilities across our economy. This need to acquire deep skills is supported by the national SkillsFuture movement started in 2014.

Lastly, it must be noted that these trends do not necessarily just pose threats to the employment of persons with disabilities, but can present opportunities too. The CFE has identified growth sectors in Singapore, e.g., finance, healthcare technology, logistics, and in digital economy sectors such as information and communications technology (ICT), media, cybersecurity, data analytics and digitisation. Getting persons with disabilities to be part of the national discourse would be important to help them secure opportunities in the growth sectors and jobs. It is also critical to put in resources to train, upskill and better prepare persons with disabilities for employment in these areas. For example, United Overseas Bank's Scan Hub has trained and placed persons with autism to support the digitisation of documents (Hong, 2017).

3rd Enabling Masterplan

The 3rd Enabling Masterplan outlines several strategic directions to support the disability sector. In particular, Strategic Direction 4 focuses on the importance of "Improved Access to Enhanced Pathways for Employment and Lifelong Learning Opportunities", wherein the committee made four recommendations (3rd Enabling Masterplan Steering Committee, 2016):

i. To develop and enhance vocational preparation pathways to better cater to persons with diverse support needs;
ii. To develop a spectrum of open, supported and customised employment models to provide more pathways to employment;
iii. To strengthen efforts to provide lifelong learning opportunities for persons with disabilities; and
iv. To scale up efforts to build employers' capabilities in hiring and managing employees with disabilities.

SG Enable's key initiatives to support students with disabilities to transit from school to gainful employment are consistent with these four recommendations. The next portion of this chapter will examine the impact of the four transition programmes run by SG Enable previously outlined.

Special Education (SPED) Schools

For students from SPED schools transitioning from school to work, it was noted that many experienced a 'cliff effect', where they faced difficulties in securing employment and ended up unemployed and staying at home, whereupon the lack of social interaction and meaningful activity further resulted in the deterioration of their work readiness and their motivation to work. The need to better support SPED students in this transition was therefore identified as a key area of focus (2nd Enabling Masterplan Steering Committee, 2012).

Every year, about 300 students graduate from the SPED schools (Lim, 2017). Some of them are able to receive additional vocational training based on their academic performance; these students either go on to further education with Metta School or Delta Senior School, or progress to mainstream educational institutions such as the Institute of Technical Education where they work towards a certificate as part of their training (Ministry of Education, 2018). With the additional training and certification provided by these programmes, many of these students are able to secure employment with minimal additional support.

SPED students who do not go on to further education will then graduate at the age of 18 years, and can either go on to open employment, sheltered workshops or a day activity centre (Ministry of Education, 2018). It was noted in the 2nd Enabling Masterplan (2012–2016) that there was a need to provide more support to help increase the percentage of graduating SPED students being placed in open employment, and that SPED students do face significant challenges in attaining open employment as they lack both vocational and soft skills (2nd Enabling Masterplan Steering Committee, 2012).

School-to-Work Transition Programme

Cognisant of the need to provide more support to graduating SPED students, the pilot School-to-Work (S2W) Transition Programme was launched in 2014. The programme is a multi-agency collaboration by the Ministry of Education (MOE), the Ministry of Social and Family Development (MSF) and SG Enable, in partnership with the prototype SPED schools, to offer customised training pathways and work options for students with diverse disability profiles who have the potential to work. The programme aims to provide such students a 'bridge' to transit from school to employment.

Pre-programme assessment and profiling

The programme starts in the last two years of SPED school, through the Individual Transition Planning (ITP) process, where a multi-disciplinary school team works with each student to identify potential post-school options, and based on the student's needs and abilities, the school then encourages and supports the students to maximise their potential. Students identified with the potential to go into employment will then be assessed for their work abilities concurrently via the student vocational profiling (SVP) tool, which also provides a framework for documenting the student's background, educational and vocational information, as well as recommended areas of job training, support and accommodations needed to facilitate the transition from school to work.

Based on the students' vocational profiles and needs, they will be recommended for suitable pathways that will offer them the necessary training and employment opportunities. The recommended pathways are all geared towards employment as the eventual outcome. In addition, SG Enable engages with the parents and caregivers to assess their readiness and commitment to fully support their family members into employment, and to start preparing them to make the transition journey together with the students. This is crucial as the parents and caregivers play a key role in helping the students with their vocational learning, inculcating and reinforcing in them the positive attitude towards work (e.g., reminding them of the importance of not skipping work for no reason) and work habits.

S2W pathways

Upon graduation from SPED schools, the students enter the S2W programme proper, with most of the students going into the 'Group Internship' pathway. The programme starts with a two-month orientation programme where the trainees go through a variety of preparatory training, including work hardening to build up physical stamina, vocational skills training and soft skills such as workplace safety, punctuality and discipline and workplace etiquette.

After the orientation period, the trainees are deployed to employer work sites where they go through a work-and-learn group internship programme for 9 months. The group internship model enables employers to mentor and train a group of students at one go, supports trainees in learning from one another, and allows a more efficient deployment of job coaches to support them. SG Enable also regularly engages with the employers to elicit feedback about the trainees and to better understand whether there can be further training or accommodation that is necessary to improve the trainees' work performance.

Besides the group internship pathway, SG Enable also provided two other pathways to employment for the students. This is because some students may not benefit fully from a group internship programme (e.g., due to their inability to work well with other students), or some of them may need more customised job support. For these students, SG Enable will recommend them to either 'Further Training' or 'Customised Employment'. Students placed into 'Further Training' will be attached to train-and-place training partners who will take them on for extended periods of vocational and soft skills training before attempting to place them into jobs. For 'Customised Employment', the situation is reversed, where the student is first placed with an employer and then undergoes a 'place-and-train' programme where he receives on-the-job vocational training.

Importance of engaging with parents and caregivers

Overall, parents and caregivers had positive feedback about the programme. The parents and caregivers observed that the trainees had experienced improvements in positive feelings of self-esteem and confidence, in their abilities to learn, concentrate and execute tasks, and through the programme, the trainees had come to build a stronger relationship with their families. The parents and caregivers also felt that the programme had helped their child make a smoother transition from school to post-school life, and they observed that their children had improved in their daily living skills, e.g., able to travel independently, and learnt new skills.

Two caregivers characterised their positive feedback as:

> From the top management of SG Enable to the coaches, the fitness instructors, other staff working in the background and their partners, I can sense their sincerity and determination to walk through the journey with me and my son. This could be a once-in a lifetime opportunity for your child to gain meaningful employment or do something that he/she enjoys. If you do not let your child experience it, you would never know whether it is good for him/her.

> I hereby would like to express my thanks to the coaches for making this possible. Without your help, [my child] would still be the short-tempered, stubborn and lazy boy. You not only giving him a chance to work but also making him see himself that he still can do and have a future like others.

Results

Across the three years of the pilot (2014–2016), 84 graduates of SPED schools have completed the programme, of whom 65 have secured employment (SG Enable, 2016c). These early results are positive, and demonstrate that the model of supported employment, on-the-job training and group internships are valuable in supporting the students to transition into employment.

Beyond the successful placements, the programme also resulted in long term benefits to the employers who participated in the programme and initial feedback from co-workers and supervisors had been positive as well. Employers who participated in the programme noted in their surveys that the co-workers working with the students with disabilities learnt to be more understanding and patient, that staff morale and teamwork improved as a result of the programme, and that the students contributed meaningfully and helped with their daily workload. This meant that employers were not doing this just for social responsibility, but were also able to achieve good business value from their participation in the programme.

Job Shadowing Day

Learning from the School-to-Work Transition Programme, SG Enable has also worked with the SPED schools to introduce a Job Shadowing Day for younger students (aged 15–17) to help students better understand the concept of work and to experience different workplaces. Job Shadowing Day is a week-long event that brings together employers and SPED students, and provides SPED students with the opportunity to be attached to employees from a variety of organisations for the duration of a day.

Through Job Shadowing Day, SPED students gain valuable exposure to different job roles and types of workplace and become more attuned to the concept of employment, and this helps to inspire them to want to work after graduation. Nur Farahnisha Sahlan (from MINDS Lee Kong Chian Gardens School) was attached to Pan Pacific Hotels Group, where she joined co-workers to perform housekeeping tasks and made new friends (Yang, 2017).

Job Shadowing Day is also a good opportunity for employers to express their commitment to diversity and inclusion. At the same time, employees can gain a better understanding of how to work with persons with disabilities and the value that they can bring to organisations. As an example, supervisors at Pan Pacific Hotels Group who worked with Nur Farahnisha Sahlan were so impressed with her positive attitude that they offered her a four-month job attachment.

In September 2017, Job Shadowing Day was announced as an annual event and SG Enable intends to scale up the initiative to benefit more SPED school students.

Institutes of Higher Learning

According to MOE, "75% of our children with special needs are supported in our mainstream schools" (C. M. Ng, 2016). While the education pathways may be different, students from SPED schools and students from mainstream schools face similar challenges in transitioning from school to work.

In the post-secondary space such as polytechnics and universities, students with disabilities are supported by SEN (Special Educational Needs) Support Offices. SG Enable works closely with these SEN Support Offices to provide support to students with disabilities. While they are still in school, they can benefit from programmes such as the RISE Mentorship Programme and the IHL Internship Programme, and after graduation they can further benefit from employment and training assistance through SG Enable, as well as deepen their skillsets through initiatives such as the SkillsFuture Study Award for Persons with Disabilities.

IHL Internship Programme

The IHL Internship Programme aims to address these issues by offering students with disabilities opportunities to gain valuable and impactful work experiences through meaningful internships with inclusive companies. The programme was started by SG Enable in December 2013, and to date, 80 tertiary students with disabilities have been placed in internships with 56 companies (SG Enable, 2016c).

SG Enable reaches out to IHL students with disabilities through the SEN Support Offices. SG Enable facilitates the process in the following ways:

a. Matching each student with a suitable company based on his or her preferences;
b. Supporting the student and employer during the selection and interview processes; and
c. Providing advice to the employer on reasonable accommodation and support needs for the intern in the workplace, when and where necessary.

The students will be exposed to an actual working environment in a sector they are interested in, and these experiences will stand them in good stead when they embark on their career.

SG Enable also sees the IHL Internship Programme as a useful initiative to help employers become more ready to hire and integrate persons with disabilities in their workforce. For employers who may not be as ready to hire right away, taking in interns with disabilities can be a useful and lower risk step for employers who are looking to assess their organisation's readiness to hire and accommodate employees with disabilities (Kok, 2016). Taking in interns can also provide employers an opportunity to green harvest potential talent.

Alister Ong, a graduate of the Singapore Management University, was supported by the IHL Internship Programme in 2013 and was placed in an internship with Deutsche Bank. Since then, he has grown in confidence of his abilities and he has gone on to complete internships with Accenture and the Ministry of National Development (Kok, 2016). The experience of taking on Alister as an intern also benefitted his employers; Deutsche Bank has since taken in several other interns, including Chen Jiajun, a Nanyang Technological University graduate with low vision, who interned with the bank in 2016. After his internships, Alister worked as a Sustainability Group Associate with Singtel, and now holds the position of Assistant Manager, Community Partnerships, at AWWA.

RISE Mentorship

From the experiences of supporting students with disabilities through the IHL Internship Programme, SG Enable realised that some students may need further upstream support in the form of confidence building, self-awareness and benefit from personalised guidance before they are ready to participate in internships and employment. Thus, RISE Mentorship was developed by SG Enable in 2017 to better support the transition of students with disabilities in IHLs into the workforce. The programme is adapted from the Australia Network of Disability's PACE Mentoring Programme.

RISE Mentorship aims to provide a platform for these students to gain a better understanding of their skills and abilities, build networks and become more confident in seeking future employment. Students with disabilities are matched with experienced business managers and professionals from inclusive employers and undergo 12 weeks of mentorship with their matched mentors. Through the programme, mentees will be able to gain a better understanding of their skills and abilities, build professional networks and tap into their mentors' wealth of knowledge and work experience.

RISE Mentorship also serves as another platform for employers to learn how to become more inclusive, and be more confident in interacting and supporting persons with disabilities in the workplace. Through mentoring, mentors will share their knowledge and expertise with their mentees, and in doing so, gain awareness in communicating, interacting with and supporting persons with disabilities. Similar to the IHL Internship Programme, RISE Mentorship is also another platform for employers to identify talent; some mentees in RISE Mentorship have gone on to do internships with their mentor companies.

Before the start of mentoring, mentors will participate in SG Enable's training on disability awareness and the RISE Mentorship Programme. The training focuses on disability etiquette and tips on communicating and supporting persons with disabilities. Similarly, mentees will also attend a briefing session which outlines their roles and expected commitment, and helps them to set out their expectations and goals for mentoring.

Jaslyn Tan, a graduate from Temasek Polytechnic in Finance and Accounting, participated in RISE Mentorship in 2017, and was paired with a Finance Director from Singtel. Through the programme, she "learnt a lot about working life" and had the chance to hone her soft skills through "mock interviews and resume-vetting sessions" (W. K. Ng, 2017). The experience also benefitted her mentor, and he was able to better understand how to support and communicate with Jaslyn, who is deaf. SG Enable plans to expand the programme to benefit more students with disabilities and employers.

Looking Ahead

Students with disabilities can benefit from better support to participate meaningfully in today's economy and workforce. SG Enable hopes that its four key transition programmes can support students with disabilities better in their transition from school to work. Nonetheless, more can be done for students with disabilities, and this can be realised by greater collaboration and support from partners such as Social Service Agencies (SSAs), SEN Support Offices and government agencies.

SG Enable will look to work more closely with the government. For example, following the initial success of the pilot School-to-Work Transition Programme, SG Enable will continue to work closely with MOE and MSF to expand the programme to more SPED schools. Secondly, SG Enable hopes to work with the SEN Support Offices to reach out to more students with disabilities, especially those from IHLs, to benefit from transition programmes and other services offered by SG Enable. Thirdly, SG Enable hopes to work with partners to build up the capabilities of the sector, such as the disability employment professionals.

Technology can also be a key enabler for persons with disabilities. To stay future-ready in today's employment landscape, it is important for employers and jobseekers to readily adopt technology and acquire new skills. Thus, it is important for SG Enable to work closely with the government (in line with the national SkillsFuture initiative) and other stakeholders to better support persons with disabilities to upskill and upgrade themselves, especially those who are working in industries where automation may reduce the need for intensive manpower. Secondly, it is also important to improve access to technology for persons with disabilities. To support this, SG Enable manages Tech Able with SPD, which aims to promote the awareness and adoption of assistive technology, and also manages the Tote Board — Enabling Lives Grant, which funds projects in the area of data & technology to expand opportunities for persons with disabilities (SG Enable, 2017).

To help Singapore advance towards an inclusive society, we must ensure that students with disabilities have equal opportunities to succeed and thrive. We must help them to demonstrate their abilities and be an equal participant in the labour market.

References

2nd Enabling Masterplan Steering Committee. (2012). Enabling Masterplan 2012–2016. Retrieved from https://www.ncss.gov.sg/NCSS/media/NCSS-Documents-and-Forms/Enabling-Masterplan-2012-2016-Report-%288-Mar%29-%28EM2%29.pdf

3rd Enabling Masterplan Steering Committee. (2016). 3rd Enabling Masterplan 2017–2021: Caring Nation, Inclusive Society. Retrieved from https://www.ncss.gov.sg/NCSS/media/NCSS-Documents-and-Forms/EM3-Final_Report_20161219.pdf

CFE. (2017). Report of the Committee on the Future Economy. Retrieved from https://www.gov.sg/~/media/cfe/downloads/cfe report.pdf?la=en

Hong, J. (2017, July 22). Banking on people with disabilities. *The Straits Times.* Retrieved from https://www.straitstimes.com/singapore/banking-on-people-with-disabilities

Human Resources. (2017). 70% of Singapore residents retrenched in Q3 2017 were PMETs. Retrieved September 3, 2019, from http://www.humanresourcesonline.net/70-of-singapore-residents-retrenched-in-q3-2017-were-pmets/

Kok, X. H. (2016, July 7). Opening career paths for the disabled. *The Straits Times.* Retrieved from https://www.straitstimes.com/singapore/opening-career-paths-for-the-disabled.

Lim, J. Q. (2017, January 18). Life after graduation: Special education students at work. *Channel NewsAsia.* Retrieved from https://www.channelnewsasia.com/news/singapore/life-after-graduation-special-education-students-at-work-7574950

Ministry of Education. (2018). Figure 1: Pathways for Educational Placement of Students with SEN. Retrieved October 4, 2019, from https://www.moe.gov.sg/docs/default-source/document/education/special-education/images/sped-pathway.pdf

Ministry of Education. (2019). SPED Curriculum Framework. Retrieved September 2, 2019, from https://www.moe.gov.sg/education/special-education/special-education-schools/sped-curriculum-framework

Ng, C. M. (2016). Speech by Ng Chee Meng, Minister for Education (Schools) at SPED Conference 2016. Retrieved October 4, 2019, from https://www.moe.gov.sg/news/speeches/20161104-speech-by-ng-chee-meng-minister-for-education-schools-at-sped-conference-2016

Ng, W. K. (2017, June 7). Work mentoring scheme for special students a hit. *The Straits Times.* Retrieved from https://www.straitstimes.com/singapore/work-mentoring-scheme-for-special-students-a-hit

SG Enable. (2014). Inclusive Society. Enabled Lives. Financial Year 2014: SG Enable Annual Report. Retrieved from https://www.sgenable.sg/pages/content.aspx?path=/about-us/

SG Enable. (2015). Inclusive Society. Enabled Lives. Financial Year 2015: SG Enable Annual Report. Retrieved from https://www.sgenable.sg/pages/content.aspx?path=/about-us/

SG Enable. (2016a). Funding and Support for Employers. Retrieved October 3, 2019, from https://employment.sgenable.sg/employers/open-door-programme/

SG Enable. (2016b). Get Trained. Retrieved October 3, 2019, from https://employment.sgenable.sg/employers/get-trained/#anchor1

SG Enable. (2016c). Inclusive Society, Enabled Lives. Financial Year 2016: SG Enable Annual Report. Retrieved from https://www.sgenable.sg/pages/content.aspx?path=/about-us/

SG Enable. (2016d). Online HRM Series for Employers. Retrieved October 3, 2019, from https://employment.sgenable.sg/employers/online-hrm-series/

SG Enable. (2017). Inclusive Society, Enabled Lives. SG Enable Annual Report 2017. Retrieved from https://www.sgenable.sg/pages/content.aspx?path=/about-us/

Yang, C. (2017, October 14). Initiative to help special needs students discover job interests to be scaled up. *The Straits Times*. Retrieved from https://www.straitstimes.com/singapore/education/initiative-to-help-special-needs-students-discover-job-interests-to-be-scaled-up

© 2021 World Scientific Publishing Company
https://doi.org/10.1142/9789814667142_0012

CHAPTER 12

Disability and Employment: Confronting Challenges in Contemporary Singapore

Vimallan Manokara

ಚ಼ೞ

Introduction

The World Health Organisation and World Bank estimate that 15 per cent, or about a billion people of the world's population lives with a disability (United Nations Enable, n.d.; WHO and World Bank, 2016). Of the world's poorest, persons with disabilities are disproportionately represented in this category as a consequence of unemployment. About 80 per cent of people with disabilities of working age are unemployed (United Nations Enable, n.d.). When people with disabilities do find employment, the situation is bleak. For persons with congenital disabilities, their experience with unemployment is longer compared with those who acquire their disability (Burchardt, 2000; Martin, White & Meltzer, 1989).

For persons with congenital disabilities, their experience with unemployment is longer compared with those who acquire their disability (Burchardt, 2000; Martin *et al.*, 1989). In terms of salaries, employees with disabilities earn less than the average income

(Konrad *et al.*, 2013). About 50 per cent of people with disabilities have incomes below the national median wage, of which women with disabilities bear the brunt of the disparity (Burchardt, 2000; Martin *et al.*, 1989). It is also not unusual that people with disabilities experience higher underemployment (Markel & Barclay, 2009). For example, persons with disabilities are under-represented in professional and managerial occupations.

By contrast, persons with disabilities tend to be concentrated in entry-level and part-time jobs (Schur *et al.*, 2009), semi- and unskilled occupations (Burchardt, 2000; Martin *et al.*, 1989). Women with disabilities tend to be found in routine clerical and personal service work, and also tend to work from home, finding themselves socially isolated and in low paid jobs (Jolly, 2000). The generally bleak employment experiences and barriers reported of persons with disabilities in accessing and sustaining paid work is a perennial global problem. With a growing recognition that employment is considered a key factor in the process of empowering individuals towards inclusion (Tripney *et al.*, 2015), it is vital and timely for social service agencies (SSAs) in Singapore who provide job placement and support programmes to review the employment provisions for persons with disabilities in Singapore.

This chapter examines disability employment by first considering the international landscape of employment and the evolving pressures confronting work in contemporary economies, and what they suggest for all workers including those with disabilities. Set against this background, international trends and milestones in disability employment are next reviewed in order to provide a context for understanding developments and challenges in disability employment in Singapore.

Background

A generation of development, policy, technology, improved delivery mechanisms and demonstrations of significant progress has not yet provided sufficient clarity and procedures to assure that all people with disabilities have a good chance getting real jobs. Furthermore, there have been troubling signs that the integrated work enterprise is stalling, resulting in ever-increasing numbers of individuals with disabilities, especially significant developmental disabilities, being served in segregated work and day programmes (Rusch & Braddock, 2004). Hence, internationally, efforts are being made to understand how persons with disabilities can be sustained better in the open employment market and be contributing members of society. There are well documented examples of people with substantial impairments enjoying the benefits of good work over many years of fluctuating labour market conditions (Brown, Shiraga & Kessler, 2006). Unfortunately, these success stories have not been generalised as employers and job support agencies continue to struggle with increasing the rate of employment of persons with disabilities.

The importance of having persons with disabilities as contributors of the economy in the open labour market is understated. According to the United Nations (UN), about 10 per cent of the world's population is disabled at any one time. However, this 10 per cent underestimates the impact of disability. When disabled persons are not fully integrated into society and the economy, they pose added costs on their families, for example more demands on their time which may preclude time spent in other productive pursuits (Mont, 2004). Additionally, the current greying world population is expected to increase the prevalence of disability as disability is known to increase significantly with age. In the United States, for example, about 2.3 per cent of previously working 35–39 year olds have experienced the onset of a work ending disability. For 50–54 and 60–64 year olds, that rate increases to 6.2 per cent and 15.1 per cent respectively (Mont, 2004).

The effects of disability can also vary from mild to profound. This is true for intellectual, sensory or physical disabilities. Similarly, the support needs for each person with disability is also unique. Hence, when discussing open employment sustainability of persons with disabilities, it is impossible adopt a 'one-size-fits-all' approach as the support needs and concerns of people with disabilities can be quite varied. Although the literature states that regardless of the presence or type of disability, persons with disabilities should have the proper customised supports and accommodations necessary. We do not understand how to adequately apply this knowledge in employment support services so that the rate of successful open employment of persons with disabilities increases.

The shift towards the industrialisation of the global economy since the beginning of the 20th century has brought about a corresponding shift in the landscape of employment. While presenting new changes and opportunities, this evolution has also posed new and different challenges to societies globally. There was an evolution in the technological and social organisation of the workplace from artisanal set-ups to large, bureaucratic factories where there was mechanisation of manufacturing and the concentration of labour. The changes to industralisation and then post-industralisation have had a significant impact on organisations and their employees. Huey (1994) attributed the changes in the Industrial Revolution to four factors: flattening of the hierarchy, outsourcing, increased use of partnerships and decentralisation of work and telecommunication (Applegate, 1994).

There was also a change in the employment of people in workplaces, with more specialisations in functions and clearly defined job roles. There was a rise in demand for skilled and flexible employees which resulted in a rise in the roles of supervisors and managers (Winter & Taylor, 1996); and, on a larger scale, there was an increase in power difference between employers and workers. Organisations began placing more emphasis on training and skill development of employees so that employees have a wider skill base and can add value to their jobs. The post-Industrial Revolution period then spurred the demand of information in the economy and the consequent rise of computers, electronics workplace. The value of workers became increasingly influenced by the extent they were flexible enough to perform a range of tasks and roles (Elger, 1987).

In present times, John Maynard Keynes's frequently cited prediction of widespread technological unemployment "due to our discovery of means of economising the use of labour outrunning the pace at which we can find new uses for labour" (Keynes, 1933, p. 3) appears to be ringing true. Indeed, over the past decades, computers have substituted for a number of jobs, including the functions of bookkeepers, cashiers and telephone operators (Bresnahan, 1999; MGI, 2013). More recently, the poor performance of labour markets across advanced economies has intensified the debate about technological unemployment among economists. While there is ongoing disagreement about the driving forces behind the persistently high unemployment rates, a number of scholars have pointed at computer-controlled equipment as a possible explanation for recent jobless growth (see, for example, Brynjolfsson & McAfee, 2011). The impact of computerisation on labour market outcomes is well established in the literature, documenting the decline of employment in routine intensive occupations, i.e., occupations mainly consisting of tasks following well-defined procedures that can easily be performed by sophisticated algorithms.

Globally, social, economic and political forces have aligned to make employment more uncertain, unpredictable and risky from the point of view of the worker. The Bureau of Labor Statistics (BLS) estimates (and likely underestimates) that more than 30 million full-time workers lost their jobs involuntarily between the early 1980s and 2004 (Uchitelle, 2006). According to Brynjolfsson and McAfee (2011), the pace of technological innovation is still increasing, with more sophisticated software technologies disrupting labour markets by making workers redundant. What is striking about the examples in their book is that computerisation is no longer confined to routine manufacturing tasks. The autonomous driverless cars, developed by Google, provide one example of how manual tasks in transport and logistics may soon be automated (Frey & Osborne, 2013).

Changes in legal and other institutions have mediated the effects of globalisation and technology on work and employment relations (Gonos, 1997). Unions' influence has continued to decline, weakening a traditional source of institutional protections for workers. Government regulations that set minimum acceptable standards in the labour market have been eroded. Union decline and deregulation have reduced the countervailing forces that enabled workers to share in the productivity gains that were made by organisations and corporations, reinforcing the notion that the balance of power continues to sway heavily away from workers and towards employers.

Further, deregulation and reorganisation of employment relations have allowed for the massive accumulation of capital in the economy. Advances in information and communication technologies allow capitalists to exert control over decentralised and spatially dispersed labour processes. Moreover, the entry of China, India and the former Soviet bloc countries into the global economy in the 1990s doubled the size of the global labour pool, further shifting the balance of power from labour to capital (Freeman, 2008). Political policies in countries like the United States — such as the replacement of welfare with workfare programs in the mid-1990s — made it essential for people to participate in paid employment, forcing many into low-wage jobs. Ideological shifts centering on individualism and personal responsibility for work and family life reinforced these structural changes; the slogan "you're on your own" replaced the notion of "we're all in this together" (Bernstein, 2006). This neoliberal revolution spread globally, emphasizing the centrality of markets and market-driven solutions, privatisation of government resources, and removal of government protections for vulnerable workers (Kalleberg, 2009).

In addition, the labour force has become more diverse over time, with marked increases in the number of women, older workers and workers with disabilities. The increase in immigration due to globalisation and the reduction of barriers to the movement of people across national borders have produced a greater surplus of labour today. However, this has resulted in an entrenchment of the 'survival of the fittest' notion, thereby highlighting the growing gaps in earnings and other indicators of labour market success between people with different amounts of education. Intuitively, it is sensible that this disparity would have also existed between people with disabilities and those without.

Another evolution of the employment landscape is that the service sector has become increasingly central. This has resulted in a changing mix of occupations, reflected in a decline in blue-collar jobs and an increase in both high-wage and low-wage white-collar occupations (Kalleberg, 2009). Compounding this is the trend that layoffs have become a basic component of employers' restructuring strategies. They reflect a way of increasing short-term profits by reducing labour costs (Kalleberg, 2009). Hence, although economic expansion and technological advancements have resulted in the creation of more jobs in a way, the expansion has really been for higher level, sophisticated jobs which machines are unable to do. This, added to the shift in power from employees to employers, indicates that over the years, the evolution of the labour market is advantageous to some but less so for others. This appears to be particularly true for the vulnerable populations such as persons with disabilities and older workers.

Situation in Singapore

According to the Ministry of Manpower (MOM), technological advancements and changing social norms are significantly altering the nature of work in Singapore. Disruptive innovations have resulted in more jobs being displaced and more frequent bouts of involuntary unemployment. Digital platforms have made the coordination of components of work more seamless, timely and convenient, thereby allowing work tasks to be unbundled. Such micro-jobs offer opportunities for workers to earn supplemental income, but come with less job security. Employers that value operational flexibility may favour contingent workers and reduce their core of permanent staff to optimise labour costs. Individuals are likely to experience more frequent career transitions across companies, sectors and even types of employment, as new job opportunities emerge and existing jobs are redesigned. Workers will have to be accustomed to the prospect of less permanent and more fluid work arrangements throughout life (Lee, 2018).

The 'Future of Work' is a broad and complex topic which has spawned major streams of on-going work. In response to technological and economic disruptions, economic agencies and the Committee on the Future Economy (CFE) are looking into future areas of growth, job creation and helping companies cope. The

Ministry of Education (MOE) and SkillsFuture Singapore (SSG) are identifying the skills and training needed to keep Singaporeans relevant. At the intersection of jobs and skills are the Ministry of Manpower (MOM) and Workforce Singapore (WSG), which match individuals with the right skills to the right jobs. While Singapore has not experienced a decline in the share of permanent employment, workers may see a gradual shift away from the traditional model of lifetime employment. In future, we expect more transitions in and out of employment and learning during adulthood. Workers may move between different jobs, work arrangements and even careers, punctuated by periods of unemployment or training (Lee, 2018).

International Landscape on Disability Employment

Historically, there have long been debates about whether people with significant disabilities are capable of working in integrated environments (Black, 1992; Wehman & Moon, 1987). For example, the United States has a protracted history of segregating and sheltering workers with disabilities (National Disability Rights Network, 2011). Dating back to the opening of the first sheltered workshop in 1840, through the period of rapid expansion of sheltered workshops in the 1950s and 1960s, the stated purpose of segregated work programmes was to meet the needs of people incapable of working in the regular workforce due to the severity of their physical, intellectual or mental impairments. Workshops were viewed as protective environments "sheltered" from public ridicule, judgment and shame, where people could develop the job skills necessary to compete for traditional community jobs (Black, 1992).

A principal assumption at the time was that people with intellectual and developmental disabilities needed to move through a continuum of rehabilitation services to prepare to work in a regular job in the community (Bellamy *et al.*, 1988; Taylor, 1988). Moving through the traditional continuum of rehabilitation services meant that an individual first participated in prevocational education, then a work-activity centre, and then sheltered employment, before finally being placed in a community job. A flaw in the implementation of this readiness model was that few people were ever determined ready for community employment and the vast majority remained confined to segregated settings in perpetuity.

By the early 1980s, the axiom "special people need special places" was being challenged by reports of individuals with significant disabilities living and working successfully in the community (Mank, 1994). The notion that people with significant disabilities needed to work in separate facilities apart from workers without disabilities, where their unique needs could be met by specially trained professionals, continued to erode as advances in supported employment opened the door to community employment for many people once considered unemployable. During the past three decades, a growing body of empirical evidence from the fields of psychiatric rehabilitation and developmental disabilities has demonstrated the effectiveness of supported employment in assisting individuals achieve employment in the open labour market, while day treatment, prevocational training and sheltered employment have been shown to be relatively ineffective in preparing individuals for competitive employment (e.g., Bond, 2004; Cimera *et al.*, 2012; Marshall *et al.*, 2014).

Consistent with the international evidence, especially in developed countries such as the United States and Australia, supported and open employment for people with intellectual disability was encouraged by governments because of its positive socioeconomic impact on individuals and on its economic benefit to society (Federal Register, 1987; Johnson & Lewis, 1994; Parmenter, 2011). Governments began to make policy changes to encourage more persons with disabilities to be employed in the open labour market. For example, in the United States, the Americans with Disabilities Act (ADA) of 1990 was considered a landmark civil rights statute.

Furthermore, in a 2011 report entitled "Segregated and exploited: The failure of the disability service system to provide quality work", the National Disability Rights Network (NDRN) sought, in part, to dispel myths about the capabilities of people with disabilities to be fully employed, integral members of the US workforce. The report asserted that "Workers with disabilities can be employed and be paid equally with the appropriate job development, training, work support, and assistive technology" (p. 34). It called for an end not only to sheltered employment but also to an antiquated labour law exception that allowed workshops and other employers to pay less than minimum wages to workers with disabilities whose productive capacity was impaired by a physical or mental disability. Additionally, in 2014, the Rehabilitation Act which tended to facilitate only 'work ready' persons with disabilities to be given opportunities in the open market became incorporated as part of the broader Workforce Innovation and Opportunity Act of 2014 (WIOA), thus pushing the integrated employment agenda for youth transitioning from school to work. For the first time, competitive integrated employment was identified as the optimal employment outcome (Hoff, 2014).

Similarly, in Australia, in 2013, the Australian Government introduced the National Disability Insurance Scheme (NDIS) following a Productivity Commission Report, which found the disability support system was 'fragmented, underfunded, unfair and inefficient' and not meeting the individual needs of people living with a disability (Buys, Matthews & Randall, 2014). The aim of the scheme is to provide people with a significant disability with the supports necessary to enhance their independence and social and economic participation, but within a framework that enables them to exercise choice and control in the delivery of these supports (Buys et al., 2014).

However, despite human rights movement and policy changes by governments to include adults with disabilities in the workforce, their employment in the community remains much lower than the mainstream population (Colella & Bruyere, 2011; Parmenter, 2011). In industrialised countries, the unemployment rate among adults with disabilities of working age is 50 to 70 per cent, which is at least twice the rate of those without a disability (Parmenter, 2011). It is a dire situation in developing countries, where approximately 80 to 90 per cent of people with disabilities of working age are unemployed (Parmenter, 2011; Zarocostas, 2005).

Parmenter (2011) highlighted that the global high unemployment rate of adults with disabilities is not moderated by culture or economic status. In countries with civil rights legislation, unemployment rates are approximately twice what they are for people without disabilities. Intuitively, it can be assumed that rates are even worse in countries without such law, despite the fact that many of these people can work and want to work (Macias *et al.*, 2001). The poor employment rate of persons with disabilities globally needs to be explored with greater depth via a thorough examination of the systems and processes that facilitate and support persons with disabilities.

Singapore Landscape on Disability Employment: Challenges and Opportunities

Similar to the past and present international trends in the employment of persons with disabilities, many disabled people in Singapore want to work but are unable to find jobs. Efforts to address this issue in Singapore began as early as the 1970s and 80s. Experts from the United Nations and the International Labour Organisation were invited and commissioned reports described the best ways to increase the employment of disabled people (Disabled Persons Association, n.d.). The setting up of Disabled People's Association (DPA) Singapore in 1986, a disabled-led organisation, represented the aspirations of the disabled to guide their own destinies. Similarly, in 1988, then Minister for Education Dr. Tony Tan chaired the Advisory Council on Opportunities for the Disabled, with an entire section offering recommendations on disability employment. As reported by the council, the civil service then employed 443 disabled people out of a total pool of 131,696 employees in 1984. Despite these efforts, in 2016, only 270 disabled people were employed out of a pool of 145,000 employees (Zhuang, 2019).

To enhance the employment prospects of persons with disabilities, the Enabling Masterplans were developed to shape the policies and systems in order to facilitate persons with disabilities to transition better into the open labour market. The first Enabling Masterplan in 2007 advocated for persons with disabilities to have equal opportunities for work by being given opportunities to receive training and have relevant skills for different industries. Vocational assessments, training and job placement were important areas that were covered. In line with this, initiatives such as the Enable fund were introduced in 2006 to provide funding assistance for employers who needed to redesign jobs, modify workplaces or implement training when they hire persons with disabilities.

The second Enabling Masterplan followed in 2012. This masterplan focused on SG Enable — an agency setup by the government whose role is to drive initiatives to improve employment outcomes for persons with disabilities. The Open Door Programme (ODP), Special Employment Credit (SEC) and the Workfare Income Supplement (WIS) were introduced to support persons with disabilities, their families and employers. Enabling Masterplan 3 (EMP3), rolled out in 2017, emphasised lifelong learning and enhanced pathways for persons with disabilities to gain entry into the open labour market. It also emphasised the importance of building the capacity and capabilities of employers using technology to better support and accommodate persons with disabilities in workplaces.

The EMP3 revealed that 2.1 per cent of the population who are between 7 to 18 years of age, 3.4 per cent of people between the ages of 18 to 49 and 13.3 percent of people 50 and above years of age present with some form of disability. In Singapore, persons with disabilities comprise about 0.55 per cent of the resident labour force (Kok, 2017). These persons with disabilities are mainly employed in the hospitality, food and beverage, wholesale and retail and administrative support sectors. Although definitive data on the number of persons with disabilities in full-time and part-time employment is not available, an important gap is that we do not understand the barriers to employing persons in a wider range of industries.

The employment opportunities for people with disabilities in Singapore have increased in the last two decades because of strong economic development (DPA, 2015). In 2015, 305 people with disabilities sought the Society for the Physically Disabled's (SPD) help to find jobs, almost doubled the figure in 2013. The success rate also increased, with 127 securing jobs in 2015, compared to 37 in 2013 (HR Asia, 2016).

However, while more companies are willing to hire people with disabilities, there are still challenges when it comes to job-matching. According to SPD, small and medium enterprises make up the majority of the companies which offered employment to these people (HR Asia, 2016). There is a need to understand why employment offered to people with disabilities by bigger companies is not as common. Understanding and addressing the reasons for why bigger companies tend not to hire persons with disabilities would be crucial to increasing the employment rate of persons with disabilities as bigger companies potentially have more job places available compared to small and medium enterprises.

In 2010, only 121 job vacancies were listed for persons with disabilities which increased to 275 job vacancies in 2012 (DPA, 2015). This shows that the number of jobs available for persons with disabilities more than doubled in a two-year period. However, while some employers seem more willing to hire persons with disabilities, there is a lack of awareness of how they can successfully integrate a person with a disability into their workforce. Prior to 2013, social service agencies such as Bizlink and MINDS used to separately provide job placement and support services for people with disabilities. Since 2013, SG Enable has begun to serve as a focal point to support the needs of persons with disabilities. One of the key functions of this agency is to enhance the employability and employment options for persons with disabilities by leveraging on the strengths of existing partners and schemes. To facilitate training and employment services, it works with agencies that are funded to provide vocational assessment, job placement and job support services for persons with disabilities. However, the sustainability rates of Open Employment (OE) appear to be much lower than placement rates.

Amongst people with disabilities in Singapore, there is a high drop-out rate after placement in OE. Based on a local job placement's agency's internal data, from April 2014 to March 2015, 88 persons with intellectual and developmental disabilities had successfully been placed in OE. Of this number, there was a 25 per cent who dropped out within 6 months of placement. From April 2015 to March 2016, the drop-out rate within 6 months was higher at

31 per cent. By the end of 12 months from placement, the rate had increased to 40 per cent. Hence, it is evident by the drop-out rate that the objectives and needs of employers are not met optimally and that there is a lack of understanding of the ways job support service providers can increase the effectiveness of placement and post-placement support services. Many employers do hire and effectively accommodate and include people with disabilities. However, the specific characteristics of those employers who are open to and successful in hiring and accommodating people with disabilities have not been identified and consolidated. As such, job coaches do not have a systematic and structured way of providing consultation, education and advocacy for better employment outcomes for persons with disabilities. While employer influence remains one part of the equation, working with the student is the other. In this regard, MOE and SG Enable piloted a school-to-work internship programme drawing together a process for individual transition planning, a tool for student vocational profiling and a group internship model which has reported encouraging early results (Wong, Chong & Ng, 2020).

A key gap in Singapore's disability services is the absence of a model or framework that is based on international best practice to guide persons with disabilities, service providers, employers and caregivers in systematically placing and supporting a person with a disability on the job so that job sustainability is maximised. This lack of a model means that funding support and resources by the Singapore government are currently not channeled to specific areas according to the person's areas of support needs. Additionally, there is a lack of implementation of systematic employment outcome measures to effectively measure the impact of employment on best-practice standards such as inclusion and person-centredness.

The challenges that Singapore faces with regards to disability employment mirrors that of the international situation. There is a lack of systematic understanding of what it takes for persons with disabilities to sustain in OE post-placement. There is also a lack of a support model to guide job coaches, service providers, persons with disabilities, their caregivers and employers on effective job matching, placement and support for sustainable OE as well as a lack of effective outcome measures to measure outcomes and impact of OE upon placement.

Additionally, as technologies such as artificial intelligence and machine learning come to the forefront of the economy, it is bound to be disruptive to jobs in the labour market. The Digital Readiness Blueprint by the Ministry of Communication and Information (MCI) sets out recommendations for building Digital Readiness in Singaporeans, guided by four strategic thrusts. Through this blueprint, the government has acknowledged the importance of including people with disabilities in accessing the benefits of digital connectivity. Initiatives have spawned as a result are SG Enable's IT programme for persons with disabilities. Singapore has done well in ensuring digital access, and efforts to provide all Singaporeans with basic and appropriate access to digital technology must be continued.

As we move into the age of artificial intelligence and machine learning, disabled people face a greater challenge in obtaining and sustaining employment as there are fears that robots are taking over the jobs of people with disabilities, given that many of the jobs predicted to be taken over by robots are often the ones most accessible to disabled people. While this might be true, the reverse is also a much discussed possibility — where robots and technology can be tapped on to generate new job opportunities for people with disabilities (Wolbring, 2016). Artificial intelligence and technology, depending on how they are utilised and embedded in the workplace, can actively contribute to better inclusion in the organisation (Wisskirchen *et al.*, 2017). Hence, it is important to believe that more can be done than just providing access to technology. There is a need to ensure that people with disabilities, particularly those with intellectual and developmental disabilities, are equipped with the skills and know-how to use digital technology safely and confidently.

There is also a pressing need for greater awareness of media and information literacy skills so that Singaporeans with disabilities are able to discern, evaluate and manage information in an increasingly complex digital environment. For example, in the private sector,

Singtel has worked with TOUCH Cyber Wellness to develop a Cyber Wellness Toolkit for students with intellectual disabilities. SG Enable is also dedicated to helping persons with disabilities gain access to disability services and schemes. One of its initiatives was the setting up of Tech Able, comprising the Singtel Enabling Innovation Centre and the ST Engineering Enabling Technology Centre. Tech Able is an integrated assistive technology space at the Enabling Village which features a technology showcase for persons with disabilities and provides them with assistive device assessment services. Persons with disabilities can find out about devices that will help them in their employment or daily living activities.

While much is being done, there is still much more to be gained from coordinating the different approaches and initiatives and aligning them under a common framework to ensure that persons with disabilities continue to be given the best chance possible to contribute productively in the open labour market. In view of this, there are also other glaring gaps in terms of job support processes that need to be addressed. For example, given that the degree of fit between the support needs of the person and what is provided in the job is crucial to successful and sustainable OE, the lack of diagnostic assessments to systematically inform all stakeholders (e.g., persons with disabilities, caregivers, employers and job coaches) on the likelihood of sustainability and areas of support needs based on the fit between the person and the job, is glaring. From a person-centred perspective, the degree of fit between a specific person with disability and a specific job in the open labour market is often a crucial determinant of sustainability of the person in that particular job. A lack of understanding of this degree of fit would lead to a reactive approach with considerable 'fire-fighting' as compared to a proactive one where support areas are identified early on and measures put in place to maximise chances of job sustainability.

There is research evidence why people with disabilities make reliable employees and there are business benefits for hiring people with disabilities (Parmenter, 2011; Riches & MacDonald, 2016). However, in Singapore, little is known about the employer's environment in terms of their capacity and capability, or how attitudes and behaviour of the staff or line manager play in ensuring sustainability of open employment; and what supports they may need and how service providers can play a role in supporting employers and not just the person with disability. Anderson (2009) proposed that employment outcomes are optimised when inputs such as candidate preparation and job development are aligned with an appropriate job matched to the person's skills and competencies and the employer's needs.

In addition to a lack of understanding of the local employer environment and its response to persons with disabilities, little is also known about the caregiving environment. The caregiving environment has particular significance for the Singapore context as people with intellectual and developmental disabilities tend to live with their families for a significant portion of their lifespan, or at least till their families are unable to care for them. Hence, there is a pressing need to understand more about the family factors that influence sustainability of a person with disability in OE, after job placement. This is supported by studies from different countries. In Australia, Knox and Parmenter (1993) found that social support both within and beyond the workplace is crucial for persons with intellectual disabilities working in OE.

Economically, opportunities and support for sustainable open employment for persons with disabilities implies the underlying assumption that people with disabilities have a right to open employment and that the costs of their participation are small and easily absorbed by the private sector. However, there is a perception that work accommodations are too costly (Domzal, Houtenville & Sharma, 2008). This perception remains persistent despite studies showing that the majority of accommodations cost little or nothing, while having positive outcomes such as enhanced productivity and increased overall organisational well-being (Solovieva, Dowler & Walls, 2011). Hence, it is important to increase awareness and education amongst employers on the economic value of hiring and retaining persons with disabilities.

The implication of limiting opportunities and support for persons with disabilities to enter and sustain in the open employment market is that it gives rise to policies advocating for substitute vocational settings, such as sheltered workshops. These policies implicitly assume that people with disabilities are generally unable to fully participate in open employment and that the productivity gap between people with and without disabilities is wide enough to shift the cost of those gaps from employers to publicly funded services such as sheltered workshops. Placements of the majority of persons with disabilities in these settings are encouraged so long as policymakers feel it is a more economical alternative to the open labour market. However, substituted settings are typically frowned upon by disability rights advocates and the disability community. Also, advocates believe that lack of access to the open employment market is a barrier to the development of the social and job skills necessary for full inclusion into society, and is thus a self-fulfilling prophecy. Additionally, such policies also keep employers from being aware of the capabilities of disabled persons and can reinforce misconceptions that they cannot be valuable contributors of the workforce. Furthermore, it almost becomes a case of working in favour of service providers to keep their funding model, at the expense of working towards placing and sustaining more persons with disabilities in open employment.

However, in order to support the successful and sustainable inclusion of persons with disabilities in open employment, it is pertinent to fully understand the necessary support structures that need to be put in place when supporting a person with a disability in a job. Employment is not always inherently beneficial (Broom *et al.*, 2006) and can result in poor health and self-esteem, especially when natural supports in the workplace are missing and sustainability after placement becomes an issue (Williams *et al.*, 2016). While different studies outlined above advocate for certain variables that should be in place to help persons with disabilities sustain in their jobs, there remains an absence of a holistic and comprehensive model for successful OE in Singapore which pulls together all important factors in the important areas of person, caregiver and employer.

Conclusion

Allowing persons with disabilities in Singapore a full range of opportunities to participate in the economy and society at large is pertinent to facilitating their inclusion in society. Removing barriers to participation that plague persons with disabilities enhances their quality of life in general as well as increases productivity, lowers unemployment and reduces reliance on government transfers (Mont, 2004). Having a disability often means being socially isolated (WHO, 2011). Being employed is one opportunity to reduce this isolation.

The challenges that social service agencies (SSAs) in Singapore's disability landscape face with regards to disability employment is not dissimilar to that of international situation. Amongst job support services, there is a lack of systematic understanding of what it takes for persons with disabilities to sustain in OE post-placement beyond the stipulated job support period. In addition, there is a lack of a support model to guide job coaches, persons with disabilities, their caregivers and employers on effective job matching, placement and support for sustainable OE. It is clear that more work needs to be done to address these challenges within the employment context in Singapore to make disability employment more successful and sustainable. To do so in the most optimal manner would require all relevant stakeholders to work together and place persons with disabilities as the main drivers in confronting these challenges and opening up new possibilities for them within the local Singaporean context.

References

Anderson, P. (2009). Intermediate occupations and the conceptual and empirical limitations of the hourglass economy thesis. *Work, Employment and Society, 23*(1), 169–180. doi:10.1177/0950017008099785

Applegate, L. M. (1994, August). Managing in an information age: Transforming the organization for the 1990s. In Proceedings of the IFIP WG8. 2 Working Conference on Information Technology and

New Emergent Forms of Organizations: Transforming Organizations with Information Technology (pp. 15–94).
Bellamy, G. T., Rhodes, L. E., Mank, D. M., & Albin, J. M. (1988). *Supported Employment a Community Implementation Guide.* Baltimore: Paul H. Brookes.
Bernstein, J. (2006). *All Together Now: Common Sense for a New Economy.* San Francisco, CA: Berrett-Koehler Publishers, Inc.
Black, B. J. (1992). A kind word for sheltered work. *APA PsychNet,* 15(4), 87–89.
Bond, G. R. (2004). Supported employment: Evidence for an evidence-based practice. *Psychiatric Rehabilitation Journal,* 27(4), 345–359.
Bresnahan, T. F. (1999). Computerisation and wage dispersion: an analytical reinterpretation. *The Economic Journal,* 109(456), 390–415. https://doi.org/10.1111/1468-0297.00442
Broom, D. H., D'Souza, R. M., Strazdins, L., Butterworth, P., Parslow, R., & Rodges, B. (2006). The lesser evil: Bad jobs or unemployment? A survey of midaged Australians. *Social Science & Medicine,* 63(3), 575–586.
Brown, L., Shiraga, B., & Kessler, K. (2006). The quest for ordinary lives: the integrated post-school vocational functioning of 50 workers with significant disabilities. *Research and Practice for Persons with Severe Disabilities,* 31(2), 93–121.
Brynjolfsson, E., & McAfee, A. (2011, January). *Research Brief: Race Against the Machine: How the Digital Revolution is Accelerating Innovation, Driving Productivity, and Irreversibly Transforming Employment and the Economy.* Digital Frontier Press Lexington, MA.
Burchardt, T. (2000). *Enduring Economic Exclusion: Disabled People, Income and Work.* York: Joseph Rowntree Foundation.
Buys, N., Matthews, L. R., & Randall, C. (2014). Contemporary vocational rehabilitation in Australia. *Disability and Rehabilitation,* 1–5. DOI: 10.3109/09638288.2014.942001
Cimera, R. E., Wehman, P., West, M., & Burgess, S. (2012). Do sheltered workshops enhance employment outcomes for adults with autism spectrum disorder? *Autism: The International Journal of Research and Practice,* 16(1), 87–94. DOI: 10.1177/1362361311408129
Colella, A., & Bruyère, S. (2011). Disability and employment: New directions for industrial/organizational psychology. In N. Anderson, D. S. Ones, H. K. Sinangil, & C. Viswesvaran (Eds.), *American Psychological Association Handbook on Industrial Organizational Psychology* (Vol. 1, pp. 473–503). Washington, DC: American Psychological Association.

Disabled People's Association Singapore (DPA). (2015). Achieving inclusion in the workplace. Retrieved from https://www.dpa.org.sg/wp-content/uploads/2015/08/Employment-merged.compressed.pdf

Disabled People's Association Singapore (DPA). (n.d.). Retrieved from please provide correct website.

Domzal, C., Houtenville, A., & Sharma, R. (2008). Survey of employer perspectives on the employment of people with disabilities: Technical report. Prepared under contract to the Office of Disability and Employment Policy, U.S. Department of Labor. McLean, VA: CESSI.

Elger, T. (1987). Flexible futures? New technology and the contemporary transformation of work. *Work, Employment and Society, 1*(4), 528–540. doi:10.1177/0950017087001004007

Federal Register. (1987, August 14). The state supported employment services program. *Federal Register, 52*(157), 30546–30552.

Frey, C. B., & Osborne, M. A. (2013). The future of employment: how susceptible are jobs to computerisation? Oxford Martin Programme on Technology and Employment, University of Oxford. Retrieved from https://www.oxfordmartin.ox.ac.uk/downloads/academic/future-of-employment.pdf

Gonos, G. (1997). The contest over "employer" status in the postwar United States: The case of temporary help firms. *Law & Society Review, 31*(1), 81–110.

Hoff, D. (2014). WIA is now WIOA: What the new bill means for people with disabilities. *The Institute Brief, 31*, 1–4. Retrieved from http://www.communityinclusion.org/pdf/IB31_F.pdf

HR Asia. 2016. More disabled people finding jobs within past two years: SPD. Retrieved from https://www.hrinasia.com/news/more-disabled-people-finding-jobs-within-past-two-years-spd/

Huey, J. (1994, February 21). The new post-heroic leadership. *Fortune Magazine.* Retrieved from https://archive.fortune.com/magazines/fortune/fortune_archive/1994/02/21/78995/index.htm

Johnson, D. R., & Lewis, D. R (1994). Supported employment: Program models, strategies and evaluation perspectives. In M. F. Hayden & B. H. Abery (Eds.), *Challenges for a Service System in Transition: Ensuring Quality Community Experiences for Persons with Developmental Disabilities.* Baltimore MD: Paul H. Brookes Pub Co.

Jolly, D. (2000). A critical evaluation of the contradictions for disabled workers arising from the emergence of the flexible labour market in Britain. *Disability and Society, 15*(5), 795–810.

Kalleberg, A. L. (2009). Precarious work, insecure workers: employment relations in transition. *American Sociological Review, 74*(1), 1–22.

Keynes, J. M. (1933). Economic possibilities for our grandchildren: 1930. *Essays in Persuasion,* 358–373.

Knox, M., & Parmenter, T. R. (1993). Social networks and support mechanisms for people with mild intellectual disability in competitive employment. *International Journal of Rehabilitation Research, 16*(1), 1–12. doi:10.1097/00004356-199303000-00001

Kok, X. H. (2017, February 7). People with disabilities a focus for 2017 Budget: Indranee Rajah. *Straits Times.* Retrieved from https://www.straitstimes.com/singapore/people-with-disabilities-a-focus-for-2017-budget-indranee-rajah

Konrad, A. M., Moore, M. E., Ng, E. S. W., Doherty, A. J., & Breward, K. (2012). Temporary work, underemployment and workplace accommodations: Relationship to well-being for workers with disabilities. *British Journal of Management, 24*(3), 367–382. doi:10.1111/j.1467-8551.2011.00809.x

Lee, A. (2018, January 12). Trends and shifts in employment: Singapore's workforce: Worldwide shifts in employment patterns may challenge the assumptions underlying current manpower policies. Civil Service College. Retrieved from https://www.csc.gov.sg/articles/trends-and-shifts-in-employment-singapore-s-workforce

Macias, C., DeCarlo, L. T., Wang, Q., Frey, J., & Barreira, P. (2001). Work interest as a predictor of competitive employment: policy implications for psychiatric rehabilitation. *Administration and Policy in Mental Health, 28*(4), 279–297. doi:10.1023/a:1011185513720

Mank, D. (1994). The underachievement of supported employment: A call for reinvestment. *Journal of Disability Policy Studies, 5*(2), 1–24.

Markel, K. S., & Barclay, L. A. (2009). Addressing the underemployment of persons with disabilities: Recommendations for expanding organizational social responsibility. *Employees and Rights Journal, 21*(4), 305–318.

Marshall, T., Goldberg, R. W. Braude, L., Dougherty, R. H., Daniels, A. S., Ghose, S. S., & Delphin-Rittmon, M. E. (2014). Supported employment: Assessing the evidence. *Psychiatric Services, 65*(1), 16–23. doi:10.1176/appi.ps.201300262

Martin, J., White, A., & Meltzer, H. (1989). OPCS surveys of disability in Great Britain: Report 4 — disabled adults: Services, transport and employment. London: HMSO.

MGI (2013). Disruptive technologies: Advances that will transform life, business, and the global economy. Tech. Rep., McKinsey Global Institute.

Mont, D. (2004). Social protection discussion paper: disability employment policy. Unpublished manuscript. Social Protection Unit, Human Development Network. *The World Bank.* Retrieved from https://digital-commons.ilr.cornell.edu/cgi/viewcontent.cgi?article=1433&context=gladnetcollect

National Disability Rights Network. (2011). Segregated and exploited: the failure of the disability service. Retrieved from https://www.ndrn.org/wp-content/uploads/2019/03/Segregated-and-Exploited.pdf

Parmenter, T. R. (2011). Promoting training and employment opportunities for people with intellectual disabilities: International experience. Employment Sector. Employment Working Paper No. 103. Geneva: International Labor Organisation (ILO).

Riches, V., & MacDonald, J. (2016). Enhanced employment outcomes study. Nova Employment, Centre for Disability Studies, University of Sydney. Retrieved from https://cds.org.au/wpcontent/uploads/2016/04/NE198EmploymentOutcomes_A4FIN.pdf

Rusch, F. R., & Braddock, D. (2004). Adult days programs versus supported employment 1988–2002: Spending and service practices of mental retardation and developmental disabilities state agencies. *Research and Practice for Persons with Severe Disabilities, 29*(4), 237–242.

Schur, L. A., Kruse, D., Blasi, J., & Blanck, P. (2009). Is disability disabling in all workplaces?: Disability, workplace disparities, and corporate culture. *Industrial Relations, 48,* 381–410.

Solovieva, T. I., Dowler, D. L., & Walls, R. T. (2011). Employer benefits from making workplace accommodations. *Disability and Health Journal, 4*(1), 39–45. doi:10.1016/j.dhjo.2010.03.001

Taylor, S. (1988). Caught in the continuum: A critical analysis of the principle of the least restrictive environment. *Journal of the Association for Persons with Severe Handicaps, 13*(1), 41–53.

Tripney, J., Roulstone, A., Vigurs, C., Hogrebe, N., Schmidt, E., Stewart, R. (2015). Interventions to improve the labour market situation of adults with physical and/or sensory disabilities in low- and middle-income countries. *Campbell Systematic Reviews, 11*(1), 1–27. DOI: 10.4o73/csr.2m5.20

Uchitelle, L. (2006). *The Disposable American: Layoffs and Their Consequences.* New York: Vintage Books.

United Nations Enable. (n.d.). Factsheet on people with disabilities. Retrieved from https://www.un.org/development/desa/disabilities/resources/factsheet-on-persons-with-disabilities.html

Wehman, P. H., & Moon, M. S. (1987). Critical values in employment programs for persons with developmental disabilities: A position paper. *Journal of Applied Rehabilitation Counseling, 18*(1), 12–16.

Williams, A. E., Fossey, E., Corbière, M., Paluch, T., & Harvey, C. (2016). Work participation for people with severe mental illnesses: An integrative review of factors impacting job tenure. *Australian Occupational Therapy. Journal, 63*(2), 65–85. doi:10.1111/1440-1630.12237

Winter, S. J., & Taylor, S. L. (1996). The role of OT in the transformation of work- a comparison of post-industrial, industrial, and proto-industrial organization. *Information Systems Research, 7*(1), 6–9.

Wisskirchen, G., Biacabe, B., T., Bormann, U., Muntz, A, Niehaus, G., Soler, G., J., & Brauchitsch, B., V. (2017). Artificial intelligence and robotics and their impact on the workplace. International Bar Association Global Employment Institute. Retrieved from https://www.researchgate.net/profile/Mohamed_Mourad_Lafifi/post/World_population_and_jobs_market_where_are_we_going/attachment/5c13b4a03843b006754b5976/AS%3A703736632586245%4015447 95296667/download/AI-and-Robotics-IBA-GEI-April-2017.pdf

Wolbring, G. (2016). Employment, disabled people and robots: What is the narrative in the academic literature and Canadian newspapers? *Societies, 6*(15), 2–16. doi:10.3390/soc6020015

Wong, M. E., Chong, S. L., & Ng, H. L. (2020). School-to-Work transition: Support for students with moderate-to-severe special educational needs in Singapore. In M. Yuen, W. Beamish, & V. S. Solbergg (eds.). *Careers for students with special educational needs: Perspectives on development and transition from the Asia-Pacific region.* (pp. 249–260). Singapore: Springer.

World Health Organization. (2011). World Report on Disability: Summary, 2011. Geneva, Switzerland.

World Bank Classifications (2016). Retrieved from https://datahelpdesk.worldbank.org/knowledgebase/articles/378834-how-does-the-world-bank-classify-countries

Zarocostas, J. (2005, December 5). Disabled still face hurdles in job market. *The Washington Times.* Retrieved from https://www.washingtontimes.com/news/2005/dec/4/20051204-112759-1170r/

Zhuang, K. V. (2019, May 7). Remembering disability in our history. *Today.* Retrieved from https://www.todayonline.com/commentary/remembering-disability-our-history

CHAPTER 13

Improving the Mental Health of Students with Special Needs in Mainstream Schools

Loh Pek Ru

ೞ

Introduction

The commitment to and adoption of United Nations Convention on the Rights of the Child (United Nations International Children's Emergency Fund, 1989) and the Salamanca Statement (United Nations Educational, Scientific and Cultural Organization, 1994) have led to the development and expansion of inclusive education worldwide (Ainscow & Cesar, 2006; Allan, 2010). In this inclusive setting, students with special educational needs (SEN) that require additional supports and services are educated alongside their typically developing peers in the same classroom for most part of the time. Research in inclusive education support the associated positive outcomes for students with SEN such as better grades, improved opportunities for social engagement and enhanced development of life skills (Buckley *et al.*, 2006; Newman & Davies-Mercier, 2005; Sumi, Marder & Wagner, 2005). In this chapter, a child with SEN is defined as one being diagnosed with a disability, has greater difficulty in learning and adapting socially, and requires different or additional resources beyond what is generally available for the typically developing same age peers (Ministry of Education, 2018). The recognition of its benefits and social impact has made inclusive education widely accepted and promoted worldwide.

In line with the international movement in inclusion, Singapore has enhanced its effort in promoting inclusive education. Between 2013 and 2019, there has been a twofold increase in the number of students with SEN enrolling in the mainstream schools. This number has increased from 13,000 to 26,000. This number in mainstream schools accounts for 80 per cent of the total population of student with SEN in Singapore with the remaining 20 per cent enrolled in the 19 special schools (Teng, 2019). The common disabilities seen in the mainstream schools are autism spectrum disorders, intellectual disability, visual impairment, hearing loss, cerebral palsy and learning disabilities. (Ministry of Education, 2018).

These students with SEN in the mainstream setting will likely encounter greater challenges compared to their typically developing peers. Many of the support systems set up within the mainstream setting focused mainly on supporting these students in their learning with the aim of meeting academic goals, while the social and emotional challenges confronting these children have apparently not been adequately addressed. In recognizing this inadequacy, MOE introduced two social and emotional learning programmes in 2019 to mainstream schools targeting at improving social and emotional skill sets in students with SEN. In general, the impact of the social and emotional challenges can lead to severe psychological distress in children. Often, if unresolved, such psychological distress will affect the mental health of the child, possibly leading to future mental health problems/illness (Kimberly *et al.*, 2019; World Health Organisation, 2020).

The World Health Organisation (2004) defined mental health as "a state of well-being in which an individual realizes his or her own abilities, can cope with the normal stresses of life, can work productively and is able to make a contribution to his or her community".

In adherence with this definition, it is not surprising to see individuals with SEN, who do not receive additional support in the educational setting, having difficulty in achieving this state of wellbeing. Many studies have supported the strong link between poor mental health in childhood and poor mental health later in life (e.g., Kessler *et al.*, 2005; Richards & Abbott, 2009). Mental health problems are also strongly associated with educational failure (Riglin et al., 2013) which in turn is associated with increased rates of psychiatric disorders (Trzesniewski *et al.*, 2006). Both educational failure and psychiatric disorders in children with SEN can lead to a range of adverse life outcomes (Ramey & Ramey, 1998; Whear *et al.*, 2014) or a serious impact on life chances (Eisenberg, Golberstein & Hunt, 2009).

In recent years, Singapore has seen an increase in the awareness of mental health problems among children and adolescents in the general population. In contrast, the mental health needs of children with SEN have not received much attention in the public domain. With increasing number of children with SEN coming into the mainstream schools, it is timely to enhance the dialogue among the various stakeholders interested in addressing the mental health needs of students with SEN in inclusive education. In this chapter, an overview of the common mental health problems seen in children with SEN and the current school support is presented. Issues and gaps in the management of mental health needs in students with SEN in mainstream schools are then identified and discussed.

Mental Health Problems and SEN

Mental health is a complex concept relating to the individual's state of wellbeing. Not having mental illness does not constitute good mental health. This state of wellbeing is further broken down to emotional, psychological and social wellbeing and having any one of them being compromised will affect the mental health of the individual. Mental health influences an individual's thoughts, feelings and actions, and this in turn affect how an individual perceives and interacts with others and the environment. This state of wellbeing is important at every stage of life, from childhood to adolescence through adulthood.

Research found that having SEN put a child at six times increased risk for developing mental health problems (Emerson & Hatton, 2007) and two times increased risk for developing emotional disorders (Green *et al.*, 2005) compared to a typically developing peer. Among children and young persons without learning disabilities, the prevalence rate of developing mental health problems is found to be at 8 per cent. This rate significantly increased to 36 per cent for those with learning disabilities. Further, out of the 28 diagnostic categories in the International Statistical Classification of Diseases and Related Health Problems 10th Edition (World Health Organisation, 1992), 27 categories reported higher prevalence rates for those with learning disabilities compared to those without (Emerson & Hatton, 2007).

On specific mental health problems, Richards and colleagues (2001) reported that individuals with mild learning disabilities at ages 15, 36 and 43 years have significantly more anxiety and depressive symptoms compared to their counterparts without learning disabilities. Moreover, learning disability often has more than one comorbid mental health problem. The most common types of mental health problems among individuals with learning disabilities are depression (Cooper *et al.*, 2007) and anxiety disorders (Emerson & Hatton, 2007; Reid, Smiley & Cooper, 2011). Depression and anxiety disorders are also commonly reported in children with attention deficit/hyperactivity disorder (ADHD)(Karustis *et al.*, 2000) and autism spectrum disorders (ASD) (Leyfer *et al.*, 2006). Children with ADHD having depression or anxiety have also shown higher levels of aggression (Jensen, Martin & Cantwell, 1997). Similarly, stress experienced by children with ASD have also led to the display of aggressive behaviour, particularly when events in their social world become unintelligible and unpredictable (Carrington & Graham, 2001).

Bullying and rejection by peers are also common occurrences for children with SEN in the mainstream school setting (Thompson, Whitney & Smith, 2007). Children with ASD have reported receiving less social support from classmates, friends and parents compared to other children (Humphrey & Symes, 2010). Teachers are less likely to report positive relationships with students with ASD due to the tension generated when managing difficulties associated with ASD (Robertson, Chamberlain & Kasari, 2003). The above issues are not limited to children with ASD only and can be also seen in children with other SEN. Such poor relationships with peers and teachers largely contribute to the social isolation and psychological distress experienced by students with SEN, leading to mental health problems over time (Lang *et al.*, 2013).

Hence, with higher risk for developing mental health problems and having generally poorer life outcomes than their typically developing peers, the mental health needs of students with SEN in mainstream schools should be supported.

Supports for SEN in Mainstream Schools

With the commitment to inclusive education, The Ministry of Education (MOE) in Singapore has established a network of support within the mainstream schools to assist the integration of students with SEN.

One such area of support is the training of teachers and paraprofessionals to work with students with SEN in the mainstream setting. To meet their training needs, the Certificate in Teachers trained in Special Needs (TSN) and Diploma in Special Education (DISE) were developed at the National Institute of Education; the former aims at training teachers as part of a professional development programme and the latter at training Allied Educators (Learning & Behavioural Support; AED-LBS) to provide more targeted support for students with SEN that are having learning, social and emotional difficulties. In addition to the TSN programme, self-learning bite-size online learning modules are also created by MOE for teachers to better equip themselves to teach students with SEN. To date, there are 600 AED (LBS) working in government primary and secondary schools (Ang, 2020). Currently, there are one to two AED (LBS) in each primary school and usually only one AED (LBS) in a secondary school, although there are plans to increase the numbers. Apart from the AEDs (LBS), school counsellors, outdoor adventure educators and student welfare officers are also supporting students with SEN in the mainstream setting.

Besides training, remediation programmes are available to provide additional help to students with SEN who are experiencing learning difficulties. Students with dyslexia at primary three and four levels can attend a school-based dyslexia remediation programme to assist with their learning. A Main Literacy Programme conducted by the Dyslexia Association of Singapore (DAS) caters to students with dyslexia in other levels. Students with SEN in primary one and two, who need additional help with English Language, can attend the Learning Support programme.

In recognition of the importance of social and emotional needs in students with SEN, two new programmes were introduced to all government primary and secondary schools in 2019. Named *Circle of Friends* and *Facing Your Fears*, these programmes focus on equipping students with SEN with self-management skills, problem-solving skills, coping strategies and peer support. In the *Circle of Friends* programme, some typically developing students are selected and trained to act as peer support for the students with SEN. The primary goals of these programmes are to improve the social skills of students with SEN to cope with social and emotional difficulties.

Specifically relating to mental health support, a national outreach programme called Response, Early Intervention and Assessment in Community Mental Health (REACH) works closely with mainstream schools to serve the mental health needs of children and adolescents in their schools. This programme was set up in 2007 under the National Mental Health Blueprint and by 2011, it was serving all mainstream schools including primary and secondary schools as well as junior colleges in Singapore. The programme is designed for quick and easy access by schools to mental health professionals for assessment and intervention. The mental health professionals in REACH provide advice to teachers and school counsellors on issues concerning the mental health needs of their students. If necessary, they work together with teachers and counsellors in implementing intervention. One advantage of this programme is that it takes on a case management approach. Under such an approach, the mental health professional assigned to the case works with school, family and the community where the child resides in, providing regular follow up and liaising with other social agencies. Hence, this programme is an invaluable support for schools to address the mental health issues among students. It should be noted that REACH is not solely designed for children with SEN but serve all children and adolescents in the Singapore government school system (Lim *et al.*, 2015). Between 2011 and 2013, REACH helped to train psychologists working in all 19 special schools to address the mental health needs in students with SEN in their schools (Institute of Mental Health, 2011).

Other forms of support for students with SEN include accommodations for examinations, providing barrier-free facilities for those with physical impairments, working with social service agencies to identify needs, and incorporating the use of assistive technology devices to assist with learning (Ministry of Education, 2020).

In an effort to promote better integration of students with SEN into mainstream education, the various forms of support mentioned above were established with the aim of reducing the learning challenges faced by students with SEN and addressing any existing mental health problems in these students. However, to receive the service of REACH, a referral is required to be made by the school to this service provider. This then brings up an important issue of identifying any existing mental health problems in these students by the school — which is examined in the next section.

Recognising Mental Health Problems in SEN

Although an understanding of mental health and its management for the general population has improved significantly in the past decades, there remains challenges concerning children with SEN. One of the key challenges is the recognition of mental health symptoms in children with SEN. Due to the lack or limited understanding, changes in behaviour may not be noticed or that the presence of symptoms of mental health problems are often incorrectly attributed to the disability or assumed to be part of the atypical developmental process of SEN. Such attribution and/or assumption are common and widespread due to the complex nature of disabilities. A demonstration of this complexity can be seen in the effort to assess depression in person with ASD. The cardinal features of autism have considerable overlap with those features of depression. The characteristics of autism can also affect the expression of depressive symptoms (Stewart et al., 2006). The default assumption may lead to devastating consequences for the person with such a disorder. Bussing and colleagues (1998) reported that students with ADHD have been denied of their access to mental health services because of an acceptance of those characteristics as being an inherent part of the disorder. Misinformation about the disorder also lead teachers to view autism as an emotional disorder (Helps, Newsom-Davis & Callias, 1999). The risk of this misinformation can result in teachers perceiving emotional distress as an inherent part of the disorder rather than a separate psychological distress, thus leaving such distress unattended. Children with SEN who lack the ability to communicate or effectively expressed their distress can also contribute to this challenge. It is not uncommon that students with SEN in mainstream schools are referred for mental health assessment only when serious behaviour, such as frequent meltdowns, out of control behaviour or school refusal, occurs.

Nevertheless, schools play a critical part in helping to identify mental health problems of students with and without SEN. Like many developed countries, many of the mental health assessment referrals of students seen in Singapore are initiated through schools. Studies have shown that teachers are pivotal in detecting mental health needs in children beside the child's family (Loades & Mastroyannopoulouref, 2010). This is not surprising as most children spend a great deal of time in schools beside their homes. The author's personal conversations with some teachers in mainstream schools revealed that they are highly committed to addressing the mental health needs of their students, but they are restrained by circumstances that limit their involvement. Unlike their counterparts in the special schools, most teachers in the mainstream schools are not trained in special needs education and do not have adequate knowledge about the different disabilities/disorders. This puts them in a disadvantaged position when it comes to deciding if the behaviour they are witnessing reflects that of the disability or a behaviour associated with mental health problems. This ability to recognise mental health problems is crucial but such knowledge and skills training are currently absent in in the pre-service or in-service teacher's training programmes. Hence, to expect mainstream teachers to pick up possible signs of mental health problems in their students with SEN without any formal training is unrealistic and unfair.

Adequacy of Training and Programmes

Internationally, there has been a shift in mental health delivery from a hospital-based model to a community-based model. The reason behind such shift is to improve accessibility to mental health services and retention of clients. The mental health delivery mode for children and adolescents is now taking on a school-based model where schools are becoming a common place for providing mental health services (Caan *et al.*, 2014). Such a change can be seen in Singapore since 2007 with the setting up of REACH.

It is becoming common practice for teachers to be increasingly involved in managing the behavioural, emotional and learning problems of their students. Although supported by REACH with classroom intervention plans, most teachers are left on their own to conduct such intervention and manage these students in the classroom — a situation that is played out in many developed countries. In recognition of the important role teachers play in managing mental health issues in school children and the need for training, the government of United Kingdom rolled out in 2019 mental health training for all teachers in England and Wales (GOV.UK, 2019). Such an initiative is a logical move as it benefits both students and teachers. For students, it allows for early detection and intervention of mental health problems among school children that otherwise may go undetected by their families. For teachers, it prepares teachers to gain a better understanding of the mental health problems confronting their students, learning why their students behaved the way they did, and having the confidence to assist their students in distress. In the long term, it benefits the school as a whole when the students affected by mental health problems recover faster or that their behaviours are more manageable in schools, ultimately allowing students' learning to take place.

In Singapore, the training of teachers at the pre-service and in-service levels have yet to incorporate the mental health component in understanding the etiology, presentations, comorbidity and management of common mental health problems among students with SEN in schools. The TSN and DISE programmes mentioned earlier prepare teachers and AEDs (LBS) to work with students with SEN. However, such programmes, because of limited training time, focus primarily on managing learning needs. More attention through an expansion of curriculum in these programmes can allow the coverage of the mental health component, particularly on the social and emotional needs and their management. As good mental health allows a child to cope well with stress, adjusts better to his or her environment and facilitates learning, it makes sense to grant more attention to securing good mental health for students with SEN. Moreover, the management of a student with mental health concerns does not lie solely with the mental health professionals, for example those from REACH. The day-to-day management of students with SEN who are affected by mental health problems during school days still relies on teachers and AEDs (LBS). Hence, it is vital for teachers and AEDs (LBS) to be equipped with the necessary knowledge and skill set to work with these students in managing not just the SEN but also the mental health problems. This will prepare teachers and AEDs (LBS) to be effective in addressing the mental health problems in students with SEN with the overall goal of promoting learning in these students.

Early Intervention at School Level

Knowing that early intervention can positively change the mental health trajectories of students with SEN, early detection becomes vital. However, as stated earlier, it is unfair to expect teachers or AEDs (LBS) to identify possible mental health problems if they are untrained. The use of screening tests in the form of self-report or parent/teacher report questionnaire may be able to bridge this gap. A valid and reliable screening test is an effective way of identifying children at risk of common mental health problems such as anxiety or depression. These internalising disorders may not be very visible and can be difficult to pick up particularly if the student with SEN has difficulty with verbal interaction or is very reserved. These tests provide a quick and simple method of examining the individual where teachers and/or AEDs (LBS) can be trained to administer. Such screening tests may not be suitable for every student with SEN or for every disability. However, if a suitable screening test is used, it can reveal important information for the school to make decisions regarding referral. Another use of such screening tests is to allow the school to monitor the student's mental health progress if there is no follow up with a mental health professional. Hence, a screening test is a useful tool to assist with early detection or a way to monitor the mental health status of students with SEN.

Apart from early detection, early intervention programmes involving social and emotional learning in school is becoming a common occurrence in many developed countries. Such programmes have shown to help improve student learning. A meta-analysis study reported an increase of 11–17 percentile points on standardised tests by schools with such a programme compared to schools without such a programme (Durlak *et al.*, 2011). Currently, the newly developed programmes (i.e., Circle of Friends and Facing Your Fears) in Singapore is only offered to students with SEN in the mainstream schools. This chapter argues that the impact of such programmes on students with SEN will be wider if they are rolled out as whole school programmes. The effectiveness of using whole school programmes to change behaviour and attitude among students have received strong empirical support (Fazel *et al.*, 2014). The argument for a whole school programme rests on the fact that not many children will have the exposure to children with SEN prior to coming into the school system. Some children with SEN may look and behave differently from a typically developing child. Often, such differences are the sources of rejection and bullying. Learning to regulate one's emotion, inhibiting inappropriate behaviour, accepting differences and learning to see from other's perspective, are important skills for typically developing children to have when interacting and socialising with children with SEN (Reicher, 2010). Typically developing children will benefit from such programmes, particularly when they are learning these skill sets together with students with SEN in the same classroom. The interaction between these children provide opportunities for getting to know each other, building rapport, diminishing the physical or cognitive differences, and, more importantly, promoting empathy and acceptance. The ultimate goal here is to equip children with and without SEN with social and emotional skill sets that can contribute to the creation of a safe and accepting school environment, thus promoting good mental health among students with SEN.

However, social and emotional learning is just one part of a larger whole in the promotion or restoration of good mental health when it comes to inclusive education. There is a positive correlation between degree of inclusion and good mental health (Dunstan, Falconer & Price, 2017). If a student with SEN feels that he or she is accepted by peers and is a contributing member of the school, this acceptance and sense of belonging promotes good mental health. Understanding this relationship is important as it can guide schools to design an environment that supports inclusion and good mental health. Such an environment will have to be stable but developmentally stimulating; provides a sense of safety; is sensitive to children's physical, biological and spiritual needs; creates opportunities for supportive learning; and where interactions are emotionally responsive. In creating such an environment, a whole school programme approach can be adopted to instill an inclusive culture or target specific inappropriate behaviours such as bullying, which is a key factor in promoting poor mental health among students with SEN. Carefully engineered activities can be designed to encourage interaction between students with and without SEN to provide opportunities for mingling between them and with school personnel.

Participation by school personnel need to be taken into consideration when designing inclusion. Schools need to be proactive in working with different stakeholders to identify any enabling factors or barriers to good mental health for students with SEN in the schools. There must be a concerted effort within the school and with relevant stakeholders to design a framework of inclusion for the school and a systematic plan to roll out such a framework for action to ensure that the inclusion and promotion of good mental health are part of the norm in the school system. Only when barriers to learning are removed and the various needs of the students with SEN are met can good mental health flourish among these students. Overall, in addressing the mental health problems among students with SEN, schools play an important role in early detection, intervention and promotion of good mental health among students with SEN. Any strategies or interventions adopted in addressing the mental health needs of students with SEN will have to incorporate the concept of inclusion.

Academic Expectation for SEN in Mainstream Schools

Inclusive education is a relatively new concept in Singapore that has only gain attention over the past few years. For most parents and mainstream schools, they are still learning to adjust to this form of education for children with SEN. Prior to 2019, children with SEN who attended mainstream schools were primarily those having mild SEN. With the extension of the Compulsory Education Act to cover children with moderate to severe disabilities, mainstream schools are seeing more of these children, although the majority of children who are severely disabled are attending special schools. With such a development, the questions arise as to whether the needs of children with moderate to severe SEN be adequately met in the mainstream schools and how would this impact on their mental health?

For children with mild SEN, who receive adequate and appropriate support in school, they are likely to move through the educational system smoothly. For those with moderate to severe disabilities, even with appropriate school support, they may still find it a challenge with the current academic curriculum. Currently, students in the mainstream schools must meet the academic goals set forth by MOE. Schools provide support in the form of remediation classes, accommodation of examinations, and use of assistive technology. The curriculum, however, remains the same for all students regardless of disabilities. The progression from primary to secondary schools is dependent on meeting the academic target. This creates high levels of stress for students with SEN who are not doing well academically. Such students are more likely to experience academic failure. Stress and academic failure are well-known factors for poor mental health among students and they contribute to anxiety and depression (Kessler *et al.*, 2010).

If inclusive education is to apply to all children with any form of disability and severity, then the current system in the mainstream school does not work for those with moderate and severe disabilities. The current situation can give rise to poor mental health among these students. The issue then is how can we make it work for students with moderate to severe SEN who are learning in the same classroom as students without SEN? In countries like the United States, Australia and United Kingdom, the principle of partial participation (Ferguson & Baumgart, 1991) is applied students with disabilities in an inclusive education setting. Under this principle, an individual can be involved in any school activity even though the skill sets needed for that activity have not been learned or mastered. Attaining specific academic outcome is not the end goal but rather what is important and valued is that the participation in activities allows the student to be perceived by others as a contributing and productive member of society. This principle has relevance to the mental health of students with moderate to severe SEN. Such an approach promotes the self-esteem and self-worth in the individual, which act as protective factors against poor mental health. At the current moment, there are no easy answers to the above questions. A public discourse is needed to bring all relevant stakeholders together to explore and identify the most effective and suitable approach to inclusive education in Singapore for students with moderate to severe SEN while promoting their mental health.

Gap between Research and Practice

To assist with identifying any practical solutions to address mental health problems in students with SEN attending mainstream schools, the use of research data to inform decision-making is of utmost important. To date, local research in this area is lacking and there is no systematic evaluation of mental health interventions that are implemented for students with SEN within mainstream schools in Singapore. Of concern is that we may be using empirically well-supported interventions which originate from western countries, thereby raising questions surrounding the efficacy and cultural appropriateness of such interventions with the local SEN population.

The differing cultural and contextual factors unique to Singapore can have significant impact on the perception, acceptance, engagement, implementation and compliance of intervention, which ultimately will influence the efficacy of intervention. Such factors may also act as enabling, protective or resisting factors to interventions. Examining and understanding these factors, their processes and impact can then be extended to develop cost effectiveness studies, which can further inform schools and policy makers on the allocation of funding and resources. Such data, particularly related to understanding classroom factors, can be incorporated into teacher training to inform and prepare teachers when working with students with SEN affected by mental health problems.

Research data can have immediate impact on decision-making about the day-to-day functioning of the school as well. Relying on these data, important questions related to whether intervention should be delivered in school or in community; what strategies can be used to ensure sustainability of appropriate mental health programmes and interventions; and whether should intervention be integrated into the whole school, or just at classroom level or individual level, can be answered.

In moving toward evidence-based mental health programmes and interventions that are suitable for our local school context, an interdisciplinary and multi-agency approach to research is most desirable. Having various vested stakeholders hold conversations regarding collaboration and addressing the issue of ownership to lead research will be a good start to this research endeavour. Another important consideration to research is the issue of funding support, a factor to ensure the development and sustainability of quality research. Overall, vested stakeholders need to address issues inherent in developing research before any progress can be made on this front.

Conclusion

Securing good mental health among students with SEN in an evolving inclusive educational setting is a complicated affair. It requires the promotion of mental well-being, the prevention of mental health problems and the care of the affected individuals. Despite this complexity, the personal, social and economic benefits of attaining good mental health to the individual and all levels of the society are well documented in the disability literature.

The current approach to addressing this issue is still inadequate in Singapore. A number of gaps remain in the existing school system that prevent students from achieving optimal mental health. A move from a community-based mental health model to a school-based mental health model and the increasing emphasis on teachers managing mental health problems in students with SEN have left many teachers unprepared. Support provided within schools is not comprehensive enough to address the common social and emotional difficulties experienced by students with SEN. School curriculum and expectations of academic outcomes are not in line with the concept of inclusion. Mental health interventions and programmes delivered in schools have not been tested against local cultural and contextual factors to examine their efficacies. The lack of research to inform mental health practices within inclusive education will curtail quality service to the students with SEN. The necessary and complimentary relationship between research and practice needs to be recognised. Often, research informs practice and practice further provokes research.

This chapter has attempted to shed some light to the issues and gaps revolving around the topic of mental health and inclusive education as increasing numbers of students with SEN are enrolling in mainstream schools. Imperative to this examination, this chapter endeavours to provoke thoughts and discourse among various stakeholders to an important and urgent topic in Singapore.

References

Ainscow, M., & César, M. (2006). Inclusive education ten years after Salamanca: Setting the agenda. *European Journal of Psychology of Education, 21*(3), 231–238.

Allan, J. (2010). Questions of inclusion in Scotland and Europe. *European Journal of Special Needs Education, 25*(2), 199–208.

Ang, J. (2020, March 4). Parliament: Students with special education needs to get more help and teaching support. The Straits Times: Singapore. Retrieved from https://www.straitstimes.com/politics/parliament-students-with-special-education-needs-to-get-more-help-and-teaching-support

Buckley, S., Bird, G., Sacks, B., & Archer, T. (2006). A comparison of mainstream and special education for teenagers with Down syndrome: Implications for parents and teachers. *Down Syndrome Research and Practice, 9*(3), 54–67. http://doi.org/10.3104/reports.295

Bussing, R., Zima, B. T., Perwien, A. R., Belin, T. R., & Widawski, M. (1998). Children in special education programs: Attention Deficit Hyperactivity Disorder, use of services, and unmet needs. *American Journal of Public Health, 88*(6), 880–886.

Caan, W., Cassidy, J., Coverdale, G., Nicholson, W., & Rao, M. (2014). The value of using schools as community assets for health. *Public Health, 129*, 3–16.

Carrington, S., & Graham, L. (2001). Perceptions of school by two teenage boys with Asperger syndrome and their mothers: A qualitative study. *Autism: The International Journal of Research and Practice, 5*(1), 37–48.

Cooper, S-A, Smiley, E., Morrison, J., Williamson, A., & Allan, L. (2007). Mental ill-health in adults with intellectual disabilities: prevalence and associated factors. *British Journal of Psychiatry, 190*, 27–35.

Dunstan, D., Falconer, A., & Price, I. (2017). The relationship between hope, social inclusion, and mental wellbeing in supported employment. *The Australian Journal of Rehabilitation Counselling, 23*(1), 37–51.

Durlak, J. A., Weissberg, R. P., Dymnicki, A. B., Taylor, R. D., & Schellinger, K. B. (2011). The impact of enhancing students' social and emotional learning: A meta-analysis of school-based universal interventions. *Child Development, 82*(1), 405–432.

Eisenberg, D., Golberstein, E., & Hunt, J. (2009). Mental health and academic success in college. *The B.E. Journal of Economic Analysis & Policy, 9*(1), 1–37.

Emerson, E., & Hatton, C. (2007). Mental health of children and adolescents with intellectual disabilities in Britain. *The British Journal of Psychiatry: The Journal of Mental Science, 191*, 493–499.

Fazel, M., Hoagwood, K., Hoover, S., & Ford, T. (2014). Mental health interventions in schools 1: Mental health interventions in schools in high-income countries. *The Lancet Psychiatry, 1*, 377–387.

Ferguson, D. L., & Baumgart, D. (1991). Partial participation revisited. *Journal of the Association for Persons with Severe Handicaps, 16*(4), 218–227.

Green, H., McGinnity, A., Meltzer, H., Ford, T., & Goodman, R. (2005). *Mental Health of Children and Young People in Great Britain.* Newport: Office for National Statistics.

GOV.UK. (2019, June 17). PM launches new mission to put prevention at the top of the mental health agenda [Press release]. Retrieved from https://www.gov.uk/government/news/pm-launches-new-mission-to-put-prevention-at-the-top-of-the-mental-health-agenda

Helps, S., Newsom-Davis, I., & Callias, M. (1999). Autism: The teacher's view. *Autism, 3*(3), 287–298.

Humphrey, N., & Symes, W. (2010). Perceptions of social support and experience of bullying among pupils with autistic spectrum disorders in mainstream secondary schools. *European Journal of Special Needs Education, 25*(1), 77–91.

Institute of Mental Health. (2011, October 6). Mental health support for special education schools [Media release]. Retrieved from https://www.imh.com.sg/uploadedFiles/Newsroom/News_Releases/SPED%20news%20release.pdf

Jensen, P. S., Martin, D., & Cantwell, D. P. (1997). Comorbidity in ADHD: implications for research, practice, and DSM-IV. *Journal of the American Academy of Child and Adolescent Psychiatry, 36*(8), 1065–1079.

Karustis, J. L., Power, T. J., Rescorla, L. A., Eiraldi, R. B., & Gallagher, P. R. (2000). Anxiety and depression in children with ADHD: Unique associations with academic and social functioning. *Journal of Attention Disorders, 4*(3), 133–149.

Kessler, R. C., Berglund, P., Demler, O., Jin, R., Merikangas, K. R., & Walters, E. E. (2005). Lifetime prevalence and age-of-onset distributions of DSM-IV disorders in the National Comorbidity Survey Replication. *Archives of General Psychiatry, 62*(6), 593–602.

Kessler, R. C., McLaughlin, K. A., Green, J. G., Gruber, M. J., Sampson, N. A., Zaslavsky, A. M., …….. Williams, D. R. (2010). Childhood adversities and adult psychopathology in the WHO World Mental Health Surveys. *The British Journal of Psychiatry: The Journal of Mental Science, 197*(5), 378–385.

Kimberly C. Thomson, K. C., Richardson, C. G., Gadermann, A. M., Emerson, S. D., Shoveller, J., & Guhn, M. (2019). Association of childhood social-emotional functioning profiles at school entry with early-onset mental health conditions. *JAMA Network Open, 2*(1): e186694. doi: 10.1001/jamanetworkopen.2018.6694

Lang, I. A., Marlow, R., Goodman, R., Meltzer, H., & Ford, T. (2013). Influence of problematic child-teacher relationships on future psychiatric disorder: population survey with 3-year follow-up. *The British Journal of Psychiatry: The Journal of Mental Science, 202*(5), 336–341.

Leyfer, O. T., Folstein, S. E., Bacalman, S., Davis, N. O., Dinh, E., Morgan, J.,…… Lainhart, J. E. (2006). Comorbid psychiatric disorders in children with autism: interview development and rates of disorders. *Journal of Autism and Developmental Disorders, 36*(7), 849–861.

Lim, C. G., Ong, S. H., Chin, C. H., & Fung, D. S. (2015). Child and adolescent psychiatry services in Singapore. *Child and Adolescent Psychiatry and Mental Health, 9*, 7. doi: 10.1186/s13034-015-0037-8

Loades, M. E., & Mastroyannopoulou, K. (2010). Teachers' recognition of children's mental health problems. *Child and Adolescent Mental Health, 15*(3), 150–156.

McMillan, J., & Jarvis, J. (2013). Mental health and students with disabilities: A review of literature. *Australian Journal of Guidance and Counselling, 23*(Special Issue 2), 236–251.

Meltzer, H., Vostanis, P., Ford, T., Bebbington, P., & Dennis, M. S. (2011). Victims of bullying in childhood and suicide attempts in adulthood. *European Psychiatry: The Journal of the Association of European Psychiatrists, 26*(8), 498–503.

Ministry of Education. (2018). Which school for my child? A parent's guide for children with special educational needs. Retrieved from https://beta.moe.gov.sg/uploads/parents-guide-children-special-educational-needs.pdf

Ministry of Education. (2020). Support in mainstream schools: Types of support. Retrieved from https://beta.moe.gov.sg/special-educational-needs/school-support/mainstream/#mainstream

Newman, L., & Davies-Mercier, E. (2005). The school engagement of elementary and middle school students with disabilities. In *Engagement, Academics, Social Adjustment, and Independence: The Achievements of Elementary and Middle School Students with Disabilities*. Menlo Park, CA: SRI International. Retrieved from http://www.seels.net/designdocs/engagement/03_SEELS_outcomes_C3_8-16-04.pdf

Ramey, C. T., & Ramey, S. L. (1998). In defense of special education. *The American Psychologist, 53*(10), 1159–1160.

Reicher, H. (2010). Building inclusive education on social and emotional learning: challenges and perspectives — a review. *International Journal of Inclusive Education, 14*(3), 213–246.

Reid, K. A., Smiley, E., & Cooper, S-A. (2011). Prevalence and associations of anxiety disorders in adults with intellectual disabilities. *Journal of Intellectual Disability Research, 55*(2), 172– 181.

Richards, M., & Abbott, R. (2009). Childhood mental health and life chances in post-war Britain: insights from three national birth cohort studies. Retrieved from http://www.scmh.org.uk/pdfs/life_chances_report.pdf.

Richards, M., Maughan, B., Hardy, R., Hall, I., Strydom, A., & Wadsworth, M. (2001). Long-term affective disorder in people with learning disability. *British Journal of Psychiatry, 170*, 523–527.

Riglin, L., Frederickson, N., Shelton, K. H., & Rice, F. (2013). A longitudinal study of psychological functioning and academic attainment at the transition to secondary school. *Journal of Adolescence, 36*(3), 507–517.

Robertson, K., Chamberlain, B., & Kasari, C. (2003). General education teachers' relationships with included students with autism. *Journal of Autism and Developmental Disorders, 33*, 123–130.

Stewart, M. E., Barnard, L., Pearson, J., Hasan, R., & O'Brien, G. (2006). Presentation of depression in autism and Asperger Syndrome: a review. *Autism, 10*(1), 103–116.

Sumi, C., Marder, C., & Wagner, M. (2005). The social adjustment of elementary and middle school students with disabilities. In *Engagement, Academics, Social Adjustment, and Independence: The Achievements of*

Elementary and Middle School Students with Disabilities. Menlo Park, CA: SRI International. Retrieved from http://www.seels.net/designdocs/engagement/05_SEELS_outcomes_C5_10-3-05.pdf

Teng, A. (2019, Nov 9). Six special education schools to lower fees by at least 25 per cent for Singaporeans. The Straits Times: Singapore. Retrieved from https://www.straitstimes.com/singapore/education/three-new-schools-for-students-with-special-needs

Thompson, D., Whitney, I., & Smith, P. (2007). Bullying of children with special needs in mainstream schools. *Support for Learning, 9,* 103–106.

Trzesniewski, K. H., Donnellan, M. B., Moffitt, T. E., Robins, R. W., Poulton, R., & Caspi, A. (2006). Low self-esteem during adolescence predicts poor health, criminal behavior, and limited economic prospects during adulthood. *Developmental Psychology, 42*(2), 381–390.

United Nations International Children's Emergency Fund. (1989). The united nations convention on the rights of the child. Retrieved from http://www.unicef.org.uk/Documents/Publication-pdfs/UNCRC_PRESS200910web.pdf

United Nations Educational, Scientific and Cultural Organization. (1994). The Salamanca statement and framework for action on special needs education. Retrieved from http://www.unesco.org/education/pdf/SALAMA_E.PDF

Whear, R., Marlow, R., Boddy, K., Ukoumunne, O. C., Parker, C., Tamsin, F., Thompson-Coon, J, Stein, K. (2014) Psychiatric disorder or impairing psychology in children who have been excluded from school: A systematic review. *School Psychology International, 35,* 530–543.

World Health Organization. (2004). *Promoting Mental Health: Concepts, Emerging Evidence, Practice (Summary Report).* Geneva: World Health Organization.

World Health Organization. (2020). Adolescent mental health. Retrieved from https://www.who.int/news-room/fact-sheets/detail/adolescent-mental-health

World Health Organization. (1992). *The ICD-10 Classification of Mental and Behavioural Disorders: Clinical Descriptions and Diagnostic Guidelines.* Geneva: World Health Organization.

CHAPTER 14

Educating Students with Hearing Loss: Towards Integration and Inclusion

Christina Michael

෴

Introduction

It is a common assumption that other than the differences in hearing and the primary modality of language use, deaf and hearing children are about the same. Marschark and Knoors (2012) state categorically that teaching students who are deaf or who have hearing loss is not the same as teaching hearing learners. One reason for this is the greater heterogeneity among students with hearing loss relative to hearing students. This heterogeneity results from each student presenting a unique profile comprising factors such as causes of hearing loss, degree of loss (unilateral or bilateral), age of onset of the loss, language environment at home, with hearing or non-hearing parents, quality of hearing devices used and habilitation or rehabilitation after being fitted with devices and a whole array of other factors, each of which will have its own impact on the development of the child. Additional factors that could have a significant impact on the development of these students include language used at home, the language of instruction and communication, absence or presence of provisions necessary for learning, and school environments and the experiences they afford. In terms of school-based experiences, studies have highlighted the fact that students with hearing loss face challenges in school which affect them socially and academically (Stinson & Kluwin, 2003). Along with challenges that accompany their inclusion within mainstream educational contexts, there are also opportunities afforded for learning, growth and development for students with hearing loss.

This chapter begins with examining the educational concerns and issues for students with hearing loss, in particular on how hearing loss affects the development of language, communication and cognition, and how teaching can be adapted for their learning needs. This chapter then discusses the issues and considerations involved in the educational placement of students with hearing loss especially in light of the increasing movement internationally towards their placement within mainstream school settings. In light of this international backdrop, the next section of this chapter describes the current educational arrangements in educating students with hearing loss in Singapore and illustrates, through the case example of the Canossian School, how the values and principles of integration and inclusion have influenced and steered the direction of education for these students.

Educational Concerns of Students with Hearing Loss

Language and cognition

Language is learned through exposure to sounds. Having a hearing loss severely impedes communication for the simple reason that most interpersonal communication is conducted using spoken language. Children with even minimal hearing loss are hampered in their ability to receive the spoken language, hence, their ability to learn the language. The development of spoken language is dependent on being able to receive and hear it. When deprived of their full receptive language abilities, they become dependent on speechreading and their abilities in speech perception. Even under the best conditions, the auditory speech perception with hearing aids is never as good as "normal" hearing.

Their listening skills also influence their ability to learn to both read and write and their speech production. Of prime concern to them in their expressive language is speech intelligibility. Speech intelligibility — how well others can understand a speaker's words — is an important outcome for children with hearing loss and children who use spoken language. This might have a direct effect on daily life, especially in the area of communication and the quality and quantity of social-emotional, self-esteem and academic success. These areas of need are exacerbated for students who adopt the oral mode for communication. Deaf students can experience feelings of inferiority as a result of not being able to understand others or to be understood. These learners, more often than not, face concomitant delays in cognitive and social-emotional development which affect overall learning.

Aside from speech production, listening acuity is linked to positive outcomes in many other areas, including reading and language skills, working memory, reasoning, and executive functioning (Marschark & Knoors, 2012). Almost all deaf children have difficulty learning to read. Traxler (2000) reported that the average 18- to 19-year old deaf student is reading at a level appropriate for an 8- to 9-year old hearing student. A significant number of students leave school with inadequate literacy skills, with reading ages being at just over half their mental age, as reported by Eatough (2000).

Language comprises the following components: morphology (the way words are formed), phonology (basic sounds or phonemes), syntax (grammar), semantics (the way language conveys meaning) and pragmatics (appropriate word choice). Lederberg, Schick and Spencer (2013) in their review of existing literature on children who are deaf or with hearing loss identified some of the challenges faced in their trajectories of language development and use. The most common problem with speech production is the substitution of phonemes and in the errors made in semantics or syntax. The researchers suggested that this finding may be an effect of the children's existing vocabulary knowledge and how it is used in acquiring new vocabulary, rather than an inability to learn new words if appropriate experience is provided.

Marschark and Knoors (2014) qualify that deaf students have their strengths too, which adds to the complexities of personalising educational plans for them. However, in developing these plans, one of the greatest obstacles is attempting to make assessments of their cognitive potential. Some of the challenges faced with determining the cognitive potential of students with hearing loss begins with the inadequacies of intelligence tests administered. The tests, more often than not, are administered using the spoken (or signed) language as verbal tests are considered good predictors of academic performance. However, this is an area that these children are already in deficit and would be further challenged in performing at these tests. Non-verbal tests generally would be assumed to produce comparable scores for deaf and hearing people but results actually have been quite variable (Maller & Braden, 2011, cited in Marschark & Knoors, 2014). In addition, non-verbal intelligence scores do not exhaustively cover the range of abilities needed for the classroom. This weakens the reliance of using IQ scores of deaf learners as indicators of helping to understand their learning challenges.

It is commonly believed that there is some level of sensory compensation with deaf learners being better as visual learners as with blind people being better at hearing than sighted people. There is, however, no conclusive evidence that this holds true for deaf learners in the classroom. Deaf children have to rely on both their central and peripheral vision for cues in the environment. The part of their brains that control peripheral vision develop a greater capacity compared to those of hearing children. This does not mean that this attuned sensitivity confers real benefits to deaf learners. Peripheral visual stimuli can help them have greater situational awareness while allowing for greater distractibility as well.

In a regular classroom setting, the information that is presented verbally (either as spoken or visual language) to students will have to be presented at a pace that allows them to turn away from the speaker (or signer) to look at visual aids or cues that may be presented as supporting information (such as on slides or on computer screens). If the pacing of instruction in the mainstream classroom is not adjusted to allow for this, these students may not be able to process much of what is taught. Therefore, small group or one-to-one teaching support is so critical for remediation purposes for students with hearing loss.

Even if the pacing of instruction accommodates their needs, deaf learners need to rely much more on their working memory and the literature on cognition patterns of deaf learners frequently highlights the poorer working memory of deaf learners. In an extensive review, Ottem (1980) found that this facet of their learning is related to their semantic memory and knowledge use. Ottem also found that the vocabulary and conceptual knowledge of deaf learners have diverse idiosyncratic associations. This is one reason why they can be less able to use relevant prior knowledge across academic contexts.

In their research, Marschark and Knoors (2014) reported on studies that reveal that deaf learners remember less than hearing individuals do in a variety of memory tasks, especially in tasks that present verbal or non-verbal materials sequentially. This ability is somewhat related to the language that the learner uses. Students who have strong phonological and speech skills tended to have longer memory spans. They are less likely to use knowledge they have for problem-solving tasks and they find it hard to integrate individual pieces of information to form concepts and identify relationships while reading or solving problems.

Another area in cognition that teachers of deaf learners need to address is in the area of executive functioning of these learners. Executive functioning covers both metacognition and behaviour regulation. Metacognition has been identified as comprising three major categories: metamemory and metacomprehension, problem solving, and critical thinking (Martinez, 2006). Educational psychology researchers have confirmed a correlation between executive function development and linguistic competence. Children with poor language skills — deaf or hearing — are, therefore, limited in several cognitive domains as a result (Hauser, Lukomski & Hillman, 2008). With poor executive functioning, children are unable to approach a novel task with minimal external support. These areas of shortcoming result in them developing a reliance on direction and assistance in solving problems. Both teachers and parents, inadvertently, allow for this to continue either to achieve task completion or in the belief that this will help them learn. This underscores the need for specialised training for teachers responsible for academic learning of students with hearing loss.

Social cognition concerns the various psychological processes that enable individuals to take advantage of being part of a social group. Social cognition relies on various social signals which enable us to learn about the world. The metacognitive ability to think about memories, beliefs, desires and intentions is an aspect of social cognition, also referred to as Theory of Mind (ToM). This faculty is the basis on which social relationships are built. Its development is dependent on communicative utterances and intentions. Deaf learners, being challenged in the areas of communication, commonly have deficits in their ToM development.

Investigations into the ToM in deaf children revealed that those with deaf parents performed much like hearing children, while the children with hearing parents were significantly delayed in their understanding of a ToM (Schick *et al.*, 2002). ToM skills are important for the development of social interaction skills, particularly those skills required in schools. The authors argue that there may be a relation between children's level of ToM development and their ability to learn by instruction and collaboration. ToM and related skills are particularly important to the teaching–learning enterprise insofar as they allow children to place teachers' language and behaviour in a larger context.

Teaching students with hearing loss

Gregory (2005) contends that there is a need for a particular pedagogy that is a function of the needs of children with hearing loss. This pedagogy is influenced by their needs in language development, communication, audiological support and their pattern of cognitive abilities. She elaborates that with deafness, these students have a comparatively small spoken language vocabulary, have difficulty with some syntactical constructions, and may find one-to-one interaction problematic. They also have limited access to incidental knowledge which is gained when children participate in or overhear conversations or through the media.

Language and communication are areas of primary concern in the education of deaf students. Gregory (2005) elaborates that teachers of children with hearing loss need an understanding of how to facilitate language development and to compensate for the gaps in knowledge that can occur in normal teaching within a mainstream setting. These specialist teachers would need to take note of the audiograms of each student and the impact of their degree of hearing loss and speech perception abilities. Teachers responsible for teaching these students would have to adapt their practice, for instance, in providing more visual support, facing the class when teaching to allow for speechreading, providing handouts or chunking the delivery of content for this profile of learners. She also states that withdrawal from some lessons may be necessary.

In a similar vein, Hauser and colleagues (2008) stressed the role of specialist teachers whose strategies emphasise aspects of deaf children's visual, social, cognitive and language skills that specifically support their executive functioning. Teachers should rely more on visual modes of presentation of content, such as the use of concept maps and graphic organisers. Another strategy is the use of games or other targeted activities that help to draw similarities and differences among concepts. Overall, the strategies adopted should include strategies that are directed at focusing of attention, behaviour management, and the use of metacognitive strategies (Marschark & Knoors, 2014). There would be other strategies that would have to be used to meet the unique profiles of various groups of students. With time, continued practice of these strategies will facilitate development of both the allocation of attention and metacognition.

Luckner and Ayantoye (2013) are of the view that the specific methods for instructional and social decisions within inclusive classroom settings still need to be developed. Gregory maintains that this is an important aspect of the specialist training for these teachers.

Based on my own experience of working with students with hearing loss, I am of the belief that teachers of the mainstream classes should minimally understand and acknowledge the differences in the cognitive and knowledge base of deaf students compared to their hearing classmates. This will help them to understand the need for the different approaches for teaching deaf and hearing children within the same classroom.

In addition to customised pedagogical approaches, mainstream education for students with hearing loss necessitates measures to increase the availability of spoken language instruction. This could be done through slowing down the pace of instruction, appropriate acoustic accommodations in the classroom, preferential seating arrangements and the consistent use of the FM or other assistive devices as well as increased opportunity for listening and oracy practice. Inclusion with the provision of these facilities would help students to develop both academically and socially.

Educational placement of students with hearing loss

In most countries around the world, whether legislated or otherwise, there is an increasing trend towards the educational placement of students with hearing loss in mainstream schools. For example, the U.S. Department of Education, Office of Special Education and Rehabilitative Services, Office of Special Education Programs (2009) stated that almost 87 per cent of students with hearing loss spend some part of the school day in general education classrooms (Berndsen & Luckner, 2012). Advancements in hearing technology have made learning in a regular classroom more accessible to these students. Unfortunately, this creates a false hope in some parents that their children could be suited for a mainstream setting that may not provide the additional provision of specialist teachers or classroom support that is required.

The reality is that most of these students within mainstream classrooms are taught by general education teachers and perhaps supported by itinerant teachers. Stinson and Antia (1999) and Cawthon (2001) make the same point that inclusion of deaf students is attainable only if there is provision for them to be fully involved in all aspects of school life. Hyde and Power (2004, p. 85) explain this requires them to be involved in "classroom communication and discourse, curriculum engagement, social events within the school and in events between the school and the community."

Traditionally, there are four categories of alternative placements: (1) separate schools, (2) resource rooms and separate classes, (3) general education classes, and (4) co-enrollment classes (Stinson & Kluwin, 2003). The Australian context (and indeed that in most developed countries) has parallels to these categories, though in Australia numbers are higher among older students (Hyde & Power, 2004).

In the general education setting, students with hearing loss are placed among hearing peers in a class that is taught by a mainstream teacher. Typically, only one deaf (or very few) deaf students are placed in any particular general education class. They may be provided support through services offered by a special needs education teacher, therapist or an itinerant teacher. Children with mild-to-moderate deafness are most often included in the general education classroom. They are perceived to be most likely to be able to access auditory information with minimal support as long as they are fitted with appropriate hearing devices. It is almost always assumed that unless there are additional difficulties or comorbidities, students with permanent bilateral loss of a moderate degree or greater will cope in a mainstream education with little or no support. Often these students share the same communication approach and follow the same curriculum as hearing students (Lewis & Norwich, 2004).

Resource rooms and separate classes are located within mainstream schools and are used for pull-out sessions for students with hearing loss who are taught by a specialist teacher or paraprofessional. The principal difference between resource rooms and separate classes is the time that students leave the classes to attend lessons in the general education classes. Students in the latter receive all, or almost all, of their education within these classes with a specialist teacher. Students in resource rooms spend varying durations in the general education classes with their hearing peers and are in the resource rooms only for selected periods during the day. This is a mainstreaming process in the context of education for the deaf. Students with hearing loss receive their education within the mainstream school, but not necessarily within a mainstream class. They could be taught in separate classrooms all the time or in resource rooms for parts of the day by specialist teachers and supported by therapists, mostly speech therapists. Specialist teachers provide services in any of three ways, namely, direct teaching, regular classroom support as well as consultation to mainstream class teachers. Consultation could come in the form of tutoring students, if necessary, or to provide advice on the formulation of academic, social or behavioural goals for students who may spend time within the general education setting.

Co-enrollment classes refer to classrooms that include both deaf and hearing student, ideally in equal numbers, and a curriculum taught in both sign language and the vernacular. Co-enrollment programming holds promise for addressing the problems with access that students with hearing loss typically experience in other educational placements (Stinson, 2011). The communication policy and procedures in place in the co-enrollment programme are a combination of a bilingual/bicultural approach as both the native sign language and the spoken language are used in the classroom by the teacher of the deaf and the general education teacher, respectively. Both languages are taught and used as separate but equal languages.

In an Annual Survey on deaf students in the United States between 2009 and 2010, there were 37, 828 children of school-going age with hearing loss. Of this, 57.1 per cent are placed in regular schools, 11.9 per cent in schools with resource room facilities, 22.7% are in regular schools with self-contained rooms, with 3.1 per cent studying at home and the remaining 3.9 per cent in other settings. 95.6 per cent of the students in regular students receive some form of additional support which could include transliteration or interpretation services, sign language instruction, audiological services, itinerant teacher support, therapy support, among other services

(Gallaudet Research Institute, 2011). The survey also reported the number of hours that students were integrated with their hearing peers on a weekly basis. With an average of 30–32 curriculum hours per week, 32.2 per cent spent 0 hours in integration; 8.9 per cent had 1–5 hours, 10.8 per cent had 6–15 hours, 11.5 per cent had 16–25 hours and 36.7 per cent had more than 25 hours of integration per week.

In the United States, special schools only admit students who have hearing loss where there is an emphasis on sign communication which could take place with or without speech being used simultaneously. Students in these schools are served by teachers and a range of healthcare professionals such as audiologists, psychologists and various therapists. The curriculum may not be entirely based on the mainstream curriculum and could be supplemented by an alternative or vocational curriculum. In 2010, it was reported that 24.3 per cent are in special schools or centers with a comparable 20 per cent in separate schools in the United Kingdom (Powers, 2002). The proportion of students with hearing loss receiving their education in mainstream schools in both the US and UK is much higher than in Singapore where the two special education schools serve only 1 per cent of school-going age students (Ministry of Social and Family Development, 2017).

Does placement in a mainstream classroom facilitate academic achievement? Students, on average, come into and leave mainstream classrooms with less content knowledge than hearing peers, even when they have highly skilled teachers and sign language interpreters (Marschark et al., 2005). Hearing devices may have positive effects on academic achievement if children are fitted pre-lingually during the earlier years of the critical period for language acquisition but appear to have little impact unless teaching strategies help to overcome the delays.

The definition of academic achievement is dependent on the context. Most commonly, it measures a student's scholastic achievement in one or more content areas at a specified level of difficulty, graded by teachers responsible for granting of credentials (Marschark & Spencer, 2010). Students with hearing loss who learn in a mainstream setting attain better academic achievement than those who learn in a separate resource rooms (Holt, 1994; Kluwin & Stinson, 1993). Holt (1994) studied the achievement in standardised IQ scores of 58,000 deaf learners over 1989–1990. These learners attended general education classrooms for more than 16 hours a week. Antia and colleagues (2009) advanced an additional variable in relation to academic achievement — the issue of "academic press", where factors such as the school environment (be it teachers, school practices, pressures from stakeholders) that "press" students to perform academically at national examinations.

It should be acknowledged that there are potential benefits for receiving an education with typical hearing peers (Luckner & Cooke, 2010; Reed, Antia & Kreimeyer, 2008). One academic benefit of including students with hearing loss in a general education setting is to provide them with access to the general education curriculum and schooling experience. Metz (2013) reported in her study that the greatest benefit for students with hearing loss in an inclusive setting was interacting with teachers who had high expectations of them. Students performed the same socially, academically and linguistically as their hearing peers did at the same grade level. One reason for this was that students had the opportunity to interact on a daily basis in an environment where they felt no discrimination and had access to communication and interaction with peers. In her study, Metz (2013) noted that teachers, parents, and students commented about the sense of community and belonging fostered by the co-enrollment environment as a result of being fully included, as opposed to being pulled out of class to receive special education services.

Another benefit is that by being able to attend a mainstream school, students with hearing loss can interact with peers who act as good language models using a wide vocabulary and complex syntactic structures. They have frequent social interactions in the classroom and within the school. A third benefit is that academically, these students are taught by the mainstream classroom teacher and were expected to participate in the same learning and assessments tasks, with the necessary modifications. Finally, the social learning from school prepares them for their life in the community once they leave school. Benefits also exist for students who are hearing. They have a variety of opportunities to interact with their classmates who have a hearing loss, and as a result they have the opportunity to learn that disabilities are a form of diversity and that individuals with disabilities are people with whom they can learn and share.

As much as there are benefits, there are also barriers. The most regrettable of these is that not all students with a hearing loss receive an appropriate education. This could be due to a lack of role clarity between the teacher and the speech-language pathologist (SLP) and who would or should be attending to the specific needs of the student, as dictated in their IEPs. Another concern expressed by researchers regarding students with hearing loss in general education classrooms is their ability to actively and fully participate in classroom instruction and discussion because of their communication difficulties. Brophy (1988) found that there was a positive correlation between participation levels and academic and social achievement within the classroom.

Eriks-Brophy and colleagues (2006) conducted a series of ten focus groups with young people with hearing loss, their parents and itinerant teachers to identify facilitators and barriers to school inclusion. Facilitators and barriers to the educational inclusion of children with hearing loss mentioned by the three groups of participants could broadly be categorised into three areas — factors in school, family dynamics and the community at large.

The focus group discussions revealed the following facilitators for a school: (a) a team approach with members of different disciplines working in collaboration to meet the needs of students through the provision of quality services; (b) having resource teachers, educational assistants and speech therapists who are knowledgeable about hearing loss and the needs of students with hearing loss in integrated educational settings; (c) the use of facilitative teaching strategies adapted to the needs of students with hearing loss; and (d) the availability and support for assistive devices, hearing devices and other technology.

Some of the facilitators or barriers were found to be associated with key workers working directly with the students with hearing loss themselves. One such factor is the partnership between knowledgeable families, professionals (itinerant teachers in this case as well as the classroom teachers) and students with hearing loss themselves as well as their peers with typical hearing. Canadian researchers (Stanovich & Jordan, 1998) studied factors that influenced not only teachers' reported attitudes towards inclusion, but their actual teaching styles and adaptations in schools on an inclusion programme. Teachers who viewed disability from a more medical conception demonstrated the least effective interaction patterns. This may have to do with their understanding of the disability itself and how it impeded learning. Those who adopted a social perspective engaged in many more academic interactions and persisted more in constructing student understanding. Avramidis and Norwich (2002) contend that teachers who are willing to work with students with diverse learning needs and feel confident in their instructional and management skills, can successfully implement inclusive education.

The findings reported by various researchers underscore the notion that placement is multidimensional. Physical placement is but one area of concern and is not the end objective of inclusion but should be considered as part of a range of curricular arrangements that need to be made in pursuit of optimal educational outcomes. Programme location, appropriate accommodations and modifications, and organisational strategies all come to play in determining the educational outcomes for individual students with the emphasis being on person-centeredness, a cornerstone in special needs education. Another factor requiring further study in measuring the outcomes of these students is whether their scores can be considered comparable to those of hearing students given the accommodations they are offered — within class as well as when and how assessments are made.

The ecology of the general education classroom is often troublesome for learners with a hearing loss. In addition to this, hearing students may lack the patience or a willingness to make efforts to communicate with their peers who have hearing loss. As a result, students who are deaf or hard of hearing may experience feelings of loneliness and isolation if they are unable to participate in social activities with peers because of communication difficulties.

The Singapore Context

Local hospital sources have estimated that hearing loss may affect up to 360,000 persons in Singapore and that nearly 3,000 young persons below 19 years are born with this (Low, 2005). There is little recent local data (Daniel & Lim, 2012). Although the number of students with this disability is small, they are no less important to advancing the knowledge of educational efforts for various disabilities. In Singapore, with its student population of 460,000[1], has only about 1% per cent who have hearing loss or visual impairments (Ministry of Social & Family Development, 2017). This works out to about 1,000–1,100 students with hearing loss, of whom only about 10 per cent are studying in either of the two SPED schools with 90 per cent of the rest attending mainstream schools. A number of factors have contributed to the larger numbers in mainstream schools. Since 2001, infants born at government or government restructured hospitals undergo the Universal Newborn Hearing Screening (UNHS) which identifies babies who may need further testing for hearing loss. This is followed by diagnosis and children with either severe or profound hearing loss may be implanted with cochlear implants from as early as six months of age. Research has suggested that early cochlear implantation with intensive habilitation can improve the speech, language and academic progress of these children (Swanwick & Marschark, 2010; Antia *et al.*, 2009). With technological advancements in hearing devices that enhance the quality of auditory input and family empowerment, these children can develop on an educational trajectory similar to that of hearing children.

---

[1] Student population in Singapore is defined as those from 7–18 years of age enrolled in mainstream schools, specialised schools and independent schools.

It has been established that early detection and treatment of hearing loss are essential for the acquisition of communication competence, social skills and emotional well-being of children. The window for language acquisition occurs within the first five years of life and inadequate auditory input during this period irreversibly delays communication and reading. This has a significant effect on their listening and speaking abilities which may have a negative impact on academic and vocational achievements (Low, 2005). Low contends that parents' awareness and acceptance of early detection are lacking in Singapore and this needs to be addressed via appropriate public education. Based on the author's experience in schools, this awareness is lacking even among teachers and allied educators at local schools. With some level of intelligible speech among students with hearing loss, teachers and administrators may not attribute some of their delays or behaviours to their loss in hearing.

In Singapore, the choice of schools for students with hearing loss is largely dependent on the communication approach used: schools that cater to those who use signing for communication or schools that support those who adopt the oral approach. Under Article 24 of the United Nations Convention of the Rights of Persons with Disabilities (UNCRPD) on Education, all governments should ensure that persons with disabilities are not excluded from the education system on the basis of disability. With this as impetus, the Ministry of Education (MOE) dedicated resources and effort in enhancing the opportunities for integrating students with special educational needs into mainstream schools in a formalised manner via the Satellite Partnership Programme which began in 2007 (Ministry of Education, 2017). The satellite programme encourages mainstream schools located in the neighbourhood of SPED schools to conduct joint social and learning activities through platforms such as co-curricular activities.

Most students with mild hearing loss enrol in mainstream primary and secondary schools. Many of them are fitted with appropriate hearing devices and are supported largely by general provisions, such as specialised support by Allied Educators (Learning &

Behavioural Support) and teachers trained in Special Needs. The MOE supports these students by providing each one with a Frequency Modulation (FM) device[2]. These students are also supported by MOE funded school-based itinerant educational support services such as training services for students and teachers in the use of Assistive Technology (AT) and assessment services for national examination access arrangements.

In the case of primary-level children with moderate to severe or profound hearing loss, parents have the option of enrolling them in either a mainstream school or a SPED school. There is only one mainstream primary school for students with hearing loss who use signing as a means of communication. If their preference is to enrol their child in a SPED school, parents have two SPED schools to select from: one which offers the national curriculum and prepares students for the Primary School Leaving Examination (PSLE)[3], or another SPED school that offers a functional curriculum which leads to a vocational track at secondary level.

For those who opt for the national curriculum, upon graduation from primary education, students with hearing loss who pass their PSLE have the option of enrolling in one of three designated mainstream secondary schools. There are no SPED secondary schools catering specifically to students with hearing loss. The implication of this is that primary age students studying at a SPED school catering to hearing loss have to be prepared to receive their secondary education in either a regular mainstream school or a designated mainstream secondary school. Students attending the SPED school doing the functional curriculum move along a vocational track in preparation for employment.

---

[2] A personal frequency modulation (FM) system uses radio waves to send speech and other signals to hearing aids. There are two basic components of a personal FM system: a transmitter microphone and a receiver. https://www.healthyhearing.com/help/assistive-listening-devices/fm-systems.

[3] The Primary School Leaving Examination (PSLE) is a national examination taken by students at Grade 6 in mainstream schools for placement in a suitable school for their secondary education.

Towards integration and inclusion: Case example of the Canossian School

Reports worldwide have indicated an increase in students with hearing loss being educated in mainstream settings alongside hearing peers due to legislation and the growing movement toward inclusion (Berndsen & Luckner, 2012; Stinson & Antia, 1999). In Singapore, this global initiative on the educational placement of students with special needs within a mainstream setting was reflected as one of the recommendations of the Report of the Advisory Council for the Disabled (ACD) which stated that "whenever appropriate and feasible, special needs education should be provided within the regular educational system" (Tan, 1988, pp. 37–38). Over the next three decades after this recommendation was pronounced, the education of students with hearing loss in Singapore has evolved to establish its own rationale and direction in moving towards integration and inclusion. The Canossian School — which caters to students with hearing loss — provides a case example of how the values and principles of integration and inclusion have influenced the evolvement of theory and practice as well as milestone decisions and events in the education of students with hearing loss within the Singapore context over the past three decades.

Until the late 1980s, the Canossian School adopted Total Communication (TC) as the primary approach for educating its students with hearing loss. TC is one of the five commonly adopted communication approaches used for students with hearing loss, which include the Auditory-Oral, Auditory-Verbal, Bilingual Bicultural (Bi-Bi), Cued Speech and Total Communication approaches (National Deaf Children's Society, 2015). During this period in the 1980s when TC was still the dominant approach used at the Canossian School, the then principal, Sister Anne Tan, who did her undergraduate studies in special needs in Australia, began to emphasise new skills within the use of TC. After returning from Australia where she observed that people with hearing loss were able to speak and interact with hearing people, Sister Anne decided to incorporate speech and auditory skills within the use of TC in the school.

In 1988, Sister Anne visited an overseas school where she learned about Dr Morag Clark's work on another approach to communication, namely, the Natural Auditory Oral (NAO) approach. The Natural Auditory Oral Approach emphasises the need to maximise the use of children's residual hearing through proper amplification using suitable devices during all waking hours. With consistent use of hearing devices, children should acquire speech and language, although at a delayed rate as hearing children. In NAO, the significant adults in the child's life are encouraged to talk to their children at normal speed and manner. The switch from using TC to NAO took off when Sister Anne officially invited Dr Clark to introduce and implement NAO at the school. Dr Clark served as a consultant till 2013, during which she travelled to Singapore once or twice a year to work with teachers on their adoption of the NAO approach in the classroom.

Part of Dr Clark's consultancy work was to conduct a training programme, the Advanced Diploma in the Natural Oral Approach to the Management and Education of Children with a Hearing Loss. The National Institute of Education (NIE), the local training institute for teachers, worked with her on the programme on the request of the Canossian School, and its first run was mounted for 12 qualified teachers in 2003 (Quah, Lim & Poon-MacBrayer, 2004). The Advanced Diploma programme aimed at providing qualified primary school teachers the prerequisite competencies for the proper use of amplification devices as well as how to promote speech and language development through natural language learning. A unique component of the NAO approach was the daily Individual Conversation (IC) that was conducted for about ten minutes for every child.

Dr Clark emphasised that participating in inclusive educational programmes encourages acceptance and recognition of people with hearing loss as "full citizens" (Clark, 2007, p. 95). She went on to articulate other advantages of participation: the promotion of social interaction as well as the simulation of an oral environment with normal linguistic and behavioural models provided by hearing peers. Students who adopt the oral mode of communication benefit from inclusion primarily due to the opportunities for social interaction with the hearing world. Their hearing peers serve as typical linguistic and behavioural models; they are immersed in a stimulating and language-rich environment; they have increased opportunities for learning and access to wider curriculum possibilities than might be offered in a segregated environment (Ross, 1990). These are conditions that have been shown to have positive effects on social acceptance, self-esteem and the ability to form mature social relations (Antia, Stinson & Gaustad, 2002). These ideas and the implementation of the NAO approach at Canossian School over the past three decades have increasingly reinforced the perception of inclusion by local stakeholders as being educationally and socially desirable.

A key benefit of inclusion pertaining to the academic domain for students with hearing loss is that these students are taught the mainstream education curriculum and are expected to participate in the standard learning tasks and assessments with individualised adaptations. By living, learning, and socialising in settings with hearing people, students with hearing loss are ready to live and work in the community after they complete their formal education. Benefits also exist for students who are hearing. They are afforded a variety of opportunities to interact with their classmates who have a hearing loss and, as a result, they have the opportunity to learn that disabilities are a form of diversity and that individuals with disabilities are people with whom they can learn and share.

To aid in the understanding of the Canossian School approach to integration and inclusion, a framework on forms of integration proposed by Avramidis & Norwich (2002) would be useful. The framework is used to situate inclusion efforts based on forms of interaction between students with special needs and those from regular schools. Efforts could refer to the *locational integration* (placing children 'with special needs' physically into mainstream schools), *social interaction* (some degree of social but not educational interaction between children with 'special needs' and their mainstream peers) to *functional integration* (some unspecified level of participation in common learning activities and experiences).

These three forms of integration are elaborated by Williams (1988). In locational integration, students with special needs are taught at the same location as regular students, but not necessarily in the same classrooms. Usually there is a physical separation of learning spaces. The second form of integration is social integration. This allows for a greater degree of social interaction among neurotypical and students with special needs. Social integration includes a structured formal education that both regular and special education students participate in. Students from both groups have planned social interaction during meals, playtime and co-curricular activities. The third type of integration is functional integration. With functional integration, children with special needs attend the same classes as neurotypical students and participate in almost all activities together. The formal and informal curricula are experienced by both regular students and those with special needs.

The inclusion programme at Canossian School, as it stands today, has transcended locational integration. There is social interaction and functional integration for all students. Social integration has been facilitated through the Ministry of Education's Satellite Partnership Programme which provides purposeful and appropriate school opportunities for integration and interaction between students with hearing loss and mainstream school students, which, in turn, will help students with hearing loss to eventually transition into the larger hearing community (Ministry of Education, 2017). At this school, common learning experiences in both the social and academic domains exist for all students with hearing loss. The extent of participation in the examinable subjects (English, Mathematics and Science), however, varies for each student. The goal of an appropriate educational placement for a child with hearing loss is to match the needs of the student to the continuum of services available in a school. No single placement option can or should be considered ideal or even desirable for all children with hearing loss (Erik-Brophy *et al.*, 2006). Each child with hearing loss has needs that vary depending on degree of loss in one or both ears, the age of fitting or implantation, the exposure to language models, absence or presence of underlying comorbid conditions, home support and other related factors.

Conclusion

The education of students with hearing loss in Singapore has evolved during the past three decades in response to the growing movement worldwide towards the integration and inclusion of students with special needs within mainstream school contexts. This trend towards the educational placement of students with hearing loss in mainstream settings along with the due consideration of an appropriate education plan that is responsive to the individual learning needs and background of each student, reflects current understandings of how the growth, learning and development of these learners can be affected by their hearing loss and addressed through education.

As one of the key proponents for the inclusion of students with hearing loss in Singapore, the inclusion programme at the Canossian School began with the goal to integrate them with their hearing peers to develop competence in the spoken language through exposure to good language models as well as learn socially acceptable norms of behaviour that are essential for their eventual assimilation into society as adults. Hence this goal sought to build the foundations upon which these students, through opportunities to access, learn and participate with hearing individuals, can then transition more effectively into the larger community and be more prepared for the real world. The Satellite Partnership Programme (Ministry of Education, 2017) in collaboration with the Canossian School, seeks to also benefit the inclusion of students with hearing loss through the aim of raising the awareness and sensitivity of hearing students toward their peers with hearing loss.

An important step to embark upon in order to inform future directions in the education for students with hearing loss in Singapore, in particular, those who have received or are receiving an education in the Canossian School or other schools catering to students with hearing loss, is the engagement of research to investigate multiple school and life outcomes and what could have contributed to these outcomes. There is currently a dearth of research literature within Singapore that have studied the school and life outcomes of and issues faced by students with hearing loss and how educational and school experiences — as influenced by the trends of integration and inclusion — have contributed towards the quality of life of these individuals.

References

Antia, S. D., Jones, P. B., Reed, S., & Kreimeyer, K. H. (2009). Academic status and progress of deaf and hard-of-hearing students in general education classrooms. *The Journal of Deaf Studies and Deaf Education, 14*(3), 293–311.

Antia, S. D., Stinson, M. S., & Gaustad, M. G. (2002). Developing membership in the education of deaf and hard-of-hearing students in inclusive settings. *Journal of Deaf Studies and Deaf Education, 7*(3), 214–229.

Avramidis, E., & Norwich, B. (2002). Teachers' attitudes towards integration/inclusion: a review of the literature. *European Journal of Special Needs Education, 17*(2), 129–147.

Berndsen, M., & Luckner, J. L. (2012). Supporting students who are deaf or hard of hearing in general education classrooms: A Washington state case study. *Communication Disorders Quarterly, 33*(2), 111–118.

Brophy, J. (1988). Research linking teacher behavior to student achievement: Potential implications for instruction of Chapter 1 students. *Educational Psychologist, 23*(3), 235–286.

Cawthon, S. W. (2001). Teaching strategies in inclusive classrooms with deaf students. *Journal of Deaf Studies and Deaf Education, 6*(3), 212–225.

Clark, M. (2007). *A Practical Guide to Quality Interaction with Children Who have a Hearing Loss.* San Diego: Plural Publishing.

Eatough, M. (2000). Raw data from the BATOD Survey England, January 1998. British Association of Teachers of the Deaf Magazine, May 1–8.

Eriks-Brophy, A. D., Durieux-Smith, A., Olds, J., & Fitzpatrick, E. (2006). Facilitators and barriers to the inclusion of orally educated children and youth with hearing loss in schools: Promoting partnerships to support inclusion. *The Volta Review, 106*(1), 53–88.

Gallaudet Research Institute. (2011). *Regional and National Summary Report of Data from the 2009–10 Annual Survey of Deaf and Hard of Hearing Children and Youth.* Washington, DC: GRI, Gallaudet University.

Gregory, S. (2005). Deafness. In A. Lewis and B. Norwich (Eds.), *Special Teaching for Special Children?* (pp. 15–25). New York: Open University Press.

Hauser, P. C., Lukomski, J., & Hillman, T. (2008). Development of deaf and hard-of-hearing students' executive function. *Deaf Cognition: Foundations and Outcomes,* 286–308.

Holt, J. A. (1994). Classroom attributes and achievement test scores for deaf and hard of hearing students. *American Annals of the Deaf*, 430–437.

Hyde, M., &. Power, D. (2004). Inclusion of deaf students: An examination of definitions of inclusion in relation to findings of a recent Australian study of deaf students in regular classes. *Deafness & Education International*, 6(2), 82–99.

Kluwin, T. N., & Stinson, M. S. (1993). *Deaf Students in Local Public High Schools: Backgrounds, Experiences, and Outcomes*. CC Thomas.

Lederberg, A. R., Schick, B., & Spencer, P. E. (2013). Language and literacy development of deaf and hard-of-hearing children: successes and challenges. *Developmental Psychology*, 49(1), 15–30.

Lewis, A., & Norwich, B. (2004). *Special Teaching for Special Children? Pedagogies for Inclusion*. UK: McGraw-Hill Education.

Low, W. K. (2005). Managing hearing loss in children and adults: Singapore context. *Ann Acad Med Singapore*, 295–300.

Luckner, J. L. (1994). Performance of a group of deaf and hard-of-hearing students and a comparison group of hearing students on a series of problem-solving tasks. *American Annals of the Deaf*, 139(3), 371–377.

Luckner, J. L., & Cooke, C. (2010). A summary of the vocabulary research with students who are deaf or hard of hearing. *American Annals of the Deaf*, 155(1), 38–67.

Luckner, J. L., & Ayantoye, C. (2013). Itinerant teachers of students who are deaf or hard of hearing: Practices and preparation. *Journal of Deaf Studies and Deaf Education*, 18(3), 409–423.

Marschark, M., & Knoors, H. (2012). Educating deaf children: Language, cognition and learning. *Deafness & Education International*, 14(3), 136–160.

Marschark M., & Knoors, H. (2014). *Teaching Deaf Learners: Psychological and Developmental Foundations*. New York: Oxford University Press.

Marschark, M., Pelz, J. B., Convertino, C., Sapere, P., Arndt, M. E., & Seewagen, R. (2005). Classroom interpreting and visual information processing in mainstream education for deaf students: Live or Memorex®? *American Educational Research Journal*, 42(4), 727–761.

Marschark, M., & Spencer, P. E. (2010). *The Oxford Handbook of Deaf Studies, Language, and Education* (Vol. 2). Oxford University Press.

Martinez, M. E. (2006). What is metacognition? *Phi Delta Kappa*, 87(9), 696–699.

Metz, K. K. (2013). *Academic Engagement of Deaf and Hard of Hearing Students in a Co-enrollment Program*. Retrieved from http://libservy.nie.edu.sg.lib

Ministry of Education. (2017). *Satellite Partnership: A Handbook for Satellite Partnership Schools.* Singapore: Ministry of Education.

Ministry of Social and Family Development. (2017). Total number of persons with disabilities in Singapore. Retrieved from https://www.msf.gov.sg/media-room/Pages/Total-number-of-persons-with-disabilities-in-Singapore.aspx

Ottem, E. (1980). An analysis of cognitive studies with deaf subjects. *American Annals of the Deaf, 125*(5), 564–575.

Powers, S. (2002). From concepts to practice in deaf education: A United Kingdom perspective on inclusion. *Journal of Deaf Studies and Deaf Education, 7*(3), 230–243.

Quah, M. L., Lim, L., & Poon-McBrayer, K. F. (2004). Special education in Singapore: Celebrating the past, envisioning the future. *Association for Supervision of Curriculum Development (Singapore) Review, 12*(2), 27–33.

Reed, S., Antia, S. D., & Kreimeyer, K. H. (2008). Academic status of deaf and hard-of-hearing students in public schools: Student, home, and service facilitators and detractors. *Journal of Deaf Studies and Deaf Education, 13*(4), 485–502.

Ross, M. (1990). Overview and the long view. In M. Ross (Ed.), *Hearing Impaired.* New York.

Schick, B., de Villiers, J., de Villiers, P., & Hoffmeister, B. (2002). Theory of mind: Language and cognition in deaf children. *The ASHA Leader, 7*(22), 6–14.

Stanovich, P. J., & Jordan, A. (1998). Canadian teachers' and principals' beliefs about inclusive education as predictors of effective teaching in heterogeneous classrooms. *The Elementary School Journal, 98*(3), 221–238.

Stinson, M., & Antia, S. (1999). Considerations in educating deaf and hard-of-hearing students in inclusive settings. *Journal of Deaf Studies and Deaf Education, 4*(3), 163–175.

Stinson, M. K. (2011). Educational consequences of alternative school placements. In M. Marschark and P. E. Spencer (Eds.), *The Oxford Handbook of Deaf Studies, Language, and Education* (Vol. 1, pp. 47–62).

Stinson, M. S., & Kluwin, T. N. (2003). Educational consequences of alternative school placements. *Oxford Handbook of Deaf Studies, Language, and Education,* pp. 52–64.

Swanwick, R., & Marschark, M. (2010). Enhancing education for deaf children: Research into practice and back again. *Deafness & Education International, 12*(4), 217–235.

The National Deaf Children's Society. (2015). Making choices about communication. Retrieved from https://www.aussiedeafkids.org.au/making-choices-about-communication.html

Traxler, C. B. (2000). The Stanford Achievement Test: National norming and performance standards for deaf and hard-of-hearing students. *Journal of Deaf Studies and Deaf Education, 5*(4), 337–348.

CHAPTER 15

Sexuality Development in Persons with Intellectual Disability: A Singapore Perspective

Lohsnah Jeevanandam

⊗⊗

Introduction

The topic of sexuality in persons with disabilities first caught my attention over two decades ago when a student with intellectual disability (ID) shared with me that her neighbour frequently rubbed against her chest when she walked past his house, and he had threatened to hurt her if she were to tell her family. After a year of enduring this sexual abuse, she developed severe anxiety and refused to leave her home. She shared with me her harrowing experience several years later when she returned to the service.

This commentary chapter is based on my professional work with persons with ID, their families, as well as staff and administration leaders. I invite you to take this journey with me as I reflect on what I have learnt over time, as well as offer some suggestions on how we can embark on this journey to empower persons with ID on their sexuality development. It is the primary aim of this commentary to trigger a lively and sustained discourse on sexuality development in people with ID in Singapore. It is also imperative to add that some views articulated here have been candidly presented and may have the potential to be perceived as being controversial and so, I urge you to dwell into this commentary with a receptive mind and heart.

Intellectual Disability: Definition and Prevalence

According to the Diagnostic and Statistical Manual on Mental Disorders (DSM-5; American Psychiatric Association, 2013), Intellectual Disability is a disability characterised by significant deficits in both intellectual functioning and in adaptive behaviour, such as conceptual, social and practical adaptive skills. This disability originates before 18 years of age. ID was referred to as Mental Retardation in the previous DSM-4 (2000) and the change in terminology reflects a positive shift in attitudes. Although, one could argue that the term 'disability' is limiting in itself and I have frequently wondered if a completely different term is warranted given that ID is not entirely about intellectual impairment only!

In terms of statistics, the Singapore Ministry of Education reports that 2.1 per cent of the student population (or 460,000 students) have some form of sensory impairment, physical impairment, autism spectrum disorder and ID. The National Council of Social Service[1] reported a 3.4 per cent disability prevalence rate for those aged 18–49 years old. In an older review by the current author (Jeevanandam, 2009), the prevalence of ID across Asia was noted to be consistent with western estimates at 0.06–1.3 per cent, with the exception being China then at 6.68 per cent. Globally, the prevalence rate of ID is at around 1 per cent, and this was confirmed after a systematic review of prevalence and incidence rates of various studies conducted between 1980 and 2000 (McKenzie et al., 2016).

---

[1] Based on a random sampling of 2,000 Singapore citizens and permanent residents aged 18 and above, done by the National Council of Social Service in 2015. The self-report disability also included those with acquired disabilities due to accidents and illness.

Importance of Considering Sexuality in Persons with Intellectual Disability

Sexual abuse rates are nearly four times higher in adults with ID than those without any form of disability (Martin *et al.*, 2006; Mitra, Mouradian & Diamond, 2011). In a review of sexual abuse in children with ID (Wissink *et al.*, 2015), it was noted that they were at a 4–8 times increased risk for sexual abuse, as compared to children with average intelligence (Jones *et al.*, 2012; Spencer *et al.*, 2005; Sullivan & Knutson, 2000).

While my initial interest in this topic developed because of my desire to empower people with ID against sexual abuse, I soon realised that this was a reactive perspective where I was placing boundaries on how much my clients should learn (for example, only learning how to say no to unwanted touch or how to report abuse). Rohleder & Swartz (2009) refers to this limiting approach as a risk or protective discourse where the motivation to educate is only to prevent sexual exploitation or sexualised behaviours. I soon realised that a proactive approach or rights-based approach (Rohleder & Swartz, 2009) would be far more liberating for the very people who I was committed to support.

It was then important that I gained an appreciation of what sexuality meant. Scouring through various definitions, I found the one proposed by the World Health Organisation (WHO) to be the most comprehensive.

> "Sexuality is a central aspect of human life and encompasses sex, gender identities and roles, sexual orientation, eroticism, pleasure, intimacy and reproduction. Sexuality is experienced and expressed in thoughts, fantasies, desires, beliefs, attitudes, values, behaviours, practices, roles and relationships. Sexuality is influenced by the interaction of biological, psychological, social, economic, political, cultural, ethical, legal, historical, religious and spiritual factors" (WHO, 2015, p. 5).

It is apparent that sexuality is not only about the physical domain, but also transcends the emotional, mental and social facets.

This definition also clearly points to the fact that while sexuality is very much private, it is also impacted by one's immediate networks of family, friends and schools, as well as determinants in the outer circle, such as the society-at-large and policies about sexuality development.

Case Vignette 1

> *I once worked with a young lady with Down Syndrome who was promised love in return for sexual favours from a foreign national. Sadly, she was also lured with basic commodities such as a packet of chicken rice. When she realised that the person had deceived her, she told me "at least he was my friend for a short while... he even said I was pretty".*

This case is a telling example of how engaging in sexualised behaviours for some can be a means to meet basic needs of food, companionship and affirmation. Ultimately, sexuality means different things for different people and caution needs to be exercised so that one does not over-simplify and reduce this complex construct to only representing the physical component. Reflecting on the wise words of well-known researchers in the area of sexuality, John DeLamater and William Friedrich (2002) who asserted that "human beings are sexual beings throughout their entire lives" bring to light that ultimately, we cannot separate ourselves from sexuality. As such, it would truly be in our advantage to embrace sexuality development, rather than distancing ourselves from it.

So, my next question was then what are some position statements on persons with disability and sexuality. Disability rights organisations have been advocating for sexuality rights for over two decades. Take for example the United Nations Standard Rules for the Equalisation of Opportunities for Persons with Disabilities in 1994, which states:

Persons with disabilities must not be denied the opportunity to experience their sexuality, have sexual relationships and experience parenthood. Persons with disabilities must also have the same access as others to family planning methods, as well as to information in accessible form on the sexual functioning of their bodies (UN, 1994, p. 28).

The Convention on the Rights of Persons with Disabilities, an international human rights treaty of the United Nations aims to protect the rights of individuals with disabilities. The American Association on Intellectual and Developmental Disabilities[2], a key body in the promotion of the rights of persons with special needs in the United States, advocates for inherent sexual rights that need to be "affirmed, defended, and respected" and that there needs to be comprehensive individualised sexuality education. In the United Kingdom, Mencap[3] is the leading agency for persons with learning disability and their families and carers and strongly advocates for the sexuality rights of persons with a learning disability.

Case Vignette 2

> *Two middle-aged adults with Intellectual Disability who were working at the same work site were interested to pursue a romantic relationship with each other. However, they were repeatedly reprimanded by their family members to not even talk to each other. When I had broached the possibility of them being at least friends, a parent chided me and said, "What happens if my daughter gets pregnant! Anyway, she doesn't have these feelings...she is still a child!"*

This example illustrates that families, out of possible fear, adopted a risk or protective approach rather than a rights-based approach. Here, the two adults were denied that they could have real feelings like that of typically developing adults. In the same vein, only advocating for the rights of the persons with ID and disregarding their families' feelings and thoughts would be tantamount to not according them the very same rights to care for their adult child too. From my experience, I have found that gently lobbying for clients' rights while respecting their families views often led to more favourable outcomes.

This far, it is evident that sexuality development is an integral component for one's optimum functioning. Disregarding it has serious ramifications for one's well-being. Specifically, the sexuality

---

[2] AAIDD. https://www.aaidd.org
[3] https://www.mencap.org.uk

rights of people with ID and disability, in general have been fiercely defended by several advocacy groups. The argument then is no longer if we should support the sexuality development of persons with ID, but rather to gain an understanding of what this process would look like.

Comprehensive Sexuality Education

It is widely recognised that in order to break down the barriers in the sexuality development of people with disabilities, a Comprehensive Sexuality Education (CSE) is required (AAID, n.d.; Lohan *et al.*, 2018; Pownall, Jahoda & Hastings, 2012; UNESCO, 2013). CSE is understood as "an age-appropriate, culturally relevant approach to teaching about sex and relationships by providing scientifically accurate, realistic, non-judgmental information" (UNESCO, 2013). Within the CSE framework, some key topics are: developing self-esteem/self-awareness, communication/assertiveness, relationship skills, personal safety, body care, decision-making, emotional health, and sexual health (National Youth Council of Ireland, 2004). Some of the positive benefits of receiving CSE reported by people with ID are an increase in self-esteem, positive feelings about sexual experiences and knowledge about sexuality issues (Gardiner & Braddon, 2009; Garwood & McCabe, 2000).

Contextual Factors to be Considered in Sexuality Development

There are several key contextual factors to be considered when empowering people with disabilities in their sexuality development. Hanass-Hancock and colleagues (2018) summarised these as: physical and communication barriers (e.g., environments that are difficult to access); negative societal attitudes (e.g., that people with disabilities are not sexually active); lack of rights to consent; and staff with limited sexuality education knowledge who therefore who lack the requisite knowledge and skills to roll out these programmes. Another concern is the digital world which poses a unique threat in itself. Individuals with disabilities when exposed to pornography could develop unhealthy sexual boundaries and sexual relationships (Schaafsma et al., 2015).

In a society such as Singapore which is a melting pot of people from various countries and traditions, it is also important to reflect on the role of culture and religion on sexuality. Confucianism has a strong cultural influence among ethnic Chinese communities in Singapore (Lee, 2010). Confucianism views sexuality as a taboo topic and prohibits discourse about sex. It advocates that sex can only take place within the formal arrangement of a marriage (Go et al., 2002; Kaljee et al., 2007). From a religious perspective, Islamic, Christian and Hindu teachings emphasise female virginity before marriage. In some parts of the Singapore society, homosexual orientation is not accepted. According to Section 377A of the Singapore Penal Code[4], sex between men in private or public is illegal.

Case Vignette 3

A parent once shared with me that he wanted his teenage son to stop masturbating as it was against the family's religion.

When I further reflected on this case, I had several questions. If the family told their son that he needs to stop masturbating because of their religious views, would he comply, given that he has already discovered an enjoyable experience? If he did not stop masturbating, would this create more tension in the family? At the end of the day, there is no straightforward resolution to this dilemma. A reactive approach would be to simply instruct the individual to stop masturbating. A proactive approach would be to seek to involve the parents, the individual and relevant others (e.g., teachers, allied health professionals) in an educational process to understand family values, learn about the sexuality development of the teenager with ID, and work out possible options and solutions for the development of a positive self-image and healthy relationships with others (e.g., ways to socialise with the opposite gender), in addition to

---

[4] Singapore Statutes Online. https://sso.agc.gov.sg/Act/PC1871?ProvIds=pr377A-

addressing masturbation in itself. Overall, the desired approach centres around how we can empower the person with ID and their family with the relevant knowledge, understanding and skills.

Current Practices in Singapore Related to Disability and Sexuality

Policies and frameworks

The Enabling Masterplan[5], right now in its third version (2017–2021), is a five-year, multi-pronged plan to enhance the quality of life of persons with disabilities and support their caregivers in Singapore. Its eventual aim is to create a caring and inclusive community that empowers people with disabilities to achieve their fullest potential. Whilst there is no explicit mention of sexuality or CSE across the masterplan, there are several recommendations that can be interpreted in light of sexuality development. For example, recommendation 2 states: *"To meaningfully engage and support persons with disabilities requiring care to be as independent as possible."* Many researchers have argued that CSE provides people with disabilities many key integral skills for independence, such as personal safety, communication skills, assertiveness, etc. (Sex Education Council of the United States, 2004). However, because there is no explicit reference to sexuality development and CSE, this also means that it is left to the reader to conceptualise what they perceive to be integral skills for independence, for instance.

Disability registry

Currently, Singapore does not have a formal disability registry. Rather, there is a voluntary database called the Developmental Disability Registry (DDR) maintained by the National Council of Social Service. As it gathers only basic information from those who apply for the DDR card, the DDR cannot be deemed to be a

---

[5] https://www.sgenable.sg/pages/content.aspx?path=/about-us/enabling-masterplan/

comprehensive registry that is representative of the people with disabilities living in Singapore.

Importantly, the Census of Population 2020 by the Singapore Department of Statistics has included disability-related questions and these are similar to the Washington Group Short Set of Questions on Disability[6]. While this does not equate to a disability registry, it is nevertheless a good attempt to obtain broad-based information on disability statistics.

Special education system

Under the purview of the Singapore Ministry of Education is a unit called the Special Education Branch which specifically focuses on assisting Special Education (SPED) schools with designing their curriculum. Notably, over the past few years they have organised a series of CSE workshops by external trainers. I was one of the two trainers for a three-day CSE workshop that was held across April to May 2019. The two runs of the workshop were well attended by a total of 56 educators from SPED schools. In recognition of local cultural views on sexuality, the workshop was named with neutral undertones — 'Healthy and Safe Relationships'. I was one of the two trainers. Across the three days, the participants learnt about sexuality development in people with disability, how to assess for the functions of sexualised behaviours, what were the components of a CSE, how to go about teaching and addressing these facets, and what were some considerations for the implementation of CSE at the respective services.

The feedback from participants was resoundingly positive with some common comments being that they now felt empowered with the knowledge on what constituted a CSE and learning about relevant training resources. Personal impression of the participants was that they strongly advocated for the sexuality needs of their clients, and at the same time, some educators were unsure on how to

---

[6] http://www.washingtongroup-disability.com/washington-group-question-sets/short-set-of-disability-questions/

address sensitive topics like homosexual orientation, premarital sex and safer sex options. Another comment was that their service did not have a clear policy on how to address sexualised behaviours. In a post-course project that was presented in February 2020, it was encouraging to hear that many services had since implemented components of CSE; for example, a support group for high-risk females and a group programme to teach protective skills.

In March 2020 there was a half-day session, 'HSR: Policy and Implementation at the School Level for School Leaders' with many special schools. In this session that was co-facilitated by myself, the general focus was on CSE, namely the components, requirements for implementation, and the need for internally developed policy and frameworks. Overall, the leaders were in agreement about the importance of CSE and an important discussion was about how to adapt the programme to different levels of needs. The leaders were also in support of the CSE workshop to continue to be offered for SPED educators.

Recommendations

Comprehensive sexuality education

Training curriculum

There are several sexuality education training resources available for persons with disabilities, for example, a training curriculum called 'Sexuality Education for People with Developmental Disabilities[7]' by Katherine McLaughlin and FLASH lessons plans for Special Education[8]. However, there are challenges in using these programmes in their entirety as these are developed in the West. For example, often the pictures of people that have been used have little resemblance to Asian people (e.g., red hair, green eyes, freckled skin) and this does not make it generalisable. With video

---

[7] https://www.elevatustraining.com/workshops-and-products/sexuality-education-for-people-with-developmental-disabilities-curriculum/
[8] https://www.kingcounty.gov/depts/health/locations/family-planning/education/FLASH/special-education.aspx

resources, the accent of the English can sometimes interfere with comprehending the content too. Hence, it is vital that there is a locally developed CSE for children and adults with disabilities. There needs to be a core training structure and relevant teaching resources that cover fundamental topics in sexuality education. These materials can then be modified accordingly for the type of clients, for example, using more modelling and role-plays when teaching individuals with moderate level of ID.

Evaluation and monitoring

In order to assess the effectiveness of the training curriculum, it is essential that there is a pre-training measure, followed by a post-training measure. Furthermore, continuing to collect data longitudinally (for example, every six months) would provide critical information, such as which aspects of learning deteriorates over time, what are some continued benefits, etc.

Training and support for staff

All levels of staff working with people with disabilities should receive training. The training should be tailored to the extent of direct service provided. For instance, administrative staff should be provided training on how to encourage social skills or conflict resolution, while direct care service providers need to be empowered with the knowledge and skills to teach all CSE components. These trainings should not be one-off and there should be regular opportunities for clinical supervision too. Within each service, a team supporting CSE could be formed and their primary responsibilities would be to gather resources, teach CSE and support the service in the implementation.

Training and support for caregivers

Experts have argued that parents have the primary responsibility for educating their child on sexuality development (Isler *et al.*, 2009;

Pownall, Jahoda & Hastings, 2012). Given this monumental role that caregivers play, they should be engaged as soon as their child enters school and be continuously educated on developmentally appropriate sexuality-related information.

Parent support groups are also vital in garnering mutual support for caregivers. From my personal experience, I have observed how some caregivers are such bold advocates for their child that their enthusiasm has positively rubbed off onto other caregivers who, over time, become less fearful about empowering their young adolescent or adult child on sexuality. One such caregiver once told me, "Now that I think about it, my fear has blinded me and I have been selfish all this while. I need to start thinking about what my son truly desires and deserves."

Research

While there has been an increase in scholarship concerning persons with disability and sexuality in the Global North (namely, North America, United Kingdom, Europe and Australia), in contrast, there is a paucity of such similar research in the Global South (Chappell, 2019). In fact, Chappell (2019) points out that it is astonishing that of the one billion people globally who have disabilities, 80 per cent live in the Global South (WHO, 2011). It is imperative that rather than simply replicating previous research, local research also aims to address theoretical gaps, as well as engage in evaluation that can lead to significant practical implications. The Disability Research Coalition, which is comprised of several social service agencies,[9] was set up by the National Council of Social Service in 2017 with the primary mandate to engage in practice-led research.

---

[9] Asian Women's Welfare Association (AWWA), Association for Persons with Specials Needs (APSN), Down Syndrome Association (DSA), Cerebral Palsy Alliance Singapore (CPAS), Community Psychology Hub (CPH), Ministry of Social and Family Development (MSF), Movement for the Intellectually Disabled of Singapore (MINDS), National Council of Social Service (NCSS), National Institute of Education (NIE), National University of Singapore (NUS), Rainbow Centre, and Serving People with Disabilities (SPD).

This platform, for instance, can be used to galvanise resources to lead sexuality-related research locally and internationally.

Policies and frameworks

There needs to be clear policies and frameworks about supporting the sexuality development of people with disabilities in Singapore. A suggestion is for the next Enabling Masterplan to propose explicit recommendations on promoting, defending and advocating for the sexuality rights of persons with disabilities. From a policy perspective, it is crucial that CSE is made compulsory for children, adolescents and adults with all disabilities.

Disability registry

A disability registry that keeps count of the vital statistics of people with disabilities, such as prevalence rate by disability type and across age and gender, should be set up. The rates of different types of abuse against people with disabilities should also be documented. Overall, such information will enable relevant government agencies to more effectively plan services and programmes.

Setting up of a Healthy and Safe Relationships service

It is envisioned that this would take the form of an association or agency that supports people with disabilities of various ages in their sexuality development. Some of the services would include: disability-friendly online-information on sexuality-related matters, face-to-face consultation for individuals who are dating or/and wish to get married, financial schemes for married couples with disabilities, genetic counselling, social networking events, trainings/workshops for staff and caregivers.

    Overall, despite the presence of subtle negative sentiments in Singapore about recognising sexuality development in people with disability, it is still heartening to witness increased recognition in the past two years of the importance of CSE, for instance, through the coordinated workshops organised by the Ministry of Education Special Education Branch as well as the session with the leaders from the special schools. Taken together, these active steps strongly suggest that we are in an opportune moment to capitalise on this trajectory and to keep steering forward. In fact, a chapter on this topic appearing at this time in a Singapore edited book and not previously is testament on its own that there is surely a shift in attitudes!

References

American Psychiatric Association. (2013). *Diagnostic and Statistical Manual of Mental Disorders* (5th ed.). Arlington, Virginia: American Psychiatric Publishing.

Bennett, L. R. (2005). *Women, Islam and Modernity: Single Women, Sexuality and Reproductive Health in Contemporary Indonesia.* London; New York: Routledge Curzon.

Chappell, P. (2019). Situating disabled sexual voices in the Global South. In P. Chappell & M. de Beer (Eds.), *Diverse Voices of Disabled Sexualities in the Global South* (pp. 1–25). Cham: Springer International Publishing.

DeLamater, J., & Friedrich, W. N. (2002). Human sexual development. *The Journal of Sex Research: Promoting Sexual Health and Responsible Sexual Behavior, 39*(1), 10–14.

Gardiner, T., & Braddon, E. (2009). 'A right to know'. Facilitating a relationship and sexuality programme for adults with intellectual disabilities in Donegal. *British Journal of Learning Disabilities, 37*(4), 327–329.

Garwood, M., & McCabe, M. P. (2000). Impact of sex education programs on sexual knowledge and feelings on men with a mild intellectual disability. *Education and Training in Mental Retardation and Developmental Disabilities, 35*(3), 269–283.

Gil-Llario, M. D., Morell-Mengual, V., Díaz-Rodríguez, I., & Ballester-Arnal, R. (2019). Prevalence and sequelae of self-reported and other-reported sexual abuse in adults with intellectual disability. *Journal of Intellectual Disability Research, 63*(2), 138–148.

Go, V. F., Quan, V. M., Chung, A., Zenilman, J., Hanh, V. T. M., & Celentano, D. (2002). Gender gaps, gender traps: Sexual identity and vulnerability to sexually transmitted diseases among women in Vietnam. *Social Science & Medicine, 55*(3), 467–481.

Hanass-Hancock, J., Nene, S., Johns, R., & Chappell, P. (2018). The impact of contextual factors on comprehensive sexuality education for learners with intellectual disabilities in South Africa. *Sexuality and Disability, 36*(2), 123–140.

Isler, A., Beytut, D., Tas, F., & Conk, Z. (2009). A study on sexuality with the parents of adolescents with Intellectual Disability. *Sexuality and Disability, 27*(4), 229–237.

Jahoda, A., & Pownall, J. (2014). Sexual understanding, sources of information and social networks: the reports of young people with intellectual disabilities and their non-disabled peers. *Journal of Intellectual Disability Research, 58*(5), 430–441.

Jeevanandam, L. (2009). Perspectives of intellectual disability in Asia: Epidemiology, policy, and services for children and adults. *Current Opinion in Psychiatry, 22*(5), 462–468.

Jones, L., Bellis, M. A., Wood, S., Hughes, K., McCoy, E., Eckley, L., & Officer, A. (2012). Prevalence and risk of violence against children with disabilities: A systematic review and meta-analysis of observational studies. *Lancet, 380*, 899–907.

Kaljee, L. M., Green, M., Riel, R., Lerdboon, P., Tho, L. H., Thoa, L. T. K., & Minh, T. T. (2007). Sexual stigma, sexual behaviors, and abstinence among Vietnamese adolescents: Implications for risk and protective behaviors for HIV, sexually transmitted infections, and unwanted pregnancy. *Journal of the Association of Nurses in AIDS Care, 18*(2), 48–59.

Laurent, E. (2005). Sexuality and human rights: an Asian perspective. *Journal of homosexuality, 48*(3-4), 163–225.

Lee, M. (2010). Confucian traditions in modern East Asia: Their destinies and prospects. *Oriens Extremus, 49*, 237–247.

Lohan, M., Aventin, Á., Clarke, M., Curran, R. M., Maguire, L., Hunter, R., ... O'Hare, L. (2018). JACK trial protocol: A phase III multicentre cluster randomised controlled trial of a school-based relationship and sexuality education intervention focusing on young male perspectives. *BMJ Open, 8*(7).

Martin, S. L., Ray, N., Sotres-Alvarez, D., Kupper, L. L., Moracco, K. E., Dickens, P. A., ... Gizlice, Z. (2006). Physical and sexual assault of women with disabilities. *Violence Against Women, 12*(9), 823–837.

McDaniels, B., & Fleming, A. (2016). Sexuality education and intellectual disability: Time to address the change. *Sexuality and Disability, 34*, 215–225.

McKenzie, K., Milton, M., Smith, G., & Ouellette-Kuntz, H. (2016). Systematic review of the prevalence and incidence of intellectual disabilities. *Current Developmental Disorders Reports, 3*, 104–115.

Mitra, M., Mouradian, V. E., & Diamond, M. (2011) Sexual violence victimization against men with disabilities. *American Journal of Preventive Medicine, 41*, 494–497.

National Youth Council of Ireland. (2004). Sense & sexuality: A support park for addressing the issues of sexual health with young people in youth work settings.

Pownall, J. D., Jahoda, A., Hastings, R. P. (2012). Sexuality and sex education of adolescents with intellectual disability: Mother's attitudes, experiences, and support needs. *Intellectual Development Disability, 50*(2), 140–154.

Rohleder, P., & Swartz, L. (2009). Providing sex education to persons with learning disabilities in the era of HIV/AIDS: Tensions between discourses of human rights and restriction. *Journal of Health Psychology, 14*(4), 601–610.

Schaafsma, D., Kok, G., Stoffelen, J. M. T., & Curfs, L. M. G. (2015). Identifying effective methods for teaching sex education to individuals with intellectual disabilities: A systematic review. *Journal of Sex Research: Annual Review of Sex Research Special Issue, 52*(4), 412–432.

Sex Education Council of the United States (SIECUS). (2004). Guidelines for comprehensive sexuality education: Kindergarten-12th grade (3rd ed.) Sex education Council of the United States, New York.

Spencer, N., Devereux, E., Wallace, A., Sundrum, R., Shenov, M., Bacchus, C., & Logan, S. (2005). Disabling conditions and registration for child abuse and neglect: A population-based study. *Pediatrics, 116*, 609–613.

Sullivan, P. M., & Knutson, J. F. (2000). Maltreatment and disabilities: A population-based epidemiological study. *Child Abuse & Neglect, 24*, 1257–1273.

Timms, S., & Goreczny, A. J. (2002). Adolescent sex offenders with mental retardation: Literature review and assessment considerations. *Aggression and Violent Behavior, 7*(1), 1–19.

UNESCO. (2013). Young People Today. Why adolescents and young people need comprehensive sexuality education and sexual and reproductive health services in Eastern and Southern Africa. United Nation Educational Scientific and Cultural Organization, Paris.

United Nations. (1994). *Standard Rules for the Equalization of Opportunities for Persons with Disabilities.* New York: United Nation Press.

United Nations. (2006). *Convention on the Rights of Persons with Disabilities.* New York: United Nation Press.

Wissink, I. B., van Vugt, E., Moonen, X., Stams, G. J. M., & Hendriks, J. (2015). Sexual abuse involving children with an intellectual disability (ID): A narrative review. *Research in Developmental Disabilities, 36,* 20–35.

World Health Organization. (2011). *World Report on Disability.* Geneva: WHO.

World Health Organization. (2015). *Sexual Health, Human Rights and the Law.* Geneva: WHO.

CHAPTER 16

A Perspective from an Educator-Parent

Norman Kee Kiak Nam

☙❧

Introduction

The author is a father with three adult sons with autism. The author is also a special needs teacher educator and a researcher for more than a decade in a tertiary institution. In this chapter, the author shares his perspectives based on his observations and interactions with other parents of children with specials on salient issues affecting the lives of their children.

Global Reality of Accelerating Digital Revolution

Many parents, including the author, are genuinely concerned about the current global trend and reality of accelerated digital revolution where the changes and their impact will have profound implications on the relevance and functionality of education, vocational training and their children being able to integrate and be included in the evolving society. In Singapore, the digital revolution is a national initiative, as articulated in the digital government blueprint, where digitalisation is consider key and critical for building a digital government for citizens, businesses and public officers to address changing public and business expectations, as well as to mitigate "increasing manpower constraints and an ageing workforce" (Smart Nation Digital Government Group, 2018, p. 2).

The pertinent issue many parents are naturally facing is whether the current special education curriculum and approach will be able to sufficiently equip and empower their children with special needs to be able to function and access all necessary governmental, work support, living and community services, with the skills and independent self-efficacy, within the context of dynamic and constant local and global changes. It is observed that there is an increasing need to access, use and pay for governmental, living and community services electronically through means of the mobile phone, computer and designated kiosk. A case in point is the purchasing of popular fast food, such as from McDonalds, Burger King and Kentucky Fried Chicken, where increasingly, customers are encouraged to independently order from designated electronic kiosks. Public libraries in Singapore require users to independently loan books from kiosks and renew if needed online. Some governmental services are increasingly encouraging the use of digital identities for online application and payment (e.g., passport application and renewal, checking of central provident fund account status). It is also increasingly common for the mainstream public to search for information using Google, learn by watching videos on YouTube, play video games on mobile devices, check emails for formal communication, informally chat on the WhatsApp application and even order goods, services and food online.

Parents are aptly concerned whether the current special needs education will be able to adequately prepare their children with the knowledge, skills and competencies to safely and comfortably access the 21st century way of life and work as it evolves (Kee, 2017), especially when they 'graduate' from school. The author has proposed a transdisciplinary digital learning environment for special education in the 21st century (Kee, 2017) and the need for a paradigm shift towards functional, contextual and just-in-time curriculum to meet the ever changing educational demands for relevance and potential employment (Kee & Wahab, 2019) to mitigate the perceived challenges.

Advances in Advanced Robotics

The current local and global interest and advances in robotics with artificial intelligence is alarming for parents, as new disruptive technologies (The Straits Times, 2016) may displace their children with special needs from jobs they have been trained and are capable of working in. In general, special schools prepare their students for vocations with job descriptions which are largely repetitive, skills based, and which requires following a fixed set of behavioural rules. For example, vocational jobs like baking, food preparation, housekeeping, hard floor cleaning, hospitality services, retail and landscaping are commonly taught in special schools to prepare their students for employment in either sheltered, supported or open employment. These job descriptions are apt for robots with artificial intelligence that leverages on advanced robotics technology, and which require predictability and clarity in expected performance with clear rules of engagement for engineering usage. Perhaps the quoted paragraph below from the publicly accessible and downloadable publication, "Infocomm Media 2025" (Ministry of Communication and Information, 2015) which explicates the master plan on "Cognitive computing and advanced robotics" exemplifies why parents are seriously concerned about the developments.

> Robots will also move out of the factory environment, and be increasingly deployed across various service industries and in our midst. One such example is Nao, a 58cm tall humanoid robot developed by Aldebaran Robotics. Nao robots have been used to teach autistic children, to interact with and monitor the elderly and even to serve customers in banks. The possibilities for applying cognitive computing and advanced robotics in Singapore are endless. (para. 1.10.2, p. 13)

The author, together with many parents, are mindful and do support the need for the national initiative, which ensures the nation's ability to remain globally competitive and relevant. However, parents do also sincerely hope for considerations and provisions in the national initiative, to include people with special needs, so that they have work and are able to earn an honest living with adequate earnings to live life with dignity and with some quality of life. The author proposes consideration of reserving some of these jobs to be done by people with special needs rather than robots. Alternatively, it would be desirable to consider including people with special needs in future jobs that are still being conceptualised and developed, which leverages on their ability. A possible case for consideration may be for people with special needs to be involved in urban agriculture or urban aquaculture initiatives to address food security needs, where climate change poses clear and present danger of food supply (Woodward & Porter, 2016).

Parents "Outsourcing" Education to Special Education Professionals

The author notices over the years that significant number of parents 'outsource' the education of their children with special needs to special educators. These parents generally excuse themselves with logical and valid reasons, such as they lack the special education training and that they need to work to earn income to meet their family economic needs and survival. Most of these parents do not actively work in close collaboration and partnership with special educators. The continuity and reinforcement of learning needed for both permanence of learnt procedures and processes are thus lacking. Moreover, generalisation of learnt curriculum under different contexts needs to be managed by parents as well as teachers to cover a diverse range of curriculum for life and work, especially for those with moderate and severe conditions.

Generally, it has been personally observed over time and informally shared through my interactions with many special school administrators and teachers, that students who have jobs after graduation are mainly from parents who have actively and consistently worked with the school and their child. The close collaboration allows behavioural and learning issues that surface during the child's learning journey to be addressed timely and aptly. Most are thus ready and suitable for participation in the School-to-Work (S2W) transition program where majority of the students were able to gain employment and remain employed (Kee & Wahab, 2019).

Sustainable Cost of Living and End of Life Concerns

Parents, especially in Singapore, are acutely aware of the relatively high cost of living compared to our neighbouring countries in ASEAN and the repeated rhetoric of the need for higher productivity to justify increase in remuneration. Parents are therefore justifiably concerned on how their children with special needs will be able to have sufficient remuneration to meaningfully support themselves, even if they have work. Moreover, moving towards the end of life of the adult with special needs, the question remains on the affordability of supporting themselves in their old age as well as life arrangements when their parents are no longer physically in the world.

Lifelong Holistic Monitoring, Evaluation of Needs and Support in an Ever Changing Environment

As the country progresses, changes in governmental policy and way of life are naturally expected. These changes may not be easy to comprehend and adopt. A case in point is on the e-government initiative where many transactions require electronic means to access, such as the use of two factor security authentication for digital identification and the use of apps for electronic transactions. Many senior citizens have reported encountering challenges and thus many community projects have been initiated to provide help to support their education for the digital age. The Infocomm Development Authority (IDA) has recognised the needs of specific community groups — the elderly, low-income families and persons with disabilities to ensure that the benefits of infocomm media are available to them.

The IDA has created the Digital Inclusion Fund to increase ownership, adoption and use (Ministry of Communication and Information, 2015). However, the digital inclusion funding does not include continual monitoring and identification of those who may not be cognizant of availability of such support and to know how to access it. A case in point is on the low utilisation of many good community support programs available in Family Service Centre (FSC) to help families with school going children. Many of these families were not cognizant of the availability of such programs and were often referred to FSC by schools.

Adult people with special needs will need lifelong monitoring, evaluation of needs and support so that the mandated changes are accessible and complied with. The author's personal example faced by his children while in supported work was the introduction of two factor authentication mandated by the organisation to apply for leave and to report sick leave. Without the intentional and consistent monitoring of needs of people with special needs, the need for learning two factor authentication may not be addressed. Fortunately, there is the job coach who monitored their needs and addressed their learning needs. However, there may be many other governmental initiatives that may affect people with special needs directly, such as new e-governmental initiatives (e.g., need to use Singpass with two factor authentication for digital identity). People with special needs may not be aware or mindful of what may be publicised in printed newspapers or electronic media routes as they may not access it. The author thus proposes the needs to create an official agency that will track people with special needs over their lifetime and to continuously look into their needs, especially when new and mandated official changes in policy and procedures will affect them. Moreover, it would be good to monitor their quality of life and provide needed support, especially when their parents are elderly or no longer around.

Unknown Future Realities

The author is mindful and aware of the need for children with special needs, as with children without disabilities, to learn the metacognitive skills of the 21st century of learning to learn and to adopt the attitude to learn for life. The need arises as new and unknown future realities are expected due to accelerated digital revolution and the impact it will have on living, learning and working. Currently, the special education curriculum focuses on learning specific knowledge and specific skills under specific known contexts. The author proposes the need for a paradigm shift and approach (Kee & Wahab, 2019) where the context needs to be authentic and dynamic, where the ability to dynamically apply diverse set of skills to address any happenings are needed. Essentially, the student and the teacher will together face diverse authentic contexts where the special educator will model and address expected and unexpected happenings. The student will learn, as an apprentice, how the special educator learns or discovers new ways to addresses challenges in life and to continually learn for life. The student thus becomes an apprentice of the special educator on how to live in the ever changing environment with level best efforts.

Strong Belief, Trust and Reliance on God

The author is aware of the research on parenting stress and would like to share his understanding from many informal observations of interactions with parents that parents with strong belief, trust and reliance on God have generally better well-being and mental health than those without. There are exceptions where parents adopt problem-focused coping strategies (Lai & Oei, 2014) and are actively involved in the interventions to directly support their children with special needs. Perhaps, in the face of realities where some are changeable and some are not, a genuine belief in God provides hope and some relief and resilience (Frankl, 2000). In the research literature, such approach may be considered as emotion-focused coping (Carver, Scheier & Weintraub, 1989).

References

Carver, C. S., Scheier, M. F., & Weintraub, J. K. (1989). Assessing coping strategies: A theoretically based approach. *Journal of Personality and Social Psychology, 56*(2), 267–283. doi:10.1037/0022-3514.56.2.267

Frankl, V. E. (2000). *Man's Search for Ultimate Meaning*. New York, NY: Persus Publishing.

Kee, N. K. N. (2017). Transdisciplinary digital learning environment for special education in the 21st century. In Nata R. V. (Ed.), *Progress in Education* (pp. 43–56). New York, NY: Nova Science Publishers.

Kee, N. K. N., & Wahab A. A. (2019). Special education in the 21st century: The need for a paradigm shift towards functional, contextual and just-in-time curriculum to meet ever changing educational demands for relevance and potential employment. In Nata, R. V. (Ed.), *Progress in Education, Volume 58* (pp. 203–218). New York, NY: Nova Science Publishers.

Lai, W., & Oei, T. (2014). Coping in parents and caregivers of children with autism spectrum disorders (ASD): A review. *Review Journal of Autism and Developmental Disorders, 1*(3), 207–224. doi:10.1007/s40489-014-0021-x

Ministry of Communication and Information. (2015). Infocomm media 2025. Retrieved from https://www.mci.gov.sg/~/media/data/mci/docs/imm%202025/infocomm%20media%202025%20full%20report.pdf

Smart Nation Digital Government Group. (June, 2018). Digital government blueprint: A Singapore government that is digital to the core and serves with a heart. Retrieved from https://www.tech.gov.sg/files/digital-transformation/dgb_booklet_june2018.pdf

The Straits Times. (2016). Disruption: What lies ahead. Singapore: Singapore Press Holdings.

Woodward, A., & Porter, J. R. (2016). Food, hunger, health, and climate change. *The Lancet, 387*(10031), 1886–1887. doi: http://dx.doi.org/10.1016/S0140-6736(16)00349-4

© 2021 World Scientific Publishing Company
https://doi.org/10.1142/9789814667142_0017

CHAPTER 17
Living a Good Life

Chong Suet Ling

ଔଓ

Introduction

Transitioning into the adult world for young persons with disabilities can be overwhelming and debilitating for both them and their families. Early planning and preparation for this major milestone, with coordinated and person-centred supports from educational institutions and agencies can greatly alleviate this experience, replace anxiety and fears with hopes and dreams, and promote life enhancing outcomes for the young person with a disability.

In 2019, I had an opportunity to witness a slice of what could be possible through a national effort to promote person-centred planning and supports for the lives of persons with disabilities in the state of New South Wales, Australia. No doubt their socio-political and cultural contexts are vastly different than ours. Nevertheless, my experience left me reflecting deeply about and becoming more appreciative of inclusive disability support. The insights shared in this chapter are gleaned from visits and conversations with professionals and practitioners invested in disability support across a wide spectrum of academia, research, training, policy, service provision, education and higher learning.

A National Effort towards Person-Centredness

In 2013, the Australian government introduced a nationwide disability scheme that has been a titanic game changer for supports and services for persons with disabilities. The National Disability Insurance Scheme (NDIS, 2019) was a response to widespread dissatisfaction with the lack of quality and accessible services for persons with disabilities, generating a tsunami that propelled an entire sector toward person-centred disability support. The policy intent behind the NDIS was to ensure that every person with a significant or permanent disability under the age of 65 years received the funding for supports and services they needed, and had *choice and control* (hallmarks of person-centredness) over how they wanted to spend their funding. The policy enactment was straightforward — *individualised funding*, by diverting what was until then, block funding to service providers, directly and fully into the hands of persons with disabilities.

I recalled hearing the sentiments of disbelief and cynicism by Australians themselves, in the early NDIS years, toward what seemed quite unrealistic and unfeasible. How would persons with disabilities be able to manage their funds, and make sound decisions about the services they needed? Fast forward six years, I witnessed a comprehensive system in operation, supported by an extensive structure and processes which were clearly and widely communicated. What stood out for me were the accessible supports available to persons with disabilities and their families at every conceivable milepost of the NDIS journey, from acquiring, to spending the funds.

The process was surprisingly linear and straightforward, yet life-centred. At the outset, the person with a disability and family members would be supported to attend a coordinated 'NDIS Planning Meeting'. There they would be helped by an 'NDIS Planner' to develop an 'NDIS Plan' for their member with a disability. Medium and long term goals, the 'NDIS Goals', would be spelt out in the Plan. This process was guided by 'NDIS Planning Areas' which covered living arrangements, social participation, independence, employment, education, health and well-being. The NDIS Plan would be submitted for evaluation. Funding would be allocated to the individual Goals, which could cover wide ranging supports such as transport, assistive aides and devices, development and training, support workers, etc. Families could select from one of three levels of supported fund management options, from fully independent to fully NDIS-supported.

At this point, the individual would be ready to 'shop' for supports and services that could best meet their goals. Persons with disabilities could engage the services of an 'NDIS Support Coordinator' to help them identify appropriate services or negotiate appropriate levels of supports with service providers. To my amazement, there was no limit to the type or number of supports and services they could engage within their budget. This could range from engaging occasional help from support workers for specific living functions and needs, e.g., helping with grocery shopping or social activities; to attending a Day Centre (akin to a Day Activity Centre in Singapore) or an Australian Disability Enterprise (ADE, akin to a sheltered workshop in Singapore) (Australian Government Department of Social Services, 2019) full or part week. Individuals could choose to combine different services such as a Day Centre and an ADE, or a Disability Employment Service (DES)[1] (Australian Government Department of Social Services, 2019) and an ADE, and still engage support workers for weekend activities and needs, budget permitting! Finally, the NDIS Plan would be reviewed throughout the individual's lifespan to ensure their goals and funding were updated.

Towards Person-Centred Supports and Services

The impact of the NDIS on disability supports and services was nothing short of transformational. With the person with a disability becoming a discerning consumer holding the purse strings, the 'charity' model of operation gave way to 'business' models, as service providers had to market themselves and innovate their programme

---

[1] These are government funded services that specialise in supporting persons with disabilities find and sustain employment.

offerings to meet their 'customer' needs. Programme offerings diversified as activities, which hitherto had been largely centre-based, were increasingly pushed out into the community to support goals for community engagement and integration. I was surprised to find a Day Centre for individuals with moderate to severe needs quite empty when I visited. The manager explained that their clients were out doing different things of their choice, e.g., some went to a café, some were volunteering for meals on wheels, and some went swimming — "It's what they want". Their focus, he explained, was "all about increasing their levels of engagement with the community and building social networks and relationships." Having a programme at the Centre was "not necessary", "just a framework", as the real aim was "about coming out of the Centre", "No need to spend all their time there, like a school".

Services sought tie-ups with community partners and pooled resources with other disability services. I came across Day Centres collaborating with services for supported (ADE') and open employment (DES) to support individuals who desired both to work and receive supports in social and recreational activities.

Staff were retrained and staffing remodelled to support the interests and needs of persons with disabilities more flexibly, which included supporting activities after centre hours and on the weekends. A critical resource person was the 'disability support worker'. Support workers would provide direct and onsite support to persons with disabilities in a range of activities and settings, with the objective of increasing their community engagement and building their skills for independence. Support workers were hired for their dispositions and matched to persons with disabilities on the basis of their goals, needs and wants, as "finding the right fit where possible is important". Often, they would become their companions and friends through shared interests and activities. In one Day Centre I visited, all the staff had a One Page Profile[2] to facilitate matching them to the clients!

---

[2] A person-centred tool which allows an individual to communicate, on a single page, about themselves including their interests, preferences and strengths.

In actuality, services shifted from a *service-centred* model where persons with disabilities were *fitted* into programmes and activities; to a *person-centred* model where programmes and activities were *planned around* what the person with a disability *wanted*. This manifested as a *whole-of-life* approach toward meeting their wants and needs which accorded them the dignity of living a full life, and a life they wanted.

Planning for a Good Life

If there was one thing that was more universally espoused than the NDIS, it was the conviction that all persons with disabilities 'deserved' a 'Good Life'. This was practically the articulated raison d'etre for anyone invested in working with persons with disabilities. The explanation of the 'Good Life' was consistently resolute, a life "no different than for you and me" — one that has "purpose and meaning", "relationships and friends", "choice and control", "sense of belonging", "contribution", and "feeling valued". The terms 'Simple Life' and 'Ordinary Life' were used interchangeably with the 'Good Life' to emphasise the basic and routine activities of life like taking a shower, eating what one likes, having friends, and having a job. This was deemed "their right".

Indeed, the oft heard Australian refrain that "they are no different than us" spoke to a humanistic value base and high expectations for persons with disabilities. Incidentally, the 'Good Life' was contrasted with a life where decisions were made or things done, for them. This included following a planned schedule of programmes in traditional Day Centres. Even being taken out for community outings in groups on the "picnic bus" was seen to run counter to person-centred planning, as this severely limited opportunities for interactions and building relationships within the community.

Pathways to a Good Life

The road to a 'Good Life' was a discernible one, paved by four defined lanes which guide life visioning and goal planning for persons with disabilities — living arrangement, social and community participation, education and employment. These lanes were well maintained, as most service providers targeted their supports and services for persons with disabilities around at least one of these pathways.

Living arrangements

'Independent living' — living on one's own, with or without housemates which can include a family member, was strongly encouraged. This culturally-embedded outcome was attainable due in large part to the accessibility of support workers who can provide drop-in help with functional or social needs, e.g., getting ready for work, or attending a weekly class.

Another acceptable option was 'supported living'. I visited a group home shared amongst four persons with disabilities with two drop-in support workers. I found two members away that afternoon — one was doing her nails, another went swimming. A typical day and a slice of a Good Life!

Social and community participation

The oft repeated mantra was that community *presence* alone — just 'being' in the community, or "dropping in", was not good enough. Community *engagement* was the desired outcome, wherein *relationships* are established through getting to know and being known to people in the community. As this is likely to happen when there is a shared interest or joint activity, intentional effort was made by services to coordinate activities to meet the interests and choices of persons with disabilities, and to introduce them into the community wherever possible, such as to the regular staff at a frequented café or recreational centre. A manager related to me how three ladies who frequented a shop to get their nails done became so well acquainted with the shop owner she invited them to her daughter's wedding!

Beyond community engagement was an even more aspirational goal of having a 'valued social role' in the community, through doing something regularly, big or small, that was perceived to be of value to other people. They could be volunteering their services at a religious institution they attended, or be helping out with towels and drinks at a sports centre where they played a sport of interest. According to Wolfensberger (1983), having multiple valued social roles, or 'social role valorization', confers the "good things in life", like respect, acceptance, chance to meet people, and not to mention, the opportunity to acquire more valued roles.

Education

It was admirable to find that the pursuit of further education beyond high school was a reality for students with disabilities. This was largely possible through legislative requirements for all Registered Training Organisations (RTO) to facilitate equity of access to education for people with disabilities. In particular, at NSW's Technical and Further Education (TAFE), in response to the needs of students with intellectual disabilities, "Access" or "Supported" classes were initiated to provide inclusive higher learning pathways for them. These were designed by Disability Teacher Consultants (DTC) from the Disability Unit and could be:

(a) A course of study adapted out of a mainstream course offering, maintained at the requisite level, e.g., Certificate III. Examples were vet science, kitchen operations, business and multimedia. I attended a multi-media course which was taught by a mainstream teacher with the specialised knowledge, supported by 2 DTCs. This course was paced over 6 months as opposed to the usual 16 weeks.
(b) A specially designed course of study, pitched at a lower level, e.g., Certificate I or II. Examples were 'Access to Work and Training', and 'Retail'. I attended a course on retail which was delivered exclusively by the DTCs. Students with intellectual disabilities were practicing communication skills through role play.

All the DTCs I spoke with displayed absolute regard for the interests and choices of the students and were stalwart advocates for them — "It's what students want", "So they enjoy" and "You'd be blown away". They emphasised that it was "not about getting a qualification", but rather the life opportunity to experience learning in a higher learning environment — "like their peers". More importantly, this enabled them to develop important social skills in an authentic 'adult' environment.

Employment

Employment confers meaningful occupation, inclusion and a sense of contribution. There was a palpable national hand in supporting open employment outcomes with 'award (full) wages' for persons with disabilities. Individuals could access any government funded DES for job matching or job training at any point in their lives, including funding for workplace modifications and wage subsidies to employers. A less desired option was "Supported Employment" in an ADE, previously known as 'sheltered workshops', where persons with disabilities carry out semi-commercialised work tasks and receive 'productivity wages' based on their work outputs.

There were dedicated specialised services targeted at school leavers transitioning from school to work. Year 12 students with disabilities could access any 'School Leaver Employment Supports' (SLES) (NDIS, 2019) through their NDIS Plan for individualised supports for up to two years post school to meet their employment goals. Supports were available in the form of customised work experience, job and lifeskills training which could include travel training, communication skills, time management skills, money handling skills, etc. 'Job Support' is a reputed 'SLES' which successfully places up to 70 per cent of school leavers with moderate to severe intellectual disabilities into successful employment. I met 19 year-old Rebecca (not her real name) doing her work experience with Job Support in a kitchen at a hospital. Articulate and confident, she had been with Job Support for 5 months and was transitioning to a 'DES' which had found her a paid job working full-time at a café.

Incidentally, Rebecca also volunteered at Two Wolves Bar, a volunteer driven social enterprise, and was a swimmer for Australia!

I was particularly impressed by the 'networks' run under the 'National Disability Coordination Officer' (NDCO, 2018) Programme for the purpose of coordinating and strengthening cross linkages between education, government, disability services, training and employment to assist school leavers and persons with disabilities to access employment and training. I found these to be valuable platforms for fostering personal friendships and professional collaborations amongst professionals and practitioners from education and inter-agencies. I attended a 'Sydney Vocational Support Network' where sector updates were shared, new services broadcasted and feedback and ideas sought. It was well attended by professionals from cross sectors of education, government, disability services, advocacy services and higher education. I also sat in a 'Ticket-to-Work' (Ticket to Work, 2019) network meeting where members from NDIS, the Department of Education, Transition Support Teachers and disability services met to pool their collective knowledge and networks to brainstorm breakthrough solutions for six school leavers who were young individuals with more complicated needs.

Realising a Good Life with Paid Supports

What in reality does a 'Good Life' with paid supports look like? The scenarios offered below are compiled from my conversations with service professionals about actual persons with a range of disabilites, including intellectual disability:

Person A

- Lives in a group home run by Day Centre 1, and receives daily drop-in support from 2 disability support workers;
- A disability support worker from Day Centre 1 accompanies A to a recreational club every Saturday where he volunteers in the locker room;

- Attends Day Centre 2, 3 days a week where he enjoys activities of interest such as swimming and shopping on a weekly basis, and receives training in cooking and grooming.

Person B

- Lives in an apartment with a flatmate;
- Has a part time job at a supermarket working 5 days a week, 4 hours per day in the morning (B received job training from a SLES for 1 year after he graduated, after which he was referred to a DES which matched him to his current job);
- Has a disability support worker from a Day Centre help him with grocery shopping on the weekend, as well as accompany him to a computer class one afternoon a week.

Person C

- Lives with his family;
- Has a disability support worker from Day Centre 1 help him with his shower and dressing in the mornings, and accompany him to attend church every Sunday and thereafter accompanies him to lunch;
- Attends a Day Centre 2, 2 days a week where he enjoys activities of interest such as bowling and gardening, and receives training in personal grooming;
- Attends an ADE 3 days a week where he does horticulture related work and is receiving job training.

Transitioning from School to a Good Life

The transition from school to a Good Life post school is coordinated through a dedicated team of 'Support Teacher Transitions' (STT) appointed by the Department of Education. STTs work with their own clusters of schools and bring with them experience and knowledge in both special education and transition planning for students and families. By their appointment and itinerant nature of their function, STTs enjoy an advantageous level of autonomy and authority with their schools. By their role, STTs participate in multiple government platforms and networks for school leavers such as Ticket to Work, and are extremely well connected within the post school disability landscape. Not surprisingly, I found the STTs whom I met to be strongly self-driven and highly regarded by their schools and the families.

Transition Planning, as run by the STTs, is highly collaborative and personalised. Between Years 9–12, STTs meet regularly with students and families, together with their teachers, to gather rich understanding of the students to inform their transition goals and support their handover to post school supports and services. STTs also assist students on planning and choosing their courses of study and course electives based on their interests, or customising courses to suit their inclinations, e.g., vocational courses and work experience.

STTs offer invaluable support to families, through providing information about post school pathways and services, how to navigate them, and sourcing and engaging appropriate services on behalf of families. EXPOs[3] are a key feature of high school education in NSW. STTs guide and accompany families to disability EXPOs to learn about post school options, and connect individual families to relevant post school resources. In many instances, STTs themselves organise school-based EXPOs for easier access and networking for students and families.

An important feature of transition planning is the completion of an 'Individual Transition Plan' (ITP) for all students with disabilities by Year 12, for handover to post school services. STTs help with the development of the ITP and its handover to NDIS Planners at the NDIS Planning Meeting. Thereafter, they often continue to support school leavers in embarking on appropriate pathways such as higher education at TAFE or finding employment.

---

[3] These are typically one day events for showcasing various provisions for students including educational and higher learning institutes. Disability-based EXPO's focus largely on services for living, social and community participation, education and employment.

STTs I met emphasised that Transition Planning had to be a "whole school process… embedded, not an add on". Starting early and involving families all the way was key. Crafting of transition goals, a key aspect of the student ITP, should begin as early as possible with asking the student, "What skills do you want to have to be more independent?". Consequently, it was important that the curriculum helped students build up practical and functional skills that were geared toward helping them to be independent in real life contexts, such as communication, money skills and time-management.

Understanding Person-Centredness

Admittedly, I visited Australia looking for person-centred *practices*, *techniques* and *tools*, for working with persons with disabilities. What I experienced instead was a *culture* of *person-centredness*, which expressed itself through the frequent and spontaneous utterances of the many professionals I talked to — "no different than us", "deserve a good life", "let them decide" and "let them have a go". I came to learn about what person-centred is and is not, and gained a deep respect for what it took to carry out authentic person-centred planning, with persons with disabilities.

Indeed, the person-centred approach offers the keen practitioner an array of fascinating and user-friendly tools, e.g., Planning Alternative Tomorrows with Hope (PATH), One Page Profile, Good Day Bad Day. It is tempting to adopt them into one's practice and think that one was practicing person-centred planning. As a senior manager from 'Family Advocacy', a service which supports and champions families with members with disabilities, explained to me, the person-centred approach is "not a formula, or a planning tool… rather, a way of looking at a person". Indeed, person-centredness is "a set of *beliefs, attitudes and expectations* about the *capacities and rights* of persons with disabilities to live their lives in accordance with their own wishes, dreams, aspirations, needs and abilities" (New Directions, 2012). At its core, it is premised on a set of values that uphold the human dignity and worth of the person with a disability.

To practice person-centred planning *authentically*, professionals must imbue and exemplify these values, a step that requires introspection and openness to one's own continual growth. For we cannot support a person beyond what we truly believe them capable of. When carried out in the 'correct' spirit of person-centredness, the focus shifts away from planning *for*, to planning *with*, the individual, a process that requires deep listening and interacting with the individual, in order to discover their interests and gifts, and how they want to live their lives.

The Local Context

Transitioning from school to post school

The concept and practice of partnering students and families in planning for their futures and preparing for the transition to an envisioned future life is still fairly new in Singapore schools. In 2017, 'Transition Planning' (Ministry of Education, 2017) was introduced into special education schools in Singapore. At the same time, the Ministry of Education (MOE) also provided schools with a dedicated 'Transition Planning Coordinator' (TPC) to support a school-wide level of coordinated and person-centred supports for students and families.

A 3-phase model of Transition Planning is adopted in all special education schools. In the 'Initiating' phase (13–14 years old), schools engage families to embark on futures planning for their children. Activities center around discovering students' interests, preferences and strengths.

In the 'Planning' phase (15–16 years old), schools work with students and families to craft post school goals in living, learning and working, based on their assessed interests, preferences and strengths. A personalised Individual Transition Plan is developed for every student, and reviewed annually.

As their post school goals gain definition, these are matched to appropriate post school pathways, services and community resources to meet their aspirations and dreams e.g. pursing social activities, further learning, or a job. During this final 'Consolidating' phase (17–18 years old), schools facilitate link-ups for families, e.g., through attending roadshows, and making referrals, e.g., to the School-to-Work Transition Programme. This is done before the student graduates to achieve a seamless transition to their post school lives and services.

Post school pathways

Upon graduating from special education schools, several pathways and services are open to students depending on their assessed levels of readiness — open or supported employment, or placement in a sheltered workshop or Day Activity Centre (DAC). As my expertise is in special education, brief descriptions of these pathways are offered below. The reader is advised to seek appropriate sources, such as SG Enable, for more comprehensive knowledge of the social services landscape for persons with disabilities.

Open/supported employment

Students assessed to be work capable may enrol in a vocational certification programme at selected special education schools and be emplaced in a job upon graduation, or participate in the School-to-Work Transition (S2W) Programme. The S2W programme is a collaboration between MOE, the Ministry of Social and Family Development (MSF) and SG Enable, a national coordinating agency for adults with disabilities that offers internships and job training for up to one year post school, leading to a job placement with full pay (Wong, Chong & Ng, 2020).

Sheltered workshop

Sheltered workshops are targeted for persons who are not work ready but can carry out simple work tasks. Run by Social Service Agencies (SSA) and funded by the Government, sheltered workshops offer eligible persons with disabilities centre-based work tasks which may be contracted, semi-commercialised or sheltered enterprises. Clients attend these centres on a full time basis and receive an allowance. Centres may offer training opportunities to prepare clients to transition into open employment.

Day activity centres

DACs are targeted for persons with higher needs who may not have the capability for work. Also run by SSAs and funded by the Government, substantial subsidies are provided to lower and middle income families for this service through means testing. DACs offer a range of day programmes and activities to support activities of daily living and community living skills of persons with disabilities. These include opportunities for social and recreational outings in the community, with some centres offering work therapy and therapy services.

In addition to the programmes highlighted above, there has also been a push in more recent years to diversify the types of services and schemes that are available to persons with disabilities, to better meet their needs and those of their caregivers. For example, the drop-in disability programme provides persons with disabilities with social and recreational activities for a few hours each week. Persons with disabilities can choose the number of hours of such services they require to suit their needs. Persons with disabilities also have access to a variety of schemes that seek to enable them to live independently, including through subsidies for transport for education or work, and purchase of assistive technology devices. Apart from these funded schemes and services, various social service agencies in the disability sector also run a range of programmes to engage adult persons with disabilities, through social and recreational activities, outings and befriending activities. There are plans to build on these efforts to extend such activities more systematically to more persons with disabilities going forward.

Conclusions

What inspired me from the Australian experience was an overarching theme of 'whole-of-life', person-centred planning for persons with disabilities. This resonated for me as a compelling and aspirational vision that accords persons with disabilities the dignity of *leading full lives, beyond services*. That disability supports and services remain block funded in our local context notwithstanding, I would like to conclude the chapter with some deliberations for more inclusive supports for persons with disabilities in Singapore.

- Persons with disabilities need to be supported through a 'whole-of-life' planning perspective. The process should be *holistic* and reflect facets of everyday living such as how, or with whom, they want to self-manage, live, play, learn, stay healthy, volunteer, work, etc. It should not be service-focussed or placement-oriented, and need not be limited to what services are offered.
- Persons with disabilities can be supported to develop a 'life plan' that represents and speaks to the life they want to lead and their dreams. There should be concrete *life-centred* goals guided by meaningful 'planning areas', such as social and recreation, independence, well-being and safety, education and learning, volunteering and employment, etc. These 'planning areas' could correspond to aspects of an emergent concept of a 'Good Life', which takes due reference from the lives of average citizens in similar age groups within our local social norms and cultural contexts.
- The voices and choices of individuals and their families should be encouraged and respected in this whole-of-life planning process.
- We need to elevate our aspirations and expectations for the participation of persons with disabilities in the community, beyond merely *being* in the community, to *engaging* and *contributing*, and being *active and valued members* in the community. They could be singing in a choir, volunteering at a craft centre or assisting in activities in a church or mosque. This will require matching social activities, including the support staff, to persons with disabilities according to their interests, preferences and strengths.

Whole-of-life planning for persons with disabilities needs to start early, while the student is in school, and continue seamlessly through their lifespan.

- The Individual Transition Plan, developed during the schooling years in special education, serves as their first 'life plan' when they leave school. This plan should not cease at this juncture, but be *handed over* to the receiving service(s) to inform their planning of programmes and activities, including capacity building, for the individuals to fulfil their aspirations. Then, as they attain their goals, gain new skills or develop new interests, their life plans should be reviewed and renewed at timely life intervals, and new activities, supports or pathways determined, as appropriate or desired.

For such whole-of-life supports to be accessible to persons with disabilities, greater flexibility would be needed in the post school services landscape, such as:

- More diversification and overlaps in programme offerings across sheltered workshops and day activity centers, for example, sheltered workshops could offer social and recreational programmes, while DACs could offer some work opportunities;
- More choice for persons with disabilities on their preferred activities;
- More capacity development opportunities to allow for continual development and growth;
- Recruiting and training suitable and willing persons, including students and parents as 'support workers' who can provide supports to persons with disabilities to be actively engaged in the community;
- Providing options for partial and multiple enrolment across services, for example, a person with a disability could attend both a sheltered workshop and a Day Activity Centre, or be in open employment and attend a sheltered workshop or a Day Activity Centre, to meet their needs and wants; and
- Collaborations across services, and with community resources, for members whose life goals or needs fall outside a service provider's offerings or hours of operation

Finally, a 'whole-of life' approach for persons with disabilities needs to be supported through sustained capacity building efforts targeted at organisations, support staff, families and individuals with disabilities, starting with schools.

- MSF's third Enabling Masterplan 2017–2021 (Enabling Masterplan, 2016) advocates a person-centred approach in the planning and delivery of post school services to persons with disabilities. Indeed, for this to happen, a nationally coordinated approach for professional training in person-centred thinking and planning and supports is needed, not only amongst support professionals but for all staff, including the leadership team.
- Families are primary support systems for their members with disabilities. Professionals and support staff need to build capacities for working with families to effectively involve and empower them. Families could be supported in setting up circles or networks of supports around their members with disabilities which could include relatives, friends or support professionals who can offer valuable support and respite for the immediate families. Families could also be supported to create a vision for the lives of their family member with a disability. These person-centred processes are best started during the school years as part of Transition Planning (Sanderson, Goodwin & Elaine, n.d.).
- Self-determination skills enable students with disabilities to be more self-directed and enhance their post school outcomes (Shogren *et al.*, 2015; Wehmeyer, 2005; Wehmeyer & Palmer, 2003). These skills — making choices, expressing preferences, solving problems, making decisions, setting and attaining goals, engaging in self-managing and self-regulating and self-advocating, need to be explicitly taught in the school curriculum to equip students with disabilities to participate meaningfully in their life planning.
- A 'transition-focussed' education improves post school outcomes for students with disabilities (Kohler & Field, 2003). This

concept is premised on Transition Planning being the fundamental basis for the planning and delivery of students' educational programmes. Curriculum should be designed to prepare them successfully for the springboard to their post school goals and lives. This should include practical and functional skills important for daily independent living, e.g., meal preparation, navigating the transport system and shopping within a budget, taught in real and natural settings. Finally, students should have opportunities to develop new interests, acquire skills to reflect on their experiences and achievements, and explore and rethink their ambitions and dreams.

References

Australian Government Department of Social Services. (2019). Retrieved from https://www.dss.gov.au/our-responsibilities/disability-and-carers/programmes-services/disability-employment-services/

Australian Government Department of Social Services. (2019). Retrieved from https://www.dss.gov.au/our-responsibilities/disability-and-carers/programmes-services/australian-disability-enterprises/

Enabling Masterplan Steering Committee. (2016). Enabling masterplan 2017–2021: Caring nation, inclusive society. Retrieved from https://www.ncss.gov.sg/NCSS/media/NCSS-Documentsand-Forms/EM3-Final_Report_20161219.pdf

Kohler, P., & Field, S. (2003). Transition-focussed education. *The Journal of Special Education, 37*, 174–183.

Ministry of Education, Special Education Branch. (2017). Transition planning for living, learning and working — Making it happen: A guide for SPED schools.

National Disability Coordination Officer Programme. (2018). Retrieved from https://www.education.gov.au/national-disability-coordination-officer-programme/

National Disability Insurance Scheme. (2019). Retrieved from https://www.ndis.gov.au/

National Disability Insurance Scheme. (2019). Retrieved from https://www.ndis.gov.au/providers/essentials-providers-working-ndia/school-leavers-employment-supports-sles

New Directions. (2012). Review of HSC day services and implementation plan. Retrieved from https://www.hse.ie/eng/services/publications/disability/newdirections2012.pdf

Sanderson, H., Goodwin, G., & Elaine, K. (n.d.). Personalising education: A guide to using person centered practices in schools. Retrieved from http://eastridinglocaloffer.org.uk/

Shogren, K. A., Wehmeyer, M. L., Palmer S. B., *et al.* (2015). Relationships between self-determination and post school outcomes for youth with disabilities. *Journal of Special Education, 53,* 30–41.

Ticket to Work. (2019). Retrieved from http://www.tickettowork.org.au/

Wehmeyer, M.L. (2005). Self-determination and individuals with severe disabilities: Re-examining meanings and misinterpretations. *Research and Practice for Persons with Severe Disabilities, 30,* 113–120.

Wehmeyer, M. L., & Palmer S. B. (2003). Adult outcomes for students with cognitive disabilities three years after high school: The impact of self-determination. *Education and Training in Developmental Disabilities, 38,* 131–144.

Wolfensberger, W. (1983). Social role valorization: A proposed new term for the principle of normalisation. *Mental Retardation, 21,* 234–239.

Wong, M. E., Chong, S. L., & Ng, H. L. (2020). School-to-Work transition: Support for students with moderate-to-severe special educational needs in Singapore. In M. Yuen, W. Beamish, & V. S. Solbergg, (eds.). *Careers for students with special educational needs: Perspectives on development and transition from the Asia-Pacific region.* (pp. 249–260). Singapore: Springer.

Index

ableism, 64, 65, 66, 71
Advisory Council on Opportunities for the Disabled, 247
Advisory Council on the Disabled, 37
advocacy, 13, 15, 17–19, 21, 22, 25
allied educators, 4, 157, 265, 298
artificial intelligence, 329
assistive technology, 131–133

Canossian School, 284, 300–304
caregivers, 84, 87, 88, 91, 118, 127, 128, 133–137, 220, 226, 227, 316, 319–321
certification programmes, 201
Circle of Friends, 266, 271
cochlear implantation, 297
cochlear implants, 297
co-enrollment, 291, 292, 294, 306
Committee for Future Economy (CFE), 223, 243
Comprehensive Sexuality Education, 314
Compulsory Education act, 149

Convention on the Rights of Persons with Disabilities (CRPD), 3, 9, 313

Day Activity Centre (DACs), 337, 348, 349, 351
deaf, 283, 285–292, 294, 297, 305–308
deafness, 288, 291
Desired Outcomes of Education, 38, 39
Developmental Disability Registry (DDR), 316
Development Support and Learning Support (DS and LS) programme, 87, 105, 106, 111
Development Support Programme (DSP), 105
digital identities, 328
Digital Inclusion Fund, 332
Digital Readiness Blueprint, 251
digital revolution, 327, 333
Diploma in Special Education, 175, 265
disability employment, 238, 244, 247, 250, 255

355

Disability Research Coalition, 320
disruption, 31, 32, 46, 47
disruptive technologies, 329

early detection, 84, 85, 88, 89
early intervention, 81–93
educational counsellors, 154, 156
educational placement, 284, 290, 292, 300, 303, 304
Education for All, 32, 45
egalitarian, 59, 68
egalitarianism, 58
EIPIC, 82–85, 87, 90, 92, 102, 103
elitism, 59
elitist, 68
Enabling Masterplan, 4–6, 18, 49, 81, 83, 84, 88, 101, 102, 136, 223–225, 247, 248, 316, 321, 352
executive functioning, 285, 287, 289

Facing Your Fears, 266, 271

global economy, 240, 242

Healthy and Safe Relationships, 317
human rights, 1–3, 11–15, 17–22, 24

IHL Internship Programme, 222, 229–232
inclusionary space, 34, 35, 42–44, 48, 50
inclusive society vision, 4
Infocomm Development Authority (IDA), 331, 332
Integrated Childcare, 83
Integrated Childcare Programme (ICCP), 83, 86, 90, 103

Kindle Garden, 104, 112

Learning Support Educators, 105, 111
Lien Foundation, 49

many helping hands, 18, 122, 139
mixed ability classes, 170, 176–181, 183, 184
mixed ability classrooms, 169, 178–181, 184
model for differentiation, 170
model of disability, 16
multiple pathways, 45

National Disability Insurance Scheme (NDIS), 246
Natural Auditory Oral Approach, 301
Natural Auditory Oral (NAO) approach, 301
neoliberal, 64, 66, 67
Normal (Academic), 172, 173
Normal (Technical), 173

Open Door Programme, 221
open employment, 239, 240, 245, 249, 253, 254, 338, 342, 349, 351
Outstanding Special Education Teacher Award (OSTA), 125

parenting stress, 333
person-centred, 335–339, 346, 347, 349, 352
post school, 194, 195, 199, 204, 215, 216, 342, 344, 345, 347, 348, 351–353
preschool children, 81

Primary School Leaving Examination (PSLE), 36, 40, 171, 202, 299
problem-solving, 150, 153–156, 161, 162
problem-solving approach, 150, 153, 155, 156, 162
Professional Practice Guidelines (PPG), 159
psychological services, 150–160, 162–164

quality inclusive practices, 107, 108, 110, 111

REACH, 158, 266, 267, 269, 270
reading specialists, 154, 156
religion, 315
Report of the Advisory Council for the Disabled, 300
Report of the Advisory Council on the Disabled: Opportunities for the Disabled, 121
RISE Mentorship, 222, 229, 231, 232
RISE Mentorship Programme, 222, 229, 232
Robotics, 329

Salamanca, 99, 109, 116
Salamanca Statement, 2, 4, 7, 261
Salamanca Statement and Framework for Action on Special Needs Education, 32, 44, 99
Salamanca Statement and its Framework for Action, 45
Satellite Partnership Programme, 46, 298, 303, 304

school-based dyslexia remediation programme, 266
School-to-Work (S2W) transition program, 202, 204, 205, 222, 225, 228, 232, 331
Self-determination, 352
sexuality education, 313, 314, 318, 319
sheltered workshop, 244, 254, 342, 337, 348, 351
Singapore Pre-School Accreditation Framework (SPARK), 109
SkillsFuture, 41, 42, 221, 223, 229, 233, 244
social and emotional, 262, 265, 266, 270–272, 276
social cognition, 288
social model, 13, 14, 16, 19, 24
social model of disability, 13, 14, 16, 19, 24, 98
social service agencies, 6, 103, 118, 119, 127, 131, 133, 136, 138, 140, 238, 249, 255
Social Service Training Institute (SSTI), 126
special education curriculum, 328, 333
special education (SPED) schools, 119–128, 130–132, 137–141, 147, 149, 200–203, 205, 222, 224–226, 228, 229, 232, 317
streaming, 171–174, 177
subject-based banding, 174

Teachers trained in Special Needs (TSN), 157, 175, 265
Tech Able, 221, 233, 252
Theory of Mind, 288

The Report of the Advisory Council for the Disabled: Opportunities for the Disabled, 5
Thinking Schools, Learning Nation, 39, 40
tiered system of support (TSS), 150, 156, 160–162
Total Communication, 300
transition planning, 198, 199, 204, 212, 213, 344–347, 352, 353
TSS structure, 162

United Nations Convention on the Rights of Persons with Disabilities (UNCRPD), 4, 6, 8, 32, 44, 99, 298
United Nations Convention on the Rights of the Child, 261

United Nations Educational, Scientific and Cultural Organisation, 2
United Nations Standard Rules for the Equalisation of Opportunities for Persons with Disabilities, 312
Universal Declaration of Human Rights (UNDHR), 1

vocational certification programmes, 201, 202
vulnerability narrative, 47, 48

World Health Organisation, 237, 262, 264, 311

www.ingramcontent.com/pod-product-compliance
Lightning Source LLC
Chambersburg PA
CBHW070307230426
43664CB00015B/2655